Practical information policies

Second edition

Gower

First edition published in 1990 as *Practical information policies: how to manage information flow in organizations* by Gower Publishing Company Limited.

This edition published by
Gower Publishing Limited
Gower House · Croft Road · Aldershot
Hampshire · GU11 3HR
ENGLAND
and
Gower
Old Post Road · Brookfield
Vermont · 05036
USA

British Library
Cataloguing in Publication Data
Orna, Elizabeth
    Practical information policies
    – 2nd ed.
    1. Information resources management
    2. Information technology – Management
    3. Title
    658.4′038

    ISBN 0−566−07693−4

Library of Congress
Cataloging-in-Publication Data
Orna, Elizabeth.
    Practical information policies / Elizabeth Orna.
    – – 2nd ed.
       p. cm.
    ISBN 0−566−07693−4 (alk. paper)
    1. Communication in organizations.
    2. Information technology.
    3. Industrial management. I. Title.
HD30.3..O76 1998
658.4′038−−dc21   98−40510
                                             CIP

The design, drawings and the computer page make-up of this book are by Graham Stevens. Printed in Great Britain by Cambridge University Press (Printing Division) Cambridge.

Contents

Acknowledgements

Though I accept full responsibility for all the imperfections of this book, it could not have been written without the generous help of many people who were prepared to give time and careful thought to sharing their experience with me, answering my questions, and listening patiently to my ideas. My first and greatest debt is to the organizations which consented to be the subject of case studies, to the people in them who contributed so generously, and in particular to Joanne Marshall and Sue Westcott who undertook the writing of their own case studies (Health Canada and MAFF, Legal Department).

Institutions

AMNESTY INTERNATIONAL, INTERNATIONAL SECRETARIAT
Graham Bennett, Director of Information Resources (on sabbatical leave from late 1997). *Sue Westcott,* Director Information Resources (on secondment to Amnesty International from late 1997).

AUSTRALIAN SECURITIES AND INVESTMENT COMMISSION
Tom Davies, National Information Manager. *Keith Inman,* National Intelligence Coordinator (now at the National Crime Authority).

BRITISH LIBRARY
David Bradbury, Director General, Collections and Services. *Stuart Ede,* Director of Acquisitions Processing and Cataloguing. *Alan Gomersall,* Director of Science, Reference and Information Services. *Sue Howley,* Assistant Director, Research and Innovation Centre. *John Mahoney,* Director of Information Systems. *David Russon,* Deputy Chief Executive. *Geoff Smith,* Head of Modern Collections. *Robert Smith,* Assistant Director of Bibliographic Services and Document Supply. *Andy Stephens,* Head of Corporate Planning and Secretariat.

CREDIT UNION SERVICES CORPORATION
Karen Nelson, Information Management Consultant.

HEALTH CANADA
Professor Joanne Marshall, Faculty of Information Studies, University of Toronto (author of the case study).

MINISTRY OF AGRICULTURE FISHERIES AND FOOD, LEGAL DEPARTMENT
Sue Westcott, Librarian (at the time the case study, of which she is the author).

NATWEST MARKETS
Victoria Ward, Spark Knowledge. *Claudine Arnold,* Spark Knowledge. *Bruce Greenhalgh,* NatWest Group Operations. *Conrad Thompson,* IBM Consulting. *Philippa Thompson,* KPMG.

NATIONAL HEALTH SERVICE
Dr Judith Palmer, Director, Health Care Libraries Unit, University of Oxford;
Director, Health Libraries and Information Network, NHS Executive, Anglia
and Oxford Region. *Pam Prior,* Regional Librarian, West Midlands Evidence
Supported Medicine Union. *Veronica Fraser,* NHS Library Adviser.

OGILVY & MATHER
Yvette McGreavy, Information Director.

QUEENSLAND INFORMATION PLANNING BRANCH
(Government Infrastructure and Coordination Division, Dept of the Premier
and Cabinet, Queensland, Australia) *Caroline Gordon,* Senior Consultant.

SINGAPORE PRODUCTIVITY AND STANDARDS BOARD
Mr Woon Kin Chung, Divisional Director, Planning and Corporate
Development Division. *Ms Aleth Wee,* Director, Planning and Research
Department. *Ms Lena Soh,* Senior Officer, Planning and Research
Department.

SURREY POLICE
Kevin Miles, Information Manager. *Phil Scutchings,* Director of Information
Services. Bracken Associates, external information consultants: *Graham
Robertson* (Principal), *Tim Sparrow, David Streatfield.*

THOMAS MILLER LIMITED
Mark Holford, Information Strategist. *Jacqueline Rees,* Group Director
of Information.

UNIVERSITY OF NORTH LONDON
Judy Evans, Head of Management Information. *Roy Williams,* Director of
Information Systems and Services.

Individuals

I am also grateful to colleagues and friends who have contributed from their
knowledge, and have helped my thinking forward, in particular: *Simon Bell,
Suzanne Burge, Rose Dixon, Professor Clive Holtham, Dr Forest Woody Horton, Jr,
Professor Donald Marchand, Rosemary Miller, Meirwen Pride, Professor Philip
M'Pherson, Graham Robertson*

to members of Aslib Information Resources Management Network, for being
information-strategy guinea pigs, and to participants in courses on information
auditing here and in Australia, who have helped me to develop my ideas about
the process.

I am especially indebted to friends and colleagues in Australia and Singapore,
who gave me the opportunity of trying out ideas on their students at just the
right time, particularly to *Barbara Poston Anderson, Hilary Yerbury, Sue Burgess,
Jan Houghton* and *Joan Parker* of the Department of Information Studies at the
University of Technology, Sydney; and to *Michael Middleton* and *Ross Harvey*
who introduced me to excellent and tolerant case study contacts.

As always, it is a pleasure to thank *Graham Stevens* for his deep understanding
of book typography and his grasp of the author's intentions and of complex
content, which result in design that encourages and supports the reader.

I do not think there are many authors who chivvy their publishers about keeping to schedule. I do, and I have to thank *Suzie Duke* and *Solveig Gardner
Servian* for bearing with it remarkably well, and for keeping me in order.

Before we begin...

These are the definitions which I use for the main concepts in this book. Some of them will appear again later, in extended form, but I hope it will be useful to have them here for easy reference, as well as for reflection before starting to read the book.

Knowledge

Knowledge is what we acquire from our interaction with the world; it is the results of experience organized and stored inside each individual's own mind in a way that is unique to each (though there are features common to how we all do this). It comes in two main kinds: knowledge *about* things, and *know-how*, and our knowledge is available to us at various levels from 'tacit' – what we know and use without expressing it in words, to 'explicit' – what we can readily formulate and explain (for more about tacit knowledge, see Cooley, 1987 and Nonaka and Takeuchi, 1995). We make it our own by *transforming* the experience that comes from outside into internal knowledge. Knowledge belongs to us more surely than most of our possessions, and is indeed the most precious and essential of all possessions, because it is what we use to guide our actions in accordance with our values.

Knowledge also depends on *memory* – and memory too comes in two kinds: *internal* – inside our heads, and *external* – knowledge put into external stores like libraries or databases or reference books so that we don't have to try to carry everything we need in our heads.

Information

Information is what human beings *transform* knowledge into when they want to communicate it to other people. It is knowledge made visible or audible, in written or printed words, or in speech.[1]

From the point of view of the *user,* information is what we seek and pay attention to in our outside world when we need to add to or enrich our knowledge in order to act upon it. So we can also usefully think of it as the *food of knowledge* because we need information and communication to nourish and maintain our knowledge and keep it in good shape for what we have to do in the world. Without the food of information, knowledge becomes enfeebled.

The transformation of information into knowledge, and knowledge into information, forms the basis for all human learning and communication; it allows ideas to spread across space and time, and links past and present in a

---

[1] 'Information allows you to express, transfer and convey knowledge', as Marchand (1997) puts it.

network that embraces generations and cultures over millennia. By virtue of that quality, it is also fundamental to the working of organizations of all kinds.

'Two distincts, division none' (Shakespeare, *The Phoenix and the Turtle*)

Knowledge and information are separate but interacting entities; we transform one into another constantly, and according to circumstances one or other will be to the fore. As Samuel Butler is said to have remarked (quoted in Gould, 1991, page 268), 'a chicken is merely the egg's way of making another egg'. The critical distinction is that before information can be used it has to be transformed into knowledge in human minds, and then applied by them to affect both the material world and the ideas of others.[2] For these reasons, the policies and strategies discussed in this book need to take into account both information and knowledge, and the term 'information policy' should be understood in that light.

Organizational information policy

An *organizational information policy* is founded on an organization's overall objectives, and the priorities within them, and defines, at a general level:
- The objectives of information use in the organization, and the priorities among them
- What 'information' means in the context of what the organization is in business for
- The principles on which it will manage information
- Principles for the use of human resources in managing information
- Principles for the use of technology to support information management
- The principles it will apply in relation to establishing the cost-effectiveness of information and knowledge.

An information policy is a dynamic tool which can be used:
- As the basis for developing an organizational information strategy (see below)
- To relate everything that is done with information to the organization's overall objectives
- To enable effective decisions on resource allocation
- To promote interaction, communication and mutual support between all

[2] Nonaka and Takeuchi (1995, pages 58, 59) make a similar distinction: 'Knowledge is essentially related to human action.' Information is what 'provides a new point of view for interpreting events or objects, which makes visible previously invisible meanings or sheds light on unexpected connections. ... It affects knowledge by adding something to it or restructuring it.'

parts of the organization, and between the organization and its 'customers' or 'public'

- To provide objective criteria for assessing the results of information-based activities
- To give feedback to the process of developing corporate policies.

Information strategy

Information strategy is the detailed expression of information policy in terms of objectives, targets, and actions to achieve them, for a defined period ahead. Information strategy provides the framework for the management of information. Information strategy, contained within the framework of an organizational policy for information and supported by appropriate systems and technology, is the 'engine' for:

- Maintaining, managing and applying the organization's information resources
- Supporting its essential knowledge base and all who contribute to it, with strategic intelligence, for achieving its key business objectives

Information management[3]

In the context of information policy, *information management* is the implementation of an information strategy in order to meet information objectives within the overall constraints of available resources. It is therefore concerned with:

- How information is acquired, recorded and stored
- Where information resources are located in the organization, and who has responsibility for them
- How it flows within the organization and between the organization and its outside world
- How the organization uses it
- How people who handle it apply their skills and cooperate with one another
- How information technology supports the users of information
- What information costs and the value it contributes
- How effectively all these information-related activities contribute towards achievement of the organization's objectives.

Knowledge management

While the term is currently almost too popular for its own good, definitions are a little on the thin side as yet (sometimes it seems to mean no more than having what in the early 1970s was called an 'index of expertise' – a card index to the various kinds of specialist knowledge and skill available in the organization, kept handy on the librarian's desk), and there is quite a determined, if

---

[3] This scope of this definition is very close to that of the definition of Information Resource Management, adopted by the Aslib Information Resource Management Network (see Willard, 1993)

misguided, attempt to hijack it into the camp of technology. In my understanding, knowledge management is concerned with:

- What the people who make up organizations need to know to act successfully in their organization's interests
- The actual resources of knowledge and skill belonging to the people who work in an organization, which collectively constitute its knowledge base
- Ensuring that these resources are maintained, safeguarded and developed in accordance with the emerging needs of the organization
- Ensuring that people understand the obligations implicit in their contract with the organization in using their knowledge to achieve the organization's goals. These obligations cover applying knowledge effectively, transforming it into information to make it accessible to others inside and outside the organization, negotiating interchanges of knowledge and information, maintaining their knowledge in good condition, adding it to the organization's knowledge base, and passing it on to their successors in appropriate ways when they leave
- Equitable arrangements between the organization and the people it employs which respect the rights of both in the matter of knowledge
- Systems and technology to support people in using their knowledge in these ways
- The value which the use of knowledge contributes to the assets of the organization.
  (For thoughtful contributions on the concept, see Skyrme, 1997 and Wilson, 1998.)

Organizations

This definition is designed to be applicable to any kind of organization, from social club to government department; from manufacturing firm to service business; from pressure group to educational institution.

Organizations are groupings of people into 'socio-technical systems' (Eason, 1988), for explicit or implicit purposes, which include creating 'offerings' of products, or services, or combinations of the two. They interact both internally and with their environment; they seek 'sustenance' to keep in being; and they have a structure and a boundary.

Process

The process view of organizations, as defined, for example, by Best (1996, page 4) – 'For practical purposes we may regard a *process* ... as the set of resources and activities (whether undertaken by people or by machines) necessary and sufficient to convert some input into some output' – sees them as an interlocking series of activities devoted to creating outputs, instead of a set of functional departments within the bounds of which self-contained activities take place – the metaphor is a river, rather than a stack of boxes.

This book takes a process approach in two ways. First, it looks at the business of developing information policy and strategy as an overall process, containing a series of processes and sub-processes, in all of which human minds, assisted as necessary by technology, use knowledge to convert what exists into something new. Second, it follows Davenport (1993) in seeing information as something that enters into all business processes, and that is essential for integrating all the processes that make up an organization.

References

BEST, D. (ed.), (1996), *The Fourth Resource: Information and its Management,* Aldershot: Aslib/Gower

COOLEY, M. (1987), *Architect or Bee? The human price of technology,* London: Hogarth Press

DAVENPORT, T. H. (1993), *Process Innovation. Reengineering work through information technology,* Boston, MA: Harvard Business School Press

EASON, K. (1988), *Information Technology and Organisational Change,* London: Taylor & Francis

GOULD, S. J. (1991), *Ever since Darwin,* London: Penguin Books

MARCHAND, D. (1997), 'Competing with information: know what you want', *FT Mastering Management Reader,* July/August 1997

NONAKA, I. and TAKEUCHI, H. (1995), *The Knowledge-creating Company: how Japanese companies create the dynamics of information,* New York: Oxford University Press

SKYRME, D. J. (1997), 'Knowledge management: oxymoron or dynamic duo?', *Managing Information,* 4 (7), 24–26

WILSON, O. (1998), 'Knowledge management: putting a good idea to work', *Managing Information,* 5 (2), 31–33

WILLARD, N. (1993), 'Information resources management', *Aslib Information,* 21 (5), 201–205

Part 1 Background

Introduction

In this chapter:
- Why this book was written
- What has changed? and what has not ...
- To the reader
- How the book is organized

Why this book was written

The first edition of this book (Orna, 1990) was written because of evidence that few businesses or public organizations in the UK had a policy or strategy for using information to support the achievement of their key business objectives. The incident that finally decided me to write it was the response at a conference of information managers to a speaker's question about how many of their organizations had a strategy for what they did with information (only four out of over a hundred could answer yes), but that was the culmination of a long period of personal experience and attention to the experience of others in the field. It seemed important to write it then, because the end of the 1980s was a time at once of opportunity and of danger for those concerned with the management of information, and for the organizations that employed them.

My purpose in writing it was threefold:

1 To show why organizations should develop such a policy; the dangers of being without one, and the benefits of having one
2 To provide practical help for information managers and others in developing and implementing information policies and strategies
3 To show examples of actual organizations in the UK and elsewhere which had taken steps to develop policies, how they set about it, and the results.

The first edition has gone at least some way to fulfilling its purpose, in that it seems to have been helpful in practice to some organizations and for some individuals – which is about as much as one can realistically hope for a book. That in itself, however, is not sufficient to merit a new edition; justification for that lies in both what has changed in the situation as compared with 1989, when I started writing, and in what apparently remains the same (though everything is in constant change and flux, and even those situations and beliefs that look as though they are set in concrete are susceptible to change, and sometimes the transitions can be very rapid – and that in itself provides a reason for writing about information as a protection against being ambushed by unexpected change).

What has changed? and what has not ...

Some of the changes and non-changes are in the world with which the book deals and to which it is addressed; others are in my own thinking, as a result of trying to keep pace with the changes in the world and of many conversations, face to face and via e-mail, with friends and colleagues in the UK and elsewhere. I shall try to summarize them here, so that readers can consider them in the light of their own experience and understanding. Most of the changes I shall describe were under way at the end of the 1980s, but they are highlighted here because they have all developed strongly since then.

In the world

Here, there are several key themes; for each, there are both dynamic and static aspects – evolving ideas and actions in some places, and the old familiar ones in others. Information policy at the level of the enterprise is not such a rare bird as it was at the time of the first edition, and it still seems that there is a better chance of producing a workable policy for information within individual organizations than at national level. There are hopeful developments at that level, such as the work in the UK of the Library and Information Commission, which has as one of its tasks advising government on the feasibility of a national information policy, and which appears to be taking the realistic line of recommending, rather than a single overall policy, a framework of principles into which existing government departmental policies should be fitted. But there is still far to go; as Browne (1997 a and b) and Rowlands (1996) among others suggest, ideas about national information policy still lack a strong intellectual basis, are driven by different values in different societies, and suffer from confusion about its scope and nature.

The role of knowledge and information in organizations

Changing. During the late 1980s and throughout the 1990s there has been a strong development in organizational theory in this area – particularly in the United States, where it is described (Nonaka and Takeuchi, 1995) as an explosion. In fact, many related ideas have been around for a good deal longer; the concept of the 'learning organization', which depends on intelligent use of information, dates back to the 1950s and 1960s (Argyris, 1993, for example, has been writing on it since 1953).

The emphasis is now, however, particularly on knowledge as the active force for organizational success. Recent developments of the ideas include Choo's (1996) concept of the 'Knowing Organization' which:

> ... possesses information and knowledge so that it is well informed, mentally perceptive, and enlightened. Its actions are based upon a shared and valid understanding of the organization's environments and needs, and are leveraged by the available knowledge resources and skill competencies of its members. The Knowing Organization possesses information and knowledge that confers a special advantage, allowing it to manoeuvre with intelligence, creativity, and occasionally cunning. (Choo, 1996, page 339)

Nonaka and Takeuchi (1995) develop the idea of organizations as creators of knowledge, through a 'knowledge spiral' (see Figure 1.1 on page 17). The ideas are not confined to the written word; the recent works cited quote examples of leading businesses which are actually trying to realize them in practice.

A prediction I made not long ago may be coming true. I suggested (Orna, 1996a) that if information and knowledge resources turned out to be a great deal more valuable than had been assumed, the world of organizational values

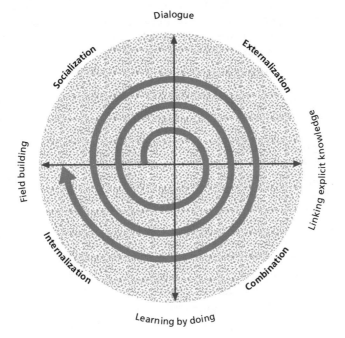

'A knowledge-creation spiral … emerges when the interaction between tacit and explicit knowledge is elevated dynamically' from a lower level to higher levels

The process is driven by four modes of thinking, each triggered by a different kind of interaction with others:

1 Socialization
Field building – the creation of 'forums' for interaction, and experience sharing

2 Externalization
Dialogue – the articulation of tacit knowledge, putting it into the outside world

3 Combination
Networking – bringing together newly created knowledge and existing knowledge

4 Internalization
Learning by doing, so that the new knowledge fully belongs to the individual and the organization

Fig 1.1   **The knowledge-creation spiral**

might be turned upside down, and people ambitious for advancement might seek to take over the hitherto despised territory of the information profes- sional. The job title of 'Knowledge Manager' is today one of high prestige, the technology vendors are making a bid for information and knowledge manage- ment as part of the IT and systems domain,[1] and one even hears of manage- ment consultants eager to learn about what information managers do.

At the same time, information science itself has been moving in a similar direction, not only in placing increasing emphasis on human cognition and the transformation of information into knowledge (for example, Ingwersen, 1992, 1994), but also in recognizing the importance of action as a result of the transformation. As Pickering (1996) puts it, information science is fundamen- tally 'the study of the knowledge system; the nature of knowledge and the way in which it is acquired and imparted. It is also about the contact between one mind and another, and the interrelationships between information and human attitudes and behaviour ... we generally impart knowledge (ie we inform) in order to influence the current or future actions of others, and we ourselves acquire knowledge (ie are informed) in order to form attitudes and act.' So, by implication, what constitutes knowledge and information for each person or institution is based on the values they hold.

At the practical level, the professional associations of librarians and infor- mation managers are joining forces with professional management bodies and technology companies to run conferences with such titles as 'Increasing Cor- porate Power through Knowledge Management'.

Not much change. While phrases like 'the learning organization' or 'the organi- zational knowledge-base' now trip easily from many managerial lips, and get enshrined in mission statements, few organizations yet have a clear definition of what knowledge and information mean in terms of what they are seeking to achieve. Abell's pilot study of firms for research on information and business performance (Owens et al, 1996) concluded that while 'information as a *con- cept* has become a central issue for most firms... the interpretation of the con- cept varies considerably from person to person'. Over the past few years, I have asked a good many audiences if they know any organizations which have asked and answered the question 'What does information consist of for *our* business?' – but have found no affirmative answers. The terms still slide by without examination, on the assumption that we all know what information and knowledge are – this quotation from *The Economist* of 1990 still has truth in it: 'One of the ironies of the "information revolution" is that so few of those involved can give any definition of what information is' (quoted in Fisher and Sless, 1990).

Things get particularly confusing when we encounter talk which purports to be about the information revolution and using knowledge dynamically, but which is actually less concerned with knowledge and information than with the wonders, in particular the speed, of the technology. The claim to novelty

---

[1] A recent survey of information management in over 200 organizations, by Interactive Information Services (reported in *Inform*, May 1998), found that IT departments, closely followed by Finance departments, con- sider themselves to have the main responsibility for information and its management.

actually rests on nothing more than a modern version of the Red Queen's exhortation to run ever faster to stay in the same place. The Chairman of IBM UK LIMITED was reported recently (Temple, 1996) as claiming that 'Managers want information yesterday and if they can't get it that quickly, they don't want it. So time is becoming more important than cost, and as a result things will get faster...;' the lesson for the people who have to provide the information yesterday (another Alice touch, that), who 'could go mad as companies rethink the whole concept of employment' is none other than the old exhortation that dates back to the first Wilson government: 'We will all have to re-skill several times in our careers.'

The cost and value of information; information as an asset

Changing. Convincing arguments for the value to organizations of intangible assets, with examples from the practice of a range of businesses, have been advanced for the past decade, notably by Itami and Roehl (1987). They identify information as lying 'at the heart of invisible assets', and divide it into three categories: environmental (from the organization's outside world); corporate (flowing outwards from the organization and 'creating invisible assets stored in the environment', including reputation and brand and corporate image); and internal (circulating within the organization).

Within the past few years, awareness of the potential value of the 'information assets' of businesses has increased greatly among senior management in some areas. Serious efforts to promote a 'Board agenda' for information, centred on persuading businesses to assign a value to their information resources, have been initiated through the IMPACT initiative and the Hawley Committee (1995) which developed from it; businesses like Reuters (1995) have sponsored research on information as an asset; and the British Library has funded research on the relationship between information use and business success (Owens et al, 1996). A possibly related development is the increasing popularity of information auditing (see Chapter 4) among a great variety of businesses and organizations.

Abell (1996), on the basis of her involvement in a range of projects concerned with how business and industry use information and how they perceive its value and effect on performance, concludes that the growing interest in company knowledge as an 'intangible balance sheet asset' has coincided with a wish to bring together a wider range of information resources than before, including 'operational data, company intelligence and external information'.

Meanwhile, convincing research evidence has accumulated on the contribution which properly managed information makes to innovation, productivity and competitiveness and on the negative contribution of the contrary (see Herget, 1995 and Crawshaw, 1994 for concrete examples of what Herget calls 'the cost of (non-) quality').

A striking development in the mid-1990s has been the growing interest (coming from a variety of disciplines, including accounting, management, systems engineering and information management) in methods of assigning costs and value to intangibles such as information, so that their contribution to overall assets can fairly be set alongside that of traditional material assets.

Burk and Horton (1988), who were first in the field with their Infomapper
software, have recently updated it (Horton, 1994); McPherson's (1994, 1996)
original IVM™ methodology has found applications in a number of contexts
in the UK and elsewhere; and other methodologies for setting a value on intangibles such as the Skandia Navigator, Sveiby's Intangible Assets Monitor, and
the IC-Index™ are becoming well known (see Skyrme, 1998). This represents a real leap forward after a long period of fairly unproductive attempts
to get there through a combination of conventional economic theory and
information theory *à la* Shannon and Weaver (for a summary, see Orna,
1996a).

Not much change. Here, too, while such phrases as 'valuing information assets',
'accountability for information' and 'managing information as a resource'
have become very acceptable additions to the managerial vocabulary, the
evidence suggests that not many organizations have got far along this road,
and that not all who use the words have grasped the inwardness of the ideas.
Telephone interviews with 500 companies, carried out for Reuters Business
Information (1995), for example, suggest that while a quarter of them considered information their most important asset (and indeed one in ten thought it
more important than the people they employed!), only one in six was currently capitalizing information on its balance sheet, 25 per cent were prevented from doing so because they found it too difficult to quantify and a similar
number advanced the same reason for not tracking the costs of collecting and
maintaining information.

Strategic use of information

Changing. Interest in the idea of an information strategy aligned with the overall business strategy, to support key business objectives, or 'core competencies', especially in those areas which are most distinctive and unique to the
organization, continues to grow and to find expression in actual attempts to
develop and apply such a strategy. It is interesting to note the change over
time in the approach of some organizations to information systems strategy,
which, as Galliers (1993) observes, has moved away from technical issues, and
towards organizational and information concerns. (Recent case studies of
major museums, such as Orna and Pettitt, 1998, provide examples of institutions which started from trying to develop an information systems strategy
and came to realize in the process that what they needed as a foundation for
ISS was a strategy for information itself.) There is a potential contradiction
between, on the one hand, a co-ordinated information strategy, and on the
other the trend towards decentralised management of information implicit in
the praiseworthy attempt which some organizations are making to get all managers to accept information management as part of their job. The solution will
demand intensive work on structure and culture and ingenious support from
systems and technology.

Not much change. While senior managers, as Marchand (1997) recently pointed out, are accustomed to use information as an essential part of their own
management activity (managing 'with' information), they often fail to define

what they are using as 'information', and to grasp that information itself requires management (management *of* information). And surveys of businesses suggests a degree of confusion about the subject. The most recent (Library Association, 1996) survey (a random sample of nearly 1000 chief executives in the UK) found, to use its own moderate wording, that 'In many cases the management of information appears to be evolving somewhat haphazardly.' While 60 per cent of respondents claimed that their company had a strategy or policy for managing its information, only 38 per cent said it was discussed at board level, and only just under 20 per cent were aware that their company had an overall information budget. And only 6 per cent of respondents were confident that the term 'information' was a category in the company accounts (66 per cent were unsure of the answer to this question).

Other research for Reuters Business Information (1994) produced a yet more depressing response on information policy: over 60 per cent of a sample of 500 larger firms had no policy for information, while of the 37 per cent of the respondents who claimed that their business had a policy, 9 per cent did not know what it was.

Understanding between different professional groups

Changing. There are some encouraging instances of *rapprochement* in the work situation between practitioners of IS/IT and of information management, and of contributions to thinking on these matters from outside the usual range (for example from systems engineering, organizational behaviour, and so on), which give hope that one day there may be a comprehensive body of ideas enriched from many sides, and that mutual understanding and interdisciplinary negotiation and cooperation in the strategic use of information may come to prevail among those who have often seemed to be unaware of one another's existence.

Not much change. While many individuals are breaking down the walls of assumption and of terminology which have concealed the fact that different disciplines are actually living in the same space and thinking similar thoughts, many practitioners are still deep in their bunkers, believing themselves to be the only ones alive in the territory. It is still easy to find, for example, discussions of information retrieval conducted purely in terms of programming, without apparent awareness of the literature from the domain of information science. A recent conference on 'Information Stewardship: implementing accountability for the data resource' was announced as intended for an audience of 'CIO's, I/S Management, Corporate Management responsible for I/S, Data Administration and Data Resource Management staff, Data/Information Stewards, business people involved in managing or using information', and an earlier article by the main speaker (English, 1993) makes it clear that, while he has sensible ideas about the concepts of information ownership, guardianship and stakeholding, he has apparently no idea that there are other professionals whose business it is to manage information, who are familiar with the ideas he discusses. From the other end of the scale, a work of deep scholarship, on 'information space' (Boisot, 1995), which is far from technology-oriented, draws on ideas from many disciplines, but shows no signs of acquaintance with the literature of information science proper – all the author cites in that area is the 'information theory' of Shannon and Weaver.

Technology that supports human minds in managing information

Changing. Electronic tools for doing things with information continue to appear on the market at a rate more rapid than human minds with other problems to think of can comfortably absorb. They are on the whole, however, tools which are better fitted to the activities for which people need to apply them, and to the way minds actually work. Abell (1996) accurately summarizes the nature of the changes as a move from 'the delivery of hardware and software specified by the IT department, to a user requirement driven approach'. This new approach is embodied in two main changes:

- from operational, financial and design software to groupware and communications
- from creation of databases to document management to work flow and imaging.

(For useful summaries of recent and current developments in the technology available for information management, see Parsons, 1996 and Thom, 1996.)

Today there is also greater potential than ever before for organizations to make integrated use of all the kinds of information they need to manage their affairs successfully, via integrated systems, which, as foreshadowed by Booth (1991), allow a common input mechanism and a common interface to external information systems, corporate systems, function-based systems, other internal information systems and office systems. Applications like Lotus Notes are, as Abell (1996) says, 'increasingly being used as a platform for integration, enabling users to contribute to, as well as access, the central knowledge base'.

And, of course, there are intranets – the application of Web browser technology to internal information resources – which became the fashionable bit of the technology in 1996. The good news is that at least some serious thinking is being invested both in finding appropriate technological support for managing corporate information on intranets (see, for example, De Smith and Boniface, 1997; and Wodehouse, 1997).

Some of the changes in this area express themselves in the form of disillusion with what had earlier been thought to be 'silver bullet' solutions. Disenchantment with the results of investment in IT has been well documented (Galliers, 1992 provides a number of telling quotations and references; and Collins, 1998, in the aptly titled *Crash*, gives hair-raising accounts of costly IT disasters resulting from all too human mismanagement). The mid-1990s saw the start of a retreat from faith in the late 1980s remedies of downsizing and short time horizons. Keegan (1994) quotes Hamel and Prahalad (*Competing for the Future*, Harvard Business School) who argue that the US and Britain have produced a generation of managers who are concerned only with downsizing, rather than creating markets for the future, while Tapscott (1996) concludes that the expected dramatic improvements to the bottom line have not materialized from business process re-engineering and staff cuts: 'Neutron bombing your company is not a strategy for the new economy.' (Hammer and Champy, whose *Reengineering the corporation* has a good deal to answer for in this respect, in a revised edition published in 1995, take pains to make it clear that 'Reengineering is not restructuring or downsizing' (page 48) – it just means doing less with less, by making processes simple and jobs more complex!)

Not much change. There are, however, still plenty of decision makers who believe that investment in IT makes investment in thinking about what you want to do with information unnecessary, and plenty of encouragement from the IT side for them to think that way. So the new developments in the technology mentioned above, which have greater potential than their predecessors for more congenial and innovative use of information – provided hard thinking about the information and what you want to do with it is invested first – are still being promoted and purchased as solutions in themselves.

And what can only be described as pernicious rubbish is still being peddled about how human beings have to submit themselves to the procrustean bed of IT and jump to it ever faster without pausing to ask questions (pursuing that mixed metaphor suggests that anyone who has had the Procrustes treatment isn't going to be in much of a state to jump anywhere). An 'Employee handbook' (Pritchett, 1994), punctuated with soundbites about the number of computers, mobile phones, fax machines, pagers, and so on now in use, and designed to 'change employees' outdated and dangerous mindsets', urges workers to 'operate with a strong sense of urgency. Accelerate in all aspects of your work', accept whatever the information revolution brings, and 'Take no part whatsoever in resistance to change'.

Information managers: how they see themselves; how others see them

Changing. There appears to be greater confidence today than there was in 1989 among those information managers who are willing to confront the situation and evaluate it – especially when they have a forum like that provided by the Aslib Information Resource Management Network which allows them to reflect collectively and share experience. There is less willingness to accept managerial brush-off, and more readiness to take initiatives, to be good opportunists, and to be ingenious in gaining recognition for their professionalism and space to exercise it properly. At least some well-placed observers in the business take an optimistic view; Coopers and Lybrand Vice Chairman and Chief Knowledge Officer, Ellen Knapp (1998) recently claimed that 'as organisations sort out their technology and cultural issues they will then realise the true value of information skills – and information specialists are going to get rich very soon.'

Not much change. Because information and the kind of management it needs are still not properly defined by senior managers in terms of what their organization is in business for, the core skills and knowledge of information professionals are still not generally understood. The research for the Library Association mentioned above revealed that only 39 per cent of the companies in the survey provided an in-house library or information service; and more than 60 per cent of the respondents from those companies were unable to say what position the person in charge of it held in the company structure – a confirmation of Abell's (1996) reflection that 'generally, the corporate information person is not viewed as part of the business', and Davenport's (1993) observation that the traditional assumption in business is that information acquisition, analysis and distribution 'is work better managed by subordinates'.

Developments in my own thinking

In the years since writing the first edition of this book, I have become more certain that the only convincing argument for investment in information resources and information management will be a demonstration that it is possible to make a reliable assessment of the value that information contributes to the overall assets of the organization. Therefore the key problem to crack is a credible method; such methods are becoming available, and information professionals should concern themselves energetically with becoming knowledgeable in this area, and with educating senior management about it.

I think I now have a clearer view of the relative roles of information policy and strategy, and of the process of moving from policy development to strategy development and implementation. I have also come to see the central role of information auditing as a means of establishing a baseline of knowledge of the actual situation, and a reasonably secure platform for both strategy development and establishing the contribution that information and knowledge make to the total assets of organizations (Orna, 1996b).

I still subscribe to these propositions:

- Knowledge in human minds is the only means by which information is put to use and gains in value.
- The human owners of the minds in organizations need to interact and negotiate in using information.
- Technology and systems should form a supportive infrastructure that helps rather than hinders human minds in doing what they need to do.
- If organizations define what they need to know to survive and prosper, they are well on the way to understanding what information they should acquire and use about their outside world and themselves.
- For a cheap, cost-effective and low-risk investment, you can't beat thinking.

To the reader

This book was written with three main groups of readers in mind:

1 Information managers who are responsible for libraries and information services and other information resources in organizations – in the hope that it will help them to apply their professional knowledge and their knowledge of their own place of work to move their organizations closer to an 'information culture'

2 Managers and executives, especially those with overall responsibility for information resources – in the hope that it will help them towards fuller understanding of the potential of this unique, complex and fascinating

resource, so that they can apply their own specialist knowledge to bringing it closer to the centre of the organization

3 Students of information science, librarianship, information management and kindred subjects – in the hope that it will form something of a bridge between theory and practice as they prepare for their careers and move out into the world of employment.

How the book is organized

The next chapter looks at why organizations need a policy for managing whatever constitutes 'their' information, the benefits they can gain, and the risks and costs they can avoid by it. It also considers who should be involved in policy making, development and implementation.

The major part of the text is then devoted to the processes involved in creating and implementing organizational information policies and strategies, and in making use of them to help the organization develop, meet change, and learn from experience so that it continues to survive and prosper in the terms it sets itself. I shall not use the currently fashionable term 'leverage', because the mental image I have is not of the simple mechanical principle of the lever, but of a more subtle, dynamic and organic rotating spiral, each turn informing the next above, and with feedback flowing back down again in a constantly descending and ascending path. The spiral represents the total process, and each turn a contributing process, which itself consists of sub-processes.

I move aside from the account of the process to consider four critical areas for the successful development and application of information strategy: human resources (though I prefer to call them people); the IT and information systems infrastructure which should support them in what they do with information; appropriate methods for measuring the costs of information, and the value that it contributes to organizational assets; and the role of information and knowledge in mastering, rather than being at the mercy of, change.

The final part of the book consists of true stories – case studies of organizations, of various kinds in a variety of places here and abroad, which are at some point in the process of developing information policies and strategies. I have deliberately looked for organizations at different stages, doing the job in different ways, because I know from readers of the first edition that a range of different stories gives a chance of finding something that connects with their own situation.

References

ABELL, A. (1996), 'The information professional in 1996', *Information Management Report*, January, 1–6

ARGYRIS, C. (1993), *On Organizational Learning* (a collection of papers on the subject from 1953 to 1991), Oxford: Blackwell

BOISOT, M. H. (1995), *Information Space. A framework for learning in organizations, institutions and culture*, London: Routledge

BOOTH, A. (1991), 'The implementation of integrated information systems', *Information Services & Use*, 11, 203–211

BROWNE, M. (1997a), 'The field of information policy: 1. Fundamental concepts', *Journal of Information Science*, 23 (4), 261–275

BROWNE, M. (1997b), 'The field of information policy: 2. Redefining the boundaries and methodologies', *Journal of Information Science*, 23 (4), 339–351

BURK, C. F., Jr and HORTON, F. W., Jr (1988), *Infomap: a complete guide to discovering corporate information resources*, Englewood Cliffs, NJ: Prentice Hall

CHOO, C. W. (1996), 'The knowing organization: how organizations use information to construct meaning, create knowledge and make decisions', *International Journal of Information Management*, 16 (5), 329–340

COLLINS, T. with BICKNELL, D. (1998), *Crash. Learning from the world's worst computer disasters*, London: Simon & Schuster Ltd

CRAWSHAW, S. (1994), 'Infomat – building a quality organization', *Congresboek Kwaliteitsorg in informatiedienstverlening*, Rotterdam

DAVENPORT, T. H. (1993), *Process Innovation. Reengineering work through information technology*, Boston, MA: Harvard Business School Press

De SMITH, M. and BONIFACE, A. (1997), 'Managing information on an intranet', *Managing Information*, 4 (1/2), 27–29

ENGLISH, L. (1993), 'Accountability to the rescue', *Database Programming & Design Magazine*, April, 53–59

FISHER, P. and SLESS, D. (1990), 'Information design methods and productivity in the insurance industry', *Information Design Journal*, 6 (2), 103–129

GALLIERS, R.D. (1992), 'Information technology – management's boon or bane?', *Journal of Strategic Information Systems*, 1 (2), 50–56

GALLIERS, R. D. (1993), 'Research issues in information systems', *Journal of Information Technology*, 8, 92–98

HAMMER, M. and CHAMPY, J. (1995), *Reengineering the Corporation. A manifesto for business revolution*, London: Nicholas Brealy/HarperCollins

HAWLEY COMMITTEE (1995), *Information as an Asset. The Board Agenda. Checklist and explanatory notes* and *Information as an Asset. The Board Agenda. A consultative report*, London: KPMG IMPACT Programme

HERGET, J. (1995), 'The cost of (non-) quality: why it matters for information providers', *FID News Bulletin*, 45 (5), 156–159

HORTON, F. W., Jr (1994), 'Infomapper revisited', *Aslib Proceedings*, 46 (4), 117–120

INGWERSEN, P. (1992), 'Information and information science in context', *Libri*, 42 (2), 99–135

INGWERSEN, P. (1994), 'Information science: opening up Pandora's Box', *Inform*, January/February, 1–2

ITAMI, H. with ROEHL, T. W. (1987), *Mobilizing Invisible Assets*, Cambridge, MA: Harvard University Press

KEEGAN, V. (1994), 'The sack by any other name would taste just as bitter', *The Guardian*, 3 October

KNAPP, E. (1998), Keynote address to EBIC 98, *TFPL Newsletter*, Issue 6

LIBRARY ASSOCIATION (1996), 'New research shows business fails to manage information effectively', *Information for Business*, 3, 1–2

MARCHAND, D. (1997) 'Competing with information: know what you want', *FT Mastering Management Reader*, July/August 1997

McPHERSON, P. K. (1994), 'Accounting for the value of information', *Aslib Proceedings*, 46 (9), 203–215

McPHERSON, P. K. (1996), 'The inclusive value of information', 48th Congress of the International Federation for Information and Documentation, Graz, Austria, 25–28 October

NONAKA, I. and TAKEUCHI, H. (1995), *The Knowledge-creating Company: how Japanese companies create the dynamics of information*, New York: Oxford University Press

ORNA, E. (1990), *Practical Information Policies. How to manage information flow in organizations*, Aldershot: Gower

ORNA, E. (1996a), 'Valuing information: problems and opportunities', in D. BEST (ed.), *The Fourth Resource: Information and its Management*, Aldershot: Aslib/Gower

ORNA, E. (1996b), 'Information auditing', *Singapore Libraries*, 25 (2), 69–82

ORNA, E. and PETTITT, C. W. (1998), *Information Management in Museums*, Aldershot: Gower

OWENS, I., WILSON, T. with ABELL, A. (1996), *Information and Business Performance. A study of information systems and services in high performing companies*, London: Bowker-Saur

PARSONS, J. (1996), 'Information – the fourth resource' in D. BEST (ed.), *The Fourth Resource: Information and its Management*, Aldershot: Aslib/Gower

PICKERING, W. R. (1996), 'Principia informatica: conversations with R T Bottle', *Journal of Information Science*, 22 (6), 447–456

PRITCHETT, PRICE (1994), *The Employee Handbook of New Work Habits for a Radically Changing World. 13 ground rules for job success in the information age*, Washington, Tyne & Wear: Pritchett & Associates Inc.

REUTERS BUSINESS INFORMATION (1994), *To Know or not to Know: the politics of information* (research commissioned from Taylor Nelson, AGB), London: Reuters Business Information

REUTERS BUSINESS INFORMATION (1995), *Information as an Asset: the invisible goldmine* (research commissioned from the Industrial Research Bureau), London: Reuters Business Information

ROWLANDS, I. (1996), 'Understanding information policy: concepts, frameworks and research tools', *Journal of Information Science*, 22 (1), 13–25

SKYRME, D. (1998), 'Valuing knowledge: is it worth it?', *Managing Information*, 5 (2), 24–26

TAPSCOTT, C. (1996), *The Digital Economy*, New York: McGraw (quoted in DiMATTIA, S. S. 'Downsizing: the next generation', *Library Journal*, 15 March, 36)

TEMPLE, N. (1996), 'Winners & Losers', *TFPL debates ...*, London: TFPL Ltd

THOM, W. (1996), 'Managing the fourth resource', in D. BEST (ed.), *The Fourth Resource: information and its management*, Aldershot: Aslib/Gower

WODEHOUSE, LORD (1997), 'The Intranet – the quiet (r)evolution', *Aslib Proceedings*, 49 (1), 13–19

Organizations and information

In this chapter:

- What makes an organization?
- What do organizations need to know to survive?
- Why organizations need to define knowledge and information for themselves
- Why organizations need a policy and a strategy for information
- Whose business is information policy and strategy?

[1] This has similarities with Scarrott's (1996) definition of an 'organised system' as 'an interdependent assembly of elements and/or organised systems', and of information as 'what is inter-changed between the elements of an organised system to effect their interdependence.' It encourages me, because Scarrott arrived at it from reflecting on information in the light of a lifetime's experience in electrical engineering, which made him dissatisfied with the approach to information typical of his profession.

What makes an organization?

Organizations are everywhere today; input 'organization' as a subject or title search term to the OPAC of any academic or large public library, and you will get hundreds of hits; add 'organizational' and you will get a few hundred more, from 'organizational behaviour' to 'organizational structure' via 'organizational culture' and 'organizational learning'. But had you made the search 60 years ago, you would not have found anything like that; as Drucker (1995a, page 76) reminds us, the word 'organization' did not come into common use in that sense until after the Second World War (though according to the *Shorter Oxford Dictionary*, it was used to mean 'an organized body, system or society' in 1873).

We all know what organizations are; we work for them, we use their services, pay our taxes to them, belong to them to pursue our hobbies or hobbyhorses. And yet ... not long ago I had occasion to try to find an acceptable definition that would cover any kind of 'organization', from business to religious body, from charity to pressure group, as a preliminary to trying to define what all organizations need to know. In the end, I arrived at the 'necessary and sufficient conditions' which are set out on page 11; here they can be summarized as:[1]

- A grouping of human beings
- For explicit or implicit purposes
- Creating 'offerings' of products and/or services
- Interacting, internally and with its environment
- Seeking sustenance to keep itself in being
- Having a structure and a boundary
- Embodying both social and technical systems.

This seemed to make sense when tried out on people interested in organizations and information in the light of their own experience, so I offer it here as the basis for thinking about what organizations need to know, the information they need to maintain their knowledge in good health, and the reasons why each organization needs its own definition of information and its own policy/strategy for using it.

What do organizations need to know to survive?

If those are the distinguishing characteristics of organizations, then in order to keep alive and well, there are certain things that every organization needs to know, as shown in Figure 2.1 on page 30:
- What is happening inside its boundaries

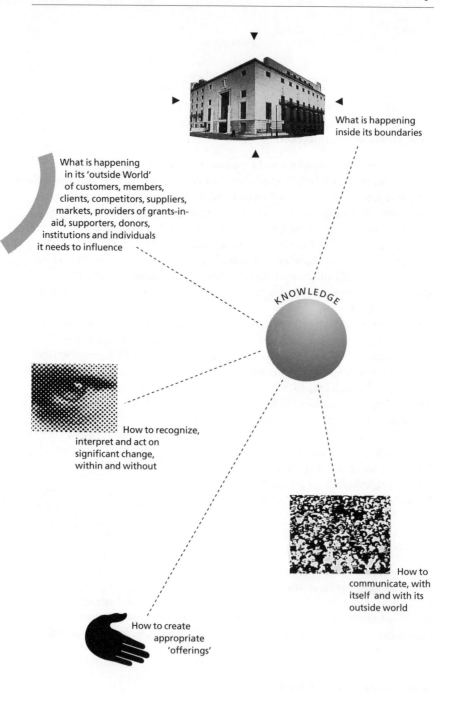

What is happening
inside its boundaries

What is happening
in its 'outside World'
of customers, members,
clients, competitors, suppliers,
markets, providers of grants-in-
aid, supporters, donors,
institutions and individuals
it needs to influence

KNOWLEDGE

How to recognize,
interpret and act on
significant change,
within and without

How to
communicate, with
itself and with its
outside world

How to create
appropriate
'offerings'

Fig 2.1   **What every organization needs to know**

- What is happening in its 'outside world' of customers, members, clients competitors, suppliers, markets, providers of grants-in-aid, supporters, donors, institutions and individuals it needs to influence
- How to recognize, interpret and act on significant change, within and without
- How to create appropriate 'offerings'
- How to communicate, with itself and with its outside world.

These are what is inside the 'KNOWLEDGE' component in Marchand's (1997) model of the factors on which successful organizational strategies depend (see Figure 2.2 on page 32).

Why organizations need to define knowledge and information for themselves

For a long time, I have been trying to find an organization that has formulated its own definition of what information means for it, in the light of what it needs to know in order to succeed in its purposes, but so far I have not found one. This is odd, because if you start from the top-level definition that fits any organization, you quickly realize that the content of each clause will be different for each organization: organizations will seek people of different specialisms, skills and values according to their various purposes; their offerings will differ; so too will their internal structures and external environments and the kind of interactions appropriate to their purposes; the nature of the sustenance they need, and its sources, will vary; and both the internal social relationships and the technology will differ from one to the next. That being so, the *content* of the knowledge and know-how – and consequently of the information they need to maintain it in good health – will also be highly specific to how individual organizations define what they are in business for.

The next chapter will set out in some detail a process for arriving at an organizational definition of knowledge and information, of how the organization needs to use them, and of how they need to flow inside the organization, and between it and its outside world. Here, it is sufficient to quote two examples of very different organizations (see Table 2.1 on page 33), from the case studies which form Part 3 of this book, to show just how different are the kinds of information which they need to take in from their outside world to maintain their knowledge. They exemplify the points made by Drucker (1995b) that core competencies vary according to the nature of the organization; so too does the environmental information which he says is neglected in many companies, though necessary for strategy development – as exemplified by US companies which went into Europe in the 1960s without even asking about labour legislation.

I have come to believe that many of the conceptual difficulties which organizations, and especially their senior managers, experience in trying to come to grips with information arise from being content with a general belief that it is quantitative, about the past and present of their own organization, and lives in databases, and from being unaware of the full range that emerges once one starts 'unpacking' the meaning of mission statements or corporate objectives. As Farkas-Conn (1989) put it, 'Managers subscribing to the notion that

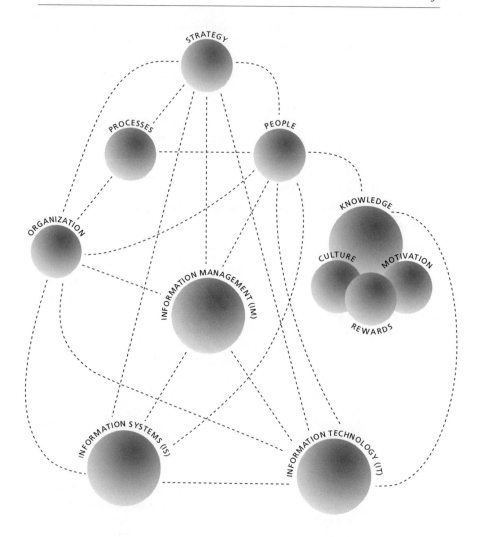

STRATEGY

PROCESSES

PEOPLE

KNOWLEDGE

ORGANIZATION

CULTURE

MOTIVATION

INFORMATION MANAGEMENT (IM)

REWARDS

INFORMATION SYSTEMS (IS)

INFORMATION TECHNOLOGY (IT)

Key

Small spheres:
= factors in the traditional
model of organizations

Large spheres:
= factors in the new model:
'invisible assets'

Based with kind permission on 'Competing with information: know what you want'
by Don Marchand. *FT Mastering Management Reader*, July/August 1997

Fig 2.2   **Traditional and new models of the factors on which organizational strategy
depends. The new model introduces knowledge, information management,
and information systems and technology.**

Credit Union Services Corporation	Surrey Police
Credit Unions, in Australia and world-wide	Trends in crime – local, national, international
Developments in the economy, finance, industry, socio-demographic trends	Local population: age profile, employment
Legislation and compliance requirements	Local geography, land use, vehicle movements
Relevant IT developments, e.g. Internet banking, electronic commerce	Local industry and commerce
Customer response to products	Relevant IT developments, e.g. for tracking crime, imaging
Competitors – banks and building societies	Research in criminology
Existing and potential markets	Local organizations/institutions
Contacts and organizations it needs to communicate with/influence	Legislation
	Other police forces in the UK and abroad
	Contacts – individual, and in local and national organizations

Table 2.1   **Information from the outside world as defined for two organizations**
(Credit Union Services Corporation, Australia; Surrey Police)

companies must use their capabilities and their resources to the fullest are still thinking of information in a disjointed manner of collections, interactions, and a growing world of hardware and software, rather than of an interconnected dynamic whole ... we must now develop an extended view of what constitutes corporate information.' (For other evidence in support of this analysis, see Reuters, 1995; Hayward and Broady, 1995.)

Yet an appropriate definition of knowledge and information for *this* organization at *this* point in its development is an essential part of the foundation for any attempt to create and apply an information policy or strategy. If you haven't worked out what you ought to know, how can you decide what you ought to be looking for, or what you ought to do with it when you have found it? (For further exploration of this in relation to information auditing, see Chapter 4.)

Why organizations need a policy and a strategy for information

If the knowledge organizations need, and the information resources they need to keep their knowledge in good health, are so extensive in range, and so specific and individual in content, the management of them must be based on a clear policy. The investment of effort in developing first a policy and then a strategy for using knowledge and information can bring both avoidance of dangers and positive benefits.

Situation	Consequent risks and losses
Uncoordinated information activities and systems	Incomplete exploitation of information, anarchic use
Information activities controlled by people with restricted understanding of organizations and information	Important kinds of information overlooked entirely, or managed without professional skills to exploit them
Inappropriate information activities; inappropriate formats for information	Organization wastes time on things it no longer needs to do; people's time wasted in disentangling information they do need from inappropriate presentation
Poor communication of essential information for creating organization's offerings	Failures in attempts to innovate
Systems and IT investment without strategy related to overall business objectives	Systems and IT cannot make maximum contribution to core competencies of organization
Not possible to bring together relevant information from different sources	Bad decisions, missed opportunities for initiatives, losses
Managers don't fully understand what they need to know to foresee dangers, how to get the information they need, how to make good use of it.	Inability to anticipate and respond appropriately to internal or external threat
Organization doesn't understand the importance of accurate and ethical use of information in dealing with its outside world	Loss of reputation, of customers, of money in compensating and rectifying

Table 2.2 **Risks and losses that information policy can help to avoid**

Risks/losses to avoid

It is a commonplace today to speak of information as a potentially profitable resource, and so it is indeed. But without a policy that compels attention to the nature and extent of the resource, how it is used, and how it contributes to corporate objectives, the potential will go unrealized and loss rather than profit will be the likely outcome.

These are some of the dangers identified from actual observation of enterprises (Table 2.2, above summarizes them):
• Uncoordinated information activities and systems, resulting from lack of policy about the use of information technology, with left hands and right hands unacquainted with one another's actions, leading to incomplete exploitation of information, and to anarchic use of information.
• The control of information activities by people who have, by the nature of their professional background, a limited understanding of how organizations work and are managed, and a restricted conception of what information is, and how it can be used. There are, for example, a lot of people with

'information' in their job titles, who are well qualified in such fields as math-
ematics, computing, accountancy, and engineering, but whose education
and work experience has not included the theoretical basis of information, or modern methods of handling the textual information which is such
an important part of the information resources of enterprises. (Davenport,
1993, suggests that as much as 85 per cent of the important information in
organizations is too unstructured to be captured or distributed electronically – and argues from this against the common managerial assumption
that information acquisition, analysis and distribution is low-level work.)

- Inappropriate information activities, unrelated to the organization's main
  objectives: for example, information products which once had a justification, but which no longer serve any useful purpose; or the presentation of
  information in formats that make it very difficult for those who need it to
  use for their own purposes.
- Failures of attempts to introduce innovative products or processes. Rothwell in the 1980s (1983, 1984) analysed a number of such failures in British
  industry, and found that poor communication of information was a major
  cause of failure in all of them. The weaknesses included poor internal communication of technological, management and economic information; poor
  communication with external sources of scientific and technological
  information and with users about what they needed; deliberate ignoring of outside advice; and failure to provide information to the users of the
  product. Sillince (1994) suggests, in a study of production management
  systems in relation to innovation and organizational design, that to succeed
  in innovation, organizations need to develop an 'information model which
  considers the following elements: work units, information needs, goals,
  inputs, and outputs', which needs to be continually monitored and updated.
  And a recent book on technology, globalization and economic performance
  argues that the 'short-termism' characteristic of British shareholders operates against the production and use of knowledge for innovation in UK firms
  (Michie, 1997).
- Systems and IT investment pursued without a strategy related to overall
  objectives, and so unable to make its maximum contribution to the organization's 'core competencies' where it could add most value. Holohan's
  (1992) research on how organizations defined the performance indicators
  presented on their Executive Information Systems shows the consequences:
  'Unfortunately, not one organization which took part in the research mod-
  elled its EIS on its overall business strategy, thus limiting the use of their EIS
  to that of a glorified fire extinguisher rather than using it to help bridge the
  gap between formulating and implementing a business strategy.'
- Inability to bring together relevant information from a number of different
  sources and disciplines in a coherent form to bear on problems to which
  they are relevant. For example, plant investment proposals unsupported by
  in-depth marketing information, and strategic plans which are short on
  information about the human resources and training requirements on which
  their fulfilment depends.
- Inability to anticipate and respond appropriately to threatening situations, internal and external. King's (1996) study of declining and failing

Situation	Benefits promoted by information policy
Integrated information activities	All resources of information can contribute to all organization's objectives
Information policy integrated within corporate policies and priorities	Decisions about resources for information activities can be taken in relation to how they contribute to corporate goals
Policy embodies criteria for assessing how information contributes to achieving organizational objectives	Off-the-cuff decisions to cut information resources become less likely, because likely effects can be predicted
Policy brings together distributed knowledge of all information resources and activities	Promotes cooperation, negotiation and openness among people responsible for different aspects of information management
Information flows more freely	Innovation, productivity and competitiveness are better supported
Options for investment in systems and IT can be evaluated in relation to key organizational goals, and to what people need to do with information to achieve them	Basis for sound systems and IT strategy, supporting corporate goals, and allowing productive use of technology
Intelligence gathering and constant monitoring of internal and external environment as part of information policy	Not only timely response to change, but chance to initiate change so as to take advantage of changing environments

Table 2.3   **Positive benefits which information policy can help to promote**

medium – large firms in the United States, for instance, indicates that 'failures are often caused from within the company and by intrinsically interrelated factors that frequently are rooted in the faulty acquisition and use of information by managers'.

- Loss of reputation among customers and the community, resulting from not having a policy for ethical use of information, or from having a policy but failing to ensure that staff follow it in their dealings with customers. The insurance industry, for example, will not quickly forget the damage and loss that certain companies suffered through the dishonest and misleading use of information by pensions salesmen.

Benefits to gain

The advantages are much more than just the avoidance of the dangers of being without a policy. The best demonstration of them lies in the case studies which form Part 3 of this book. Here, they can be expressed briefly as follows (see Table 2.3 above for a summary):

- It becomes possible to integrate all information activities, and to mobilize all sources of information to contribute to the totality of the organization's objectives.

- The information policy provides the basis for objective decision making about resources for information activities, and about the management of information, because it is integrated within the framework of corporate objectives and priorities. So any proposed development in the management of information can be considered in relation to how it will contribute to overall objectives and priorities.

- A policy for information allows for continuity in development; it reduces the danger of information initiatives being cut short, and the resources invested in them wasted – a hazard to which information services are particularly susceptible in organizations in search of quick cuts in apparent expenditure. The fact that the policy embodies criteria for assessing the contribution that information makes to fulfilling the objectives of the enterprise means that it is possible to judge the real gains and losses that would follow from a proposed change in resources. (For a study of the importance of continuity and development in using knowledge to the success of leading professional firms, see Liestka et al. 1997.)

- Because an information policy is developed by bringing together distributed knowledge of all information resources and activities in the organization, it is capable of promoting cooperation and openness rather than hostility or concealment among those who are responsible for different aspects of information management. (There is a lot of uplifting managerial talk these days about information sharing and being a learning organization, but it will stay at the level of cynicism-promoting talk without an actual policy for information.) It is also an essential step on the way to combining the benefits of diffused responsibility for knowledge and information with a dynamic, unified view of the organization's total resources, and with ready access to all of them.

- The free flows of information that result favour successful innovation, as suggested both by the Rothwell studies mentioned above, and by more recent research such as that presented by Bowden and Ricketts (1992), which indicates that the factors associated with effective implementation of innovation are parallel to those associated with effective implementation of information policy, for example cross-functional teams, and good intra- and inter-firm communications. They also support productivity and competitiveness. Koenig's (1992) studies of productivity in the pharmaceutical industry revealed differences in the information environment of more and less productive firms, with the more productive showing greater openness to outside information, less concern with protecting proprietary information, greater effort devoted to developing information systems and more uses of them by end-users. Bowonder and Miyake (1992) made similar findings, with particuar emphasis on the importance of environmental scanning, about the relationship between information management and competitiveness in Japanese companies. (See also Ginman, 1987, on the positive correlation between a highly developed information culture and successful business performance in the metalworking industry; and Itami and Roehl, 1987, on invisible assets as the focal point for strategy development and growth.)

- An information policy makes the basis for a sound strategy for investment in information systems and technology, because it allows the options to be evaluated in relation to the organization's key objectives, and to its human resources (see the case studies in this book of Amnesty International, page 186, of the University of North London, page 350, and of Surrey Police, page 325).
- Finally, the constant monitoring involved in applying an information policy means that the organization is capable not only of timely response to changes in the internal and external environment, but of moving ahead to *initiate* change that will allow it to take advantage of changing environments. 'A strategist who understands that changes will occur need no longer formulate policy that simply reacts passively to external and internal factors. Because strategy can influence these factors, it can initiate and even create the changes it desires.' (Itami and Roehl, 1987).

Whose business is information policy and strategy?

Information policy and strategy are too important for the well-being of the organization to be left to a limited group of people, or developed without close attention from top management and/or board level. The process should involve everyone who manages resources of information which are essential to the organization in the light of its definition of what it is in business for; the senior managers to whom they are responsible; representatives of 'stakeholders' who use or contribute to the resources; and those who manage the systems and technology which support people in doing things with information. And it should be under the aegis of the top management team.

This is in line with ideas advanced by Marchand (1997) and by Japanese-American thinkers like Nonaka and Takeuchi (1995) about the value that can be created by diffusion of responsibility for knowledge and decision making throughout organizations, rather than concentrating it at the top (see the case studies of the University of North London, page 350, and of Thomas Miller & Co. Ltd, page 343, for examples of organizations which are seeking to develop this approach through their information strategy).

Summary

- The essential features that make an organization: a grouping of human beings for a purpose; which creates 'offerings'; interacts internally and with its environment; seeks sustenance to keep in being; has a structure and a boundary; embodies social and technical systems.
- Those features mean that all organizations need to know: what is happening inside, and in the 'outside world' that is significant for them; how to recognize significant change; how to make their offerings appropriate; how to communicate.
- 'Information' means something special and different for each organization, so each needs to formulate its own definition of information in the light of what it seeks to achieve.

- Organizations need a policy and a strategy for information both to avoid risks and losses and to gain positive benefits.
- Information policy and strategy are too important to be left to one limited group, or developed without close support from the top. The process of developing them should involve the whole range of people responsible for essential resources of information, stakeholders in the resources, and the people who manage information systems and technology.

References

BOWDEN, A. and RICKETTS, M. (1992), *Stimulating Innovation in Industry. The Challenge for the United Kingdom,* London: Kogan Page/NEDO

BOWONDER, B. and MIYAKE, T. (1992), 'Creating and sustaining competitiveness: information management strategies of Nippon Steel Corporation', *International Journal of Information Management,* 12, 39–56

DAVENPORT, T. H. (1993), *Process Innovation. Reengineering work through information technology,* Boston, MA: Harvard Business School Press

DRUCKER, P. (1995a), *Managing in a Time of Great Change,* Oxford: Butterworth Heinemann

DRUCKER, P. (1995b), 'The information executives truly need', *Harvard Business Review,* January–Febuary, 54–62

DUCKER, J. (1992), 'Information and the getting of wisdom', *Intelligent Enterprise,* 1 (9/10), 24–7. (Examples of using wrong information, ignoring relevant information)

FARKAS-CONN, I. (1989), 'Information as a corporate resource', *Information Services and Use,* 9, 205–215

GINMAN, M. (1987), 'Information culture and business performance', *IATUL Quarterly,* 2 (2), 93–106

HAYWARD, T. and BROADY, J. E. (1995), 'The role of information in the strategic management process', *Journal of Information Science,* 21 (4), 257–272

HOLOHAN, J. (1992), 'Use of executive information systems in measuring business performance', *Journal of Information Technology,* 7, 177–186

ITAMI, H. with ROEHL, T. (1987), *Mobilizing Invisible Assets,* Harvard: Harvard University Press

KING, A. S. (1996), 'Organon of business failure: phase model of organizational decline', *Journal of Information Science,* 22 (4), 259–276. (Useful analysis of how lack of strategic use of information contributes to decline and fall of businesses exhibiting various syndromes)

KOENIG, M. E. D. (1992), 'The importance of information services for productivity "under-recognized" and under-invested', *Special Libraries,* Fall, 199–210

LEISTKA, J. M. et al. (1997), 'The generative cycle: linking knowledge and relationships', *Sloan Management Review,* 39 (1) (Fall), 47–58

MARCHAND, D. A. (1997), 'Managing strategic intelligence', *Financial Times Mastering Management,* London: Financial Times/Pitman ('sharing strategic intelligence rather than processing it centrally encourages a diversity of interpretations and views about the future'; helps to cope with rapid change in the environment; strategic intelligence should not be confined to the top of the company, but should be distributed in line with more lateral approaches)

MICHIE, J. (1997), 'Innovation the key to growth for any nation' (article on ARCHIBUGI, D. and MICHIE, J. (eds), *Technology, Globalisation, and Economic Performance,* Cambridge: Cambridge University Press) *The Guardian,* 21 April

NONAKA, I. and TAKEUCHI, H. (1995), *The Knowledge-creating Company: how Japanese companies create the dynamics of information,* New York: Oxford University Press

REUTERS BUSINESS INFORMATION
(1995), *Information as an Asset: the invisible
goldmine* (research commissioned from
the Industrial Research Bureau), London:
Reuters Business Information. (Findings
show that the information businesses
referred to was mostly internal; they made
little mention of external information)

ROTHWELL, R. (1983), *Information and
Successful Innovation*, British Library R&D
Report 5782, London: The British Library

ROTHWELL, R. (1984), 'Information and
successful innovation', in *Information for
industry: the next ten years*, British Library
R&D Report 5802, London: The British
Library and the Technical Change Centre

SCARROTT, G. G. (1996), 'The purpose
and nature of information', *Information:
instrument for the survival of society. Report of
a workshop held at the IEE*, 6 December

SILLINCE, J. A. A. (1994), 'A management
strategy for innovation and organizational
design: the case of MRP2/JIT production
management systems', *Behaviour &
Information Technology*, 13 (3), 216–227

Part 2 The Process

Establishing the ground

In this chapter:

- A basis of understanding, and why we need it
- Initiatives for starting
- Extracting meaning from objectives
- 'What should be'
- What organizational structure and culture can tell us
- Resources for an investigation
- Using the output

A basis of understanding, and why we need it

Whatever we aim to do about the way an organization uses information, and wherever the initiative comes from, before we take any decisions we need as clear an understanding as we can get of the organization: what it seeks to achieve, where it is trying to go, how it sets about its business, and how it sees itself and its outside world. That is the only safe basis for action designed to lead to change in how it uses information and applies knowledge.

The positive gains from starting in this way are:

- A picture of 'what should be' – if this is what the organization is trying to do, with this structure and this culture, then this is what it ought to be trying to do with information and knowledge
- Some first ideas about how that could be expressed in a policy for information, and a first definition of what information means for the organization
- Practical leads for the next steps in the process, for example an information audit, or development of an information strategy:
  - Where to concentrate effort
  - Where to start
  - Key people to involve; potential management supporters, allies to cultivate, foes to neutralize
  - The right questions to ask
  - Benefits to look for
  - Appropriate ways of setting about the job.

Initiatives for starting

The opportunity for starting this process may come in a number of ways. The initiative may come from management, or it may originate from senior professional staff who are particularly concerned with information. It may arise out of a range of situations: a clearly formulated intention to move towards a corporate strategy for information; management's fancy being taken by a new topic such as 'knowledge management', or a fashionable technique like information auditing; a response to a particular question – such as how to give a geographically dispersed and professional staff direct access from their desktop to essential business information; or even a negative and threatening situation, where enterprising people use crisis as 'the coin of opportunity'.

If the initiative comes from the top, these days it is quite likely to be for the development of a strategy – either for information or for information systems/ IT, thanks to the IMPACT programme and the Hawley Committee (see page 19) and to similar developments specifically addressed to board level, which have helped to create more information awareness at the top of enlightened organizations. Many initiatives, however, will still be in response to a particular situation with an information aspect, often defined in terms that are far from expressing the real problem. It is one of the aims of this book to encourage decision makers to use specific situations as an opportunity for starting an investigation which will lead to a picture of what the organization as a whole should be doing with information, and to the beginnings of a policy, and which will, by virtue of that, have a much better chance of yielding a productive solution to the original problem.

Another aim is to encourage experienced information professionals who hold a position of authority in the management structure, and have won respect for their judgement by their achievements, to take initiatives of this kind, and to see it as part of their role to educate management and their colleagues in the gains to be made through strategic management of the organization's resources of information and knowledge. The first edition of this book noted the loss of self-esteem that the information profession seemed to be suffering; there is still quite a lot of that about, and still evidence of great ignorance of the significance of information and the capabilities of information professionals among the managers of many organizations. Abell (1996), for example, reports that, while many companies are becoming more interested in information utilization, real innovation and developments are being driven by people other than information professionals, and that the latter are not seen as being part of the business. On the other hand, recent experience, particularly from the organizations which form the subject of the case studies, suggests some positive changes. I have certainly encountered more information professionals exercising high levels of authority, who are taking and making opportunities to move their organizations towards information strategy, often in new alliances with colleagues from different professional backgrounds.

Extracting meaning from objectives

We have to start here before we can begin to think about what the organization does with information, because its objectives and priorities – its own definition of what it exists for – make the framework within which everything we learn about it will be interpreted, all possible courses of action evaluated, and all decisions implemented. And if we don't fully understand what it thinks it is in business for, we risk misinterpreting what we find at later stages, assigning inappropriate values to information resources, and choosing information solutions that are so bad a match that they harm its interests rather than furthering them. An associated problem is the well-attested fact that even when organizations have detailed statements of their objectives (and that is not universal), it can't be taken for granted either that everyone knows about them, or that there is general agreement on what they mean. None the less, objectives make a startpoint, and the very fact of making and presenting a reasoned analysis of their knowledge and information implications can provide a focus for productive discussion of their meaning.

Table 3.1 on page 45, presents a 'worked example' based on the objectives of one of the case study organizations. We start from the top level set of objec-

Objectives	Knowledge requirements
	About:
• Maintain and improve the performance of companies and the securities and futures markets	The companies and markets covered by its remit The economic and financial context in which they operate, home and worldwide Government policies in relation to them The work of comparable institutions in other countries
• Maintain investor confidence in the securities and futures markets by ensuring adequate investor protection	Investors, institutional and individual, and their investments Risks against which investor protection is needed
• Achieve uniformity in the way it performs its functions and exercises its powers	How it defines its functions and powers and how it carries out the functions and uses the powers
• Administer laws effectively, with a minimum of procedural requirements	The laws which it has to administer The methods and procedures it uses in doing so
• Process and store documents and information which people give the Commission efficiently and quickly	The documents and information it collects from its 'outside world' How it manages their processing and storage How it makes them available to the public
• Ensure that they are available to the public as soon as possible	How well it meets their requirements
• Take whatever action is necessary to enforce the law	How it identifies when action is needed, decides on what to do, takes action The results

Table 3.1   **The objectives of an organization (The Australian Securities and Investments Commission[1])**

tives, and we ask of each of them: 'To achieve this objective, what knowledge and/or know-how do we require?'

The set of answers to that question provides the basis for the next question: 'What information do we need to draw on to maintain the knowledge we require?' As will be seen from Table 3.2 (on pages 46 to 48) the answers become more complex and detailed when we get to this level, and more meaning starts to emerge from the original objectives.

[1] See Case Study 2, page 197
The Commission's overall aim is 'to protect the interests of companies and investors … ensure fair play in business, prevent corporate crime, protect investors and help Australia's business reputation abroad.'

Knowledge requirements	Information required to maintain knowledge	
About:	Content	'Containers'
• The companies and markets covered by its remit	Ownership Structure Performance data	Relevant external databases Internal databases Internet Specialist press Statistical series
	Products and services	Company information products
• The economic and financial context in which they operate, home and worldwide	National and worldwide economic situation Market conditions	Relevant external databases Internet Specialist press Statistical series
• Government policies in relation to them	Legislation Planned developments	Government publications Government websites Parliamentary debates Reports of government bodies Contacts in federal and state governments
• The work of comparable institutions in other countries	Location, constitution, methods	Annual reports Contacts, correspondence
• Investors, institutional and individual, and their investments	Who they are Their investments Their experience and views of companies and markets	Specialist press Reports on research by Commission and others Reports from staff in contact with investors
• Risks against which investor protection is needed	Ways in which investors have suffered loss Opinion of protection afforded	Specialist press Internal database Records of complaints Reports on research by Commission and others
• How it defines its functions and powers and how it carries out the functions and uses the powers	Current definition and proposed changes in scope	Legislation establishing the Commission Reports of government bodies
• The laws which it has to administer	Existing law and proposed changes	Relevant legislation Reports of government bodies

Table 3.2 **The information (content and 'containers') which the Commission needs to draw on to maintain its knowledge.** *Continued on opposite page*

Knowledge requirements	Information required to maintain knowledge	
About:	**Content**	**'Containers'**
• The methods and procedures it uses	Methods and procedures established by the Commission	Manuals, minutes, guidance instructions
	Performance criteria and results	Standards and criteria statements; reports on performance in meeting them
	People responsible for these activities; qualifications, skills, training	Personnel and training records held in database
	IT and systems used to support them	Reports on IT/IS management Specialist press for keeping track of relevant development
• The documents and information it collects from its 'outside world'	What companies tell investors about their products/services, activities, results	Prospectuses, company reports, takeover documents, etc.
	Records of Commission's dealings with companies	Internal database of companies and Commission's transactions with them
• How it manages their processing and storage	Information management strategy	Strategic Information Plan
• How it makes them available to the public	Information systems strategy	Corporate IT Strategy Plan
• How well it meets their requirements	Questions put by inquirers	Records of transactions with inquirers via electronic inquiry service; reports
	Their views of service offered	Reports of user surveys; information audits, etc
	Performance criteria and results	Standards and criteria statements; reports on performance in meeting them
	People responsible for these activities; qualifications, skills, training	Personnel and training records held in database
	IT and systems used to support them	Reports on IT/IS management Specialist press for keeping track of relevant development

Table 3.2   *Continued on page 48*

Knowledge requirements	Information required to maintain knowledge	
About:	Content	'Containers'
• How it identifies when action is needed, decides on what to do, takes action	The Commission's transactions with investors and companies	Correspondence; records of transactions; visit reports; reports of investigations
	Decisions and rationales for them	Internal reports Communications with Director of Public Prosecutions
• The outcomes of action	Results and lessons from them	Internal reports; database; Annual Report
	Performance criteria and results	Standards and criteria statements; reports on performance in meeting them
	People responsible for these activities; qualifications, skills, training	Personnel and training records held in database
	IT and systems used to support them	Reports on IT/IS management Specialist press for keeping track of relevant development

Table 3.2   *end*

We now have to think about what the Commission's staff have to do with the information it needs in order to achieve its objectives. Here things become yet more complex, because we have to consider not only who needs to use the information, but also the information flows and interactions that are required both within the Commission and between it and its outside world. Table 3.3 (on pages 49 to 54) starts from the kinds of information the Commission has been identified as requiring, and sets out for each how it needs to flow, and the people who need to interact with one another in order to transform it into knowledge and act on it.

So far as I know, this is an exercise seldom if ever undertaken in organizations, though it seems quite an obvious step. Experience shows that people concerned with information management have no difficulty with the concept, or with deriving knowledge and information needs from the objectives of their own organization. And it usually takes no more than a few hours to produce the answers.

Given that in any organization there will almost certainly be different interpretations of objectives, and different degrees of knowledge of them, a straightforward analysis of this kind makes a good starting point for discussion of what they mean, and of what information means for the organization. Using

Companies and markets covered by its remit

People involved

- Company staff responsible for supplying information to the Commission
- Industry associations
- Local business communities

- Programme managers and specialist staff responsible for contact with companies
- Intelligence and Analysis Service
- Staff responsible for company records
- Librarians and other information specialists
- Systems / IT staff [1]
- Staff responsible for publicizing the Commission's work

Interactions/information flow

between • Company staff responsible for supplying information to the Commission • Industry associations • Local business communities	*and*	• Programme managers and staff responsible for contact with companies	
between • Staff responsible for contact with companies	*and*	• Intelligence and Analysis Service • Staff responsible for company records • Librarians and other information specialists • Systems / IT staff • Staff responsible for providing information about the Commission's work	

[1] Systems / IT staff are concerned in nearly all information interactions, because they are reponsible for ensuring that systems and IT support people in using information in the ways that they need

The economic and financial context in which they operate, home and worldwide

People involved

- Suppliers

- Intelligence and Analysis Service
- Librarians and other information specialists
- Decision makers about strategy; those responsible for implementing it
- Systems / IT staff

Interactions/information flow

between • Intelligence and Analysis Service • Librarians and other information specialists	*and*	• Suppliers • Decision makers about strategy; those responsible for implementing it • Systems / IT staff	

Table 3.3 **The information flows and interactions among people that are necessary in order to make effective use of the knowledge and information the Commission requires**
Note: All information flows in both directions. *Continued on page 50*

Government policies

People involved

- Government; public service
- MPs

- Decision makers and staff responsible for government contacts
- Intelligence and Analysis Service
- Librarians and other information specialists
- Systems/IT staff

Interactions/information flow

between
- Government; public service
- MPs

- Decision makers and staff responsible for government contacts

and
- Decision makers and staff responsible for government contacts

- Intelligence and Analysis Service
- Librarians and other information specialists
- Systems/IT staff

The work of comparable institutions in other countries

People involved

- Staff of comparable institutions

- External relations staff
- Programme managers
- Librarians and other information specialists

Interactions/information flow

between
- Staff of comparable institutions

and
- External relations staff

between
- External relations staff

and
- Programme managers
- Librarians and other information specialists

Investors, institutional and individual, and their investments

People involved

- Investors

- Staff responsible for investor contacts
- Staff responsible for publicising the Commission's work
- Intelligence and Analysis Service
- Librarians and other information specialists
- Systems/IT staff

Table 3.3   *Continued on page 51*

Investors, institutional and individual, and their investments

continued

Interactions/information flow

between • Investors

and • Staff responsible for investor contacts
• Staff responsible for providing information about the Commission's work

• Staff responsible for investor contacts
• Staff responsible for providing information about the Commission's work

• Intelligence and Analysis Service
• Librarians and other information specialists
• Systems/IT staff

Risks against which investor protection is needed

People involved

• Investors
• Companies

• Staff responsible for investor and company contacts
• Intelligence and Analysis Service
• Librarians and other information specialists
• Staff responsible for publicizing the Commission's work

Interactions/information flow

between • Investors
• Companies

and • Staff responsible for investor and company contacts

between • Staff responsible for investor and company contacts

• Intelligence and Analysis Service
• Librarians and other information specialists
• Staff responsible for providing information about the Commission's work

How it carries out its functions and uses its powers

People involved

• All staff of the Commission
• Staff responsible for monitoring performance
• Systems/IT staff

Interactions/information flow

between • Staff responsible for monitoring performance

and • All staff of the Commission
• Systems/IT staff

Table 3.3   *Continued on page 52*

The laws which it has to administer

People involved

- Legislators
- Professional legal staff
- Staff responsible for contacts with companies and investors

Interactions / information flow

between • Legislators	*and*	• Professional legal staff
between • Professional legal staff	*and*	• Staff responsible for contacts with companies and investors

The methods and procedures it uses in doing so

People involved

- All staff of the Commission
- Staff responsible for developing and maintaining methods and procedures
- Staff responsible for monitoring performance

Interactions / information flow

between • Staff responsible for developing recording and maintaining methods and procedures • Staff responsible for monitoring performance	*and*	• All staff of the Commission

The documents and information it collects from its 'outside world'
How it manages their processing and storage
How it makes them available to the public

People involved

- Providers of documents and information
- Members of the public who make inquiries

- Staff responsible for collecting documents and information
- Staff responsible for processing and storing them
- Staff responsible for making them accessible
- Staff who need access to them
- Staff who deal with inquiries from outside
- Systems / IT staff

Interactions / information flow

between • Providers of documents and information	*and*	• Staff responsible for collecting documents and information

Table 3.3 *Continued on page 53*

**The documents and information it collects
from its 'outside world'
How it manages their processing and storage
How it makes them available to the public** *continued*

between	• Staff responsible for collecting documents and information	*and*	• Staff responsible for processing and storing them • Staff responsible for making them accessible
between	• Staff responsible for processing and storing them • Staff responsible for making them accessible	*and*	• Staff who need access to them • Staff who deal with inquiries from outside • Systems/IT staff
between	• Members of the public who make inquiries	*and*	• Staff who deal with inquiries

**How well it meets the requirements
of inquirers**

People involved

- Members of the public who make inquiries

- Staff who deal with inquiries
- Staff responsible for managing documents and information
- Staff responsible for monitoring performance
- Systems/IT staff

Interactions/information flow

between	• Members of the public who make inquiries	*and*	• Staff who deal with inquiries
between	• Staff who deal with inquiries	*and*	• Staff responsible for managing documents and information • Systems/IT staff
between	• Staff who deal with inquiries • Staff responsible for managing documents and information	*and*	• Staff responsible for monitoring performance • Systems/IT staff

**How it identifies when action is needed,
decides on what to do, takes action**

People involved

- Companies
- Investors
- Director of Public Prosecutions
- Civil courts

Table 3.3 *Continued on page 54*

How it identifies when action is needed, decides on what to do, takes action

continued

- Staff responsible for contact with companies
- Staff responsible for investor contacts
- Staff responsible for initiating action
- Intelligence and Analysis Service
- Staff responsible for company records
- Systems/IT staff

Interactions/information flow

between • Staff responsible for contact with companies • Staff responsible for investor contacts	*and*	• Staff responsible for initiating action • Intelligence and Analysis Service • Staff responsible for company records • Systems/IT staff
between • Staff responsible for initiating action	*and*	• Director of Public Prosecutions • Civil courts

The results

People involved

- Staff responsible for initiating action
- Staff responsible for contact with companies
- Staff responsible for investor contacts
- Staff responsible for company records
- Staff responsible for publicizing the Commission's work

Interactions/information flow

between • Staff responsible for initiating action	*and*	• Staff responsible for contact with companies • Staff responsible for investor contacts • Staff responsible for company records • Staff responsible for providing information about the Commission's work • Staff who deal with inquiries

Table 3.3   *end*

something like this as a starter helps people who are not much in the habit of thinking about such topics to grasp them and relate them to their own work.

'What should be'

Let us now develop from this analysis a brief statement of its implications for what the Commission should be doing with information in order to maintain the knowledge it needs in good health and ready for effective action.

What the Commission needs to know

The most important knowledge for the Commission is that about:
* Companies
* Markets
* The economic and social context
* Relevant government policies
* Investors and their investments
* Risks against which investors should be protected
* Its own functions and powers and how it exercises them
* The laws it has to administer, and how it does so
* The information it collects from its 'outside world'
* How it manages that information
* How well it meets the requirements of the public
* How it takes action, and the results.

The information resources it needs to feed its knowledge

To maintain its knowledge, the Commission needs to acquire and have ready access to:
* Information about the companies and markets covered by its remit, internal and external databases, textual and numeric forms
* Qualitative and quantitative reports generated from its own activities
* Externally originating reference and information products relevant to its 'outside world', in various media, print-on-paper and electronic
* 'Intelligence' products, resulting from in-house work, and bought in
* Information about its own resources of knowledge and expertise
* Information about its own performance and the criteria by which it is judged
* Archives and records.

The human resources the Commission needs to manage the information resources

The Commission needs people who can manage acquisition and maintenance, and provide access to the various resources of information, who can gather strategic intelligence and interpret it, who can integrate and add value to the whole range of information resources, and who understand existing information needs and are able to anticipate emerging ones in the light of the Commission's key business objectives. It also needs to assign responsibility for awareness of the totality of information resources and information activities, and for promoting their integrated use. And, besides those with special responsibility for managing information, everyone who uses it needs to understand their own obligations and what they owe to their colleagues in that respect.

The information interactions the Commission needs

The value of information to organizations is realized only when human minds transform it into knowledge, combine it with what they already know, and, supported by appropriate information technology, act on it in cooperation – the process which Skyrme (1992) describes as 'knowledge networking'. So information flows, interactions and negotiations between people are the most critical part of 'what should be'. The analysis of Table 3.3 could be taken into yet more detail, but even at the present level, it is obvious that the Commission needs to provide organizational structures and cultural encouragement for many interactions, both internally and between itself and the outside world. To take only the interactions necessary to achieve the first objective concerning the performance of companies (see page 46): they require the participation of company staff, industry associations, local business communities, programme managers and staff responsible for contact with companies, Intelligence and Analysis Service, records managers, information professionals, systems/IT staff, and those responsible for Commission publicity. See Figure 3.1 on opposite page.

The systems and information technology infrastructure the Commission needs

If we follow through all the information interactions which are required for achieving the Commission's goals, it quickly becomes obvious that in almost all of them the contribution of systems and IT is essential to support people in reaching the information they need, and in using it for their own purposes. It is important to observe the 'chronology' of this contribution. Systems and IT cannot make their input effectively until the organization has defined the information it needs to support people in using their knowledge; that has to be the basis of the brief for creating the technical infrastructure and the applications that do the right job. This seems so obvious that it is almost embarrassing to mention it – but not quite; there are too many examples of management failing in its obligations to create the brief, and leaving systems and IT to do the best they can, often with less than happy results. Sillince (1994), for example, shows how implementation of a systems change in production management in manufacturing companies (the introduction of hybrid MRP2/JIT – Materials Requirements Planning/Just In Time – systems) is undermined by lack of attention to information needs and use, combined with structural and cultural factors.

On the other hand, Abell (1996) reports that organizations are becoming less dependent on IT departments to develop information strategies, and more interested in an information systems or information utilization focus. Certainly over the past few years I have come across organizations which have started by

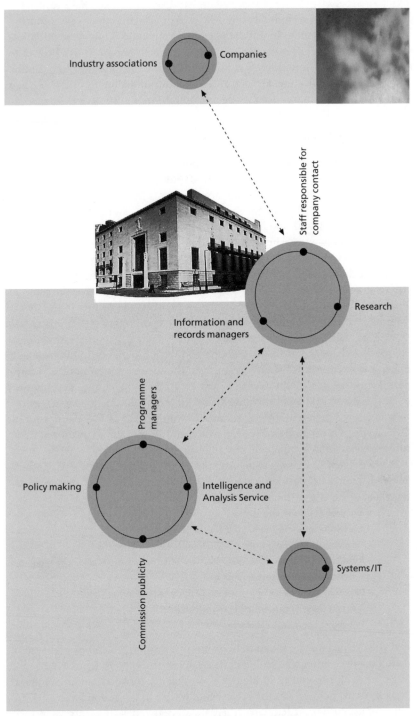

Fig 3.1   **Information interactions and information flows necessary for meeting goals concerning the performance of companies** (See Tables 3.1 to 3.3)

trying to develop an 'information systems strategy' and which have realized in due course (often prompted by systems staff) that what they really need is a strategy for information. In this connection, Symon et al. (1992) provide some interesting insights; they describe an action research approach to a project to develop a hospital information system which took into account information interactions, organizational structure and organizational culture, and led to a framework of information needs and an implementation strategy.

What organizational structure and culture can tell us

Analysis starting from what the organization says it is trying to do can, as we have just seen, take us a long way, but it's not to be relied on by itself. We need to look at it in the light of the organization's history, structure and culture, because that will cast into relief the strengths we can build on, the threats we shall have to avoid, the impregnable bastions which will withstand direct attack, and the strategic alliances to be sought.

Many researchers have described features of organizations which seem to favour productive and profitable use of information. A programme to study the relationship between information culture and business performance in Finland (Ginman, 1987) observed linkages between the factors of the CEO's information culture, company culture, the 'life cycle' stage the company was at, and its business performance (see Figure 3.2 on page 59). Ginman concludes that there seems to be 'a strong connection between intellectual and material resource transformation' and that 'the supply of information to companies must be designed to comply with their prevailing culture and requirements.' (page 105). Her observations, particularly about the importance of the CEO in promoting an information ethos, are confirmed in follow-up work by Owens and Wilson (1996). (See also Abell and Winterman, 1993 for a literature review on information culture and business performance.)

Skyrme (1992), writing from experience of Digital Equipment Corporation's attempts to develop knowledge networking, describes the organizational factors that go with success as:

- A degree of informality
- Knowledge authority rather than position authority
- Openness of communications; willingness to share information
- A belief that co-ordinating expertise from different people is better than going it alone; co-operation not competition
- Developing a network of individuals with shared visions and goals
- A strong sense of responsibility to co-workers
- Self-regulation of the network.

If you are fortunate enough to be in an organization which has that kind of structure and culture, the path will be relatively smooth, and you will be able to get on with the matter in hand without having to worry too much about organizational politics. On the other hand, if your organization has a long tradition of jealously guarded departmental autonomy, deriving from its history, then direct attempts to sell the virtues of 'information sharing' will be about as successful as telling a bunch of toddlers that it's nice to share their toys. Nor

Degree of interest in information,
relative market share, rate of feedback

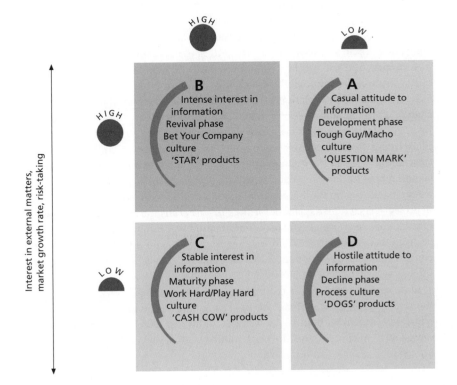

Interest in external matters,
market growth rate, risk-taking

Fig 3.2 **Linkages between CEO information culture, company culture, life cycle and business performance**

will proposals to introduce centralized management of information have much luck.[2]

In an organization where IT has a strongly entrenched position, and where top management sees information as synonymous with information technology, you won't get far without finding a management champion to educate about the distinction, and without trying to build a strategic alliance with IT and information systems colleagues in which both sides have something to gain. If, on the other hand, information has a bad name in the organization because it's been equated with IT and there have been some heavy losses from ill-judged and badly managed investments, it is no good going straight in with a proposal for a large investment in human resources for information management; once again you have to start by getting the distinction clear in management minds, and you will need to reinforce it by demonstrating some low-cost quick wins from doing something sensible with information.

If an organization is planning a major change in direction, the nature of the change is critical, and has to be taken into account in any information initiatives. As Marchand (1997) reminds us, it is particularly critical for organizations trying to change their orientation and/or culture to be aware of the information risks in the change and to seek to avoid them, as well as understanding how information can contribute positively to successful change. For example, an organization seeking to move towards innovation, and changing to project-centred management for the purpose, runs the risk, as project teams disband, of losing useful information that could be exploited in future; for successful change, its information management will need a particular focus on conserving the memory of successes and failures and making it accessible for future use.

If we do not pay heed to these intangible but significant characteristics of the organization in which we are operating, the result may well be wasted effort, investment without visible return, disillusion, and loss of credibility for the people concerned; and the opportunity of doing something useful about information may be lost for years.

Questions about structure

We need to answer such questions as:

- What formal units is the organization divided into? Companies, divisions, departments?
- Do the main sub-divisions have a degree of autonomy, or is the organization highly centralized?
- Where does the structure come on the line between hierarchy and network (see Figure 3.3 on page 61).
- What are its decision-making bodies, and what are their functions?

[2] As Davenport et al (1992) put it, 'Unless the politics of information are identified and managed, companies will not move into the Information Age. Information will not be shared freely nor used effectively by decision makers ... [that] will take what politics always take: negotiation, influence-exercising, back-room deals, coalition-building, and, occasionally even war.'

Organization characteristics

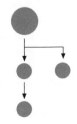

Vertical hierarchy
– Fixed decision rules and chains
   of command
– Centralized decisions
– Little horizontal communication

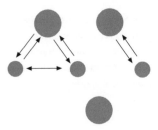

Autonomous divisions
– More decision points
– Information flows up as well as down
– But little flow between autonomous
   groupings

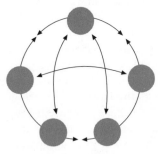

Network
– Multi-directional information flows
   and feedback
– Adaptable

Fig 3.3   **Organizational structure and characteristics**

- Does the organizational structure provide meeting places for interchange of information among people from different functions who contribute to the same process?
- Who are the senior managers and what are their formal responsibilities?
- How do their responsibilities relate to authority and accountability?
- Who takes what decisions?
- Who has power to override decisions?
- Are there differences between what the organization chart depicts and the reality in day-to-day operations?

As you will observe, some of the questions relate to what the organization says about itself, and others to what it does in practice and to how the two diverge. This is sometimes perilous territory; and that is why its exploration has to be undertaken by people with experience of the organization, and good standing in it, with the backing of senior management. It is part of the environment of human interactions, ideas and feelings against which initiatives for change have to be considered and evaluated. The degree to which the organization's structure matches its priority objectives can either smooth the path towards developing information policy and strategy, or make it very hard going. For example, an organization which combines a very hierarchical structure and slow decision processes with objectives that demand quick and flexible response to environmental changes will have difficulty in achieving a policy for information, or indeed for anything else. And if a policy is to be successfully introduced in such a situation, it will inevitably have structural consequences of the kind outlined by Horton (1987, page 267):

> The introduction of the information management idea into organizations implicitly carries with it very substantial structural change consequences. For one, the integration of information technologies, operating information programs, and ongoing information services into a cohesive policy and operational framework implicitly means reshuffling people and blocks on the organization chart.

Questions about culture

The other essential questions we need to answer are not about what the organization says or does, but *how* it does it. As Eason (1988, page 154) says, 'Any organization has its own, more or less explicit, culture and values; not what it does but the way that it does it.' The culture embraces the way the organization regards itself, the people who work for it, and its outside world; the way it presents itself to them; the way it treats them; and the 'stories' that are current in the organization to explain and account for what it does, and to help people make up for the deficiencies in what it provides to help them do their work. (For an account of the significance of stories in organizational life and learning, see Brown and Duguid, 1994.) The culture therefore has a potent influence on how the organization values information, on the way it flows, and on how it is used, and so it will condition the resources it is prepared to devote to developing information policy and strategy, and affect the success of any such endeavours.

The questions that can elicit a picture of how the organization manages are of this kind:

- Does it have a Mission and Vision statement? How is it phrased? How do staff take it? Seriously? Cynically? As a bad joke?
- Does it rely heavily on short-term contracts, and if it does, what provision does it make for job handover and transfer of knowledge?
- Is its 'human resources' policy devoted to keeping people in their proper boxes and doing exactly what their job description says, or to encouraging initiatives, flexibility and development?
- If it claims to encourage flexibility, does that mean in practice that it expects employees to accept every proposed change in work content and conditions without question?
- Are there sharp boundaries between staff at different levels, or is collective and cooperative endeavour valued and rewarded?
- Are there policies on staff development and training? If there are, to what are they directed, and are they implemented in practice? Do staff take part in formulating their own training needs and training plans?
- How are industrial relations managed? Is the trend authoritarian, cooperative, or capricious?
- Does the organization commit itself formally to openness and maximum access to information? If it does, how does this work out in practice?
- Has it an ethical policy to guide its conduct towards the outside world and its own staff?
- Is the main direction in which information travels from the top down, with responses going up through the prescribed channels?
- Is lateral movement of information encouraged, or does rumour flourish in its absence?
- Do different functions and departments keep themselves to themselves and clutch their knowledge tightly against prying eyes, or is there free interchange and cooperation between them?
- Are professional staff encouraged to meet and discuss with colleagues in other organizations, with the expectation that they will have the good sense and loyalty to know where to exercise discretion; or are such exchanges frowned on[3]
- How does the organization take its decisions? Does it actually make use of the available information for assessing the various options, or does it look for information that will support the one it has already decided on? Does it draw on the expertise and knowledge available among its staff? (Has it any means of knowing what *is* available?)
- How good is the organization at knowing when to be cautious and when to be ready to take risks?

[3] There is plenty of research evidence over the last 20 years or so to show that businesses which encourage such exchanges are not only happier places to work, but also succeed better in innovation and compete more successfully. See, for example, Olson (1977), Koenig (1992) and Bowonder and Miyake (1992).

Resources for an investigation

One of the advantages of the approach recommended in this chapter is that it makes only a light demand on resources, and it is one where information managers can readily take an initiative. The analysis of information implications of objectives in particular is primarily desk research, requiring mainly thinking time. Knowledge of the organization and contacts with people in different parts of it are the main essentials for the consideration of organizational structure and culture; here the output from the analysis of what the objectives mean in terms of information can be used as the basis for discussions that should enrich understanding. While there is advantage in keeping the process fairly informal and low key, management support and understanding is essential from the start, and there is advantage in establishing protocols at this stage which will serve as a model for later more formal and extended projects.

The essential resources are:

- Commitment of top management to the defined purpose of the investigation (for example: 'To analyse the implications of key business objectives in terms of how the organization needs to use information and knowledge to achieve them, and to recommend appropriate action')
- Person(s) of sufficient knowledge, experience, judgement and standing to carry it out
- An adequate allowance of time for doing the job
- Access to appropriate people and documents
- Agreed methods of managing and reporting on the investigation.

Readers should be able to judge what those resources would amount to in their own organization; in any case, at this stage it is wise to limit the number of people involved and to keep the time span short, because this is the start of a learning process, and it needs to be kept manageable. The qualities required of people who carry out this first investigation (and subsequent ones) are:

- Breadth of knowledge about the organization that extends beyond their own department or professional specialism
- Long enough experience in the organization to be aware of its character, and to be known to those from whom they will be seeking information
- Capacity to establish mutual professional respect with colleagues, to interact with them in a calm and courteous way, and to acquire information from them without wasting time
- Ability to analyse and synthesize information derived from both text and conversation
- Sufficient openness of mind to preserve them from prejudging and from interpreting what they are told in the light of their own preconceptions
- Ability to present the outcome in an accessible way, and to make a well-argued case for any recommendations arising.

Using the output

The output can be used as a basis for information auditing, or for initiating development of an information strategy, or for making a case for taking information use into account in any planned change initiative. And even if it appears to lead nowhere at the time, it is worth keeping on hand to bring forward on another occasion – one of the lessons of experience is that climates and views change, people who look like immovable obstacles go to exercise their talents elsewhere, and it is worth watching for opportunities to have another go. The next chapter looks at making use of the output as the foundation for information auditing.

Summary

- Before taking any decisions about information policy, we need to understand the organization for which it is to be designed: what it seeks to achieve, how it manages, how it sees itself and its outside world. (Rowlands', 1998, representation of information policy making on a national scale as 'a process of negotiation, bringing together competing value frames and resolving conflicts,' is also valid at the organizational level.)
- That helps us to work out what the organization ought to be doing with information and knowledge, what the principles of its information policy should be, and the kind of systems and IT infrastructure it needs in order to support it.
- It also gives useful practical pointers for information auditing: where to start, what to look at, who to talk to, questions to ask.
- The organization's objectives make a useful starting point for asking and answering three questions:
  1 What do the organization, and the people in it, need to *know* to achieve its objectives?
  2 What *information* does it need to draw on to maintain the required knowledge?
  3 How does the information need to flow and how do people need to *interact* in order to turn it into knowledge and act on it?
- Organizational structure and culture may favour developing information policy, or make it difficult.
- Organizations which are seeking to make a major change in orientation need to pay special heed to the information risks entailed, and to understand how information can contribute positively to successful change.
- This approach makes only a light demand on resources, and it is one where information managers can take initiatives, and establish their credentials for further development of information policy.

References

ABELL, A. (1996), 'The information professional in 1996', *Information management report,* January, 1–6

ABELL, A. and WINTERMAN, V. (1993), *Information Culture and Business Performance. Literature Review and Feasibility Study,* HERTIS Information and Research, Hatfield: University of Hertfordshire

BOWONDER, B. and MIYAKE, T. (1992), 'Creating and sustaining competitiveness: information management strategies of Nippon Steel Corporation', *International Journal of Information Management,* 12, 39–56

BROWN, J.S. and DUGUID, P. (1994), 'Organizational learning and communities of-practice: toward a unified view of working, learning and innovation', in TSOUKAS, H. (ed.), *New Thinking in Organizational Behaviour,* Oxford: Butterworth Heinemann

DAVENPORT, T. H. et al. (1992), 'Information politics', *Sloan Management Review,* Fall, 53–65

EASON, K. (1988), *Information Technology and Organisational Change,* London: Taylor & Francis

GINMAN, M. (1987), 'Information culture and business performance', *Iatul Quarterly,* 2 (2), 93–106

HORTON, F. W., JR (1987), 'The impact of information management on corporate cultures', *Aslib Proceedings,* 39 (9), 267–274

KOENIG, M. (1992), 'The importance of information services for productivity "under-recognized" and under-invested', *Special Libraries,* Fall, 199–210

MARCHAND, D. (1997), 'Competing with Information: know what you want', *FT Mastering Management Reader,* July/August

OLSON, E. E. (1977), 'Organizational factors affecting information flow in industry', *Aslib Proceedings,* 29 (1), 2–11

OWENS, I. and WILSON, T. with ABELL, A. (1996), *Information and Business Performance. A study of information systems and services in high performing companies,* East Grinstead: Bowker-Saur

ROWLANDS, I. (1998), 'Some compass bearings for information policy orienteering', *Aslib Proceedings,* 230–237

SILLINCE, J. A. A. (1994), 'A management strategy for innovation and organizational design: the case of MRP2/JIT production management systems', *Behaviour & Information Technology,* 13 (3), 216–227

SKYRME, D. (1992), 'Knowledge networking – creating wealth through people and technology', *The Intelligent Enterprise,* 1 (11/12), 9–15

SYMON, G. et al. (1992), 'The process of deriving requirements for a hospital information system', *Behaviour & Information Technology,* 11 (3), 131–140

Information auditing: from initial analysis to doing the audit

4

In this chapter:

- Not a new invention
- Definitions and what they imply
- What can organizations expect from information auditing?
- The benefits
- The audit process

Creative tension comes from seeing clearly where we want to be, our 'vision', and telling the truth about where we are, our current reality. The gap between the two generates a natural tension ... an accurate picture of current reality is just as important as a compelling picture of a desirable future. Peter M. Senge. (1990)

Not a new invention

Though it is only in the last three or four years that information auditing has started to become popular with organizations, and to be the subject of articles and courses, it is far from being a new invention. I first made an 'information audit' – though it was not called that – more than 20 years ago, and reference to the term dates back to at least 1982. A paper of that date by Taylor describes 'an audit of the formal information activities and their effect on the organisation' looking at how well they help people to do their jobs. Taylor also says that it is essential to understand what the organization does, its history, the place it occupies in its industry, and its market share; to know about its customers, its clients, and its 'public'; and to be aware of organizational 'dynamics' and 'culture' and how they influence the flow of information. And he says that eventually the audit should 'become an ongoing analysis of the benefits and costs of each major activity'. In short, he presents a very farsighted view of information auditing, which is well ahead of some current rather simplistic approaches to the topic.

Information audits are being done today in a wide range of businesses and organizations in the UK, from pharmaceutical firms, banks, and the health service, to charities and cultural organizations such as museums. Their popularity probably has something to do with the accountancy associations of the word 'audit', the emphasis placed today on accountability and value for money in the matter of information services, and the interest which large businesses are currently taking in setting a value on information assets. That makes it important to have a clear account of what the process entails, the resources it needs, and what organizations can reasonably expect to gain from carrying it through.

Definitions and what they imply

The brief definition which is becoming current in the UK today was developed by the Information Resources Management Network of Aslib (the Association for Information Management); it sums up the essentials in these terms:

> A systematic examination of information use, resources and flows, with a verification by reference to both people and existing documents, in order to establish the extent to which they are contributing to an organization's objectives.

We can expand this into a more detailed outline of what the information audit examines:

1 The information an organization holds – on paper, in machine-readable form, and in the minds of the those who work for it – which can be turned into knowledge by people and applied in their work to meet its objectives
2 The resources for making information accessible to those who need to turn it into knowledge
3 The ways in which it uses information to further its objectives
4 The people who are involved in using information
5 The 'tools' it uses for doing things with information – from the simplest non-electronic indexes and filing systems to the most sophisticated computer applications and systems
6 The criteria it uses to assess the costs and values of information.

The definitions have some important implications:

1 As the aim of the audit is to find out how the organization is using information to meet its objectives, the starting point has to be the organization's objectives, and what they imply about the information it needs to achieve them, and how it needs to use that information. Consideration of key business objectives should yield a basic statement of 'How It Should Be' in the matter of information and its use, which will form the reference point from which the audit starts. (Chapter 3 has dealt in detail with this process of defining what the organization should be doing with information.)
2 The audit process is a matter of asking appropriate questions to find out 'How It Actually Is' in respect of the matters outlined above.
3 The output of the audit consists of the results of matching how it should be against how it is.
4 Action on the output is a matter of interpreting the results, and deciding what to do to bring the organization's use of information closer to what its objectives require.

Unfortunately organizations do not always realize that it is dangerous to start an audit without the essential first step of looking at the information implications of their objectives. Not long ago I encountered an organization which had undertaken an audit without this preliminary, at a time when it was undergoing a good deal of pressure; when the audit was completed, they found themselves perplexed as to how to use the results because there was nothing against which they could match them.

Booth and Haines (1994) provide an example of a more thoughtful approach, with their account of an information audit of a regional health authority within the UK National Health Service. The strategy which they developed at the start was to:

1 Identify and review the corporate objectives of the authority
2 Decide what information is required to meet them
3 Do an information audit to determine if this information currently exists in the authority and, if so, to describe how it is currently used
4 Address any immediate information gaps and problems
5 Develop an information management policy to ensure appropriate resources,

organizational structures and training to meet the information requirements of the authority's corporate programme.

What can organizations expect from information auditing?

While information auditing can make a valuable contribution and bring benefits, there are dangers in undertaking it without knowing what one is letting oneself in for, so it is important to understand what organizations can reasonably expect to get out of doing it, what resources they need to put into it, and what they need to do with them if they are to get benefits. Any organization that initiates an information audit has to be prepared to think carefully about what information it needs, and what it needs to do with it in order to survive and succeed in meeting business objectives, ask the right questions to find out what information it actually has and how it is being used, and analyse the results honestly, and, finally, take appropriate action.

Nor is an audit something to be undertaken out of the blue and as a one-off operation. If the effort invested in it is to pay off, it has to be a stage in a carefully planned process. Organizations will get maximum value from information auditing if it is used as the starting point for an ongoing cycle of evaluating what they are doing with information, and learning from the process.

Figure 4.1 (on page 72) shows information auditing in the context of strategic goals, information policy and information strategy.

The benefits

The best way of looking at information auditing is as a key that can unlock the door to benefits. Because it gives us a map of what the organization is actually doing with information, and allows us to measure how well the reality matches what the organization ought to be doing with information, it provides a sound foundation for a range of benefits and initiatives, short- and long-term.

In the short term, the results of the audit allow:
- Attention to immediate threats, risk avoidance
- Cost savings from more rational management
- Quick gains from making information more accessible or usable for those who need it.

Over the longer term, the experience of the auditing process can promote valuable cultural changes, and provide a strong platform for policy initiatives:
- Enriched understanding of what information and knowledge mean for the organization – at the top, and throughout the organization
- Interaction and negotiation among the 'guardians' of information resources and the stakeholders in them
- Development of a strategy for managing knowledge and information
- Better use of information in supporting key business processes, and in initiating and responding to change
- Integrated management of the organization's complete range of information, supported by appropriate systems and technology
- Reliable assessment of the cost-effectiveness of information and its use, and

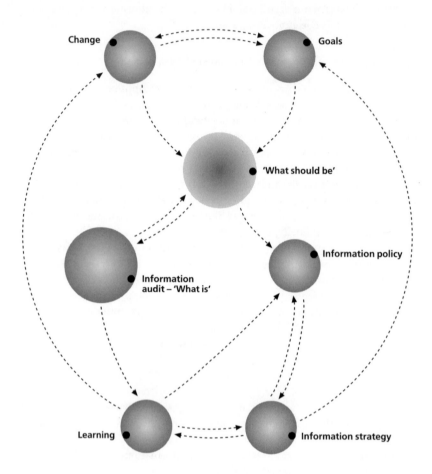

Change
Goals
'What should be'
Information policy
Information audit – 'What is'
Learning
Information strategy

Change
What do we need to know
to manage the changes we
face successfully?

Goals
What do our objectives mean
in terms of the knowledge
and information we need?

'What should be'
What we *should* be doing
with knowledge and
information

Information policy
Basis for a top-level
information policy

Information audit – 'what is'
What are we doing with
knowledge and information?
How does 'What is' match
'What should be'?

Learning
What can we learn from
the audit?
What changes do we need
to initiate?

Information strategy
Basis for developing and
implementing information
strategy

Fig 4.1   **Information auditing in the context of information strategy and change management**

of the proportion of the organization's total valuable assets which is contributed by the use of knowledge and information.

The audit process

There is as yet no standard for how to do information audits. Probably the way forward lies in establishing standards for what the audit should look at, while leaving organizations free to decide how they meet the standards, in the light of their definition of information and what they need to do with it, in relation to their key strategic objectives. At the same time, it is important that organizations should have access to relevant examples and case studies which they can draw on in planning their own audit. I am not convinced that the auditing model of the accountancy profession, with its certificates and signing off, is wholly appropriate here, because the purpose of information auditing is to establish a foundation for using information strategically, rather than to see that figures add up and things are being done 'correctly'. There are, however, other aspects of the practice of financial accounting which should be drawn on, especially meticulous attention to detail, and making the audit a repeated exercise.

While there is no 'standard' procedure (which worries some people unnecessarily), there is by now a fairly well-established common core of modern thinking about information auditing, which can be summarized in these terms:

1 It matches:
   – What organizations are doing with information against
   – What they should be doing with it in order to achieve their goals
2 Things you need to know before starting an audit:
   – What the organization does and how it does it
   – Its market, customers, clients, public
   – Its culture: how it manages, how it sees itself, its staff, its role
   – Its present orientation: where it's trying to go now
   – Changes in orientation it seeks: where it wants to go in future
3 Auditing looks at:
   – Information services, systems and products (including the often disregarded products which the organization uses to carry information about itself and its offerings to the outside world it depends on, seeks to serve or to influence; and those it uses to convey information internally)
   – How they support people in their work in order to see how effectively information serves organizational objectives
4 It provides a basis for:
   – Setting a value on the contribution that information makes to the organization
   – Decisions about changes in ways of using information and benefits to be sought
5 It should be an ongoing process, not a one-off
6 It is best managed from in-house, though outside help is often useful.
   The process shown in Figure 4.2 (page 75) is based on these ideas.

The first step – analysis of the information implications of what the organization is aiming to do – has been dealt with in detail in Chapter 3, so there will just be a brief reminder of it here. The rest of this chapter looks at steps 2–7 (that is, up to and including the process of doing the audit), identifies key issues, and suggests some approaches to them, some of which are exemplified in the case studies. The remaining stages – from interpreting the results and presenting them through to deciding on action and setting up monitoring – form the subject of the next chapter.

A further point to make about this sequence of activities is that it represents a practical principle which can be applied for other purposes besides information auditing; readers will meet it again, in various guises, on the road to information policies and strategies.

Step 1: Analyse the information implications of key business objectives

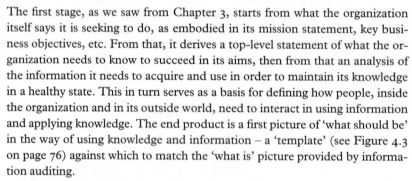

See Figure 4.2

The first stage, as we saw from Chapter 3, starts from what the organization itself says it is seeking to do, as embodied in its mission statement, key business objectives, etc. From that, it derives a top-level statement of what the organization needs to know to succeed in its aims, then from that an analysis of the information it needs to acquire and use in order to maintain its knowledge in a healthy state. This in turn serves as a basis for defining how people, inside the organization and in its outside world, need to interact in using information and applying knowledge. The end product is a first picture of 'what should be' in the way of using knowledge and information – a 'template' (see Figure 4.3 on page 76) against which to match the 'what is' picture provided by information auditing.

It also gives invaluable clues to:
* What resources of information to look for
* Key people to talk to
* Information flows to seek
* Technological support needed
* Questions to ask
* How to ask them
* Useful starting points for audit pilots or projects.

Except in very small organizations, it is becoming the usual practice to identify projects which can be used to gain experience of the process at low risk and low cost, with the chance of gaining some practical demonstrable improvement (the Surrey Police case study – page 325 – is an example). If this approach is adopted, the first top-level analysis can be taken to more detail for the areas in which auditing is going to be piloted.

Step 2: Ensure support and resources from management

See Figure 4.2

Experience from all sides tells us that this step is a condition for success. If you don't ensure that top management understands what an information audit entails, and makes a firm commitment to it, there is little if any chance of success. So in the early stages a lot of time and effort needs to be devoted to initiatives and interactions with management. This requires a high level of

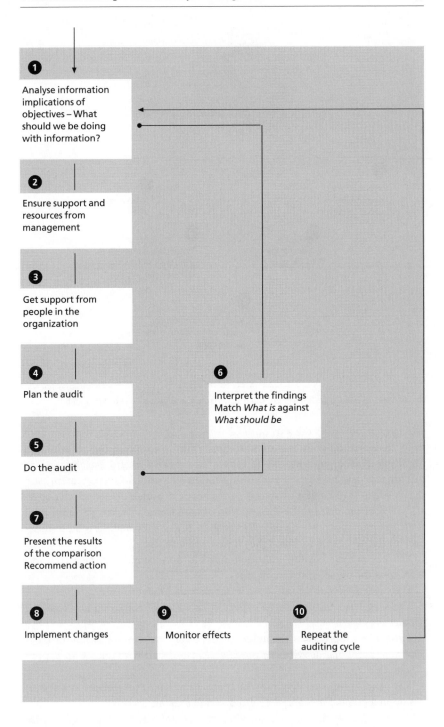

Fig 4.2 **The information auditing process**

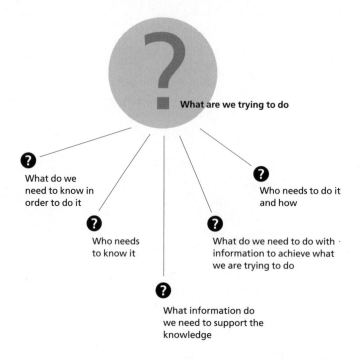

What are we trying to do

What do we need to know in order to do it

Who needs to know it

What information do we need to support the knowledge

Who needs to do it and how

What do we need to do with · information to achieve what we are trying to do

Fig 4.3   **The answers to these questions make the output from the first stage: 'what should be'**

skill in negotiation on the part of those responsible for the audit, together with deep understanding of the organization. The analysis of the information implications of organizational objectives can make a useful introduction to this process, and help in the basic information education of management, and that is why it is recommended as the first step. Corporate objectives can, after all, safely be assumed to be the creation of management, who are committed to them (and if not, they can hardly say so!), and so they make a solid foundation for the new ideas to which they have to be introduced.

The key points that top managers need to understand and give commitment to at the outset of the audit are:

- The objectives of the audit, both immediate and longer-term
- The long-term benefits to be expected, in terms of achieving key business objectives
- The scope proposed: is the audit to cover the whole organization, or parts of it, or particular activities or processes? Is it to start with one or more pilot projects?
- The phases proposed: the audit plan should be based on realistic steps, with stopping points for evaluation and decision making
- The benefits from each phase: what the organization can expect to gain from each step
- The timescale, expressed both in person days and the total elapsed time to completion

- The deliverables, for example progress reports and presentations at the end of each phase
- The resources required.

  The essential resources are:
- Support from top management
- People who possess knowledge, experience, judgement and standing to run the audit
- A proper time allowance for them to do the job
- Guaranteed access to people and documents
- A clear reporting line to the top level of decision making – the audit needs a management champion, who can be 'educated' by the people doing the audit, and who can in turn educate the rest of the senior management team.

See Figure 4.2

Step 3: Get support from people in the organization

It is not only top management who need to understand what is being proposed. When they have given formal agreement on the points outlined above, it is essential that everyone in the organization who will be affected should be fully informed, and have the opportunity of asking questions, expressing any anxieties and receiving explanations. If this essential courtesy is not extended to them, and if the first they hear of it is a memo telling them to expect to be interviewed on a given day, they are more than likely to feel threatened, and will not make the essential contribution from their knowledge of their own work – and so the quality and reliability of the audit findings will suffer. The people who will be involved should also receive a guarantee that they will be able to take part in discussing the audit findings, so that they can contribute to the ultimate decisions. Without that, they will not be committed to change, and the investment in the audit is less likely to succeed and may well be wasted. Time given to this step is time well spent, because, as well as gaining commitment and interest for the audit, it helps people to set a value on their own knowledge, to understand the part that information plays in their work, and to appreciate their mutual responsibilities for interchanging it and negotiating about it.

See Figure 4.2

Step 4: Planning the audit

Experience suggests that the lowest-risk and most productive approach is to select projects to start off the auditing process. This allows you to learn about doing the job in a more or less controlled environment, with minimal risks, and, if you pick your projects with care, to make a useful and quick contribution to improving information use, which gives tangible benefits.

Characteristics of information	Score (5 = Absolutely critical, 1 = Low significance)				
Example: Customer information	5	4	3	2	1
Key strategic aims can't be achieved without it	●				
Essential for a desired change in the organization's orientation		●			
Essential work can't be done without it	●				
Legal requirements can't be met without it				●	
Essential for planning and monitoring processes				●	
It has to flow between people for a key process to take place	●				
Potential for use in cost saving or revenue generation		●			

Table 4.1   **Identifying strategically important information**

Criteria for successful audit projects

There are some straightforward criteria for selecting potential audit projects. In the first place, look for areas where information has high strategic importance and where it has high potential for adding value. Here, once again, the preliminary analysis of the information the organization needs to achieve its aims makes a useful starting point. For each of the types of information identified, ask if it has any of the characteristics shown in Table 4.1 above, and score its level of significance on each characteristic.

The other criteria for potential projects are:
1 The area should have a clear boundary and not be too large
2 There should be potential for some 'quick wins'
3 There should be a fair proportion of staff in it who are information-aware.

An example: A project in an international information business. The area selected for an information audit pilot was the company's directory publishing operation. At that time the products were traditional printed volumes, but the company was planning to change its orientation towards electronic products. The audit looked at the processes of collecting, verifying and editing information for a range of directories, and at the technology in use to support the work; to see how well they were serving the objectives of maintaining the company's leading position in the market, and preparing for the move towards electronic products. The area was selected mainly because it seemed probable that organizational culture had an impact on the way in which information for the directories was collected. Details of organizations that figured in the directories were mostly collected by sales staff whose main job was selling these same organizations advertising space in the directories, and who therefore did not want to endanger good relations with customers by making too much fuss about the quality of the information they provided. Many of the senior executives had themselves come up via sales; they understood the value of good relationships with customers who bought advertising, but had less idea of the damage potential of poor-quality information.

As a project, it met the criteria listed above: the quality of the information that went into the directories was critical for competitive success and for reputation; the relationships between the organizations that supplied information and the company were crucial; there was a clear boundary; there was potential for quick wins (especially via upgrading the support given to editorial staff by replacing some antiquated systems); and the nature of the work ensured that editors as a whole were information-aware.

In deciding on projects, it can also be useful to combine the judgement of the people responsible for the audit with a general or selective invitation to submit possible projects (see, for example, the Surrey Police case, where this was done). If people have something they particularly want to look at, their knowledge and motivation can be a strong advantage, though it will usually need to be supported by intensive training and help.

Key people

Who does the audit? This is a key decision; there are those who think it should be done by outside consultants, because they alone have a breadth of knowledge and expertise to which no one inside the organization can aspire. My own view (as a consultant) is that this is expecting a lot of consultants (and rather more than most of us are likely to be able to deliver), and insultingly little of those who work in organizations. The more I see of the process, the more convinced I am that it should be managed and controlled from inside the organization, and carried through by people who work there. Outside help is certainly useful; appropriate consultants can offer experience of other audits, provide specialist support in such areas as questionnaire design or analysis, or training and support through regular discussion with the audit team of problems and progress (see the Surrey Police case study for an example of this kind of outside help), but the invaluable component is the knowledge which people have of their own organization. And they are the ones who will have to live with the results and put them to use.

The core audit team who will be responsible for managing the audit should be chosen for their strategic understanding of the organization's business, and their ability to interact with a wide range of people – especially to listen to them; and they should be of good standing in the organization. It is essential to ensure that they all have the same understanding of what they are doing – so the programme should provide for frequent team meetings, careful initial training, and feedback. Booth and Haines (1994) give an account of very thorough training for an information audit in the health service. If the audit is being carried out as a series of projects, with the work on each done by a group which has a particular interest in the area, it will usually be necessary to pay particular attention to 'induction training' to help them get to grips with the underlying concepts, and with the management aspects of doing the job. They will need support from the core audit team in this, to ensure that all projects run on comparable lines so that the results can be treated with the same level of confidence – especially important where projects cover different stages of the same process, or gather evidence on it from different parts of the organization. In large and diverse organizations, it may also be necessary to have a steering group to oversee the whole audit process (see, for example, the University of North London case study, page 349).

None of this, however, should deter small organizations which can afford only the time of one person for information auditing. If the person has the appropriate qualities, and is freed for the period of the audit from at least a proportion of their normal workload, it is a feasible undertaking. Of course the scale has to be limited, and the investment of effort targeted, but that is no bad thing, and at least the one-person audit manager has minimal problems of project administration and none at all in team building and supervision. (See the MAFF case study, page 274 for a successful example of a one-person audit.)

Who do the auditors need to talk to? There are two main groups with whom the people carrying out the audit will need to interact; and again, the analysis of the information implications of objectives should give pointers to them:

1 People who are given responsibility by the organization for being 'guardians' (some organizations call them 'stewards') of specific kinds of information, or for managing it on behalf of the organization, together with the managers to whom they have ultimate responsibility. For example:
   – Those who have responsibility for acquiring, making accessible, and disseminating certain kinds of information
   – Those whose permission has to be asked for using particular forms of information
   – Those who have the right to update and change databases.
2 'Stakeholders' in information, that is, the people who have a legitimate need for particular kinds of information in their work, and whose voice therefore needs to be heard in decisions about it.

Methods

A variety of methods can be used in information auditing. They include: study and analysis of documents and of databases used in conveying information; observation of how people carry out information tasks; structured interviews; informal meetings of work groups to identify key problems; questionnaires; mapping and other forms of visual representation (see Figure 4.4 opposite); and Soft Systems Analysis (see Chapter 5, page 95 for an example). Table 4.2 on pages 82 and 83 suggests where they are useful, and things to bear in mind about them.

The choice of methods is again something on which sound knowledge of the organization and its culture should be brought to bear. Methods need to be worked out very carefully in advance; the people applying them should have appropriate training and practice, and professional advice should be sought if necessary on such matters as developing and testing questionnaires; interviewing techniques; and software for analysing results or presenting data visually (see the Australian Securities and Investments Commission and the

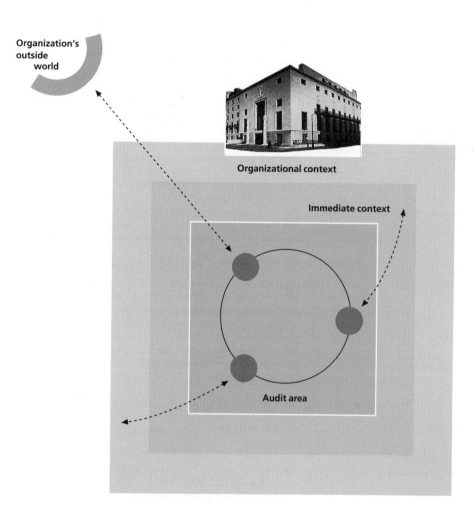

Organization's outside world

Organizational context

Immediate context

Audit area

Information resources:

? What's in them?
Who are
   The guardians?
   The stakeholders?
What comes in?
What goes out?

Fig 4.4   **A visualization of the audit area**

Methods	What they are useful for
Analysis of documents and data-bases	Useful preliminary before taking up people's time with interviews or questionnaires Good basis for deciding what questions to ask
Observation	Useful for spotting where systems or presentation of information make tasks difficult. NB Get permission from the people you are going to observe and make sure they're happy to be watched.
Trying things out for yourself	Useful for spotting possible obstacles to getting at and using information that people need in their work; a good basis for deciding on questions to ask
Structured interviews	Useful for tapping into people's knowledge, learning how they use information in their job, how information flows, difficulties in getting/using what they need *(I'm not convinced of the value of working to a fixed script in the information auditing situation; probably a more informal structure which covers the main points but allows the people involved to make their own decisions will produce better results.)* NB Give people an outline of the topics of interest beforehand; meet them in their own territory if possible; let them take the lead in talking; ask them about what they do and what they need to know to do it, *not* about what information they use.
Informal meetings of work groups	Useful for identifying problems as they perceive them in the area of the audit Helpful as a basis for deciding on questions and where to address them
Questionnaires	Use with care, and don't try to find out more than you can analyse. Useful for quantitative data, and for gathering experience and views on key topics Keep them short; make them easy to fill in without error (you'd be surprised at how many wrong ends to a stick respondents can find) and easy to extract data from for analysis. Plan them in cooperation with whoever will do the analysis For qualitative information use a 5-point scale with meaningful phrases to describe the points (informal meetings should yield some pointers to these). Keep open-ended responses to a minimum

Table 4.2   **Methods and where they are useful.** *Continued on opposite page*

Methods	What they are useful for
Mapping and other visual methods **(see Figure 4.4 on page 81)**	Simple visualizations of the audit area; information resources in it; the immediate and wider organizational context, and the 'outside world'; and information flows are helpful in disentangling the reality from strings of words. They can be supported by summarized answers to such questions as: • What's in this information resource? • Who is its guardian? • Who are the stakeholders? • What comes in? • Who from? • What goes out? • Who to?

Table 4.2   *end*

University of North London case studies – pages 197 and 349 – for examples of the use of appropriate software to support audits). If your organization has specialists in any of these areas, it can help to spread understanding and win allies to consult them – we all like to have our expertise recognized, and we feel kindly towards colleagues who appreciate it. At this stage in preparing for the audit, it is essential to take basic decisions on the kind of analyses to be made of the results; simplest and strongest is probably the best advice. Information auditing is more craft than scientific research. Better a limited set of statements and a small number of correlations in which it is possible to have reasonable confidence than a complex analysis of dubious reliability which acts as an obstacle to interpretation and action.

It is essential to remember that information auditing is not just a technical task. Whatever methods we use must, of course, be reliable and properly applied, but doing an audit is not just a matter of counting and statistics; it is primarily a job of interacting with people, in some quite sensitive areas, so selection and preparation of the audit team, preliminary presentation to people in the organization, and all subsequent interactions with them deserve the utmost attention. And planning needs to include how and when progress reports will be given.

If, on the other hand, you wish to kill an audit stone dead, here are four simple steps to doing it:
1 Try to cover too much at once
2 Ask more questions than you need
3 Make sure the audit team don't share the same view of what they're doing
4 Make sure that the people on the receiving end don't understand the purpose of the process.

See Figure 4.2

Step 5: Finding out

We come, at last, to actually 'doing the audit'. This is the stage when we ask a parallel set of questions to those asked at the start in order to define what knowledge and information the organization needs to achieve its objectives, and how it needs to use them (see Figure 4.5 on page 85).

There are five key areas, which are relevant to any audit project:

1 Information resources (both content and 'containers')
2 Guardians and stakeholders
3 Information flow and interactions
4 Technology and systems to support the use of information
5 How the cost-effectiveness of information is assessed.

For each area, there are essential questions which the audit has to seek an answer; the basic form of these questions is outlined below, but the detail, the emphasis, and the way in which they need to be asked is the critical element, and you have to make your own decisions in the light of your knowledge of your own organization.

Another set of decisions at this stage concerns how to record the findings; they need to be taken before the finding out begins, not while it is in progress. The aim is to make it easy to record accurately and economically, to minimize effort in preparing reports on the findings, and to make them intelligible to the people they are presented to. Since the whole purpose of information auditing is to allow us to match what the organization *should* be doing with information, and what it *is* doing, so as to see how well it is contributing to meeting its objectives, the recording of findings should aim to make the comparisons easy. If the first stage of analysing the information implications of the organization's objectives has resulted in a formal statement, the sections of that should be used as a guide to developing the materials for recording audit findings.

Where you are looking for quantitative results that lend themselves to being turned into tables or graphs, plan the recording forms so that they make it easy to extract and key data from them. For recording qualitative results about people's experience or opinions (from interviews or questionnaires) use five-point scales as far as possible, and limit open-ended questions to where they can throw useful light and yield telling quotations. Where the audit involves observing processes or systems, or examining documents, establish checklists of critical criteria related to the purpose for which people use them in their work, and identify how well they support people in doing the job.

Pre-test everything you plan to use in recording:

• Is it understandable for the people who will be doing the recording?
• Is it easy for them to fill in?
• Is it easy to extract data from it, or to analyse?
• Is it easy for people participating in the audit to understand, without ambiguity?
• Does it allow people to answer easily and without errors?

If you find anything that fails these tests, amend it until it passes; otherwise what you get from the audit may be unreliable.

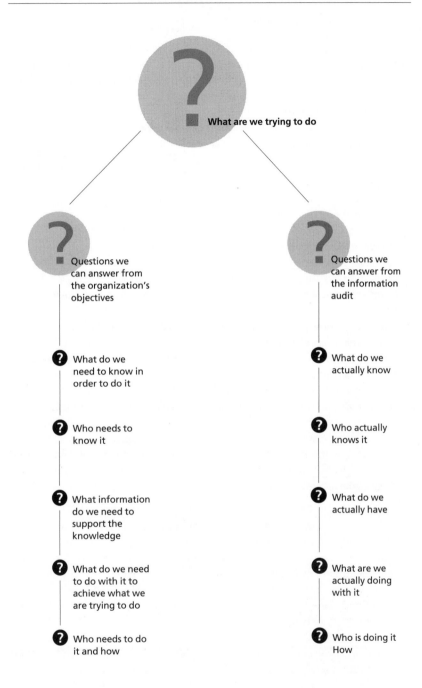

What are we trying to do

Questions we can answer from the organization's objectives

Questions we can answer from the information audit

What do we need to know in order to do it

What do we actually know

Who needs to know it

Who actually knows it

What information do we need to support the knowledge

What do we actually have

What do we need to do with it to achieve what we are trying to do

What are we actually doing with it

Who needs to do it and how

Who is doing it How

Fig 4.5   The original set of questions (see Figure 4.3), and the parallel 'What do we actually know?' set

Key questions on information resources

We have to be prepared to find information resources in every part of the organization, not just in formal repositories like libraries or information systems, and not just in those functions where people spend a lot of time reading, writing, or interacting with computers. The touchstone for identifying information resources is:

Is this something, which holds information that people need to apply in their work, to achieve their, and the organization's, objectives?

The things that meet this criterion will obviously differ according to the business of the organization; allowing for that, they will include such resources as:

* Customer records
* Information from and about suppliers
* Information about operating budgets
* Financial results
* R&D reports, from its own operations, and from outside
* Competitor information: how they are doing financially; what they are producing
* The information products of the organization itself, for the world outside, and for the internal audience of its own staff
* Information from and about its 'constituency', its market, its target audience, or its clients
* Information about subject areas of importance to its work, for example: the industry sector it belongs to; the education system; science and technology; processes, materials, plant, or equipment
* Information from the monitoring of its production processes
* Information about the broader environment in which the organization operates: the economy, legislation, government and European Union regulations, social change, demography, etc.

In the wording of this list, I have been careful to avoid referring to the particular physical forms in which information may be embodied. It could be in books, periodicals, internal reports, market research reports, brochures or correspondence, or held in machine-readable form in databases, but for the purpose of identifying information resources the form is irrelevant, though it can become relevant later on when we start evaluating how well resources serve the users and their purposes. Readers may also notice that the list does not treat as separate categories information which comes from outside and that which originates inside the organization. This too is deliberate – though enlightened organizations set themselves the aim of being able to search all their diverse information resources as if they were a single database, many organizations still needlessly hamper their work by not letting the left hand of external information see what the right hand of internal information is doing. They organize their databases or collections of material according to where the content originates from, keep them physically separate, use different ways of structuring them and looking for information – and in the process lose the chance of letting them interact and illuminate one another. Of course it is essential to be able to identify where particular pieces of information come from, and to group things from a specific source physically. But it is a perverse waste of potential value to put large obstacles in the way of finding all the relevant information on any issue, regardless of whether it came from outside or inside.

The basic questions about information resources are:

- What are they?
- Where are they?
- Who is responsible for them?
- What kind of information do they contain?
- How do the people who manage them define the users and the way they are used?
- What do the users themselves say?
- Are there other people who could make good use of this resource who
  - Don't know about it?
  - Know about it, but don't have access to it?

Key questions about guardians and stakeholders

The information audit brings us into personal contact with the people who are entrusted by the organization with managing the resources of information, and with those whose work needs make them interested parties – guardians and stakeholders. It provides the opportunity of mapping the lines of control, the placings of focal points for information management within the organization structure, and the interrelation between them. In large organizations, it is quite likely that services and systems for handling information will have developed separately within autonomous companies or divisions; alternatively, the parent organization may have set up a range of separate central services covering different functions or physical forms of information. It is also important to find out the division or department in which 'information resource entities' are located, the source of their funding, and the provision – if any – for formal or informal links and information exchange between them.

At the level of 'organizational culture', it is necessary also to be sensitive to which grouping or individual is accepted to be 'top dog', where they stand in relation to information resources and their management, and how willingly or otherwise the other 'dogs' concede the leadership. This is important, because if changes are recommended as a result of the information audit, the power structure of the present management of information will need to be taken into consideration.

The questions to be asked about guardians and stakeholders are:

Guardians

- What is their place in the organization's structure?
- What are their reporting lines?
- What is their work specialism?
- What training/experience have they in information management?
- What are their contacts
  - With the guardians of other information resources?
  - With stakeholders in the information they manage?

- What knowledge do they have of the work of other guardians, and of stake-holders?

Stakeholders
- Who are they?
- How do they use information in their jobs?
- What contacts do they have with the guardians of the information they use?
- Are there information resources that would be useful to them which they
  - Can't get at?
  - Don't know about?

Key questions about information flow

When we investigate what people do with information, we quickly become aware that it is a fluid element – its nature is to flow (though it also sometimes goes straight down the drain, or gets dammed up in stagnant ponds, or disappears underground never to emerge again). But it is not just something that goes through the plumbing; human minds interact with it, they consume it and transform it into knowledge; it is also a means by which people interact with one another and exchange ideas. Without that kind of interaction, information would be of little use to the organization, and would generate no changes or advances (see Table 3.3, pages 49 to 54).

The essential things we need to find out are: Who gives what information to whom? and how does the information people get match what they need in order to do their job? So the questions to ask people in the audit are:
- What information do you receive as part of your job from:
  - People inside the organization?
  - People outside the organization?
- How does what you receive match what you need to do your job?
- What information do you give as part of your job to:
  - Other people in the organization?
  - People outside the organization?
- What contact do you have with the people
  - To whom you give information?
  - From whom you receive it?
- Are you able to discuss information needs with them?

Key questions about technology

Throughout this book, readers will notice that IT is always considered after information content, information use, and the people who use information. That sequence is a deliberate choice, because it is the logical order. We have to know what material we want to work on, and what we want to make with it, before we can decide what are the right tools for the job (and it is worth remembering once again that even today not all tools are, or need to be, electronic ones). Of course it is true that information technology is qualitatively different from earlier technologies because of its potential for adaptive interaction with its users, intertwining with human thought, and enabling new ways of thinking – but the first steps to interaction still have to be initiated by humans. And the humans who do the work that the technology is meant to support are the ones who should make the most important contribution to specifying what the technology should be able to do to help them. These ideas are more widely accepted today than when the first edition of this book appeared, but there are still too many examples of disastrous 'collusion' among those who design and market hardware and software, those who make the decisions to buy, and those who manage IT and information systems, in which all the parties are unaware of:

- The significance of information for the organization
- What it really needs to do with information
- Basic principles of managing information.

The information audit can be a first step towards a policy for IT and systems that not only avoids the disasters of ignorance but capitalizes on the knowledge resources of those who work for the organization. The aim at this stage is not just to make an inventory of IT and systems, but also to see how people use them for all aspects of managing information resources throughout the organization.

The essential questions about the technology centre on how it supports people in using information in their work:

- How is it being applied in doing things with information?
- How appropriate is it for the tasks people have to use it for?
- How easy is it to use? How reliable is it?
- What say did users of particular systems have in specifying what they should do for them?
- How compatible is it with other systems being used?
- Who makes the purchasing decisions?
- Who manages the technology? What are the interactions between them and the people who use it to manage information?

Key questions about how the costs and value of information are assessed

There are those who think an information audit should provide an estimate of actual cost and value of information to the organization. It seems to me that this represents an attempt to go too far too fast, because this is a very complex area (see McPherson, 1994 and Orna, 1996, for an overview). But an audit *can* usefully find out what the organization's current practice is in this respect.

- What kind of information costs are taken into account? Purchase of equipment, actual information? Staff costs?
- Is any account taken of costs saved by having and using information, for example in staff time, risk avoidance?
- How are the costs and benefits of proposed information investments assessed?
- Does the organization try to evaluate information resources in relation to how much and how well they contribute to key business objectives?
- Does it value information in such terms as those proposed by Burk and Horton (1988)?:
  - Quality (for example accuracy, comprehensiveness, relevance)?
  - Utility (for example accessibility, ease of use, quality of presentation)?

– Impact on productivity (for example contribution to decision making, product quality, time-saving)?
– Impact on effectiveness (for example contribution to new markets, customer satisfaction)?
– Impact on financial position (for example cost reduction or saving, substitution for more expensive inputs, increased profits, return on investment)?
• Does it recognize 'intellectual capital' (the knowledge and know-how of those who work for it, their ideas and initiative) as a driving force in its business?

It has to be said that not many organizations show up strongly here, but the subject is increasingly engaging the interest of decision makers in business who are aware that information and knowledge probably have a large potential value, though ideas about how to set a figure on it are mostly rather vague. So the audit can bring a degree of clarity by at any rate establishing what the organization's actual practice is, and that in turn will make an essential basis for any future attempt to establish the value contribution of knowledge and information (see Chapter 8, page 139, for further consideration of this topic).

Summary

Having followed the audit process through to the point where the job of finding out is completed, it is time to take a break, to summarize the story so far, and to look ahead to the next stages, which are the subject of Chapter 5.
• The information audit is a process of matching what should be with what is.
• So before starting, we need to establish what information resources the organization should have, and what it should be doing with them.
• Don't start without (a) support and guaranteed resources from the top, (b) understanding from the people who will be affected.
• It's not a once-for-all job; it needs to be a regularly repeated process.
• In itself it can bring some immediate benefits, and it can unlock the door to longer-term ones, by virtue of providing a solid basis of knowledge for policy initiatives.
• It is best done in stages, or by a series of projects – to minimize risk and maximize learning from experience.
• It should be managed from within, drawing on the organization's own knowledge of itself, not handed over to outsiders to carry out.
• Information auditing is a process of interacting with people, not just a technical exercise.

References

BOOTH, A. and HAINES, M. (1994), 'Information audit: whose line is it anyway?', *Health Libraries Review*, 10 (4), 224–232

BURK, C. F., Jr and HORTON, F. W., Jr (1988), *Infomap: a complete guide to discovering corporate information resources*, Englewood Cliffs, NJ: Prentice Hall.

McPHERSON, P. K. (1994), 'Accounting for the value of information', *Aslib Proceedings*, 46 (9), 203–215

ORNA, E. (1996), 'Valuing information: problems and opportunities'. in D. BEST (ed.), *The Fourth Resource: Information and its Management*, Aldershot: Aslib/Gower

SENGE, P. M. (1990), 'The leader's new work: building learning organisations', *Sloan Management Review*, 32 (1), 7–23

TAYLOR, R. (1982), 'Organisational information environments', in G. P. SWEENEY (ed.), *Information and the Transformation of Society*, Amsterdam; Oxford: North-Holland Publishing Company

Reading list

DAVENPORT, T. H. et al. (1992), 'Information politics', *Sloan Management Review*, Fall, 53–65

DAVENPORT, T. H. (1993), *Process Innovation. Reengineering work through information technology*, Boston, MA: Harvard Business School Press

DIMOND, G. (1996), 'The evaluation of information systems: a protocol for assembling information auditing packages', *International Journal of Information Management*, 16 (5), 353–368

DRUCKER, P. (1995), 'The information executives truly need', *Harvard Business Review*, January–February, 55–62

FARBEY, B. et al. (1995), 'Evaluating business information systems: reflections on an empirical study', *Information Systems Journal*, 5, 235–252

GINMAN, M. (1987), 'Information culture and business performance', *Iatul Quarterly*, 2 (2), 93–106

HAWLEY COMMITTEE (1995), *Information as an Asset. The Board Agenda. Checklist and explanatory notes*, KPMG Impact Club

HAYNES, D. (1995), 'Business process reengineering and information audits', *Managing Information*, 2 (6), 30–31

HAYWARD, R. and BROADY, J. E. (1995), 'The role of information in the strategic management process', *Journal of Information Science*, 21 (4), 257–272

HERGET, J. (1995), 'The cost of (non-)quality: why it matters for information providers', *FID News Bulletin*, 45 (5), 156–159

McPHERSON, P. K. (1995), 'Information mastery', *Aslib Proceedings*, 47 (3), 109–116

MARSHALL, J. (1993), *The Impact of Information Services on Decision Making: some lessons from the financial and health care sectors*, Information Policy Briefings No. 1, British Library Research and Development Department

ORNA, E. (1996), 'Information auditing', *Singapore Libraries*, 25 (2), 69–82

REUTERS BUSINESS INFORMATION (1994), *To Know and not to Know: the politics of information*, based on research conducted by Taylor Nelson AGB

REUTERS BUSINESS INFORMATION (1995), *Information as an Asset: the invisible goldmine*, based on research conducted by the Industrial Research Bureau

ROBERTSON, G. (1994), 'The information audit: a broader perspective', *Managing Information*, 1 (4), 34–36

Information auditing: interpreting and presenting the findings

---

In this chapter:
- Interpreting the findings
- Presenting – a selling job
- From audit to action plan

Facts do not 'speak for themselves'; they are read in the light of meaning.
Stephen J. Gould (1991)

Introduction

The last chapter took us as far as the process of finding out. Now we move on to making sense of the findings, telling the organization about what they mean, and recommending action. Of course this is not a straight linear progression; within the broad movement forward, there are doublings back and anticipations of what comes next, and people who have been closely involved in the process will inevitably find they are extracting possible meanings from what they find as they go on. This can be put to good use; supplementary questions can be asked to test the validity of interim interpretations. But final judgements need to be suspended until the full picture is available from whatever the audit has undertaken to look at.

⑥

See Figure 4.2

Step 6: Interpreting the findings – matching what is with what should be

We return now to the steps in the audit process. Interpretation of the audit findings is as important as the findings themselves, and the quality of the interpretation is critical for the success of the action that follows from the audit.

Matching what is with what should be

As explained earlier (see page 70), the heart of information auditing is a matching process between what the organization's goals imply it should be doing with information, and what the audit has shown it is doing. The focus for interpretation is the points where the two differ and those where they match, because these are the most significant for the contribution information makes to achieving organizational objectives.

Burk and Horton (1988) provide a useful means of identifying these significant points, as shown in Figure 5.1 on page 94.

Two examples will help to make the point clear:

1 A situation where information is of high strategic importance, but there is a mismatch between how it is being used and the key objectives.

A chamber of commerce

Main goal: To retain existing members, and recruit new ones, by providing relevant products/services

Strategic importance of information to achieving this goal: **High**

audit findings to organizational objectives

❷ **1** *What objective does this information resource/activity contribute to*

❷ **2** Strategic importance of that objective to organization's success?   High   High

❷ **3** Strategic importance of this information resource/activity to the objective?   High   High

❷ **4** How effectively does it contribute?   Well   Poorly

          Good news   Bad news

Fig 5.1   **Questions to help in relating audit finding to the organization's objectives** (based on Burk and Horton, 1988)

What should be:
- High-quality information about members and potential members
- Easy access to information about their business interests

What is:
- Elderly membership database
- Allows only for limited information about members
- Needs special reports to extract information about their business
- Staff responsible for database haven't time/don't understand why colleagues want it

    Interpretation: High strategic importance of information is undermined by:
- Lack of access to essential information
- Poor IT support
- Failures of understanding and communication

    Score for this aspect of information use: **A minus;** a threat to the organization's future if it continues

2 A situation where the high strategic importance of information to achieving a key objective is well matched by how the organization is using information.

A firm manufacturing quality sports clothing
    Main goal: To maintain competitive position by developing new products, matching customers' needs
    Strategic importance of information to achieving this goal: **High**

What should be:
- High-quality information about customer response to products, lifestyle, preferences
- Flowing well between customers and the business

What is:
- Good relations and information flow between:
  - Customer care staff and customers
  - Sales staff and customers
  - Customer care, sales, marketing and R&D
- Sophisticated customer database

Interpretation: High strategic importance of information is supported by:
- The kind of information collected
- The ways in which people use it and interact with information and with each other
- IT and systems

Score for this aspect of information use: **High;** there are potential lessons here for other areas of the business.

When it comes to interpreting the range of findings in a way that gives a sense of the whole picture, there are various possibilities. The Australian Securities and Investments Commission (see page 197) used the well-tried SWOT analysis (Strengths, Weaknesses, Opportunities, Threats) very effectively in presenting its information audit findings. Booth and Haines (1993) provide an interesting example of using the 'holistic' soft systems methodology in an information audit to define the current information system as perceived by staff of the organization. A 'rich picture' of the systems and groups of people making up the organization and its environment, created from information gathered during interviews and discussions, was used to devise 'root definitions' of:
- **C**lients or customers of the systems
- '**A**ctors' responsible for the main activities
- **T**ransformation processes by which inputs are modified and outputs produced
- '**W**orld view' – that is, the 'philosophy' informing the systems
- **O**wnership of the system – who has the controlling power
- **E**nvironment in which the system operates
  (The initials make up the acronym CATWOE which is often used as a shorthand expression for this aspect of the soft systems approach.)

The rich picture and the root definitions were used in interpreting the audit findings.[1]

---

[1] I recently enjoyed the experience of helping to run a practical course which combined information auditing with the soft systems approach. Besides generating a lot of hilarity, the experience of creating a rich picture and root definition for their own organizations illuminated them from a new direction for participants, who were then able to use the insights constructively in planning an information audit.

Another approach to interpreting the whole picture takes up the initial analysis of what the organization needs to know to achieve its goals, the information it needs to support that knowledge, and the information interactions it requires in order to act on the knowledge (see Tables 3.1 to 3.3 pages 45 to 54). This means using the 'what should be' statement directly as a framework for presenting the findings about 'what is', so that each statement of the desirable state of affairs is immediately followed by the actual situation. Table 5.1 on page 97, shows an example based on an analysis similar to that of Tables 3.1 to 3.3, for a company.

Directly relating the actual and the desirable makes it possible to move on to visualizing where they converge and diverge; Figure 5.2 on pages 98 and 99 shows an example. A graphic representation makes a good starting point for planning the report on the audit, which is the next topic for consideration.

❼

Step 7: Presenting the audit findings: a selling job

See Figure 4.2

If we do not pay heed to how we make the knowledge acquired in the course of the audit visible and manageable for others who have not shared in the process, we run the risk of burying it under a heap of words and wearying the reader into exasperation or misunderstanding of the essential message. And in that case, we shall have great difficulty in selling the product, which is what we must do if the organization is to get a useful return on the effort it has invested in the audit.

Reporting on the audit

The report is all too often the stage at which value, instead of being added, is subtracted. The main dangers are:
- Too much prose: prose is good for developing arguments and telling stories; but it acts to obscure relationships of numerical information, and it is often unhelpful when we need to draw attention to particular points or to summarize conclusions.
- Too much detail: it is easy to forget that material through which we can find our way with easy familiarity is likely to be an impenetrable thicket for all but those who are closely involved in that particular aspect of the organization's work.
- Not enough signposts: readers need to know where they are going, where they are at present, and where they have already been. Most reports give them little help in the way of an informative contents list, carefully structured heading hierarchy, and cross-references.
- Not enough stopping points: readers need the chance to pause at the end of each step in the argument, and to review where it has brought them.
- Not enough aids to verification: it is a courtesy to readers to refer them to the places in the report where they will find the evidence that supports particular arguments.
- Discourtesy, or downright insult, to the eye: badly reproduced reports, lines far too long for comfortable reading, inappropriate typefaces, ill-prepared graphics, and tables that make it hard to identify and compare critical data –

Knowledge and know-how requirements	Information required to maintain knowledge	
	Content	**'Containers'**
• About customers	Who and where they are Products bought Transactions Retention rates/losses	Database, allowing access via multiple features
	Findings: *Database acknowledged to be unsatisfactory for access to information now required; intensive efforts and investment being made to upgrade system.*	
	Views of value and quality Level of satisfaction with products/services New requirements	Reports from people in regular contact with them Reports of special research
	Findings: *Effort has recently been put into developing feedback, including training for staff in this area, but information needs and interactions are not yet clearly defined.* * Research commissioned in the past hasn't always been satisfactory; briefs sometimes not clear; where findings have been relevant, often not acted on.* * Awareness on the part of managers now improving; research strategy under development.*	
• About economic and social context in which the company works	Demographic trends Age structure of population Economic situation Employment patterns Lifestyle/social trends	Appropriate statistical series Periodicals and press Research reports On-line external databases Internet
• About competition and innovation in the industry	Situation of competing companies Their products and services	Periodicals and press 'Intelligence' reports compiled from various sources
	Findings: *Press and PR section within External Relations provides cuttings service; some periodical subscriptions; access to one on-line business database, but used by few people.* * Awareness among some senior managers that much more external information of significance to the business is needed, and that there is a big information gap here.* * No manager with specific responsibility for developing information resources of this kind, and no staff with relevant professional qualifications.*	

Table 5.1   **The information which a company needs: what should be and what is**

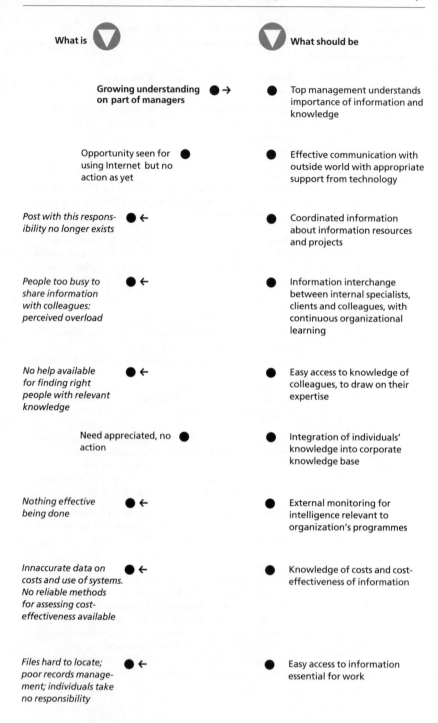

What is ▼   ▼ **What should be**

What is		What should be
	Growing understanding on part of managers ● →	● Top management understands importance of information and knowledge
	Opportunity seen for using Internet but no action as yet ●	● Effective communication with outside world with appropriate support from technology
Post with this respons- ibility no longer exists ● ←		● Coordinated information about information resources and projects
People too busy to share information with colleagues: perceived overload ● ←		● Information interchange between internal specialists, clients and colleagues, with continuous organizational learning
No help available for finding right people with relevant knowledge ● ←		● Easy access to knowledge of colleagues, to draw on their expertise
	Need appreciated, no action ●	● Integration of individuals' knowledge into corporate knowledge base
Nothing effective being done ● ←		● External monitoring for intelligence relevant to organization's programmes
Innaccurate data on costs and use of systems. No reliable methods for assessing cost- effectiveness available ● ←		● Knowledge of costs and cost- effectiveness of information
Files hard to locate; poor records manage- ment; individuals take no responsibility ● ←		● Easy access to information essential for work

Fig 5.2   **What should be and what is – convergence and divergence**
continued on opposite page

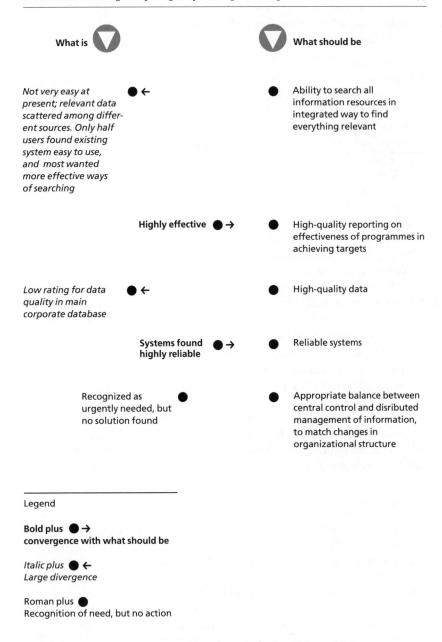

What is ▼   ▼ **What should be**

● ← *Not very easy at present; relevant data scattered among different sources. Only half users found existing system easy to use, and most wanted more effective ways of searching*

● Ability to search all information resources in integrated way to find everything relevant

Highly effective ● → ● High-quality reporting on effectiveness of programmes in achieving targets

Low rating for data quality in main corporate database ● ← ● High-quality data

Systems found highly reliable ● → ● Reliable systems

Recognized as urgently needed, but no solution found ● ● Appropriate balance between central control and disributed management of information, to match changes in organizational structure

Legend

Bold plus ● → **convergence with what should be**

Italic plus ● ← *Large divergence*

Roman plus ● Recognition of need, but no action

Fig 5.2   *end*

all these are still too common, and readers who meet them are likely to be consciously or unconsciously influenced against the content.

Reports should:
- Not demand too much reading time (an executive summary at the beginning is a good investment; willingness to read is generally inversely related to how exalted the reader is in the organization)
- Express the findings in the language which the people to whom it is addressed use and are accustomed to (they will not learn information-specialist speak, so it is the obligation of authors to translate anything esoteric into their terms)
- Emphasize: opportunities for using information to bring benefits to the organization's most important goals; and threats and risks that need immediate action
- Give examples of: good use of information that adds value; poor use that causes loss of value; beneficial changes ('quick wins') which have already been made during the audit as a result of what has come to light (see the ASIC case study, page 197, for an example)
- Present proposals for: short-term low-risk changes that can bring 'quick wins'; the next stages of auditing (if the audit is being done by stages); longer-term changes and phases towards them.

And finally, it should take every opportunity to sell thinking as a low-risk and highly cost-effective activity (for an example of a successful national institution which believes this and acts on it, see the British Library case study, page 213). Decisions on structure, format, layout etc. are best taken by the writers of the report, in the light of their knowledge of the organization and of the people they are addressing, and drawing on whatever professional expertise is available to them. (See the case studies of the ASIC, University of North London and Surrey Police for examples of approaches to reporting on audits.)

Communication

Presenting the audit findings and recommendations for action on them is a critical point in the process because it determines whether the audit will be acted on, or added to the tally of dead and unceremoniously buried initiatives. The process of face-to-face presentation is a combination of communicating information and selling a course of action. The people who have managed the audit should take the lead in presentation and in arguing for their recommendations; and the findings should be presented to those who have participated, as well as to the top management team, in fulfilment of the undertaking to give them the opportunity of discussing the findings and contributing to decisions on action.

The assets which the presenters can draw on are the knowledge gained from the audit, which is their unique property until it is presented, the authority which comes from knowledge, and the relationship they have built up with the 'management champion' and with colleagues throughout the organization during the audit.

Preparation

Because presentation to the top management team is such a critical stage, it is essential to devote adequate time to preparing and trying it out. If, as in some of the case studies, there has been a steering committee, they are the ideal audience for a 'dress rehearsal'. Otherwise the critical observer for the trial run will have to be the 'management champion'. Whoever fulfils the role, their job is to pick up things that are likely to be misunderstood, to give rise to questions or to hostile responses, or to be seen as threats to power structures – and to suggest alternative approaches, different ways of putting the same point, how to deal with opposition, and what arguments to address to potential allies and to likely opponents. It is particularly important to discuss possible structural changes implicit in the findings and recommendations and their 'political implications', and to develop strategies for presenting them. Fortunately, the experience gained during the audit process is likely to have deepened the audit team's insight into power structures and prevalent 'world views'.

As with a written report, so too with presentation it is good sense to choose techniques that are familiar to and approved of by the people addressed. It is equally important to make sure you know how to use them really well, and that they work on the crucial occasion. Readers will certainly have experienced manifestations of the rule that computer-based demonstrations which work perfectly in rehearsal fall over on the night. (This sort of thing actually happened long before computers were invented; my father used to tell me about the advice he was offered as a pupil teacher 80 years ago by his science master, when learning how to demonstrate the principles of distillation to a class – 'Put a spoonful of brandy in the collecting vessel before you start'.)

Presentation outwards into the organization, as well as upwards to top management, should, as recommended earlier (see page 77), be provided for in planning the audit. It is of equal importance to the 'upstream' presentation, and demands a different approach, with no less rigorous preparation. The aim is not only to inform and to sell ideas for action; it is critical to use this occasion as a forum for interaction and exchange of views on an equal basis, where people who have contributed information to the audit are able to consider what use has been made of it, to see how their contribution matches other inputs, correct inaccurate representations, discuss the conclusions drawn and recommendations made, and propose alternative or additional courses of action. This outward presentation is an opportunity for spreading knowledge of the audit process through the organization, and for identifying and drawing in new people to work on the next stages.

Making the presentation can be a challenging experience; but those who undertake it should remember the advantage they have acquired by becoming the people who are most knowledgeable about what the organization does with information. That gives them the authority to be heard when they propose action based on what they have learned, and it lends merited value to their judgements. So, if it comes your way to be the presenter of the results of an information audit, remember:

• Your audience will take you at the value you set upon yourself

- Use the authority of honestly gained knowledge
- Make sure they see the view you want them to see – it is part of the role entrusted to you to be a reliable guide.

See Figure 4.2

Steps 8 to 10: Following up the audit

At this point the first round of information auditing is completed, but, rather than an end, it marks the beginning of new activities – covered in later chapters, as well as another cycle of the auditing process.

The presentation of audit results should flow without interruption into decisions, and decisions into action. The outcome of presentation should be an action plan, which should aim for:

- Essential changes to avoid any immediate threats
- Quick benefits in key areas, to keep up the momentum and maintain commitment to change
- Maintaining the communications links established in the audit
- A definitive statement of the organization's information policy (see Chapter 6, pages 105–108)
- A start on developing an organizational information strategy to ensure that the business strategy benefits from an 'organizational knowledge base' which is kept constantly up to date
- Establishing appropriate criteria for monitoring and evaluating changes as they are implemented
- Making the information audit into a regular exercise.
- Regular reporting on information developments at the top level as a feed into business strategy development
- Starting to assess the cost-effectiveness of information use and its contribution to the value of the organization's assets.

Summary

- The heart of information auditing is the matching of 'what is' with 'what should be'.
- The focus for interpreting the findings from an audit is the points where:
  1 Information is of high strategic importance for the organization and there is a big difference between the reality and what should be
  2 Information is of high strategic importance for the organization and there is a good match.
- Presenting audit findings is a selling job, and deserves full attention and intensive preparation, so that the decision makers understand the message and buy it, and the organization gets a useful return on the effort put into auditing.
- Presentation outwards into the organization is as important as presentation upwards to top management.

- In both face-to-face and written presentation, probably the most important factor in selling the ideas is to express them in the language which the audience uses.
- And the most important idea to sell is: Thinking is a low-risk and highly cost-effective activity!

References

BOOTH, A. and HAINES, M. (1993), 'Information audit: whose line is it anyway?', *Health Libraries Review*, 10 (4), 224–232

BURK, C. F., Jr and HORTON, F. W., Jr (1988), *Infomap: a complete guide to discovering corporate information resources*, Englewood Cliffs, NJ: Prentice Hall

GOULD, S. J. (1991), 'The validation of continental drift', *Ever since Darwin*, London: Penguin

From information audit to information policy

In this chapter:

- Refining the information policy
- What an information policy should cover
- Who drafts the policy?
- Selling the policy
- The policy as a foundation for information strategy

Introduction

In Chapter 3 (page 43) I argued for the positive gains that come from starting with an understanding of the organization 'what it seeks to achieve, where it is trying to go, how it sets about its business, and how it sees itself and its outside world'. Among those gains were:

> A picture of 'what should be' – if this is what the organization is trying to do, with this structure and this culture, then this is what it ought to be trying to do with information and knowledge
>
> Some first ideas about how that could be expressed in a policy for information.

The last two chapters have been devoted to the business of finding out what the organization is actually doing with information and knowledge and matching it against the 'what should be' picture, so as to make well-founded decisions about action to capitalize on good matches and improve bad ones. We agreed, I hope, that it was important not to lose the impetus, and for decisions to flow without interruption into actions. One of the first and most significant actions should be to refine whatever ideas about information policy we developed initially, in the light of what we now know, and to make that policy a firmly stated part of the organization's guiding principles.

Refining the information policy

We defined organizational information policy (page 9) as:

> A policy founded on an organization's overall objectives, and the priorities within them, which defines, at a general level:
>
> • The objectives of information use in the organization, and the priorities among them
>
> • What 'information' means in the context of whatever the organization is in business for
>
> • The principles on which it will manage information
>
> • Principles for the use of human resources in managing information
>
> • Principles for the use of technology to support information management
>
> • Principles it will apply in relation to establishing the cost-effectiveness of information and knowledge.

Let us now look in more detail at what a policy should cover and how it might be expressed.

What an information policy should cover

What follows is an example of what an information policy could cover. It is based in part on actual policies developed in some of the case study organizations, and in part on experience and reflections over the past eight years. It is not offered as a model for copying, rather as a source of ideas about what might be appropriate for specific organizations. I doubt if any organization would wish to take the whole lot on board at one go; most, I guess, will be happier to start with a few basic principles which they see as particularly relevant to their own situation, and there's nothing wrong with that. An information policy can, and should be, revisited from time to time, and further refined in the light of experience. What *is* important is that the policy should be expressed in terms that match the organization's goals and character (see 'Nailing down the basic principles' below, page 108), and that it should be used throughout the organization as a focus for thinking about how it uses knowledge and information.

▼

Name of organization
Policy for the use of information and knowledge

Basic obligations

1 Information resources are the property of the organization as a whole, not of individuals or groups within it.

2 It is part of the job of everyone in the organization to:

• Be aware of what they need to know to do their job, and of the information needs of the people with whom they interact in their work

• Use information in order to keep their knowledge in an appropriate state to support their work

• Interchange information and knowledge with colleagues and with people outside the organization to help it achieve its aims

• Manage conscientiously any resources of information for which they are responsible.

3 It is the organization's obligation to provide education, training and support to enable them to do so.

4 The organization will respect knowledge in the minds of people as their own permanent property; in return, they will use it to support their work and that of their colleagues, and make it available to the organization's knowledge base on leaving the organization.

The policy

We will:

1 Define what knowledge we need to achieve our goals, the information we need to maintain the knowledge, and the ways in which people in the organization need to use knowledge and information.

2 Keep the definitions up to date as our goals evolve and change.

3 Audit our use of information and knowledge regularly to ensure that we have what we need and are using it appropriately and to good effect.

4 Ensure that appropriate information is acquired from outside, and generated inside, to allow us to do what we need to do with information and knowledge

5 Exploit it fully, to meet all current needs, and to help us develop to meet changes in our goals and in the environment in which we operate.

6 Ensure that it reaches, on time, and in the right format, all the people who need to use it

7 Identify the people responsible for managing specific resources of information, and those who are 'stakeholders' in them, and ensure that the authority of the managers of information resources matches the responsibility they carry

8 Provide for a coordinated overview of our total resources of knowledge and information

9 Promote information interchange between managers of information resources, and between them and stakeholders

10 Develop and maintain an infrastructure of systems and information technology to support the management of information resources and information interactions with the organization and between it and the outside world

11 Use knowledge and information ethically in all our internal and external dealings, so as to preserve and enhance our reputation [1]

12 Pursue maximum openness of access to information inside the organization and for our 'outside world'

13 Safeguard our resources of information – current and historical – so that they remain accessible for use at all times

14 Ensure preservation of the organization's 'memory' in the form of its knowledge base [2]

15 Provide appropriate education and training to enable all members of staff to meet their responsibilities in using knowledge and information.

16 Develop and apply reliable means of assessing the costs and value of information, and the contribution it makes to achieving our objectives

17 Provide appropriate human and financial resources for managing and developing the use of information and knowledge

18 Seek to use knowledge and information to support the management of change and the development of change initiatives to benefit the organization, and to create new knowledge [3]

19 Use this policy as the basis for information strategies which will support our businesss strategy

[1] The Institute of Information Scientists (1998) has recently published helpful draft guidelines for professional ethics.

[2] For a useful review of thinking about 'organizational memory', see Stein (1995):
... organizational memory concerns the knowledge-base of the organization ... the means by which knowledge from the past is brought to bear on present activities ... An improved organizational memory can benefit the organization in several ways:
• It can help managers maintain strategic direction over time.
• It can help the organization avoid the nightmare of cycling through old solutions to new problems because no one can remember what was done before.
• It can give new meaning to the work of individuals if such efforts are retained.
• It can facilitate organizational learning.
• It can strengthen the identity of the organization.
• It can provide newcomers with access to the expertise of those who preceded them.

[3] See Nonaka and Takeuchi (1995) and Choo (1996).

Appendices:
- The definition of information for this organization (a brief statement of what constitutes information from the point of view of the organization's goals)
- Its information resources (a list of the resources it holds and maintains to support its use of knowledge and information in achieving its goals).

Nailing down the basic principles

We cannot afford to let even the broadest statement of an information policy be in such general terms that everyone can assent to it and nobody feels under any obligation to do anything about it. The policy statement has to nail down the principles in a way that commits the organization to doing something sensible that will be of benefit to it where most needed. This example, from an actual organization (it was the subject of a case study in the first edition – Orna, 1990, page 281), shows one instance of doing it. The organization made its living by analysing the advertisements in trade and technical and consumer periodicals, and selling reports based on the analysis to publishers and editors in this area of the industry as a guide to what the competition was doing. At the time of the information audit whose findings are described in Table 6.1 (see page 109), it was in some trouble.

So the principles about getting information on time and in the right format to the users, training in the appropriate information skills, and information interchange were expressed in terms of:
- Defining the key production jobs to take account of the information-based nature of the organization's activities
- Establishing appropriate measures of quality control
- Promoting the necessary flows of information, and communication within and between different functions
- Providing appropriate training for staff, supported by self-help training and reference products.

Again, if the mapping of the findings of the audit on to the organization's objectives has shown that failures to communicate essential information between different parts of the organization are hindering the achievement of objectives, then the information policy statement should emphasize bringing together staff from different areas to explain their work and information needs to one another, and to negotiate how to promote information interchange.

As a final example, the ways in which the organization tells its markets or its public about what it has to offer, or gives its staff the information they need to do their jobs, may emerge as a crucial area for success and a current cause of failures. In that case, the information policy objective of getting information in the right format to those who need to use it should be formulated to put emphasis on such activities as analysing the target markets for its information products, relating them to their role in meeting its objectives, and applying appropriate expertise to develop products that meet the needs of users.

Key objectives	Findings
To deliver reports to clients to the agreed schedule and at required level of accuracy	Neither timing nor accuracy requirements being met because: • Information about clients' requirements badly managed • Nature of data analysis tasks not understood by management; staff doing it did not understand its significance; no training in principles of indexing, which in fact is essence of the job • No standards for day-to-day communication of information • No adequate procedures for schedule maintenance • No standards for quality control
To sell the company's products to new clients, and ensure that existing ones stay with the company	Little difficulty in selling the products, because there is a recognized need for stay them, but a lot of difficulty in keeping existing clients, for the reasons indicated above
To support production and product development with an efficient and effective computer system	• Problems of interface between users and the system (and the system manager), lack of training. • Software not appropriate for the job • Hardware, especially printers, not up to requirements; liable to disastrous breakdown

Table 6.1 **Example of key objectives and the findings from an information audit**

Who drafts the policy?

Given the emphasis on continuity and maintaining the flow of action, it is sensible for whatever grouping has managed the stages which have led to this point to take responsibility for drafting the information policy. If there has been a steering group, for example, it would become their next responsibility, and they would delegate the actual drafting to the individual(s) or group who ran the audit or other earlier initiatives. The brief for the draft should be on these lines:
• Short
• Clearly linked to what the organization is trying to do, and to where it is seeking to go
• Focused on key points
• Providing a framework on which people can grow their ideas based on their knowledge and experience
• Expressed in ways appropriate for its character and culture
• Visually well designed and accessible.

Existing structures developed for information auditing will allow for discussion of the draft with 'management champions' who can prepare the ground for its presentation to the top management team. This is a stage which should be completed as quickly as is consistent with due consideration, because it marks a 'milestone' in the journey towards strategic use of information and knowledge, and because the output is a tangible and saleable product.

Selling the policy

In this and subsequent stages of the journey, the earlier investment of time in establishing working groups, reporting structures and protocols begins to pay off. It doesn't have to be done again! And the structures created at the beginning will have been enriched and strengthened by the experience of shared work, and by the links and interchanges developed during the work throughout the organization. There is rather less explaining to do; it becomes possible to refer back to ideas that have started to take root in the organizational compost (see the case study of Surrey Police, page 325, for an illuminating account of the length of time this can take). And there should be some attractive if small benefits already gained, as well as the prospect of future ones, as an incentive to buy into the next stages of the process.

The long-term benefits are substantial ones; they can be summarized as shown in Table 6.2 on page 111.

Presentation

Once again, as with the results of the information audit, presentation both upwards and outwards, to top management and branching outward into the organization is essential; and in this case it is even more important to pull out all the stops and make an impressive job of it. The fact that the foundations have been laid, and that the audience have absorbed some of the key ideas and know the people involved, makes it a rather easier task, and so does the fact that the product is a compact one.

With top management the main aim is to get them to sign up to the policy, to write a reference to it into corporate objectives as an essential element in them, and to accept it as the basis for further development of organizational information strategy. Perhaps the most creative and valuable results can come from presenting the policy outward into the organization, and using it as an 'educational product'. It can form the basis for group discussions, focusing on specific points of the policy, in which people look at the policy in relation to their own work and interpret it creatively in the light of their own knowledge and experience, start negotiating with one another over information use, and commit themselves to participating in information strategy development, which is the real engine that will drive the organization's progress to full and productive use of its information and knowledge resources.

Benefits	Leads to ...
Integration of all information activities	Information can make its full contribution to meeting organizational objectives
Decision making on resources for information activities can be objective, because it's based on the organization's objectives and priorities	Effective deployment of resources; long-term planning becomes possible; continuity in developing use of information promoted, and wasted investment avoided
Cooperation among those responsible for managing information resources, and between them and stakeholders, is promoted	Enriched use of knowledge and information through inter-functional and inter-disciplinary cooperation; reduced unproductive time on dog-in-a-manger behaviour; discovery of new possibilities for productive use of knowledge and information
Enhanced chances of successful innovation and competition	Improved return on R&D investment, increased market share, better competitive position
Sound decisions on investment in IT and systems	IT and systems support information objectives; permit productive developments in information use; promote internal and external information interactions; support people in using knowledge and information; upgrading of skills; increased job satisfaction
Constant internal and environmental monitoring and intelligence gathering makes possible anticipation of change, flexible response, and productive change initiatives	Information activities continue to be appropriate for what the organization seeks to achieve; new situations can be evaluated on the basis of knowledge; threats avoided; information can be used to plan change initiatives

Table 6.2 **Long-term benefits from an information policy**

The policy as a foundation for information strategy

Looking at the policy in this way, in relation to key business objectives, and especially to the changes in orientation which it seeks to make, will give indicators of focal points for information strategy development, just as considering what the organization is and does gives pointers to what an information audit should look at (see page 70).

Figure 6.1, on page 112, shows the path we have travelled so far, a spiral one which starts from understanding the organization's aspirations and character; goes on to define what, in the light of them, it should be doing with knowledge and information; matches that against what it is really doing, through information auditing; and uses the output to refine its ideas about how it should use knowledge and information, into an information policy. That policy in turn will form another 'landing' on the route towards information strategy which expresses the policy in actions directed towards achieving its aims over defined periods of time.

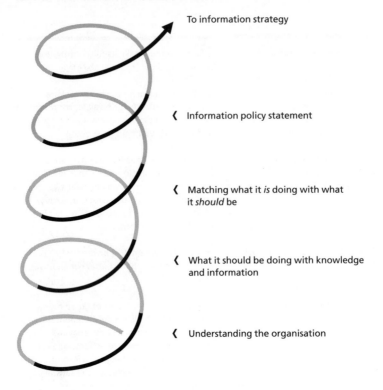

To information strategy

❬   Information policy statement

❬   Matching what it *is* doing with what
    it *should* be

❬   What it should be doing with knowledge
    and information

❬   Understanding the organisation

Fig 6.1   **The path we have travelled so far**

Summary

- Finalizing an organizational information policy and getting it accepted is an essential first follow-up to an information audit, and it should be done speedily, on the principle of striking while the iron is hot.
- A wide range of commitments *can* go into the policy.
- But it is for the people in the organization to use the knowledge gained so far to decide what is feasible for *their* policy and how to formulate it.
- The policy should be drafted by those who have done the preliminary work of organizational analysis and information auditing.
- It should make a compact and attractive product for selling throughout the organization.
- In planning presentation, use the structures and contacts built during the audit.
- In presenting the policy, sell it on quick wins already achieved through using information, and on long-term benefits to come.
- The aim of presenting the policy upwards is to get top management to sign up to it and what follows from it – information strategy development; the aim of presenting it outwards is to get people to enrich it with their knowledge and experience, and to join in developing information strategy.

References

CHOO, C. W. (1996), 'The knowing organization; how organizations use information to construct meaning, create knowledge and make decisions', *International Journal of Information Management,* 16 (5), 329–340

INSTITUTE OF INFORMATION SCIENTISTS (1998), 'Draft IIS Guidelines for professional ethics for information professionals', *Inform,* January/February, 4–6

NONAKA, I. and TAKEUCHI, H. (1995), *The Knowledge-creating Company,* New York: Oxford University Press

ORNA, E. (1990), *Practical Information Policies,* Aldershot: Gower

STEIN, E. W. (1995), 'Organizational memory: Review of concepts and recommendations for management', *International Journal of Information Management,* 15 (2), 17–32

Interlude

In the series of processes that have formed the subject of Chapters 3 to 6, we have reached the point where an information policy has been formulated and accepted. The emphasis has been very much on process, on ways of doing things so as to achieve the next step in a desired direction.

I hope this book is fulfilling the claim of its title to be 'practical', but it does not set out to be a cookbook; it doesn't tell its readers 'Do this, then this, and then that, and you will have an information policy.'

It requires inputs of thought and knowledge from both parties to the transaction, readers and author. If practical action is to give the desired results, it needs to be informed by ideas, just as ideas need to stand the test of being put into practice before they can claim to be any good.

So it is important to take pauses for thinking and putting our thoughts into the outside world where we can see them and judge whether they are acceptable as a basis for action (see Figure 1 below).

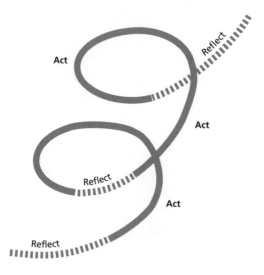

Fig 1   **Pauses for reflection and phases of action**

That is why, before going on to the activities of developing and implementing an information strategy, I think we should take a rest from 'how to do it' and pause to reflect on four main concerns of information strategy, which have to be taken into account both in developing and in using it.

They are:

1 People as creators of knowledge, users and transformers of information, agents who apply knowledge in action, and negotiators about information

2 Technology and other tools which help people to do things they need to do with information and knowledge

3 The value which information and knowledge resources, and their use, add to the organization

4 The changes which organizations encounter, originating within or without, anticipated or unexpected, and the use of knowledge and information to foresee change, avoid danger from it, maximize advantage, initiate change to create new knowledge, and gain new advantage.

Each of these themes could make a book in itself, but I shall exercise restraint. In the next chapters, I shall propose brief arguments, supported by some examples and stories, for why and how information strategy needs to take them into account. For those who want to consider them further, there are references to sources I have found helpful.

The main purpose is to help readers to consolidate their own thinking, bring the light of their knowledge and experience to bear on these ideas, and to make their own judgements about how they apply to their organizational situation as they interpret it.

Perhaps the best way of doing this is to go back to first principles of what makes an organization and what all organizations need to know to survive and prosper, as set out in Chapter 2 (see Figure 2.1, page 29).

If we look at what they imply for the key concerns of a strategy for information and knowledge (see Table 1 on pages 116 and 117), we find that a combination of the four elements is essential to keep them alive and well.

What makes an organization	Implications for what information and knowledge strategy must be concerned with	
• A grouping of human beings	How they think, feel, act and interact in respect of knowledge and information	❶
• For explicit or implicit purposes	The organization's purposes, goals and values, and how intangibles such as knowledge and information contribute to achieving what it most values (the 'business value model')	❸
• It interacts, internally and with its environment	The content of the interactions – what is critical knowledge and information for the organization	
	How people interact in respect of knowledge and information	❶
	How technology can support the essential interactions	❷
• It seeks sustenance to keep in being	The value of knowledge and information in gaining sustenance and keeping the organization successful	❸
• It has structure and a boundary	Structures that promote information flows and interactions among people inside the organization, and between them and its outside world	❶
	How technology can support the structure and the information flows	❷

Key:

❶	People as creators of knowledge, users and transformers of information, agents who apply knowledge in action, and negotiators about information and so on	The intangible value which people, aided by technology, create/add/subtract for the organization by what they do with knowledge, and how the organization assesses it	❸
❷	Technology and other tools which help people to do things they need to do with information and knowledge	The changes which organizations encounter, their use of knowledge and information to foresee change, avoid danger from it, maximize advantage, initiate change to create new knowledge, gain new advantage.	❹

Table 1   **The nature of organizations, what they need to know, and the implications for an information and knowledge strategy.** *Continued on opposite page*

What all organizations need to know	Implications for what information and knowledge strategy must be concerned with	
• What is happening inside, and in its 'outside world'	Identifying critical knowledge and information for the organization, and managing it	❸
• How to recognize, interpret and act on significant change	Monitoring and scanning the internal and external environment for intelligence	❸
	Interpreting it to detect significant change	❹
	Taking advantage of change to avoid risk and gain advantage	❹
	Initiating change and creating new knowledge	❶ ❹
	How technology can support people in these activities	❷
• How to create its 'offerings'	Appropriate skills and knowledge and how those who need them learn	❶
	Intelligence about its markets, and the flow of information about them	❸
	How technology can support people in creating the offerings	❷
• How to communicate	Information interactions internally and between the organization and its outside world	❶
	Appropriate skills and knowledge and how those who need them learn	❶
	How technology can support people in communicating and gaining access to the knowledge embodied in their communications	❷

Table 1   *end*

That marks the end of the interlude; the next chapters will look briefly at the four key factors, and how information and knowledge strategies should take them into account and

in **Chapter 10** we shall return to the process of developing and implementing information strategy,

with, I trust,

minds refreshed and ready for more work.

People and technology: battlefield or creative interaction?[1]

In this chapter:

- Why people are the really essential resource
- How information strategy needs to be concerned with them
- A human resources strategy as part of information strategy
- Systems to support people in using information and knowledge
- The reality
- Towards successful information systems/IT strategy
- Building and implementing the strategy

[1] Some of the material in this chapter is based on a chapter on 'Human resources in information management' in Orna and Pettitt, 1998.

Whereas information recorded in the old technology of writing was static, the com-
puter allows data-structures to be articulated and animated. This new power to cre-
ate and handle new kinds of signs represents an advance to civilisation which may
be as great as the invention of writing, but, of itself, it does no more to create arti-
ficial intelligence than did the ancient innovation of writing. Intelligence, knowl-
edge and meaning are more appropriately regarded as the products of the social
system. Any formal system that we are likely to be able to create is trivial in com-
plexity compared with the encompassing social system that uses it. Only by correctly
embedding the computer-based system in the social system can the data it contains
have any meaning, express knowledge or support intelligent behaviour.
Ronald Stamper (1996)

Introduction

This chapter deals with the interaction of people and technology in organizations, and it deals first with people. I have chosen to look at it in this way for a
number of reasons:

1 The balance needs redressing: far more is still published about using IT to
manage information than about how human beings can take control of the
process; in many organizations information management is automatically
equated with information systems and technology; and today, when 'knowledge management' is the current fashion, IT is staking an exclusive claim to
that too. As Davenport (1994, page 129) puts it, 'we have yet to address
fully the role of people in information management work'; and as Galliers
(1992, page 54) observes 'many have tended to assume that [IT] will provide the answers automatically. It is unfortunately the case that we have not
spent anything like the same amount of effort on understanding the nature
of our changing information requirements, nor on ways and means of integrating IT into the value-adding processes of business ...'.

2 Human beings can exist without information technology, and so can organizations, though today it is part of the working life of most. People have
been organizing themselves successfully without it since prehistoric times
by just talking to one another, and 'This is still the most important technology in any organisation where most of the organised behaviour is informal
in character' (Stamper, 1996). The ways in which we think and interact
with one another were laid down long before IT was invented. As McArthur
(1986) reminds us, writing is just over 5000 years old, printing a mere 500,
and electronic computation no more than a few decades. See Figure 7.1 on
page 120.

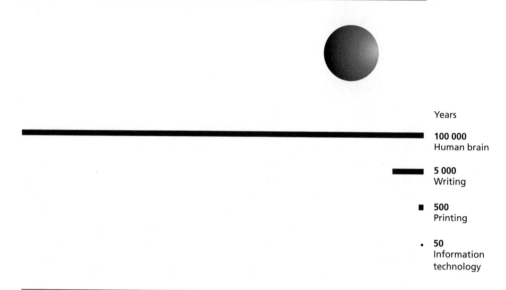

Years

100 000
Human brain

5 000
Writing

500
Printing

50
Information
technology

Fig 7.1   **The timescale of human information storage**

3 The interaction between the two is still treated in too shallow a way, and too often presented as one in which humans have to look sharp and adapt themselves to whatever technology is brought into the workplace. Already at the start of the 1990s, evidence had accumulated that 'Computer-based systems have too frequently been designed and introduced with little concern for the social, organizational and political contexts in which they are supposed to operate, for the human-resource implications of the IT-based systems design', and the fact that it was a management problem had been disregarded (Willcocks, 1991, page 121).

4 Interactions between the people who manage systems/IT and the rest of the organization are not sufficiently considered; 'And IT people have been left to deal with the increasingly complex problems associated with meeting changing information requirements and organizational imperatives, with little support or interest on the part of their management colleagues' (Galliers, 1992, page 54). This deficiency also exists as regards relations between them and the people who manage information resources. So it is not surprising that the role of information systems and technology is not often related to the overall strategy of organizations.

5 Systems and IT cannot yet exist without people, and may never do so; for the foreseeable future people will create both the hardware and the software. Those who design electronic products for use by people in their work need to have a rich understanding of human interactions, which is often lacking – the model of human beings that many computer systems seem to imply is still more like a cardboard cut-out than a 3-D living person. And those who use the systems need to be able to contribute from their knowledge of their own work to how they are designed and applied – but they do not often get the chance.

Why people are the really essential resource

Plenty of lip-service is paid today to the importance of people, but without much evidence of grasp of the simple and self-evident fact that the only agency which can turn information into knowledge, and act constructively upon it, is the human mind. It is only human beings who can make sense of information and manage it to good purpose. Unfortunately, human minds are a costly resource, and the value of what they do with information is intangible and hard to calculate in concrete terms, as are the costs of failures in performing these tasks effectively. This probably accounts for the fact that talk about the value of human resources is often accompanied by action in the form of 'down-sizing', replacing human work by information technology, short-term contracts, and various other 'cost-saving' devices, whose main effect is to undermine the sense of self-worth, create insecurity and deprive organizations of the value that is added through the exercise of human knowledge, experience and skills. As van der Spek (1998, page 46) argues, however:

> One of the biggest mistakes many companies make is to see knowledge management as a way of replacing people – they assume that if they can create systems to capture knowledge they will no longer need resident experts. In fact, knowledge and learning are the opposite of downsizing and re-engineering. They are tools for growth. They are about creating fat, not about getting leaner. And they are about having greater, and not fewer, resources.

There is indeed a well-established body of thinking, going back many years, by respected practitioners in business management which points to 'invisible assets' (including information and knowledge resources, corporate culture and management skills) as, in Itami's (1987) words, 'the most important resources for long-term success'. Money cannot buy:

> an instantaneous change in corporate culture or employee morale. Accumulation of these resources requires on-going, conscious, and time-consuming efforts; you cannot just go out and buy them off the shelf ... The important features of invisible assets – they are unattainable with money alone, are time-consuming to develop, are capable of multiple simultaneous use, and yield multiple, simultaneous benefits – make it crucial to carefully consider strategies for accumulating them ... People are important assets of the firm ... because much of the invisible assets of the firm are embodied in people; people carry and exchange the information necessary for strategic fit. (pages 13–14)

The case studies in this book would not have been possible without interaction with people in a variety of organizations – through conversations, demonstrations of how things are done, and reading documents composed by people. The experience goes to underline that organizations are indeed 'socio-technical' systems[2] in which the 'socio-' element comes first, and in which human knowledge, human interactions, and people's perceptions of the organization, of their colleagues and of themselves, are critical to what the organization can achieve.

---

[2] See Eason (1988) for an excellent and still valid study of organizations as socio-technical systems and designing technical systems for human use.

How information strategy needs to be concerned with people

Our analysis of the nature of organizations, what they need to know, and the implications for information and knowledge strategy (see page 116) suggests that such a strategy needs to be concerned with people in these ways:

- Understanding how they think, feel, act and interact about knowledge and information, and helping them to do so constructively, to their own benefit and that of the organization.

Most organizations still have a long way to go in this respect. As Drucker (1995, page 96) says:

> Few executives yet know how to ask 'What information do I need to do my job? When do I need it? In what form? And from whom should I be getting it' ... Practically no one asks 'What information do I owe? To whom? When? In what form?'

Yet, as Davenport et al. (1992) point out, in a wise study of organizational information politics:

> Information management must become something that all managers care about and most managers participate in. They must view information as important to their success and be willing to spend time and energy negotiating[3] to meet their information needs.

It is certainly encouraging to note from a number of the case studies in this book (see, for example, the studies of Thomas Miller & Co. Ltd and the Australian Securities and Investments Commission) that the organizations concerned are taking active steps to bring this about, by, for example, including information responsibilities in job descriptions. (See Leistka, et al., 1997 for an interesting study of the importance of this approach in high-performing professional service firms, where collaboration between people with deep technical expertise in one area, coupled with ability to link their work with that of others, leads to generating new ideas.)

- Creating organizational structures that promote information flows and interactions among people inside the organization, and between them and its outside world, by such means as establishing 'meeting places' – which may be actual physical environments or electronic forums where cross-functional teams, networks or groups can interchange ideas (see, for example, the case studies of NatWest Markets and the British Library).
- Initiating change and creating new knowledge (see Chapter 9).
- Helping people to acquire and maintain the skills and knowledge they need for creating the organization's offerings. If organizations seek to be competitive and innovative, as so many today claim they do, the people who develop the products and services on which their success depends need to have their knowledge constantly reinforced by feedback from the

---

[3] 'Constructive negotiation' over information needs is a much more accurate and realistic way of putting the desired outcome than the currently popular 'information sharing', with its motherhood, apple pie and nice children associations. It has to be worth people's while to interchange information; and it is important to learn the skills of positive interaction over information in which both parties to any transaction get something useful from it. (See Davenport and Prusak, 1998, for an excellent chapter on reciprocity over the exchange of knowledge in the organizational 'knowledge market'.)

'customers', monitoring of the relevant environment, and interchanges of ideas inside and outside the organization. They also need to be aware of new methods, techniques and technologies that they could apply, and to gain skills in using them (see the case studies of Thomas Miller & Co. Ltd, and NatWest Markets for examples).

What people in organizations need to understand about information and knowledge

It is also evident that, if any organization is to achieve its aims, the people who work for it need to:

1 Be aware of the aims, and of the organization's interpretation of the knowledge and information it needs to support their achievement.
2 Define for themselves, in cooperation with management and colleagues:
   • What their own knowledge and information requirements are
   • What they need to do in order to meet them
   • How they need to use knowledge and information in their own work
   • The support they can get from and give to colleagues
   • The interactions they need with the organization's 'outside world'
   • The support they need from information systems to maintain and use their knowledge effectively.
3 Take and implement decisions to ensure that they get what they need and use it constructively.
4 Monitor the process and negotiate changes to make it work better, and to keep it in line with developments.

Information roles

Most people in their work have many roles related to information and knowledge (though they may not be aware of all of them); they can be creators of knowledge, users of information, agents who apply knowledge in action, negotiators of deals over access to information, transformers of information into products and services for internal or external clients, etc. When we look at organizations in this way, it becomes evident that people in a wide range of jobs – customer relations, competition analysis, product development, financial management, sales, human resources, public relations, for example, as well as libraries and information services – are responsible for managing and using significant resources of information. Apart from that, an overall information management role – as distinct from a 'Chief Information Officer' whose remit is specifically systems and IT – needs to be provided for.[4]

4 An interesting straw blowing in the wind is suggested in a quotation from Yves-Michel Marti (Evans, 1997), who predicts that 'smart organisations' will start spending more on able and knowledgeable people, including corporate librarians – a 'source of great human knowledge few organisations exploit fully ... Despised or ignored by top management [they] have years of training and experience specifically addressing how to structure, cross-reference and access knowledge.' Davenport and Prusak (1998, page 29) make a similar point about corporate librarians as 'natural knowledge brokers'.

Though it is still rare to encounter such a role, the case studies provide some good examples (see the studies of the Credit Union Services Corporation, the Singapore Productivity and Standards Board, and the Australian Securities and Investments Commission). The person who fulfils it has to be aware of the full range of the organization's information resources, to know and to communicate on terms of mutual understanding with the guardians and stakeholders of each resource, and to take responsibility for developing the organization's strategy for using information. As the case studies show, the people who fulfil this role can be drawn from many different functions and backgrounds, and have various job titles. It is essential, however, if the job is to be done properly, for the holder to be at a level of authority which matches the responsibilities that go with it.

Taking care of knowledge

The definition of knowledge set out at the start of this book (see page 8) means that knowledge cannot exist without people who know. Knowledge in the human mind is a wonderful, dynamic force, with amazing potential for making connections and for speedy retrieval and application. It is, alas, also a desperately fragile, vulnerable, and easily wasted resource, as we may see from daily experience in all kinds of organizations. People with deep knowledge of particular fields which are important for the business of their organization can find themselves prevented from putting it to the fullest use by cost-cutting measures which mean they have to spend large parts of their time on procedural, clerical or administrative activities. Such expedients may achieve a required short-term saving of n per cent on the budget, but they offend against the sound economic principle that people should spend the largest possible amount of their working time using the specialist knowledge for which they were employed, and represent a long-term loss.

An aspect of knowledge not often considered is provision for the transfer of the 'tacit knowledge' acquired in the course of experience in the job, as part of the process before people leave organizations where they have worked for some time. Some organizations have a policy for retirement preparation which includes 'succession planning' and briefing by the retiring job holder of the person who will succeed him or her. This, while useful, leaves out of account people moving to other jobs, or taking early retirement, or made redundant, whose knowledge effectively goes with them. It would be worth con-sidering a negotiated 'transfer of knowledge' contract in such cases. It could take various forms: for example, the training of less experienced colleagues; written or electronic products embodying knowledge; 'knowledge-elicitation' sessions of a more productive kind than those conducted by non-specialists trying to embody expert knowledge for artificial intelligence purposes. The purpose would be to put the 'tacit knowledge' into the outside world, where it would be accessible for transformation to knowledge within the minds of others and embodiment as part of the organizational knowledge base. An important part of the knowledge that should be transferred is that which constitutes the organization's memory of its own history, a resource whose value is today beginning to be recognized in the business world (see, for example, Palmer, 1995).

The institution of a contract of this kind would help to preserve the continuity and relevance of the knowledge base, to avoid risks arising from lack of essential knowledge, and to prevent the costs of re-creating lost knowledge and of finding new information sources. It would also mitigate the losses that arise from the demoralization of both those who leave those who and are left behind.

There are other common situations where attention to making the knowledge held by individuals accessible to their colleagues is critically important. When hitherto separate businesses or organizations come together through merger or acquisition, the people who work in them can be at a loss to know where to turn for the information which is critical for successful performance in the new situation. The case study of NatWest Markets is an example of an intelligent approach to the consequences of a turbulent period of acquisition, through the simple expedient of giving staff an authoritative reference source to 'Who knows about what'.

A human resources strategy as part of information strategy

Organizations increase the chance of success for their information and knowledge strategy if they have a related human resources strategy, because it can create understanding and commitment for developing and implementing information strategy, and ensure that there are people available to contribute knowledgeably to the process.

These aspects of human resources should be taken into account:
- The resources of human knowledge and skills which the organization needs in order to achieve its aims
- The existing resources of knowledge embodied in the people who work there (a 'knowledge audit')
- How to maintain the continuity of knowledge resources, and protect them from loss, in the face of normal changes in the composition of the organization's staff, and of major developments in policy and ways of working
- The groups of people who need to cooperate in using knowledge
- The organizational structures to allow and encourage their cooperation
- The education and training that the organization needs to provide for its staff in order to develop and maintain their knowledge
- The role of technology in supporting the people in using and interchanging knowledge
- The promotion of 'organizational learning' – the capacity for the organization as a whole to learn from experience, and to apply what it has learnt in developing its work.

Such an approach, it is worth noting, is consistent with ideas being developed (by the World Bank among others) about the need for 'national balance sheets measuring the stock of the nation's physical and intellectual capital' (Hutton, 1996). GDP measures, which leave out of account all non-market transactions – both those which add value, and those which (like the waste of skills of unemployed people) are in effect a loss – 'offer only an indifferent guide to policy'. The World Bank's new 'wealth accounting system' includes, besides natural capital and produced assets, human resources and 'social capital'.

Burack et al. (1994) make a similar point in relation to the individual business: 'New paradigm companies recognize that ... business strategies require counterparts for human resources, often involving significantly changed roles for the human resources function.' So institutional policies which take account of the value of people in managing their resources of knowledge are realistic rather than utopian.

Systems to support people in using information and knowledge

The ways in which people in organizations need to use information, and to interact with one another in respect of information and knowledge, suggest the nature of the support they should be able to rely on from the technology. It should help them to:
- Store information neatly and elegantly
- Get back to it whenever it is relevant
- Reach people who know and converse with them
- Retain the results of experience (of failure as well as of success) and learn from them
- Interchange ideas and information informally
- Capture the essentials from informal exchanges for long-term use
- Scan all information resources as if they were one
- Keep track of change in the outside world and within the organization which is significant for their work.

And it should
- Remind them to do things in time
- Remind them of those to whom they should communicate information
- Present information in formats acceptable and helpful to the users
- Do routine things effectively and efficiently, without making users jump through hoops.

If systems make it easy to get at information which is managed by a different department, to tell colleagues what we are doing, or to ask them for help or information, they are likely to promote the habit of using them for that purpose. So, when new systems are being planned, the planning should take account of the interchanges of information which people need to make in order to achieve the organization's objectives. The various kinds of information that most organizations handle have a relationship of mutual support – not only are all of them essential, they have to interact if the organization is to get full value from them. And that interaction has to take place through people, supported as far as possible by the available technology.

The reality

Since the first edition of this book, there have been extraordinarily rapid changes in the technology (see Chapter 1) which have had an impact on the lives of all organizations and most individuals; the most significant are probably those associated with the development of the Internet, the application of web technology to internal resources of information in the form of intranets,[5] and the attempt to integrate the full range of external and internal information sources thus made available.

Many of them have great potential; as Wilson and Wilson (1994, page 179) express it:

> Information technology may be understood as a means of facilitating the development of post bureaucratic organizational characteristics. Computer-based information and communication technology may allow a greater diversity and dispersion of control structures to emerge.

Some organizations are making imaginative use of the technology in this way. But ...

- There are still plenty of organizations where technology is expected to deliver solutions without much intervention from human thought or any contribution from either the intended users or people with understanding of information management. Many of them probably figure in the 90 per centof IT projects which, according to a recent study (OASIG, 1996), fail to meet all their objectives, or in the 40 per cent of projects which fail totally.

- The long history of such failures suggests that a further failure – to learn from experience – compounds their effects. Ewusi-Mensah and Przasynski (1995) describe the findings of a survey addressed to top computer executives of large companies in the USA which suggests that most organizations do not keep records of their failed projects, and make no formal effort either to understand what went wrong or to learn from the failure. This is perhaps hardly surprising, given that Western culture is generally ashamed of failure, which leads those concerned with failed projects to seek to bury them from view, rather than regarding them as an opportunity for learning.

- Developments in access to vast electronic resources can lead to yet another example of the current enthusiasm which both businesses and government show for handing costs and responsibilities down the line to end users. The costs to them of wandering round huge quantities of unstructured material can be both financial and intellectual. As Holtham (1996, page 54) puts it, 'The problems of information overload are approaching epidemic proportions. The inability of Western societies to resolve the informational dimensions of the technology that will support a future information revolution, could be of profound strategic significance to whole societies if we remain

---

[5] White (1997) gives a well-timed warning about the dangers to corporate health lurking in intranets: 'users begin to assume (usually incorrectly) that conscious decisions have been made about content, and that all their information needs can be satisfied ... Without due care an intranet is likely to become the 1990s equivalent of the Management Information System of the 1970s and the Executive Information System of the 1980s.' (See also White et al., 1998.) A 1998 survey of IT, marketing and human resources managers in 300 of the UK's top 1000 companies (by David Lewis Consultancy for FT Publishing, quoted in *Managing Information*, 5 (5) page 5), suggests that they are not using intranets as strategic business tools; the information on them is tactical and not necessarily relevant, and most companies are not exploiting available resources, e.g. very few respondents reported having competitive information or industry news on their intranets.

incapable of recognizing the distinctions between data and information and between analysis and judgement', and it is far from certain that modern tools of data handling, high quality though they may be, 'will in fact alleviate the information crisis. It can also be argued that much of the problem lies in inadequate skills and competence in managing information'.

The distinctions Holtham mentions, and the limits to the scope of the technology, seem to be unknown to many of the purveyors of IT and systems. A random sample of recent publicity for seminars and conferences from a variety of institutions yields some interesting claims:

> Learn from the experts how to build an information management strategy that will ensure your company's long-term survival.
> (Brochure for a two-day event sponsored by a computer periodical and software firms)

> Data Mining or Knowledge Discovery in Databases (KDD). This involves the use of machine learning, statistics or database technology as components of large-scale data analysis to extract new knowledge.
> (Publicity for a report on data mining costing £495)

> An extensive technology suite, which is based on a powerful underlying technology architecture, offers ... automatic knowledge acquisition, concept and context analysis, and discovery.
> (Description of a software company's product; background to a talk by its Vice President for Systems Integration at a conference on knowledge management)

> ... a knowledge-based computer system for solvency analysis of commercia credit customers. The bank also uses datamining to analyse historical customer data, knowledge that gives a unique insight into the mind-set and behavioural patterns of each customer.
> (Background to a talk by a banker at a conference on increasing customer loyalty through knowledge management)[6]

There is a particularly determined IT attempt to take over the knowledge management bandwagon; we learn from a recent issue of *Information Strategy* (April 1998, 10–11) of a 'new breed of intelligent agent software' which 'has the potential to make knowledge management a painless and even effortless process', by monitoring information on employees' computer screens and building up a profile of their areas of interest and expertise 'without any human involvement'.

I am waiting for the day when the IT industry discovers common sense and tries to take that over from human beings. Meantime, it is refreshing to know that not everyone is taken in by this particular lot of emperor's new clothes – for some sharp observations on 'The knowledge backlash' see the collection of pieces under that title by Tate, Angell, Bottomley and Kautto-Koivula (1998). One quotation to give the flavour: 'perhaps worst of all, the knowledge man-

---

[6] As an antidote, try Davenport (1998): 'Contrary to much data mining hype, firms seeking customer intelligence have to go well beyond software, and employ a lot of intelligent people'; and see his excellent book on *Information Ecology* (1997) – 'Our fascination with technology has made us forget the key purpose of information: to inform people.'

agement movement is underpinned by a marriage of two of the world's most powerful "spin" machines – global management consultancy and the IT industry – both dedicated to developing new ways of doing business to keep companies in profit, especially themselves.'

I wrote in the first edition that 'Ill-considered introduction of information technology can be the last straw that reveals structural weakness in enterprises – disrupting social systems based on mechanistic theories of management and control.' People are fortunately rather good at saving bad human managers from the consequences of their ineptness, getting some entertainment out of the process, and making unworthy systems function. But if human taskmasters seek to delegate control to electronic systems, the whole structure can start falling apart. Many managements – even, or maybe especially, those who claim to be committed to 'empowerment' – are, however, still deeply unwilling to consider organizational forms that involve relinquishing close control, making room for autonomy and responsibility of work groups, and using the technology creatively to support them. As Mumford put it in 1986 (page 61), 'There are the managers and the managed and firms do not want to disturb this clear relationship by confusing the two roles. Some groups do things, others have things done to them or are told to do things.' And no longer ago than yesterday, I heard the founder of McKinseys complaining in a radio interview that many managements still stand in their own light by clinging to this principle – at 95, he is evidently a good deal more advanced in his thinking than they are.

Two contrasting scenarios for information technology featured in the first edition of this book: one showing the process of acquiring and implementing and the outcomes 'As it often is', the other 'As it might be'.

The first ran from technology development depending on simplified and erroneous views of users and their work; through hard-sell advertising which pretends the product is a substitute for thought; to purchase decisions by Fat Cats with limited knowledge of both the technology and the jobs of the people who will use it; to systems designed without reference to the social values of the organization and implemented without proper explanation or training; to outcomes in disasters, losses, demoralization, and human adaptability over-exploited and intelligence insulted. The 'As it might be' version started from technology development based on understanding of real work situations and respect for how people work; it progressed through dialogue between well-informed customers and vendors, to purchase decisions made on the basis of a specification drawn up jointly by users and IT specialists, with realistic cost justification; to systems design with full participation of ultimate users, phased implementation, fully monitored, with appropriate training. The end results of this utopian scenario were:

> Technology in its proper place, as a supportive infrastructure; social and technical systems working together instead of against each other; users involved in making decisions on organizational change; agreed safeguards to employment and guarantees of re-training, embodied in 'New Technology Agreements'; opportunities for people to develop skills and negotiate new ways of working; upgrading of the enterprise's performance; and innovation, development of new products, services, markets. (Orna, 1990, page 97).

Not all is gloom, however; there are organizations which are 'doing different' in thinking about the relationship between people, information and technology, and among them are a number of the case study organizations in this book (see, for example, the development of information strategies which integrate information and IS/IT by the Australian Securities and Investments Commission, Amnesty International or the Productivity and Standards Board of Singapore; the NatWest Markets approach to knowledge management; the long-term work on building understanding of information in Surrey Police; the British Library's emphasis on strategic thinking; the appreciation by Thomas Miller & Co. Ltd that people's knowledge is the strength of the business and technology the tool to help them apply and benefit from it).

Towards a successful information systems/IT strategy

What has been said in this chapter so far points towards the need for planning IS/IT strategy at the highest level in the organization. Careful thought is therefore needed about the structure of the bodies that take the decisions.

First, they need a senior-management presence, so that there is a direct link with the policy-making function of the organization, with all that it implies in two-way flow of information and in evidence of management commitment. Second, they must bring together the stakeholders and the experts who understand the specialist issues. Neither group on its own can produce a successful strategy; their interaction is a necessary, if not a sufficient, condition for success. The stakeholders should include the managers of information resources, including in-house information service/library, and records, and a representative of those responsible for the organization's information products, both hard-copy and electronic. Third, IS/IT management structures must be able to change as the organization develops, and as it gains confidence and familiarity with the structures and procedures themselves. (It is encouraging to note that a course is now being offered by a leading training organization on 'Creating technology partnerships', between the supplier, the information manager, the IT department and the end user.)

Corporate objectives and priorities

The presence of top management and of senior managers from major divisions or departments on the bodies that make the IS/IT decisions is the best guarantee that the organization's priority objectives will be used as the framework for deciding on IS/IT strategy.

The objectives of IS/IT strategy

The objectives which an organization seeks to achieve from the use of IS/IT may range from resource savings (of staff, stock or equipment), cost reduction, productivity (more efficient use of resources), or minimizing risks, to support for individuals, adding value, intelligence gathering, or innovation.

The choice of IT objectives needs first to match the key corporate objectives. There is a basic distinction between those objectives which are at the resource deployment end of the range (savings and productivity) and those which are closer to work enhancement (those which support individuals in their work, or help the organization to develop new products or services, etc.). In some situations one or other end of the spectrum may clearly match corporate objectives; in others, both ends may be called for, in relation to different key objectives. (As Marchand, 1997 points out, characteristically most investment in information systems and technology goes to those areas where return on investment is low, rather than to supporting the organization's most distinctive competencies, where the return is potentially higher.)

Corporate culture

Whatever objectives are sought in the IS/IT strategy, it is important to look at their implications for the organization's existing social system, and whenever possible to move the impact of the choice towards the use of technology as a tool, controlled by people, rather than as an instrument of control used on people.

When contemplating new uses of information technology, organizations must be aware of the features of their organizational culture which they most value, and then make sure that any application they consider will not undermine those features. By the same token, they should look at those features that may make a negative contribution to corporate well-being, and consider whether a suitable choice of IT might help to see them on their way. For example, if departmental boundaries are too rigid, technology that positively encourages interaction and cooperation across boundaries may help towards a better culture in this respect.

Cost justification

Deciding IS/IT strategy on the basis of corporate objectives also has important implications for decisions about what is an acceptable cost for planned investment. If the use of IT is being considered at policy-making level, it makes no sense for the costs to be scrutinized at traditional accounting level.

Matching the existing technology

When strategy for investing in new technological developments is being developed, decisions are needed about the technology currently in use. The relevant questions include:

* What features of the existing technology must the new be compatible with?
* Can the new technology be used to make better use of the potential of what we already have?
* What features of the existing technology are causing difficulty in work and holding people back?

- Can the new technology help to overcome the difficulties? Or should the parts of the existing technology that are causing them be scrapped?
- What lessons can we draw from the history of our existing technology and the ways in which it was decided on, so that at least we avoid making the same mistakes twice?

Building and implementing the strategy

In this section I draw on the book by Eason that has already been quoted; though published in 1988, it still holds its place for good sense. Its thesis is that 'Until we learn to design socio-technical systems rather than technical systems' the information revolution – driven as it is by technical imperatives – will go on creating failures and distortions.

Socio-technical design

The essence of the approach is contained in these propositions, which form a sound basis for an IS/IT strategy

1 The successful exploitation of information technology depends upon the ability and willingness of the employees of an organization to use the appropriate technology to engage in worthwhile tasks.

2 The design target must be to create a socio-technical system capable of serving organizational goals, not to create a technical system capable of delivering a technical service.

3 The effective exploitation of socio-technical systems depends upon the adoption of a planned process of change that meets the needs of people who are coping with major changes in their working lives.

4 The design of effective socio-technical systems will depend upon the participation of all relevant 'stakeholders' in the design process.

5 Major benefits will only result if the socio-technical developments are directed at major organizational purposes where there are opportunities to be taken or problems to be resolved.

6 The specification for a new socio-technical system must include the definition of a social system which enables people in work roles to co-operate effectively in seeking organizational purposes and provides jobs which incumbents perceive as worthwhile.

7 Information technology systems must be designed to serve the functional needs of the organization by serving the functional needs of individual users in a usable and acceptable way.

8 The effective exploitation of information technology requires a major form of organizational and individual learning.

9 The exploitation of the capabilities of information technology can only be achieved by a progressive, planned form of evolutionary growth.

10 To be successful, socio-technical design concepts must as far as possible complement existing design procedures and organization change practices.

System design principles

- Both technology specialists and the users have valid expertise to contribute to system design, and a legitimate interest in the solutions adopted. The team structure therefore needs to give all its members roles that allow them to contribute their expertise.
- The consequences of planned changes can best be understood if the possible options for meeting the needs of the IS/IT strategy are assessed at an early stage for their impact on all the users who would be affected: not just the full-time or occasional users of the technology, but also the people who will need to use its outputs.
- Detailed specifications for systems options should be prepared from both technical and social points of view, and the tasks that any system will affect must be analysed. The outcome should be a statement of what the system should be able to do, and the criteria it will need to meet to be usable and acceptable to the users.
- Prototypes of the system, or key parts of it, which create, or simulate, the behaviour of the real thing should be available for users to try. Full value can be derived from a prototype only if the ultimate users of the system can get their hands on it and try performing their normal tasks on it, and see how they feel about it.
- The first essential for any system is that it should make it possible to do the tasks concerned. Then, beyond functionality, it needs to be usable. The people who do the tasks should be able to use the system to carry them out without being made to perform contortions unfitting for human minds; the system should enable them to use the knowledge and skills that are relevant to their jobs with minimum interference.
- Systems should respect the discretion of the users and support them in the development of their work. Evidence from the field is, as Eason points out (page 149), all to the effect that users prefer the role of master rather than servant in relation to the system – and reasonably enough. When the system demands that users perform tasks in a particular way or sequence, which is in fact not the most effective way of doing it, they are not likely to feel kindly towards it. Nor are they if it monitors the rate at which they do their work, especially if the monitoring is then used as a basis for payment of bonuses.

Implementation principles

- The process of bringing into operation individual projects in fulfilment of IS/IT strategy should involve a cycle of implementing and monitoring, and a 'cascade' process of drawing in more and more people. As Eason (page 166) expresses it, it should be a process of 'integration of the technical system into the organisational fabric'. As such, there is a strong case for the management of the process to be taken over by the users, with a senior user manager in control, and the user representatives who have participated in designing the system as coordinators in their own particular work areas.

- The design of proper training for people whose work involves using IS/IT should be part of the human resources aspect of information policy. The users of systems should take part in designing their own training programmes; and when they are trained should act as a training and advice resource for their colleagues.
- Both cognitive and affective aspects should be provided for in training. When training is planned, it should be broken down into short manageable stages, to avoid the memory overload that sets in very quickly with unfamiliar material, and what has been learned should be applied at once.
- Many users of unfamiliar systems suffer from deep anxiety and lack of confidence – feelings that can make learning difficult or impossible, and that can lead to disastrous loss of self-esteem and collapse of work performance. To avoid such trauma, there should be opportunities to work with the system in a non-threatening situation, and with the support of fellow users who can empathize with the difficulties.
- In the development of the information infrastructure it is necessary to provide for regular assessment by the users. The purpose is to show both whether systems are bringing the intended results, and whether they are aiding the users as effectively as they should. A third outcome of consistent evaluation can be pointers towards future development – new requirements arising from users' experience, and ideas for new ways of using the technology, which in turn may feed into the development of corporate information policy. This should be part of the total effort of the organization to review its own development in relation to its objectives, and to the environment in which it functions – constantly and as part of its normal activity, rather than as some exceptional effort undertaken only when disaster threatens.
- Evaluation and feedback should be part of the system design and development pattern from the start, and should never be skipped as a tiresome time-consuming stage. Qualitative rather than mechanistically quantitative assessment should be the goal.

Summary

- It is only human minds which can turn information into knowledge and act constructively upon it.
- So information strategy needs to be concerned with:
    - How people think, feel, act and interact over knowledge and information
    - Creating organizational structures that promote information flows and interactions inside the organization and between it and the outside world
    - Helping people to acquire and maintain the skills and knowledge they need
    - Taking care of the organization's knowledge resources.
- A human resources strategy covering these concerns should be part of the organization's information strategy.
- An information systems and IT strategy should be a support to the people in the organization in using information and knowledge to achieve its goals, not a substitute for them or a dictator to them.

- It should be designed in the light of what the organization seeks to do, what knowledge and information it needs to do it, and what people need to do with knowledge and information.
- Decisions about systems and IT, and their implementation, need the participation of senior management, information managers and stakeholders, along with the systems and technology experts.

References

ANGELL, I. (1998), 'The knowledge scam', *Information Strategy*, July/August, 23–24

BOTTOMLEY, A. (1998), 'Jumping on the bandwagon', *Information Strategy*, July/August, 25–26

BURACK, E. H. et al. (1994), 'New paradigm approaches in strategic human resources management', *Group and Organization Management*, 19 (2), 141–159

DAVENPORT, T. H. (1994), 'Saving IT's soul: human-centred information management', *Harvard Business Review*, March–April, 119–131

DAVENPORT, T. H. (1998), 'Getting intimate; are companies finally making serious attempts to get to know their customers?', *Information Strategy*, April, 53

DAVENPORT, T. H. with PRUSAK, L. (1997), *Information Ecology. Mastering the information and knowledge environment*, New York: Oxford University Press

DAVENPORT, T. H. and PRUSAK, L. (1998), *Working Knowledge. How organizations manage what they know*, Boston, MA: Harvard Business School Press

DAVENPORT, T. H. et al. (1992), 'Information politics', *Sloan Management Review*, Fall, 53–65

DRUCKER, P. (1995), *Managing in a Time of Great Change*, Oxford: Butterworth Heinemann

EASON, K. (1988), *Information Technology and Organisational Change*, London: Taylor & Francis

EVANS, R. (1997), '1998 We won't get fooled again', *Information Strategy*, December 1997–January 1998, 24–27

EWUSI-MENSAH, K. and PRZASYNSKI, Z. H. (1995), 'Learning from abandoned information systems development projects', *Journal of Information Technology*, 10, 3–14

GALLIERS, R. (1992), 'Information technology – management's boon or bane?', *Journal of Strategic Information Systems*, 1 (2), 50–56

HOLTHAM, C. (1996), 'Resolving the imbalance between information and technology', in D. BEST (ed.), *The Fourth Resource: Information and its Management*, Aldershot: Aslib/Gower

HUTTON, W. (1996), 'Priceless assets amount to folly', *The Guardian*, 11 March

ITAMI, H. with ROEHL, T.W. (1987), *Mobilizing invisible assets*, Boston, MA: Harvard University Press

KAUTTO-KOIVULA, K. (1998), 'The pitfalls of knowledge', *Information Strategy*, July/August, 26–27

LEISTKA, J. M. et al. (1997), 'The generative cycle: Linking knowledge and relationships', *Sloan Management Review*, 39 (1), 47–58

MARCHAND, D. (1997), 'Competing with information: know what you want', *FT Mastering Management Reader*, July/August 1997

McARTHUR, T. (1986), *Worlds of Reference*, Cambridge: Cambridge University Press

MUMFORD, E. (1986), 'From bank teller to office worker: the pursuit of systems designed for people in practice and research', *International Journal of Information Management*, 6, 59–73

OASIG (1996), *Failing to Deliver – the IT Performance Gap*

ORNA, E. and PETTITT, C. W. (1998), *Information Management in Museums*, Aldershot: Gower

PALMER, C. (1995), 'Lest we forget …', *The Observer*, 8 January

STAMPER, R. (1996), 'Signs, Information, Norms and Systems', in B. HOLLMQVIST, et al. (eds), *Signs of Work: Semiosis and information processing in organisations*, Berlin and New York: Walter de Gruyter

TATE, P. (1998) 'The knowledge backlash', *Information Strategy*, July/August, 22–23

VAN DER SPEK, R. (1998), 'When Fat is a Corporate Issue', *Information Strategy*, April, 46–47

WHITE, M. (1997), 'The joy of intranets?', *Inform*, December, 11

WHITE, M. et al. (1998), *Intranet Management – A TFPL guide to best practice*, London: TFPL

WILLCOCKS, L. (1991), 'Human resource and organizational issues in the 1990s', *Journal of Information Technology*, 6 (3/4), 121–127

WILSON, F. A. and WILSON, J. N. (1994), 'The role of computer systems in organizational decision making', *The Information Society*, 10, 173–180

Reading list

ANGELL, I. O. and STRAUB, B. H. (1993), 'Though this be madness, yet there is method in't', *Journal of Strategic Information Systems*, 2 (1), 5–14
Systems and IT are unsympathetic to organizations they are supposed to serve; argues for a sociological approach; tidy methodologies versus untidy life; methodology should be a servant not an agent.

BAKER, B. (1995), 'The role of feedback in assessing information systems planning effectiveness', *Journal of Strategic Information Systems*, 4 (1), 61–80
Most research concentrates on planning rather than implementation, and assumes rationality in planning practices. To be effective, information systems planning needs to take into account intangible as well as tangible characteristics.

BALCOMBE, J. (1993), 'Knowledge is the only meaningful resource today', *Aslib Information*, 21 (10), 378–380
'We must persuade top management not only that information is a corporate resource … but also that, for the new age organization to work, the empowered employees must have information skills.'

CHARAN, R. (1991), 'How networks reshape organizations – for results', *Harvard Business Review*, September–October, 104–115
Examples of organizations with permanent networks of managers cutting across hierarchies and functions, with autonomy to initiate, and the role of building 'soft' changes and promoting interaction, negotiation and free flow of information.

DOYLE, D. A. and du TOIT, A. (1998), 'Knowledge management in a law firm', *Aslib Proceedings*, 50 (1), 3–8
Use of intranet technology to further knowledge management. They can influence organizational learning via knowledge acquisition, information distribution, information interpretation, organizational memory. Importance of content organization and design of visual presentation which reflects mindset of target audience.

FARBEY, B. et al. (1995), 'Evaluating business information systems: reflections on an empirical study', *Information Systems Journal*, 5, 235–252
Case studies on behalf of a systems vendor showed fewer than half the organizations claimed to have IT strategy; IT investment decisions were made piecemeal; few of the projects took intangible benefits into account; evaluation did not look at the full impact of the system on the organization.

GOLDMAN, S. L., NAGEL, R. N. and PREISS, K. (1994), *Agile competitors and virtual organisations: strategies for enriching the customer*, New York:Van Nostrand Reinhold (cited in BONAVENTURA, M., 1997, 'The benefits of a knowledge culture', *Aslib Proceedings*, 49 (4), 82–89)
'If it is true that organisations sell the skills, knowledge and expertise of the people who work for and with them, and if it is also true that those people think, learn and innovate only 5 to 15 percent of the time, then it seems possible to triple the effective output of an organisation by moving the effectiveness in thinking, learning and innovating from 15 to 45 percent … In agile competition, thinkers are the basis for success; it is the nonthinkers who can destroy the system.'

JOHANNESSEN, J. A. et al. (1997), 'Information management in negotiations: the conditions under which it could be expected that the negotiation partners substitute a competitive definition of the situation for a co-operative one', *International Journal of Information Management*, 17 (3), 153–168
Factors which lead to win–win outcomes include: extensive exchange of information which is 'emotionally interesting, concrete, provocative and close in time and space'; extensive information about the value system involved, developing positive emotions, and 'framing the situation in order to gain profit' rather than to escape losses.

McGRATH, G. M. et al. (1994), 'Planning for information systems integration: some key challenges', *Journal of Information Science*, 20 (3), 149–160
Research evidence suggests that attempts to integrate information systems are likely to fail if they don't take into account the effects on the balance of organizational power

POWELL, P. (1993), 'Causality in the alignment of IT and business strategy', *Journal of Strategic Information Systems*, 2 (4), 320–334
Argues that often lip service gets paid to the strategic nature of IT when it comes to making a case for investment, and that strategic justification has become 'a tool for securing investment in IT by circumventing established organizational policy on investments'.

REPONEN, T. (1994), 'Organizational information management strategies', *Information Systems Journal* 4, 27–44
Presents an interactive framework for 'evolutionary information systems planning', based on integration, interaction and learning, and drawing on understanding of the business vision and strategy, IT, information management, and practical experience of applying IT

SISTLA, M. and TODD, J. (1998), 'Warning: a killer mistake in business – Don't let technology drive your requirements', *Information Outlook*, June, 19–24
Useful guidelines for developing information strategies to match organizational needs.

How knowledge and information create value for the organization

---

In this chapter:

- Why information strategy must seek a reliable value for information and knowledge
- Value factors that relate the organization's interests to its use of knowledge and information
- Oddities and problems of intangible assets
- Overcoming the problems
- Objective methodologies

---

[1] 'Sustained' is the critical word; I get worried when terms like 'knowledge management' become fashionable, and organizations start boasting of their 'Chief Knowledge Officer'. What has been in fashion this year can go out of fashion next, unless a thorough basis of understanding has been established to make the mode into the norm!

Why information strategy must seek a reliable value for information and knowledge

We are concerned here with the intangible value which people, aided by technology, create, add (or subtract) for the organization through what they do with information and knowledge, and with how we establish its value in a way that allows it to be set alongside other assets that organizations traditionally measure in financial terms.

This is a notoriously difficult subject, which economists have grappled with rather unsuccessfully for many years, but it is essential to find a solution to valuing such intangibles as knowledge and information. If we can't find a way of putting them in the same framework as physical resources, they will not get serious sustained attention [1] from decision makers and controllers of resources – and so they will not receive the investment they need for putting them to productive use.

The only thing likely to bring a real change is methods for putting a reliable and acceptable figure on what knowledge and information contribute to the total assets of organizations. That is why the information audit should look at how (or whether) the organization tries to establish the cost-effectiveness of its use of information and knowledge. Fortunately, a number of such methods are now available (see Skyrme, 1998, for a useful outline of the Skandia Navigator and Value Creation Model, Sveiby's Intangible Assets Monitor, and the IC-Index™, as well as the McPherson IVM™ which is discussed below), and they are becoming more widely known and applied by business.

Their development has coincided with a constructive interest taken by businesses at the top level. The KPMG IMPACT Programme – 'a club of major organizations seeking to share experience in information management', with a committee (the Hawley Committee) drawn from senior executives of a number of large businesses and other organizations, has done useful work on selling the ideas of 'Information as an Asset' and a 'Board Agenda' for information. The IMPACT Programme has gone on to fund research on an 'Information Health Index' – a set of indicators designed to give a 'broad measure of how an organisation, business unit or profit centre is managing, making best use of, and safeguarding, its information assets' (IMPACT Programme Ltd, 1998). A number of works which aim to guide businesses in realising the value of 'intellectual capital' have also been published.

Value factors that relate the organization's interests to its use of knowledge and information

The table on pages 116 and 117 identified a number of points where the well-being of all organizations is linked to the value which knowledge and information can confer:

- The organization's purposes, goals and values, and how intangibles such as knowledge and information contribute to achieving what it most values (the 'business value model')
- The value of knowledge and information in gaining sustenance and keeping the organization successful
- Identifying critical knowledge and information (i.e. that of highest potential value) for the organization, and managing it
- Intelligence about its markets, and the flow of information about them.

Davenport (1993) amplifies this list, with his account of organizational activities where information is both an essential element without which they could not take place, and has the potential to confer value; they are:

- Monitoring how processes are performed – businesses that are effective in managing/monitoring information about quality have a competitive advantage
- Integrating different business processes, and integrating stages within individual processes – information is the 'glue' that holds the organizational structure together
- Customizing products and services – when information about customers is managed to create offerings tailored to their needs, it gives a competitive edge to the organization (as leading supermarket chains have demonstrated)
- Supporting strategic decision-making processes with vital unstructured and externally originating information – which is much more relevant than the 'historical' financial information from accounting systems which is generally used
- Creating information products, as the primary output of the business. More and more businesses have these as their main output; those that use their resources of information fully to support the process of creating such outputs are most likely to succeed.

Marchand (1997) takes the useful approach of identifying four ways of 'using information to create business value' (see Figure 8.1 opposite):

1 Minimize risks
2 Reduce costs
3 Add value (typically through market/customer orientation)
4 Create new reality (innovation, new markets, customers, products).

Each requires different types of information, different actions in using information, different processes, different organizational structures, and different applications of IT/IS.

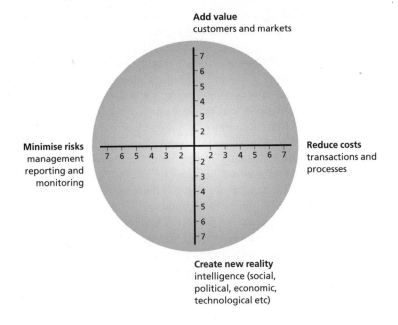

Fig 8.1   **Four ways of using information to create value**

Oddities and problems of intangible assets

Information and knowledge have some peculiarities which make them different from material resources when it comes to value:

- To have value, information has to be transformed by human minds into knowledge, without which no products of tangible value can be created or exchanged
- If information is exchanged and traded, the value from using it can increase for all parties to the transaction
- The value of information is not diminished by being used; it can be transformed into knowledge and used many times by many users for adding value to many activities and outputs. As Itami and Roehl (1987) put it, 'free rides' are to be had when resources accumulated in one part of the company are used simultaneously and at no additional expense by other parts. 'The essence of invisible assets is information, and it is this characteristic, which is not shared by other resources, that makes a free ride possible. Only information-based assets can be used in multiple ways at the same time ...'. Information 'can be used simultaneously, it does not wear out from over use, and bits of it can be combined to yield even more information.'
- Information has no inbuilt value; it has to be used to acquire value – which is another way of putting the point about needing human minds to transform it to knowledge and act on it
- It is a diffused resource, which, as Davenport (1993, see above, page 140) points out, enters into all activities of businesses.

Apart from these unusual features, there are other factors which add to the difficulty which organizations have in getting to grips with valuing their information resources:

* Very few, if any, organizations appreciate that they need to make their own definition of information in relation to what they are trying to do. And if you haven't defined 'your' information, how can you establish criteria for valuing it? (Whenever I speak about these matters, I ask if anyone knows an organization which has done so; so far nobody has told me of one – it will be a real pleasure to hear from any reader who knows such a phoenix.)

* Information is a combination of 'containers' and content (for example a content of trade statistics, in a container of a database), and the only hard figure readily available is what we pay for the combined package. Traditional accounting can't cope with repeated use of content, or its use by many people; nor can it trace the process of adding value once people have transformed information into knowledge and applied it.

* The problems are compounded by the tendency – now well recognized, but still alive and well in many organizations – to identify information with IT and systems, and that adds to the difficulty because of the present widespread discontent with the results of investment in costly systems.

Qualitative and quantitative value from knowledge and information

In spite of the difficulties, there is a large body of indirect but convincing evidence of the value of information in promoting productivity, competitiveness and innovation; and in avoiding risk and reducing uncertainty (see, for example, Koenig, 1992, and Griffiths and King, 1993, on the contribution of information services and libraries; Bowonder and Miyake, 1992 on information management and competitiveness; Bowden and Ricketts, 1992, Fransman, 1992 and Newby, 1993 on the relation between information use and successful innovation). But while the research is thorough and the qualitative evidence impressive, it still cuts little ice with most top decision makers.

There is also some direct financial evidence, from the fairly rare cases where it is comparatively easy to set a figure on the costs of using low-quality information, in terms of lost customers, staff time in rectifying errors, and so on. Herget (1995), for example, looks at the 'negative value of non-quality' – both to the supplier of information products and to customer. His case study of a company which provides its customers with tailor-made information products shows very clearly how that negative value manifests itself in the loss of clients (see Table 8.1 on the opposite page).

Fisher and Sless (1990) provide similar figures for the costs of error rates in completing forms to an insurance company and the value added by redesign to make them easier to complete correctly.

Harris and Marshall (1996) offer a useful example of building a business case, with actual cost details, as an approach which makes it possible to demonstrate the value of library services in a way that 'addresses the financial and strategic concerns of the organization'.

	Cost (ECU)
Lost clients (40/y at 5000 ECU), of which 50pc due to quality failure	100 000
Quality inspection	16 000
Editing costs	20 000
Feedback	10 000
'Defensive' visits to clients	25 000
Internal firefighting	25 000
Internal administration	10 000
Total cost of 'non-quality'	**206 000 ECU**

Table 8.1   **The 'negative value of non-quality'** (Herget, 1995)

Overcoming the problems

Happily, methods which can support proper valuation of intangibles are being developed. In accounting the UK Advisory Council on Science and Technology pointed out in 1993 that business's objection to action that can't be shown directly to enhance the bottom line is 'being undermined as accountancy principles embrace the need to value intangibles'. More recently the Danish Ministry of Business and Commerce has launched a project to define a national standard for Intellectual Capital account statements, while the International Accounting Standards Committee (IASQ) UK was reported in mid-1998 as planning to publish an International Accounting Standard on accounting for intangible assets.

A number of methods specifically oriented to valuing information are now available. They depend in various ways on a combination of informed human judgement of the significance of various information resources to achieving the organization's goals, with a computer application which 'interprets' the judgements to establish the extent of their value contribution.

The value triangle

Underlying the judgements is the basic idea that establishing the value of anything is always an indirect process, which involves finding appropriate equivalents and standards; not necessarily just in money terms. As Figure 8.2 on page 144 suggests, it is a three-way relationship. It always involves a human judgement, which is based on the relationship between the object of value and the human who is doing the judging, and that relationship centres on the use to which the human puts the object – whether that is to acquire security against ill-fortune, or to achieve some desired purpose, or to feel superior to others who do not possess it.

Value judgements also imply criteria – 'this is more important to me than that, because ...'. When it is an organization rather than an individual which is making the judgements, finding appropriate criteria is hard enough, as it involves both thinking and feeling, and often conflicting interests; while applying them is exceedingly difficult, especially where there are multiple criteria

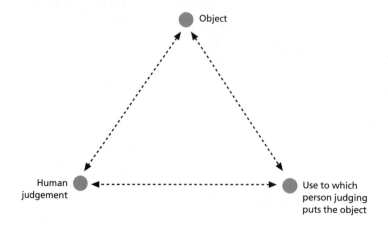

Fig 8.2   **Value triangle**

(as in the organizational context) that are so complex as to be beyond the capacity of unaided human memory.

And of course there is the problem implicit in that statement of what: goes on when we set a value on things: the 'subjective' nature of human value judgements; how can we use them to arrive at an account of the value of an intangible which can safely be counted in with 'hard' monetary values? Some help with this one is at hand from the unified theory of value (axiology), which argues that it is possible to have an objective methodology that separates value perspectives in the user's mind from the evaluation framework – 'the analysis is logical and neutral while the perspectives' of the people involved 'can be partisan', as McPherson (1991) puts it.

Objective methodologies

The well-known Infomapper software (Burk and Horton, 1988) can probably be counted the first in the field. While the principal purpose for which it was designed was to help organizations to get an overview of their information resources, it also allows them to be ranked in value. Its basis is an 'information resources inventory' (a parallel to information auditing). The resources are then ranked in terms of their overall value to achieving the strategic objectives of the organization (see Figure 5.1, page 94). These activities depend on human judgements for inputs to the software in order to get out valid rankings. Unlike some more recent methodologies, this one yields relative values, and does not provide for their expression in terms, for example, of the proportion they contribute to the total value of the organization's assets.

The methodology with which I have first-hand acquaintance is the Integrated Value Manager (IVM), which has been developed by McPherson (1994, 1996) over the past five years or so as an instrument that measures the value of an asset, system or organization. It has now been employed in a number of

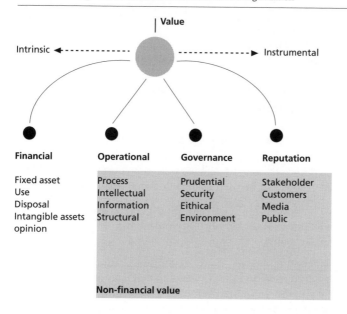

Fig 8.3a   **Aspects of value**

businesses, for such purposes as cost justification and business case for a major IT system development whose outputs contained significant intangible contributions benefiting managerial effectiveness; and extending corporate strategy of a public utility to include intangible factors as well as financial projections (for example strategic fit over political, market, competitive technical indicators, analysis of exposure to environmental and ethical risk, indicating the cost of compliance with environmental and ethical criteria). Based on the ideas mentioned above about a structured framework which is independent of the inputs of subjective human perspectives, it depends on the combination of the two, and both are essential. The strength, rigour and objectivity of the methodology are derived from its use of measurement theory to combine many different kinds of value contribution into proper indications of achieved value.

The basic ideas underlying the method are these:
* All organizations are systems for creating value
* The value they create is not just financial, and not only the organization is concerned; its activities have value effects for others – not only customers or shareholders, but also the wider community affected by its operations – and these reflect back in its reputation.
* There are, as shown in Figure 8.3a above, four essential value dimensions, one financial and three non-financial:
  1 Financial (which includes both tangible assets and those which, while intangible, have direct financial value)
  2 Operational (including processes, intellectual assets, information and organizational structures which support the creation of value)

3 Governance (including prudent management, security, ethical conduct, and respect for environmental values)

4 Reputation (in the eyes of stakeholders, customers, the media, and public opinion)

- All four dimensions must be observable and measurable; therefore, as shown in Figure 8.3b on the opposite page, we need a comprehensive methodology to deal with:
  - Evaluation and combination of value in the three non-financial dimensions
  - Combination of monetary and intangible value so that overall value added on all four dimensions can be used as a decision variable, and for subsequent financial analysis (see Figure 8.4a on page 148).

Measurement methods are obviously the critical bit, and this is how McPherson approaches them\:

Inputs:
- Financial inputs of revenue and costs: conventional accounting; financial audit
- For the non-financial: a range of measurement tools, including:
  - Performance measurement, information audit
  - Governance, ethical, and environmental audit
  - Opinion surveys, market research, analysis of correspondence

Intermediate outputs:
- Financial – projections of discounted cash flow, net present value, shareholder value added
- The others: Non-financial Value Added – delivered as 'normalized utilities', and then combined to indicate 'Combined Non-financial Value' (as shown in Figure 8.4a).

Final outputs:
The final output is the amalgamation of financial and non-financial value to give an inclusive value, in which the proportions of accountable value added contributed by all four dimensions can be shown. It allows the organization to see what such intangible elements as knowledge and information are contributing, to express that proportion in equivalent money value, and to compare their actual contribution with what they should contribute (see Figure 8.4b on page 149).

So the good news for those who wish to develop information strategies that take account of the value to the organization of knowledge and information is that it is now feasible to set a reliable value on information, on the basis of methodologies which take account of knowledgeable judgements of responsible decision makers at each level of the process. Certainly the judgements have to go back to interpretation of organizational objectives; they demand hard individual thinking at detailed levels, together with negotiation, discussion, and resolution of contradictions, so applying the methodologies is no trivial matter, which may act against it being taken up widely. Spending time on thinking is not much favoured in economies and businesses dedicated to short-term payback – but on the hopeful side, there is evidence of organiza-

Figures 8.3a and b are based, with kind permission, on unpublished originals by McPherson

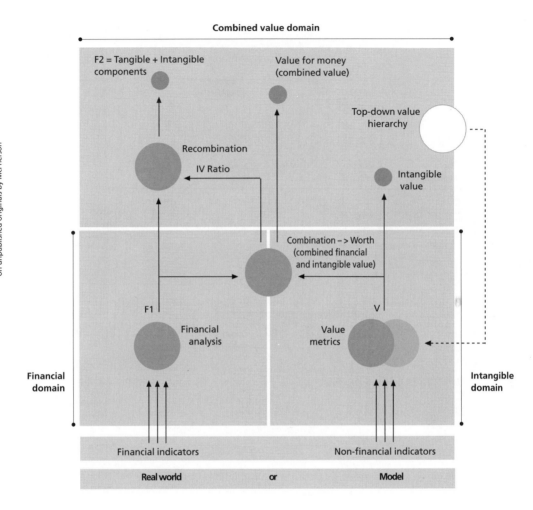

Fig 8.3b   **The IVM approach**

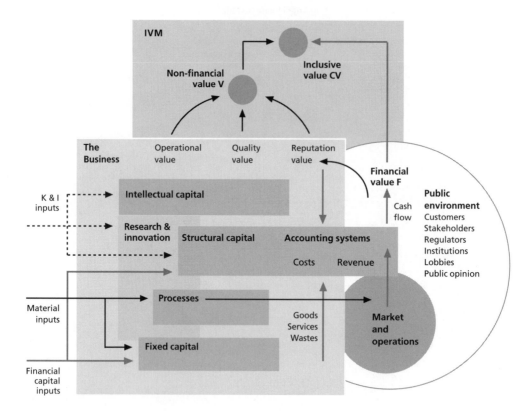

Fig 8.4a   **Measuring value with the IVM: capital and operational assets**

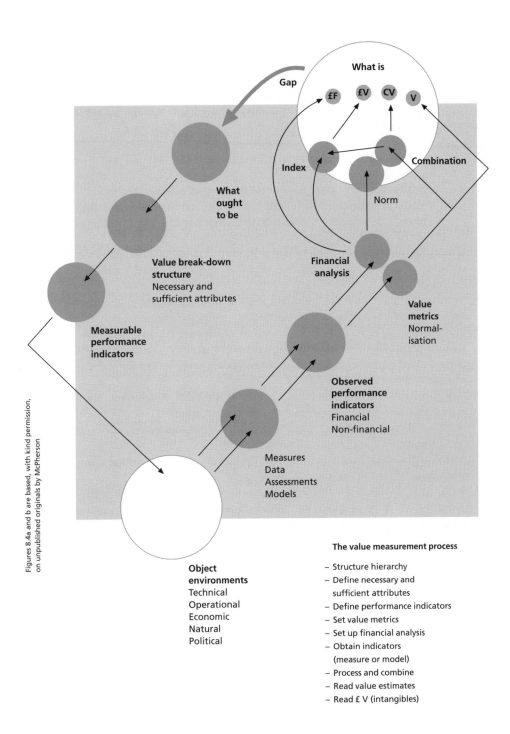

Figures 8.4a and b are based, with kind permission, on unpublished originals by McPherson

Fig 8.4b   **The value-measuring process**

tions which believe that it is a good investment for their top managers to devote time to thinking (see the British Library case study, page 230). And there is a role in this for information professionals and the libraries and information services they manage, which is there for the taking if they are prepared to exert themselves in becoming familiar with the ideas involved, and then to assert themselves in promoting, as Skyrme (1998) recommends, 'the concepts of intellectual capital and how it is measured and managed, so that they can articulate their contribution'.

Summary

* We have to tackle the intangible value which people, aided by technology, add for the organization through their use of information and knowledge, and we have to try to find a way of setting it alongside the assets traditionally measured in financial terms
* If we don't, information and knowledge will not receive sustained attention and long-term resources, and therefore will not get built into the fabric of the organization
* Information and knowledge are essential elements in a great range of organizational activities, and have potential both to confer and subtract value
* Intangible assets have some unique features which make them highly valuable. In particular, their value is not reduced by use (we can have our information cake and eat it); they can be used many times by many people to add value; they can offer 'free rides'
* Unfortunately, organizations are not usually in the habit of looking at them in ways that help them to appreciate these unique features
* However, there is much useful qualitative, and some quantitative, evidence of their value
* And now there are methods that can help to put intangibles in the same value frame as traditional material assets
* Anyone responsible for developing information strategy owes it to themselves to make these problems and the solutions to them part of their equipment as a protagonist of the value of information and knowledge.

References

ACOST (Advisory Council on Science and Technology) (1993), *People, Technology and Organisations. The application of Human Factors and Organisational Design*, London: HMSO

BOWDEN, A. and RICKETTS, M. (eds), (1992), *Stimulating Innovation in Industry. The Challenge for the United Kingdom*, London: Kogan Page/NEDO

BOWONDER, B. and MIYAKE, T. (1992), 'Creating and sustaining competitiveness: information management strategies of Nippon Steel Corporation', *International Journal of Information Management*, 12, 39–56

BURK, C. F., (Jr) and HORTON, F. W., (Jr), (1988), *Infomap: A complete guide to discovering corporate information resources*, Englewood Cliffs, NJ: Prentice Hall

DAVENPORT, T. H. (1993), *Process Innovation. Reengineering work through information technology*, Boston, MA: Harvard Business School Press

FISHER, P. and SLESS, D. (1990), 'Information design methods and productivity in the insurance industry', *Information Design Journal*, 6 (20), 103–130

FRANSMAN, M. (1992), 'The Japanese innovation system: how it works', *Science in Parliament*, 49 (4), 25–30

GRIFFITHS, J. M. and KING, D. W. (1993), 'Libraries: the undiscovered national resource', *Information Policy Briefing*, London: British Library Research & Development Department

HARRIS, G. and MARSHALL, JOANNE G. (1996), 'Building a model business case: current awareness service in a special library', *Special Libraries*, Summer, 181–194

HAWLEY COMMITTEE (1995), *Information as an Asset: the Board Agenda: A consultative report; Information as an Asset: the Board Agenda: Checklist and explanatory notes*, London: KPMG IMPACT Programme

HERGET, J. (1995), 'The cost of (non-) quality: why it matters for information providers', *FID News Bulletin*, 45 (5), 156–159

IMPACT Programme Ltd (1998), *Information as an Asset. The Information Health Index*

ITAMI, H. with ROEHL, T. W. (1987), *Mobilizing Invisible Assets*, Boston, MA: Harvard University Press

KOENIG, M. (1992), 'The importance of information services for productivity "under-recognized" and under-invested', *Special Libraries*, Fall, 199–210

MARCHAND, D. A. (1997), 'Competing with information: know what you want'. *FT Mastering Management Reader*, July/August 7–12

McPHERSON, P. K. (1991), *Note on the Axiological Basis of the SWAP Evaluation Framework*, Kenninghall, Norwich: The MacPherson Consultancy

McPHERSON, P. K. (1994), 'Accounting for the value of information', *Aslib Proceedings*, 46 (9), 203–215

McPHERSON, P. K. (1996), 'The inclusive value of information', 48th Congress of the International Federation for Information and Documentation, Graz, Austria, 25–28 October

NEWBY, H. (1993), *Innovation and the Social Sciences: The Way Ahead*, Swindon: Economic and Social Research Council

SKYRME, D. (1998), 'Valuing knowledge: is it worth it?', *Managing Information*, 5 (2), 24–26 (the same author's *Measuring the value of knowledge* –1997, London Business Intelligence Limited – should also be mentioned, as should its price of £395)

Reading list

METCALFE, S. (1997), 'Technology systems and technology policy in an evolutionary framework', in D. ARCHIBUGI and J.MICHIE (eds), *Technology, Globalisation and Economic Performance*, Cambridge: Cambridge University Press
'Innovation and information asymmetries are inseparable', and 'Creativity is intimately connected to uncertainty and the discovery processes by which firms find and exploit their own choice sets.'

ORNA, E. (1996), 'Valuing information: problems and opportunities', in D. BEST (ed.), *The Fourth Resource: Information and its Management*, Aldershot: Gower

REPO, A. J. (1989), 'The value of information; approaches in economics, accounting, and management science', *JASIS*, 40 (2), 68–95
Useful review of research on economics of information; with few exceptions it has been theoretical rather than empirical, and almost all the theoretical studies have been influenced by Shannon's 'information theory'

STEWART, T. A. (1997), *Intellectual Capital*, London: Nicholas Brealey Publishing.
If you can take the *Fortune* style ('Information and knowledge are the thermonuclear competitive weapons of our time'. 'We'll take intellectual capital and look under the hood, so to speak: to show how the stuff works and how to make it work better.'), Part 2 'Intellectual Capital', is a useful introduction

TAYLOR, R. S. (1986), *Value Added Processes in Information Systems*, Norwood, NJ: Ablex Publishing Corporation

Knowledge and information for managing change

In this chapter:

- Change: the essence of existence
- A change matrix – four kinds of change which organizations have to deal with
- How organizations deal with change
- Creating new knowledge and applying it to get the best out of change

---

[1] Support for this proposition comes from Metcalfe (1997), in the context of the relation between technology policy and economic performance. Discussing an 'evolutionary framework' for technology policy, he argues that its central concerns should be 'Process and change, not equilibrium and state'. Evolutionary policy seeks a shift towards creativity and away from efficiency because traditional competitive selection 'consumes its own fuel, destroying the very variety which drives economic change', and to encourage creativity we should be more concerned with enhancing the adaptive capability of firms.

... the dynamics of knowledge impose one clear imperative: every organization has to build the management of change into its very structure. [And they have] to do something, and not say 'Let's make another study ...' Peter Drucker (1995)

Change: the essence of existence

Change permeates human life and the world in which we live. The impetus for the earliest scientific observations which advanced the development of societies and technologies was change: change in the seasons, the weather, the night sky, plants and animals. Observation led to prediction so that people could try to act to get the things they valued, and to avoid dangers by being prepared for them; it laid the foundations for navigation, agriculture, medicine. The remarkable development of human brains and minds was advanced by being able to predict change, and to use stored knowledge from past observation to take opportunistic advantage of new changes.

The earliest technologies were based on bringing about change in order to get things of value – adding value by the application of knowledge, as we would say today: cultivation to provide a regular food supply; cooking to make the food palatable and to preserve it; working natural materials to make containers, tools, weapons, building materials, textiles, images of power and embodiments of ideas.

So change is interwoven in all life, inseparable from the world we live in, an essential part of what makes us human, and by seeking to understand and control change, the human intellect in which we take such pride evolved. Some of the most powerful theories the human mind has developed are theories of change – above all, Darwinian natural selection, which provides the most satisfying account of how living creatures adapt to survive in changing environments.

Organizations and individuals fly in the face of nature when they seek to remain unchanging;[1] that is as sad a delusion as that of the Pharaohs who believed that stuffing their corpses with pitch would keep them immortal, and as futile an endeavour as trying to make the sea stay still or rivers stop flowing. No organization is ever static, and the way in which they change over time is indeed one of the factors from which we can learn most.

Recognizing change as the essence of existence does not mean that we have to accept all change; but it does allow us to start deciding what changes to resist with all our force, where to exploit change in the outside world and turn it to our own advantage, and where there are opportunities to use what we know to initiate change to our benefit (as Edwards and Peppard, 1994, remark, probably one of the greatest barriers to change is 'the assumption that it simply happens or that people must simply change because it is necessary to do so'). So this chapter looks at the changes which organizations encounter, originating within or without, anticipated or unexpected; and at how they can make use of knowledge and information to foresee change, identify what is significant to them, avoid danger, maximize advantage, and initiate change – in the process creating new knowledge and gaining new advantage.

A change matrix – four kinds of change which organizations have to deal with

There is a rather prevalent view at the moment that change is something (usually nasty and unexpected) which is done to us; the fact that such an attitude is so common says something about the culture of the organizations with which many of us have to deal in our lives as citizens and workers. But it doesn't have to be like that.

As a start towards a rather better-founded approach to change, Figure 9.1 on page 155, sets out in matrix form four typical kinds of change, involving combinations of two factors:

1 Whether the change is expected or unexpected
2 Whether it originates outside the organization or within it.

How organizations deal with change: two questions and some answers

There are two questions to ask in looking at these examples of change:

1 What constitutes good management of this change?
2 What does the organization need to know in order to manage it well?
  (This is similar to the process of deriving knowledge and information requirements from the organization's objectives, as developed in Chapter 3, see page 44.)

Let us try to answer these questions for some of the examples in Figure 9.1.

Expected change originating in the outside world (cell 1a)

For all the examples, these are the conditions for successful management of the change:

• Anticipation, timely planning ahead
• Planning to finance essential change in new ways, for example public/pri vate collaborations, PFI (Private Finance Initiative), sponsorship
• Exchange of experience with other organizations involved in similar changes
• Monitoring the effects of the change and taking action to deal with them.

To make sure that most of the changes they encounter are indeed expected, and that only the minimum are unexpected, to anticipate change which is significant for them, and to plan ahead to deal with it, organizations need to know about:

• The existing qualifications and training of staff, so as to be able to plan any retraining they will need; local labour markets and educational institutions, so as to be able to plan recruitment if new staff are needed

Change originates:

Change is:	Outside	Inside
Expected	1A	2A
Unexpected	1B	2B

The cells of the matrix:

1A
Expected change originating in the outside world

Examples:
• New legislation
• Demographic and social change in the population the organization serves
• Changes in manufacturing technology/ materials

1B
Unexpected change originating in the outside world

Examples:
• Natural disaster affecting the supply/price of raw materials
• Premises destroyed by terrorist bomb
• Hostile takeover bid
• Competing products launched which undermine the market

2A
Expected change originating within the organization

Examples:
• Flotation of the company on the stock market
• A decision to move to a 'partnership' type of organization, with a commitment to acknowledging the organization's responsibilities to all who are involved in its activities or affected by them
• A decision to outsource IT

2B
Unexpected change originating within the organization

Examples:
• A decision by the owners to close a plant, announced without warning to its management and staff
• Losses caused by a rogue trader or dishonest manager
• High staff turnover or absenteeism caused by imposed changes in working practices

Figure 9.1 **Matrix of four kinds of change**

• Existing publicity, advertising, product leaflets for customers, and other information products, so as to check whether they need to be changed, and whether any new products are required
• Relevant developments in IT and applications software, so that they can decide on appropriate investments; their own existing systems and technology, so they can deal in time with necessary modification.
• Their own history, so that they can learn about how they dealt with similar situations in the past, and how effective it was.

New legislation

Here, successful management of the change will lie in identifying how the legislation will affect the organization's operations, and in conforming to it by:
* Changes in products, processes, ways of working, etc.
* Training or retraining staff
* Investing in new equipment.

To manage the change successfully, the organization needs to know about:
* Developments in legislation and how they affect production methods and or materials, ways of working, etc. Examples – legislation forbidding the use of dangerous materials like asbestos; legislation on full disclosure of information in selling pensions and insurance.
* Sources of advice and exchange of experience offered by government, Business Link services, libraries, industry associations, etc.

Demographic and social change in the population the organization serves

The hallmarks of successful management of this kind of change include: preparing to change the service offered to match the population change, for example more children, or more elderly people, or more people suffering from Aids.

The knowledge for successful management will depend on wide environmental monitoring for intelligence about:
* The economic situation in the organization's own country and in countries with which they do business
* Changes in demography, including age distributions
* Social trends
* Employment statistics
* Health statistics
* Health, welfare and education systems
* Customers/clients and their lifestyles/culture
* Sources of advice and exchange of experience offered, for example, by government, libraries, academic institutions etc.

Unexpected change originating in the outside world (cell 1B)

The one thing that constitutes successful change management in all the examples is a flexible, quick and appropriate response; and the knowledge which organizations require for success covers:
* Understanding of the sources of risk for their own business
* Risk management
* Disaster planning.

Natural disaster affecting the supply/price of raw materials

Successful change management will require:
* Quick location of alternative sources of materials
* Effective planning for the use of alternative materials

- Changing the nature of products to avoid bad consequences of using different materials, and if possible to take advantage of their characteristics
- Forward planning to avoid exclusive dependence in future on particular materials/suppliers.

The necessary knowledge to minimize bad effects, and get whatever advantage is possible from the change, is that about:
- Alternative materials
- Sources/suppliers of them
- Alternative products.

Premises destroyed by terrorist bomb

The bomb which destroyed much of the main shopping centre in Manchester in 1996 is an instructive example. Businesses and other organizations in the area did manage the disastrous change in their affairs successfully, by:
- Implementing 'disaster plans' prepared for such occasions
- Cooperating with other organizations affected to give and receive help.

The knowledge which helped them to manage was of:
- Methods and techniques of 'disaster planning'
- The experience of other organizations in dealing with similar disasters
- Other organizations and individuals in the area with whom to cooperate in dealing with the situation (in the instance quoted, existing good relationships among organizations and businesses in the area were a source of help, and organizations added to their good reputation by helping others).

A hostile takeover bid

A well-publicized and fairly dramatic series of events around an attempt to take over the Co-operative Wholesale Society in 1997 provides a good example of the use of knowledge by organizations to deal with unexpected change. Their successful management of the situation consisted of:
- Rapid reaction to the hostile bid
- Investigation of the group originating it and of help they had received from inside the organization
- Strong legal action to defend their position
- Publicity as the events were in progress
- Appeal to the loyalty of customers (a strong card with this very traditional business).

The knowledge they drew on was of:
- Financial institutions
- Potential corporate raiders
- The legal system, so as to be able to take quick protective action
- Their customers and shareholders.

They also used rather unexpected skills in under-cover investigation and public relations, and a good communications system with their customers.

Competing products launched which undermine the market

Successful management of this change would be marked by such actions as:
- Analysis of competing products
- Quick planning of re-launch of existing products to emphasize their distinctive features
- Longer-term planning to move into new markets, and diversify products
- Setting up competitor monitoring (they should have been doing this already; and it is to be hoped they have learned from the experience!).

The required knowledge and know-how are:
- Knowledge of competing products and of markets, so as to be able to plan the re-launch of existing products to emphasize their distinctive features
- Know-how in competitor intelligence
- Long-term planning to manage the move into new markets and diversify products.

Expected change originating within the organization (cell 2A)

In these cases, change is anticipated, and known and discussed throughout the organization, and it should be the easiest kind to manage well. It is, however, illuminating to find an account (Kotter, 1995) of a study of 100 change efforts, of which a few ended in total failure, a very few were totally successful, and most came in between, with a 'distinct tilt toward the lower end of the scale'. (His observations about what made for success are encouraging, given the recommendations made elsewhere in this book about managing such change efforts as information auditing: doing the job in phases; learning from errors on the way; a sense of urgency; creating and communicating vision; drawing people in to act on it; 'quick wins'; a 'powerful guiding coalition' and so on.)

Flotation of the company on the stock market

A typical example of this kind of change is the decision of many building societies and insurance companies to move from their traditional mutual status to that of a plc. Successful management of the change is characterized by:
- Preparatory research on the company's situation, the views of customers and intermediaries and of staff, and other companies which have taken similar steps
- Well-managed publicity and information provision inside and outside
- Staff training for the new situation of the company
- Monitoring the results of the change.

The requisite knowledge for this action is of:
- Requirements to be observed in relation to the stock market
- Attitudes of 'stakeholders' to the proposed change
- The company's financial situation

- The effects of similar changes on other companies
- The effects on the company's customers, intermediaries, staff, and its public reputation.

Unexpected change originating within the organization (cell 2B)

These are all examples of the kind of change that should not be unexpected, and of bad management. There is not much organizations can do to manage them once they have happened (think of Barings Bank, for example); more important, if the organization survives, is to learn the lessons, plan to do better in future to avoid such disastrous events, and identify what it needs to know to keep out of similar trouble in future.

In some of these cases, the change involves knowledge being unevenly distributed – top management knows something, but the rest of the organization, to its cost, does not; one member of staff knows something about what is going on, but managers who should be aware of his or her actions don't know what it is their managerial responsibility to know. In other cases, the full range of effects likely to follow from management decisions is not known; it is, for example, known exactly how much money will be saved by cutting pay or reducing the time available to do jobs, but those responsible for the decision to make the change have not anticipated that there will be other financial losses from lost time caused by stress, industrial disputes, etc. because they don't know their own workforce, are unacquainted with the industrial culture in the area, or are unaware of what happened in other businesses in the industry which have sought similar solutions.

Decision by owners to close a plant, announced without warning

To avoid such damaging changes, organizations need to:
- Know how to handle closures, redeployment, or redundancies with maximum openness and involvement of staff
- Be aware of examples of successful management of such change situations
- Have skills in human resources management, negotiation and industrial relations.

High staff turnover or absenteeism caused by imposed changes in working practices

To avoid such changes, organizations need to know about:
- Legal requirements and work practices
- Alternative ways of achieving financial savings
- The skills and potential of their workforce
- Skills in human resources management, negotiation, and managing industrial relations.

Creating new knowledge and applying it to get the best out of change

As I hope these examples have made clear, managing change successfully, and not being taken unawares by it, depends critically on human beings having essential knowledge and applying it effectively. The highest and most productive level in the strategic use of information and knowledge – as such Japanese writers as Itami (1987) and Nonaka and Takeuchi (1995) have demonstrated – lies in creating new knowledge, which can then be applied to get the best out of change, in both responding and initiating modes. Itami and his American co-author Roehl distinguish various levels of 'fit' between the organization's strategy for using what it knows. At the level of 'active fit' organizations 'can sometimes change the environment by a judicious choice of strategy or can at least anticipate external changes'. A higher level is the so-called 'leveraged fit' between the organization and its environment. Here the organization 'does more than anticipate and respond to future changes in the environment; it uses those very environmental characteristics that are seen as limiting at the passive and active levels of strategic fit to make its strategy more effective'– that is, it uses the constraints it faces as the stimulus to innovation. An example: the clockwork radio and more recently the clockwork personal computer; the constraint of lack of power supplies in rural developing countries has been the stimulus to their inventor to innovate by combining a twentieth-century technology with a medieval one. Figure 9.2, on page 161, suggests the way in which knowledge and information can help to move organizations from spending most of their time responding to unexpected change towards a situation of 'change mastery' where they use foresight and insight to initiate change. Though knowledge is a fashionable word these days in management circles, as Nonaka and Takeuchi point out, 'all this talk about the importance of knowledge … does little to help us understand how knowledge is created.' Yet it is perhaps the most important thing for organizations to understand if they wish to survive and prosper, and for our present purposes in this chapter knowledge creation is both a high-level change process in itself and the key to keeping the initiative in managing change. (It is rather saddening to find from the latest results from the Cranfield European Knowledge Survey, as reported by Tate, 1997, that nearly a quarter of UK firms, as compared with just 1 per cent in Germany and 4 per cent in France, say that creating new knowledge is not a priority for them.) What follows draws largely on the insights of Nonaka and Takeuchi (1995), with grateful acknowledgements.

Conditions that enable knowledge creation

Three conditions are necessary for knowledge to be created (op. cit., page 74):
1 A strategy for knowledge and information (to which we shall return in the next chapter)
2 A vision of what kind of knowledge the organization needs (the equivalent of 'what should be'– see Chapter 3)
3 Its 'operationalization' into a management system for implementation.

The essence of the strategy lies in developing the organization's capability to 'acquire, create, accumulate, and exploit knowledge', and the most critical

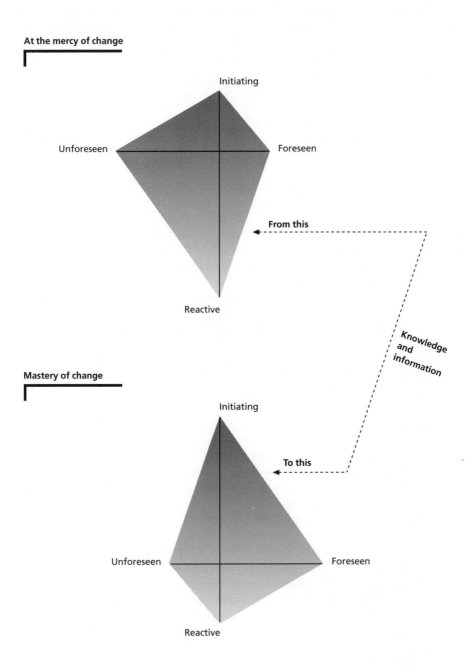

Fig 9.2   **From being at the mercy of change to mastery of change**

element is to conceptualize the 'vision about what kind of knowledge should be developed and to operationalize it into a management system for implementation'. (See also Choo, 1996; he links the creation of knowledge with making sense of the organization's situation and taking decisions.)

The Japanese approach to knowledge

There is a typical Western assumption that the only knowledge is that which is explicit, formal and systematic, which goes with the view of organizations as 'machines for information processing'. (Fortunately, not all Western writers share it; see for example Davenport, 1993 on the dangers to organizations of seeing information as limited to quantitative data that can be held in traditional database systems, and of missing the value of unstructured qualitative textual information.)

The Japanese view is quite different and much more subtle: 'Knowledge expressed in words and numbers represents only the tip of the iceberg.' It is seen as primarily tacit – not easily visible or expressible, and it includes subjective insights, intuitions and hunches. Tacit knowledge has two aspects: technical know-how, like that which is passed on in traditional craft apprenticeship, and the cognitive dimension, in which come schemata, mental models and beliefs reflecting the holder's image of reality and vision of the future (and so related to value). Again, there are Western writers who work on similar assumptions; Cooley (1987) has described his work, as an engineer, on making use of the tacit knowledge of craftsmen and technicians, and relates how organizations can benefit from using it.

The knowledge creation spiral

While new knowledge cannot be created without 'intensive outside–inside interaction', the actual creation of knowledge demands that what we have learned from others be internalized, 'reformed, enriched, and translated to fit the company's self image and identity.' (cf. the discussion in Chapter 3 of the need to understand the organization's culture).

Knowledge can be created at various levels: at the level of the individual, the group, the individual organization, and organizations working together. Nonaka and Takeuchi express this visually, as shown in Figure 9.3, through the concept of 'the knowledge-creation spiral', which 'emerges when the interaction between tacit and explicit knowledge is elevated dynamically' from lower to higher levels. The engine of the process consists of four stages or modes:

1 Socialization
2 Externalization
3 Combination
4 Internalization

The spiral progresses through the stages mentioned above, via processes that characterize the transitions from one to another:

* Field building: the creation of 'forums' for interaction and experience sharing, associated with socialization

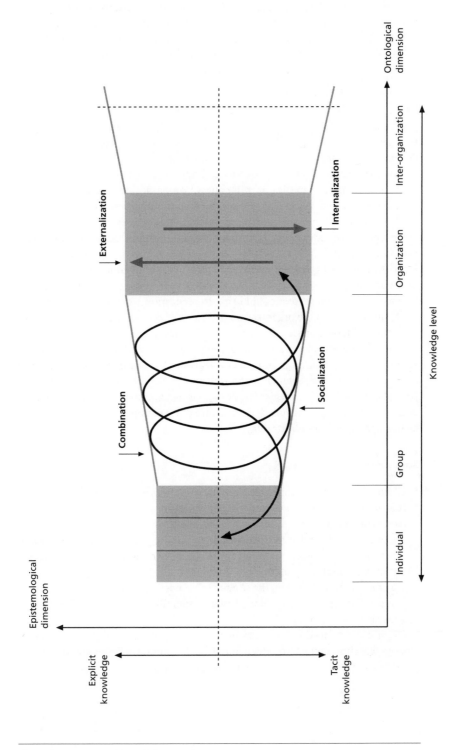

Fig 9.3   **Spiral of organizational knowledge creation**

- Dialogue: articulation of tacit knowledge, leading to externalization
- Networking: bringing together newly created knowledge and existing knowledge from other parts of the organization, which triggers combination
- Learning by doing: which triggers internalization so that the knowledge fully belongs to the individual or organization.

(The spiral is a powerful image or metaphor, which can be used in many ways; another knowledge spiral from Nonaka and Takeuchi has already appeared in Chapter 1; there are others to illustrate different processes in Chapter 6 and the Interlude, and readers will meet yet another, concerned with the development of information strategy, in Chapter 10.)

The manner in which the process can happen is described in this way (the authors give many examples from Japanese companies, related to how knowledge is created to develop new and often revolutionary products):

•→ An individual finds new information that enriches his or her own knowledge and makes ideas that have been floating around come together with new illumination. Tacit knowledge moves towards becoming explicit. •→ The individual discusses the new knowledge informally with colleagues – socialization and dialogue. •→ They realize the ideas have potential for the organization to initiate changes that could bring to realization some key aims. •→ They move outwards into the organization to network with other people – guardians and stakeholders in other information and knowledge resources. •→ The combination of ideas leads to a formal decision to try something out. A project is set up and carried through in phases – learning by doing. •→ The experience creates new knowledge which is internalized by the organization. It becomes part of what informs strategic decisions, and leads to new products, services, even to a new organization derived from the existing one, and possibly to changes in organizational strategy.

Summary

- Change is the most stable characteristic of organizations, as it is of life.
- It is not necessarily always something unpleasant which is done to us; knowledge confers greater freedom in responding to and initiating change.
- Creating new knowledge and using it to initiate change is the highest and most productive level of change; it is the key to gaining and keeping the initiative in managing change.
- To create new knowledge, the organization needs a strategy for using knowledge and information, a vision, and a system for implementing the strategy to achieve the vision.
- Organizations need to use both tacit and explicit knowledge in the 'knowledge-creating spiral', in which individuals interact with one another and the organization to create new knowledge and bring about change.

References

Choo, C. W. (1996), 'The knowing organization: how organizations use information to construct meaning, create knowledge and make decisions', *International Journal of Information Management*, 16, (5), 329–340

Cooley, M. (1987), *Architect or Bee? The human price of technology*, London: Hogarth Press

Davenport, T. (1993), *Process Innovation*, Boston, MA: Harvard Business School Press

Drucker, P. (1995), *Managing in a Time of Great Change*, Oxford: Butterworth Heinemann, pp. 70–71

Edwards, C. and Peppard, J. W. (1994), 'Business process redesign: hype, hope or hypocrisy?', *Journal of Information Technology*, 9, 251–266

Itami, H. with Roehl, T. W. (1987), *Mobilizing Invisible Assets*, Boston, MA: Harvard University Press

Kotter, J. P. (1995), 'Leading change: why transformation efforts fail', *Harvard Business Review*, March–April, 59–67

Metcalfe, S. (1997), 'Technology systems and technology policy in an evaluationary framework', in D. Archibugi and J. Michie (eds.), *Technology, Globalisation and Economic Performance*, Cambridge: Cambridge University Press.

Nonaka, I. and Takeuchi, H. (1995), *The Knowledge-creating Company: how Japanese companies create the dynamics of information*, New York: Oxford University Press

Tate, P. (1997), 'Common knowledge', *Information Strategy*, 2 (10), 21

Developing and using an information strategy

In this chapter:

- Distinctions and definitions
- The engine of change and development
- The baseline – what you need to know before starting
- Whose business is information strategy?
- Essential resources
- Other enabling conditions for success
- Where to start – focal points for strategy development
- The develop–implement–learn spiral

[1] 'Strategic intelligence can ... be defined as follows: it is what a company needs to know about its business environment to enable it to anticipate change and design appropriate strategies that will create business value for customers and be profitable in new markets and industries in the future. ... The value of strategic intelligence comes from improving the capabilities of managers and workers in a company to learn about changes in the business or industry environment which will require rethinking business practices. They must then share their perceptions, new information and insights wherever in the company such information is needed. The challenge for strategic intelligence is to increase the "intelligence quotient" of all managers and employees in a company ...'(Marchand 1997a.)

Seven key words for strategic thinking: **1 Differentiation** – *what makes the organization unique.* **2 Concentration** – *on priorities: strengths, weaknesses, opportunities, threats.* **3 Repercussions** – *how one strategic activity can lead to other possibilities for future action.* **4 Timing** – *using information to take change initiatives at the right time.* **5 Momentum** – *keeping up the initiative once it's started.* **6 Imbalance** – *'an unbalanced strategy that shakes up an organization is best for its long-term health'.* **7 Combination** – *interdependence of all the resources of the organization, so it implies integrated management of information.* Hiroyuki Itami with Thomas W. Roehl (1987)

Information strategy also means making choices, not carving out a master plan in stone. Thomas Davenport with Lawrence Prusak (1997)

Distinctions and definitions

With this, the last chapter, we return to the practicalities of the process of creating an organizational strategy for using knowledge and information which we left at the end of Chapter 6, with the completion of an information policy. I hope that the ideas offered in the intervening chapters, and readers' own reflections on them in the light of experience, will have brought some enrichment which will feed into the practical considerations.

Before we begin, a reminder, to save you having to turn back to the start of the book, of the relevant definitions and distinctions.

Organizational information strategy

Organizational information strategy is the detailed expression of information policy in terms of objectives, targets, and actions to achieve them, for a defined period ahead. Information strategy provides the framework for the management of information; itself contained within the framework of an organizational policy for information and supported by appropriate systems and technology, it is the 'engine' for:

* Maintaining, managing and applying the organization's resources of information
* Supporting its essential knowledge base and all who contribute to it, with strategic intelligence,[1] for achieving its key business objectives.

Distinctions

Information policy:
* At the level of principles
* Short statement
* Can be developed at one go
* Meant to last.

Information strategy:
* Basis for action for a given period
* Reviewed at frequent intervals
* Can be developed and implemented in stages.

Information systems/IT strategy:
* Depends on what information the organization needs, and how it needs to use it
* Deals with applications software and infrastructure to support information management
* Decisions on information policy and strategy have to come first.

The engine of change and development

As Figure 10.1 suggests (see page 169), a strong information strategy, which is well understood and has the commitment of everyone in the organization, can become the engine that:
* Drives interchanges of information internally and with the outside world
* Brings in intelligence about change
* Leads to integrated responses
* Promotes creation of new knowledge through internal interactions
* Leads to initiatives, directed both internally and to the outside world, which make for success in innovation and competition.

The baseline – what you need to know before starting

Here we need to remind ourselves of what was said in Chapter 3 about laying the foundations for the strategic use of information and knowledge.

The identity of the organization

What is its primary orientation? Is it, for example, towards:
* The market and customers?
* Risk avoidance?
* Cost reduction?
* Innovation?

If it is currently seeking to adopt a new orientation, as many organizations today, for example, are trying to become customer-focused, then that factor is of particular significance for the kind of strategy it will need to support it in the attempt.

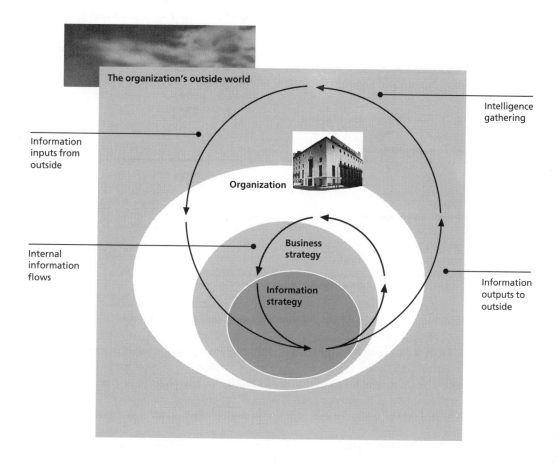

Fig 10.1   **Information strategy, the engine**

Technocratic Utopianism	A heavily technical approach to information management stressing categorization and modeling of an organization's full information assets, with heavy reliance on emerging technologies.
Anarchy	The absence of any overall information management policy, leaving individuals to obtain and manage their own information.
Feudalism	The management of information by individual business units or functions, which define their own information needs and report only limited information to the overall corporation.
Monarchy	The definition of information categories and reporting structures by the firm's leaders, who may or may not share the information willingly after collecting it.
Federalism	An approach to information management based on consensus and negotiation on the organization's key information elements and reporting structures

Table 10.1 **Models of Information Politics.** From Davenport et al. (1992)

What is its information culture? Is the emphasis on communicating and building relationships? On influencing and controlling? On problem solving and efficiency? Or on discovery, inquiry, innovation?

Does it proclaim its dedication to 'information sharing'? And if it does, how does that go down in practice? Are people willing to interact and negotiate over the information resources they hold, or do they clutch them firmly and growl at strangers who approach? What of its 'information politics'? Do they fall into any of the categories that Davenport and his co-authors (1992) identify (see Table 10.1)?

What are its key objectives, and the priorities among them (see Chapter 3)?

'What should be' with respect to knowledge and information

Next we need to answer (as we did in Tables 3.1–3.3, pages 45 to 54) these questions about the knowledge and information implications of what the organization claims it is trying to do:

- What does it need to know to achieve its objectives?
- What information does it need to maintain its knowledge?

That gives a picture of 'what should be', against which, as recommended in Chapter 4, the information audit can start finding out 'what is', in terms of information resources, where they are, what they consist of, who are their guardians and stakeholders, how they are used, and how well they support what the organization is trying to do.

The output from all that questioning and finding answers provides the material on which the information strategy developer has to work. Fortunately, if an information audit has been carried out, it should be well structured as a result of the work done on it in the course of interpreting and presenting the findings, and therefore accessible and manageable. And if the people responsible for the audit are also involved, as they should be, in strategy development, they will have an invaluable structure of knowledge and be able to move swiftly about it, and identify priorities.

Whose business is information strategy?

Information strategy is intended to benefit the whole organization in its most critical activities, and so its development needs to draw on a wide range of knowledge and experience.

1 Managers of information resources, for example:
   * Environmental intelligence
   * Customer information
   * Competitor information
   * Economic/financial information
   * Human resources
   * Information service/library/archives (these resources often seem to be overlooked when projects of this kind are being set up; but the people in charge of them don't have to accept invisibility!)[2]
   * Marketing
   * Membership
   * Contacts
   * R&D
   * Information products
2 Managers of information systems and information technology
3 Stakeholders in information resources
4 Managers responsible for the organization's corporate strategy.

Essential resources

The essential resources are similar to those needed for an information audit (they are listed briefly below as a reminder). If a properly resourced audit has been carried out in the organization, the structures, reporting arrangements, groupings and relationships in the course of that process can be built on. (Another instance of the value of setting things up properly first time round – the cost and effort next time is minimized.)

[2] Bonaventura (1997) – who works for a systems company – puts the case for their presence, and that of other essential contributors, emphatically: 'While the technology is non-trivial, it will not make or break a Knowledge Management programme: the human support infrastructure (librarians, publishers, design teams) will ... any methodology which is targeting Knowledge Management needs to address the definition and installation of that support infrastructure.'

Essentials for information strategy development are:
- A compact representative group to manage it (drawing on the constituencies mentioned above)
- Knowledge of the organization
- Top management support
- Understanding throughout the organization of what is being done
- 'Management champion'
- Straightforward reporting arrangements
- A clear brief
- Realistic phased timetable
- Appropriate resources of time and finance.

Other enabling conditions for success

In Chapter 9 (pages 160 and 162) I quoted some conditions put forward by Nonaka and Takeuchi as enablers of knowledge creation. The first of them was a strategy for knowledge and information, which is what is currently occupying our attention; the next a vision of the kind of knowledge the organization needs, which we have just discussed; and the third a management system to implement the strategy for achieving the vision. There are others, and they are worth citing here, because I think they are both a help in developing information strategy, and something which it should seek to promote and keep in being throughout the organization. In quoting them, I shall intersperse some real-life stories from the case studies and elsewhere.

The first of these enablers is maximum possible autonomy for the individuals and teams to whom the organization entrusts responsibility for new developments; this allows original ideas to develop and spread through the organization, upwards, downwards and sideways, and is part of the process described in Japanese management thinking as 'middle-up-down management'.

> ... knowledge is created by middle managers, who are often leaders of a team or task force, through a spiral conversion process involving both the top and the front-line employees ... The process puts middle managers at the very center of knowledge management, positioning them at the intersection of the vertical and horizontal flows of information within the company. (Nonaka and Takeuchi, 1995, page 127).

The case study of the Surrey Police Force (see page 325) provides an example. As described in the case study, action which led to the development of an information policy and strategy came about in that way, when ideas originating from an individual were given the opportunity of spreading upwards and outwards into the organization. The NatWest Markets case study (see page 293) exemplifies another aspect of autonomy for a self-organizing team.

The next enabler is cross-functional teams, drawing in people from a broad cross-section of different organizational activities (see the case studies of the Australian Securities and Investments Commission, page 197, and the University of North London case study, page 349, for examples of such teams).

Finally, Nonaka and Takeuchi recommend what is described as 'fluctuation and creative chaos', designed to 'stimulate the interaction between the organization and the external environment'. This is important because it introduces discontinuity, and the opportunity to reconsider values through dialogue and interaction. Such an alternation of order and chaos is not seen as something to be afraid of. The concept is very different from Western 'problem solving'; it demands the 'purposeful use of ambiguity', and can succeed only when members of the organization 'have the ability to reflect upon their actions'. It can lead to questioning of values as well as of factual premises.[3] This can take place only in a supportive environment, not in the kind of chaos which is brought on by panic and authoritarianism. It demands great self-confidence on the part of management to seek to promote this as part of organizational development, but I suspect it happens spontaneously and to good effect in the course of many projects such as those described in the case studies. Certainly these unfamiliar ideas underline the importance of allowing time for thinking and insisting that people do think, instead of the usual tacit assumption that thinking is not working, and that you have to show you're working by rushing around (the British Library case study, see page 213, is an organization where thinking among senior managers is seen as being essential for sound strategic decision making).

Where to start – focal points for strategy development

It is not possible or desirable to develop the strategy everywhere at once; as with information auditing, the 'spiral' approach, in which development and implementation interact, and in which at each turn there can be learning and diffusion further into the organization, is recommended (see below, page 175). So a choice has to be made of the points where application of an information strategy will bring most effect.

As Marchand (1997b) reminds us, when organizations invest for information management, they should concentrate on the distinctive, innovative end of their activities because that is where the return on investment is potentially higher (in contrast, most IT investment is still at the conventional end, where the return is lower). So we need to look for the organization's:

- Strengths
- Unique features
- Core competencies (the distinctive ones, what the organization is very good at, those of highest potential value to it)
- Survival essentials (including what the organization is not very good at, and areas where this constitutes a risk)
- Potential for innovation.

[3] See also Itami and Roehl (1987) on 'imbalance', as cited at the start of this chapter: the thinking here is that there should be periods when resources and talents are not in balance with current strategy; the organization should not be in equilibrium for too long or it loses momentum; it needs to progress through zigzags.

Examples of actual starting points

Some of these examples are drawn from the case studies, others from the recent experience of other organizations. Among them, they cover in a variety of ways the key concerns, discussed in Chapters 7–9, of: people in relation to technology; change; and the value of knowledge and information.

Getting the benefits of informal information interchange, without the disadvantages of once-only use

An international charity; its information strategy aims at:
Combining informal e-mail networks with more permanent databases, using IT to make it easy to contribute knowledge from the informal exchanges to a sophisticated database which allows multiple use

  Counteracting the weakness of project-centred working by making sure that knowledge and information from projects – and especially the lessons of what worked and what failed – is managed and made accessible for future use. This is a frequently encountered problem today, and part of the strategic solution may lie in structural change; if an organization's structure is solely task-force- and project-based, there is a danger of information loss because it is not appropriate for transferring the knowledge gained during projects into a robust and durable knowledge base. Nonaka and Takeuchi (1995) propose a 'hypertext organization' in which different 'layers' co-exist. When projects are completed, 'members move down to the knowledge-base layer and make an inventory of the knowledge created and/or acquired', including successes and failures.

Helping staff to be aware of their own knowledge and of its value in interaction with the knowledge of others in the organization

A specialist insurance company (see the Thomas Miller & Co.Ltd case study, page 343); its strategy aims at making it part of the job description of its highly qualified staff that they should contribute to the business's knowledge base,[4] so that colleagues and clients can use it to grow the business. The strategy involves intensive use of quite sophisticated technology, and investment in education for staff in using it.

Integrated management of all information resources

A large museum; the focus for developing its information strategy is integrated use of the whole range of its information resources, which will, for example, allow staff planning multi-media products for sale to draw on information about the collections, potential markets, visitors, possible commercial partners and competing products.

[4] An observation in this context; today a number of organizations are both seeking integrated information management and trying to get all managers to adopt information management as part of their job responsibilities. These are both reasonable things to do, but there seems to be an as yet unresolved problem of how to combine decentralized management of information with an overview of what is going on, and a coordinated strategy. The solution will demand some crafty work on structure and culture, and ingenious support from systems and technology.

Managing and using information from the organization's outside world

An international organization; it is strong on output of information, but has diagnosed a weakness in its failure to make enough use of the response which it gets from customers, clients, the public and government bodies. The focal point of its strategy development is managing incoming information so as to learn from it, plan action and develop policies.

The Australian Securities and Investments Commission (see case study, page 197)

An exercise of 'information discovery' (information auditing) in the organization and development of an information policy resulted in a Strategic Information Plan which used the findings to propose seven key strategies:

1 *Build an effective national information management framework of policy, planning, standards and collaboration.*
2 *Systematically identify and articulate core business information needs.*
3 *Improve business information processes and corporate data quality.*
4 *Develop an integrated information management structure for both electronic and physical documents and records.*
5 *Research and develop expertise to apply knowledge management tools and techniques.*
6 *Ensure that operational staff are able to make effective use of information resources.*
7 *Leverage use of the Internet.*

Amnesty International (see case study, page 186)

The focal points for developing an international information management strategy include:

• *Integrating the use of IT and the use of information*
• *Improving the quality of decisions on investment in IT to benefit users in countries with few resources*
• *Testing the effectiveness of what the organization does with information.*

Surrey Police Force (see case study, page 325)

Here the information strategy is driven by the need to use information economically, to avoid multiple inputs, to standardize, and to develop a system that allows each element of information to be accessed and used in multiple contexts. Its aim is fully integrated management of information, with maximum access and maximum openness. This approach has led to changes in organizational structure, which bring together, in one information services department, systems, information technology, library, records and registry.

The develop–implement–learn spiral

If the people responsible for developing information strategy were to try to get it complete in every detail before starting to use it, they would never see it applied. 'Analysis paralysis' would set in, with its trail of talk, working parties,

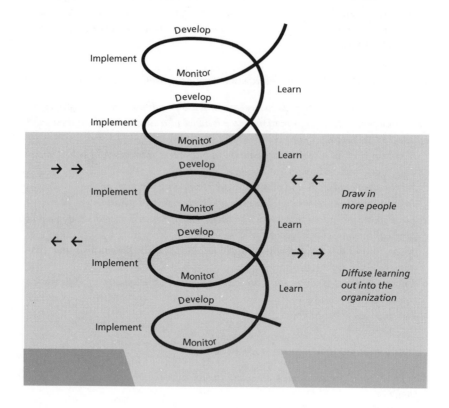

Fig 10.2   **Spiral of develop – implement – learn**

reports, heaps of documents, disillusion, all to be finally forgotten as yet another failed initiative.

So it is wise not to think of it as an end-on process of first develop, then implement. It is only by doing something that you find out if what you have planned really works. Equally, it is no good doing something unless you make sure to learn the lessons and to pass them on. That is the reasoning behind proposing interaction between developing the strategy and putting it into action. I envisage it as a spiral process, with learning at each turn of the spiral, and new people being drawn into development as it continues. It is a rotating spiral, as well, which means that there is a constant process of revisiting earlier stages to monitor and update (see Figure 10.2 above).

This prototyping approach also gives the best chance of the strategy being understood and integrated into the way the organization sets about its business, because it

- Allows you to demonstrate
  - *without taking too long about it,*
    - *or tying up too many resources,*
      - *real benefits of applying a strategic approach to information*
      - *in areas that are critical for the organization;*
    - *to measure the impact at the end of each phase;*
    - *and to learn more each time around.*

As suggested earlier, it is not reasonable to expect immediate and complete understanding at the top level (as Marchand, 1997b says, general managers are accustomed to managing *with* information, but the management *of* information is as yet a rather unfamiliar concept). Some of the case studies show the length of time that is needed for such ideas to take root in the thinking of senior managers, but it is time well spent, because it can ensure that they will contribute to developing the strategy for the areas of business which they control and know well, and will take good advantage of it. And the moral of that is to keep at it; understanding will grow as the strategy is put into effect; and the day will come when top management will start taking credit for it and even boasting of it! (For further encouragement, read Davenport's recent outstanding book on *Information Ecology* (1997); the chapter on information strategy recommends a similar approach to the one advocated here, backed up by Davenport's wide range of experience.)

What the organization stands to gain

Meantime, no opportunity should be lost of selling the benefits of the integrated management of knowledge and information in the framework of a strategy which is contained within the organization's overall corporate strategy (see Figure 10.3, page 178).

Summary

- A strong information strategy can become the engine of successful change and development for organizations.
- Before starting to develop it, you need to know about:
  - Your organization's orientation
  - Its information culture
  - Its key objectives and priorities.
- You also need to know how well what it actually does with information and knowledge matches what it should be doing – preferably through an information audit.
- Information strategy development needs cooperative effort from:
  - Managers of all the organization's information resources
  - The stakeholders in them
  - Managers of information systems and information technology
  - Managers responsible for corporate strategy.
- It needs a compact group to manage it, a management champion, understanding throughout the organization, and proper resources of time and money.

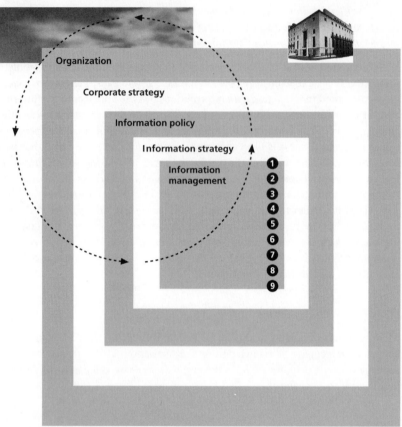

The organisation's outside world

Fig 10.3 **Integrated information management in the framework of information strategy, information policy, and organizational strategy**

❶ Helps organizations learn from experience
❷ Keeps knowledge in good form for application
❸ Allows them to take advantage of opportunities
❹ Helps them to avoid dangers by awareness of change
❺ Supports innovation, redefining problems, finding new solutions
❻ Helps gain and keep reputation
❼ Gives a sound basis for resource allocation
❽ Provides a strong framework for IS/IT strategy
❾ Makes a basis for valuing information and knowledge

- Other things that help: a self-organizing team with maximum autonomy; acknowledgement of the importance of thinking, and time for it.
- Strategy can't be developed everywhere at once; it's better to choose significant focal points for development, and work by a spiral of develop–learn–implement. That way, at each turn there can be learning, diffusion into the organization, and drawing in of new people.

References

BONAVENTURA, M. (1997), 'The benefits of a knowledge culture', *Aslib Proceedings,* 49 (4), 82–89

DAVENPORT, T. H., ECCLES, R. G. and PRUSAK, L. (1992), 'Information politics', *Sloan Management Review,* Fall, 53–65

DAVENPORT, T. H. with PRUSAK, L. (1997), *Information Ecology. Mastering the information and knowledge environment,* New York: Oxford University Press

ITAMI, H. with ROEHL, T. W. (1987), *Mobilizing Invisible Assets,* Boston, MA: Harvard University Press

MARCHAND, D. A. (1997a), 'Managing strategic intelligence', *Financial Times Mastering Management,* London: Financial Times/Pitman

MARCHAND, D. A. (1997b), 'Competing with information: know what you want', *FT Mastering Management Reader,* July/August, 7–12

NONAKA, I. and TAKEUCHI, H. (1995), *The Knowledge-creating Company: how Japanese companies create the dynamics of information,* New York: Oxford University Press

Part 3 Case studies

Case studies: topic finder

To help readers to select those case studies which may be particularly relevant to their own interests, here is a list of key topics, with a pointer to the relevant case studies

Amnesty International

Amnesty International (AI) is among a number of international humanitarian and aid organizations which are developing information policies and strategies. At the time when this case study was initiated, an information strategy was being finalized for presentation to its governing body, with a proposal that it should be implemented from the end of 1997, and monitored and evaluated in 2001; in December 1997, the strategy was accepted (the follow-up is described on pages 193 to 194).

AI's role demands that it should be an information-intensive organization; it depends on gathering intelligence from the outside world, and on a constant interchange of information within the organization, with its supporters, and with the outside world which it seeks to influence. Not only is Amnesty International information-intensive; it has characteristics that pose particular problems in managing information and in decisions on resources. In some countries it is able to run a sophisticated operation with many paid staff and advanced IT support, while in others its workers are volunteers, and they have difficulty even in getting a telephone line.

Background

Foundation and development

The foundation of what became Amnesty International 1961 by a British lawyer, Peter Benenson, was occasioned by a press report of two Portuguese students being sentenced to seven years in prison for a toast to freedom. He organized a one-year campaign to persuade oppressive governments to release people imprisoned for political and religious beliefs: those who became known as 'prisoners of conscience'. The response was so great that Amnesty became a permanent international movement.

The primary tactic was mass letter writing demanding the release of prisoners 'adopted' by Amnesty. Over time, the organization extended its mandate to campaign for fair trials in political cases and against torture and ill-treatment of all prisoners. In 1970 it took a formal position opposing the death penalty in all cases, including unlawful executions and 'disappearances'. It further extended its remit to safeguarding people seeking refuge in one country from oppressive government in another, and opposed the international transfer of equipment or expertise that could lead to human rights violations. In 1991, AI decided that it would directly address political opposition groups that commit such abuses as hostage taking or arbitrary killings, and it also took up such issues as the forcible exile of people from their own countries. In 1977 it was awarded the Nobel Peace Prize, and the following year the UN Human Rights Prize.

Objectives and mandate

AI's objective is:
- To contribute to observance throughout the world of human rights as set out in the Universal Declaration of Human Rights.

Its mandate is:
- To promote awareness of and adherence to the Universal Declaration of Human Rights and other internationally recognized human rights instruments, the values enshrined in them, and the indivisibility and interdependence of all human rights and freedoms
- To oppose grave violations of the rights of every person freely to hold and to express his or her convictions and to be free from discrimination by reason of ethnic origin, sex, colour or language, and of the right of every person to physical and mental integrity, and, in particular, to oppose by all appropriate means irrespective of political considerations:
  - Imprisonment of prisoners of conscience (provided they have not used or advocated violence)
  - Detention of any political prisoner without fair trial, and trials procedures that do not conform to internationally recognized norms
  - Death penalty; torture; cruel, inhuman or degrading treatment of prisoners (whether or not they have used or advocated violence)
  - Extrajudicial executions and 'disappearances'.

Principles of working

AI is committed to impartiality as regards countries adhering to different world political ideologies and groupings. It works through:
- Financial and other relief
- Legal aid
- Publicity for cases
- Investigations
- Representations to international organizations and governments
- Promotion and support for general amnesties.

Organizational structure and culture

AI is based on world-wide voluntary membership. The directive authority is the International Council; between its meetings, an International Executive Committee (IEC) is responsible for decision making, while day-to-day management is in the hands of an International Secretariat. Sections can be established in any country with the consent of the International Executive Committee; groups can become affiliated to AI or to Sections, and individuals in countries where there is no national Section can become members of AI. The International Council consists of members of the IEC and representatives of Sections. In accordance with its aims, AI's organizational culture is wholly democratic.

Context for the development of information strategy

In 1995 a new organizational structure was introduced for the International Secretariat, to 'give a balance between functions and areas of influence, and to de-emphasise hierarchies and divisions'. The structure is based on three Program Groups (Regional, International and Resources), the boundaries between which are seen as fluid (see Figure C1.1).

1 The Regional Programs Group: to facilitate effective action in relation to specific regions

2 The International Programs Group: to ensure development and implementation of coherent international policies, clear standards for AI's work, and an overall international programme which effectively addresses AI's mandate.

It includes these programmes:

- Legal and international organizations: advice on international law, relations with IGOs (international governmental organizations) and international NGOs (non-governmental organizations), strategies
- Media and audiovisual: media strategies, written and audiovisual products
- Campaign and crisis response: international policy on campaigning, coordinating crisis response
- Research and mandate: advice and training, policy development on the mandate
- International development: mobilizing people and institutions, human rights awareness, education and training
- Resources: developing and managing the resources needed by the International Secretariat to achieve its objectives. The resources consist of:
  - Publications Program
  - Information Resources Program
  - Office Management Program
  - Information Technology Program
  - Human Resources Program
  - Finance and Accounting Program.

The Information Resources Program is the one particularly concerned with information strategy; it is responsible for developing management strategies, information gathering, library, documentation, audiovisual materials, copyright, and archives.

Strategy development

The actual stimulus to the development of information strategy came from a 1995 International Council Meeting resolution calling for a set of interlinked information strategies at international and national level. The orientation of the information strategies called for was not specified; and it is quite possible that what the members of the International Council had in mind tended more towards IT and information systems than towards information in terms of content. In the event, however, it was the Director of Information Resources who, in agreement with the Director of Information Technology, took the lead

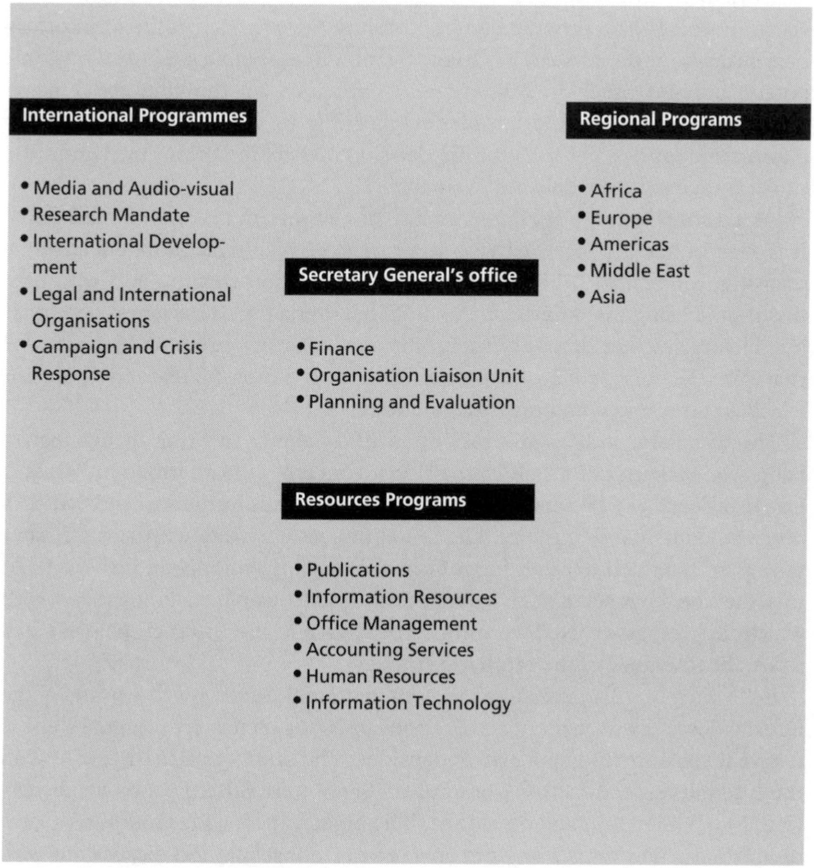

International Programmes

- Media and Audio-visual
- Research Mandate
- International Development
- Legal and International Organisations
- Campaign and Crisis Response

Secretary General's office

- Finance
- Organisation Liaison Unit
- Planning and Evaluation

Regional Programs

- Africa
- Europe
- Americas
- Middle East
- Asia

Resources Programs

- Publications
- Information Resources
- Office Management
- Accounting Services
- Human Resources
- Information Technology

Fig C1.1   **Organizational structure diagram**

responsibility for interpreting and implementing the resolution. Negotiating this presented no difficulty, as the Director of Information Resources had been pressing this issue for a long time, and the Director to whom he reported had an information background.

The resolution was seen as an opportunity to bring together a number of developments currently under way, including Internet, e-mail, archives, user-oriented library services, and provision of information through audio-visual media. It also provided an opportunity to raise the profile of information throughout the movement. Many Sections had spent a great deal on computers, but not much in training, and not much on thinking about using information, so the resolution made it possible to get people talking about information, and to get some of the decision makers to take an interest in the subject – in itself a positive achievement

Information strategy development also has important resource implications. It is seen as being concerned with using existing resources more effectively – knowing, for example, how databases are used, their quality, and who uses them – and using that knowledge to build in criteria for effectiveness and quality. This raises questions of criteria for allocating resources as between, for example, Sections which are on version 4.3 of Lotus Notes and those for which a phone line is an unrealized ambition.

The discussions about the resolution have helped to bring in not just IT people but others not aware of their own concern with information, while it has also deepened IT specialists' understanding of information and led to a more fundamental definition. The initial discussions were with IT staff; later they were extended to other programmes, including regional and research. At first the concepts seemed too theoretical, but focusing on innovations with which the people involved were concerned, such as the Internet, helped them to see the relevance of the proposed strategy.

Following the discussions in the International Secretariat, a draft of the information strategy went out to Sections; this was seen as an essential step, as it gave them something positive to consider. The draft was also discussed with the International Executive Committee. There were other forums for discussion, too, both within and outside AI. The organization-wide Computer Communications Working Group provided good feedback, as did discussions with people outside Amnesty, for example Greenpeace, and the British Overseas Aid Group – all of whose members were either starting to develop or considering information policies (it is encouraging to record that they were drawing on the first edition of this book to help them).

The draft strategy

The draft is a short document, taking up no more than six sides of A4, supplemented by two pages of appendices. It presents definitions of information management, principles for information management in AI, strategic aims of information management up to the year 2001, and proposals for implementation. The appendices set out the information management implications of AI's long-term objectives, and give an example of an information management strategy for a medium-sized AI Section.

AI's information resources

These are defined in these terms: 'on victims and violations; finances; information about AI itself, its culture, structures, its membership, its mandate, its effectiveness; country information; information about the cultural, social, political, economic and technological environment in which AI works. Such information feeds the knowledge base of AI.'

Strategic aims

The strategic aims of information management are linked to long-term objectives, and 'identify where information adds value ... The strategy will act as a map for assigning resources, and will guide decisions'. It will complement existing and future policies and strategies, for example, media and publication, and archives.

Benefits

The benefits to AI identified in the strategy include:
- Enhancing its effectiveness to protect victims and expose human rights violations
- Assisting cultural change
- Helping AI to be an organization that 'listens and learns'
- Maximum added value from information management
- Cost saving from reduced overlaps and duplications
- Facilitating effective organizational development
- Clarifying responsibility for information management
- Providing a tool for monitoring information management
- Ensuring necessary skills and knowledge to manage both information and IT
- Ensuring that parts of AI which are lacking in access to technology are not disadvantaged.

Principles

The principles set out in effect constitute an information policy framework for the strategy. Information management in AI will:
- Promote free flow of information and non-hierarchical communication, together with freedom of expression
- Conform to the general values of AI
- Contribute significantly to the pursuit of AI's objectives
- Promote sharing of information within AI
- Ensure that no part of the AI movement is excluded from access to information through barriers of technology, language, etc
- Deliver accurate, timely, concise information, relevant to the purpose of users, and in an appropriate format
- Deliver information clearly and intelligibly in straightforward language
- Adhere to security standards, protecting sources and individuals

- Minimize costs and duplication, and maximize returns on resources invested in information management
- Contribute to effective work organization
- Make full use of appropriate available technology
- Promote organizational learning and ensure that organizational memory is developed through responsible archiving and evaluation
- Follow international standards, including data protection and copyright.

Strategic aims to 2001

The aims are set out under the headings of:
- Develop people and skills for information management: including professional information management and IT staff, training for staff and volunteers, work with NGOs and other organizations to develop and train information management skills in human rights work
- Standardization in information management: including closing the information gap for the information-poor parts of AI, with minimum standards of IT capacity for all Sections; standards for hardware and software; standard systems for classifying, indexing, filing and storing documents in hard copy and electronic form
- Information sharing and access: including promotion of information resources as shared resources of the whole of AI; collaborative working through groupware etc. in key areas such as campaign planning; information dissemination systems to reflect user needs and capacities, giving control of quantity and flow to users; full implementation of archives policy throughout AI, with all parts being accountable for their archives management; systems for regular collection of standard information, including financial and development information, about the performance of AI
- Security of information: including guidelines on data protection; maintenance of confidentiality with appropriate systems; development of security classification for information; security of e-mail communication
- Resources for information management: including adequate human and financial resources for information management in international and Section budgets; inclusion of information management issues in all strategic and operational plans; decisions on IT investment in line with the information management strategy; development of income generation from AI's information resources
- Information overload and quality of information: including standards of accuracy, relevance, timeliness and clarity for all information managed by AI; monitoring users' needs to ensure they get what they need in terms of quality and quantity; use of images as valid and effective means of communicating information
- Technological innovation: including continuous research on the potential of IT for application in AI's work, exchange of experience, and adequate investment
- Communication of information: including e-mail throughout the organization to improve democratization and non-hierarchical communication;

Internet access as part of minimum IT capacity; systems for exchange of digital stills and moving images within AI.

Implementation

Responsibility is assigned for implementation at the international level, and in Sections, the International Secretariat and other relevant structures. The plan for implementation up to 2001 is on these lines:
- 1997 – International Council Meeting (ICM) to recommend on priorities for implementation and adopt strategy
- Sections, International Secretariat etc. to develop specific information management strategies in 1998
- Implementation will begin in 1998–99
- Interim report on implementation by Director of Information Resources in 1999
- Continued implementation 1999–2001
- Final implementation report to 2001 ICM for review and evaluation.

Implementation costs

Information management and IT will be a major investment in the period to 2001; the strategy aims to ensure that money is well spent. 'However, it is essential that financial provision is made at the international and Section level to support the strategy. The percentage of the international budget allocated directly to information resources in 1997–98 is 10 per cent; this level of investment will need to be maintained, and acts as a guide for Section budgets.'

Links between long-term objectives and information management

The strategy document includes a useful analysis of the information management implications of Amnesty International's long-term objectives; an example is reproduced as Figure C1.2, see page 194.

Acceptance of the strategy and start of implementation

The information management strategy was passed unanimously and without amendment at the International Council Meeting which took place in December 1997. The satisfaction of this outcome was somewhat clouded by the adverse effects of the strong pound, which places limitations on the resources which Amnesty International is able to devote to many initiatives. No extra funding could be voted for implementation of the strategy, nor for all but four of the key decisions taken by the Council (the information strategy came fifth in the voting, and this will be taken into consideration if the financial position improves). None the less, as most of the expenditure in the information management strategy was represented by the budgets of the Information Resources Program and the Information Technology Program, it is possible for most of the initiatives to go ahead, though at a slower pace or in a less ambitious way than originally intended.

AI long-term objectives	Specifics	Role for information management
1 Strengthening research and action	• To strengthen AI's research base ... • To mobilise people into action through the use of further development of existing techniques ... • In situations of human rights crises, to escalate efforts to stop human rights violations • To expand research and action capabilities on MEC and MSP.	• Ensure access to research information in all formats • Build databases to organise information • Improve speed of delivery of information to researchers • Get more information on MSP/MEC • Tap potential of IT for developing new action techniques • Exploit global electronic sources of information • Develop fast communication systems for crises, including satellite • Ensure access to real-time information in crises.
2 Mobilising people for action	• To develop the strategic role of all parts of AI • To expand the strengthen AI's capacity to influence and mobilise people ... • To use and further develop AI's expert knowledge and techniques to defend and protect victims ...	• Promote information sharing and improve access to key information resources • Build expertise in using electronic communications and IT as tools for action • Gather information on the 'State of the Movement' and communicate it for improved planning.

Fig C1.2   **Information management and Amnesty International's long-term objectives** (extract)

The view of those responsible for implementation is that the strategy represents a very good opportunity for the staff in both programmes to make a recognizable contribution to the organization, and offers 'a hook to hang projects etc. on'. Endorsement of the information management strategy by the International Council Meeting has improved the situation, since work related to an ICM decision has far better chances of being recognized and represented in the various strategic plans that are used to allocate funds. Morale among the staff concerned has benefited now that their work is firmly built into this process, and the profile of information has been raised by the importance accorded it by the Council.

Evaluation

The author of the draft strategy learned a good deal from the process. He decided to take his own line in developing it, so as to ensure that it was appropriate for the organization. From the experience, which confirmed that it was the right decision, he emphasizes three lessons:

1 Understand the organization structure and what it implies for policy and strategy development
2 Try to strike a balance between realism and ambition
3 Having something straightforward to present to people helps them to think about the subject in relation to their own experience and knowledge.

Having developed the strategy, its author had the opportunity of taking sabbatical leave and travelled abroad for a period. The follow-up was handled by an experienced information professional who came into Amnesty International on secondment. She found that the existence of a clearly written strategy and implementation plan made the handover a smooth one, and this is something worth noting, for it cannot always be guaranteed that the originator of a strategy will be there to oversee its implementation. Despite the resources problems described above, she takes a very positive view of the prospects and comments that staff in both the Information Resources and the Information Technology Programs see the strategy as a focus for the two programmes to work together, and as 'an arena to look to the future and plan the information environment we want to create'.

To set against these hopeful indicators there are some factors, mainly related to the organization's structure, which may make for difficulty in extending the information strategy outwards from the International Secretariat. Since decision making rests with the elected International Executive Committee, and the sections are essentially autonomous bodies, achieving any degree of standardization in how things are done represents something of of a challenge to the spreading of the strategy in the way it is intended to dvelop. Lack of any sanction for enforcing compliance certainly means that any policy has to show clear organizational benefits and be practical if it is to be adopted; on the other hand, this situation makes it difficult to take opportunities quickly, which in turn could lead to implementation by default of local policies on an *ad hoc* basis, and so to loss of the potential organization-wide benefits. There is also probably a good deal of educational work to be done on promoting understanding of the ideas of managing information, as opposed to managing the technology, given the long-standing tendency – which exists in many organizations – to see IT as the complete answer to all information needs, rather than as a part of the solution.

Seen from the outside, the situation is a mainly hopeful one. Other factors that should favour a good outcome include:

• Having a Director of Information Resources to implement development of the information management strategy
• The good relations prevailing between the Information Technology and Information Resources directors, and the support both received from their manager

- The wide scope of the information resources programme (bringing together information management strategies, information gathering, the library, documentation, audiovisual materials, copyright and archives)
- The open and non-hierarchical culture of Amnesty International
- The support received from similar organizations which were also interested in developing information strategies
- Adoption of the concept of a phased implementation/development spiral, with the scope that it offers for learning and for continuing monitoring and evaluation
- The insistence that the strategy should be an inclusive one, accessible to all parts of the AI movement, and excluding no part of the organization through barriers of technology or language
- The aim of spreading information management skills throughout the organization so that they become part of the equipment of those engaged in human rights work.

Australian Securities and Investments Commission[1]

Introduction

The Australian Securities and Investment Commission makes an interesting case study for several reasons: it is an information-intensive organization, making links between government, business and the public, to all of which it has obligations; it carries out multiple information transactions and uses information as the basis for action on many fronts. And during the period at which this book was being written it has travelled a significant way towards developing strategies for using knowledge and information. In this, it is part of a trend in Australian federal and state government – a number of departments are taking such initiatives as setting up units for coordinating the use of information (see Case study 6, the Information Planning Board, Queensland Government, page 266), and others are creating posts with the title of Information Manager, Information Director, or Chief Information Officer. And, as in the UK, the concept of knowledge management is emerging.

The Commission

The Australian Securities Commission was established as an independent government body in 1989, with the remit of administering the Commissions Law throughout Australia. The Commission is accountable to the Commonwealth Parliament; in each State and Territory Regional Commissioners manage its offices. Its aims are 'to protect the interests of companies and investors ... ensure fair play in business, prevent corporate crime, protect investors and help Australia's business reputation abroad' (ASC, 1997a). It defines its task as being to:

- Maintain and improve the performance of companies and the securities and futures markets, in the interests of commercial certainty, reducing business costs and the efficiency and development of the economy
- Maintain investor confidence in the securities and futures markets by ensuring adequate investor protection
- Achieve uniformity in the way we perform our functions and exercise our powers
- Administer laws effectively but with a minimum of procedural requirements
- Process and store the documents and information people give us efficiently and quickly
- Ensure that those documents and information are available to the public as soon as possible
- Take whatever action is necessary to enforce the law.

---

[1] Originally the Australian Securities Commission; the name changed in 1998 when the Commission took on some new roles.

The Commission investigates complaints, prepares criminal cases for the Commonwealth Director of Public Prosecutions to conduct, and takes cases before civil courts or administrative hearings. It sets standards for investment advice, managed investments, prospectuses, takeover documents and financial reporting, and seeks to contribute to law reform. It receives, processes and makes available to the public information about Australia's one million companies, and it uses information technology to support it in the task.

The Commission's *Annual Report* for 1996/97 records successful action in these areas: a larger than ever number of corporate criminals gaoled (23 in all, and their offences, are listed in the *AR*); over A$100 million recovered in civil actions for investors; a pilot project – based on research which showed investors had difficulty in locating and understanding the information they wanted in prospectuses – to allow investment managers to use a shorter prospectus answering key questions; and policy statements on a range of issues including electronic prospectuses.

Company information work accounts for about 20 per cent of ASIC's running costs and employs 280 full-time staff (21 per cent of the total). The company database which it maintains is open to the public, and 2.37 million company searches were carried out in 1996/97, 84 per cent of them on-line. In the same year, full company searches on the Internet were introduced (over 98 000 company searches in the first year); ASIC's company names index is also on the Internet, as are its draft policy statements, which are available for public comment. The Information Division, responsible for the public databases, is quality certified to ISO 9001 standard. By the end of the 1996/97 year 45 per cent of companies were using the Commission's electronic lodgement service to submit their annual returns. The first stage of a data warehouse has also been developed, which will allow information and intelligence staff to analyse company data for intelligence and surveillance purposes in a way not previously possible. Information technology to support immediate national communication, information sharing and workflow management is identified as critical to ASIC's effectiveness.

Communication is an essential element in the Commission's work; it consults with Members of Parliament, local business communities, national and industry associations and its own staff, and supplies information needed by investors, company directors, professional advisers, accountants and the media. This aspect of its work accounts for 2 per cent of its running costs. Members of the public may apply for copies of ASIC documents under the Freedom of Information Act 1982; categories covered include documents relating to meetings of the ASIC and its meetings with government, to Parliamentary committees and questions, and to applications from business, as well as general correspondence with members of the public. In 1996 the Commission opened its electronic Infoline service, which received about 70 000 calls.

Organizational structure

The structure of the Commission is shown in Figure C2.1 on page 200.

Moves towards an information strategy

In 1996, a proposal to establish an ASC strategic information plan was put forward and circulated within the organization. The original initiative which resulted in this proposal came from the National Coordinator for Information and Intelligence (a member of management with Senior Executive Service status); he employed an Information Manager, and they worked to 'push the Strategic Information Plan along and make it happen'. (Ultimately the Information Manager became responsible to the National Director Executive who is also the sponsor of the project.)

On the premise that the Commission is a knowledge-based organization, the proposal recommended managing its information resources according to a nationally coordinated information strategy covering a period of two to five years, within a policy framework in terms of objectives, targets and actions to achieve them. The plan would identify and clarify the operational information requirements of its programmes and help to integrate the corporate IT Strategic plan with them. Development and implementation of the plan would use a 'multiple methodology' in eight stages (see below), involving an information audit, analysis of information crucial to programme success, and development of information plans for each programme, the process to be fitted into the programme planning cycle.

Implementation of the strategy would be the responsibility of an information management specialist based in the Office of the Chairman, working alongside Information and Intelligence Programme staff in regions and the Information Technology Services Branch; part of the role of the job holder would be to build the information management skills of internal information service providers, to allow them to take on an information consultancy role for the programmes. The proposal identified the risks to be guarded against if its recommendations were adopted: conflicting demands on resources in the information intelligence programme would need to be managed carefully, as would increased expectation and demand for information from within the organization.

Part of the background to this proposal came from a study carried out two years earlier, which looked at the need for expertise and knowledge within ASC; this recognized it as an information-based organization, relying on the knowledge of specialists who 'direct and discipline their own performance through organised feedback from colleagues and clients', and by implication depending also on continuous learning in order to maintain its expertise. The capacity to learn depends not only on having a constant input and flow of appropriate information, but also on being able to manage it so that those who need it can readily get access to everything that is relevant to their work needs and easily transform it into usable knowledge – 'information optimization', as the information strategy proposal puts it, to give managers 'value-added information services: screening, summarising, synthesising, highlighting, and presenting information in [a] useful and timely manner'.

At present, as the proposal pointed out, the Commission is far from attaining this level of use of information:

Commission

Office of the Chairman
[Policy and national management]

    National Director Enforcement
    National Director Regulation
    National Director Executive
    Regulatory Policy Branch
    International Branch

Regional Offices
[Operational staff]

    Compliance Programs
    Corporate Investigations
    Small Business
    Complaints Assessment

Information Program

    Managing ASIC
    database
    Business services
    to companies
    and public

Infrastructure
[Support services, distributed throughout
all offices]

    Human Resources
    Finance, Property and Office Services
    Learning and Development
    Information Specialist:
        Information Resource Centres [including library]
        Information Management Centres
        Information Technology and Services Branch
        National Intelligence and Analytical Services
    Communications and Publishing [including Infoline]

Fig C2.1   **Organization chart**

The ASC collects vast amounts of information, either lodged with the ASC or generated internally. Despite the massive collection process we are frequently unable to describe even basic characteristics of our operating environment. For example:

– What is the demographic spread of our licensees?
– What is the primary occupation/activity of proper authority holders?
– How many companies fall into the new categorization to be introduced by the Corporate Law simplification process?
– How many complaints match the characteristics of a 'phoenix'[2] situation?

The proposal draws on a theoretical background that covers concepts of information management, information resource management, information auditing, and 'information resource entities' (Burk and Horton, 1988). It makes a clear distinction between information systems (the 'ends' for which the technology should be used), IT (the means and methods by which it is used), and information management (the rationale for using information, the people responsible, the policy directions), while arguing that they should be managed in an integrated manner, 'with clear correlation between Information Systems Strategy, the Corporate IT Strategic Plan and the Strategic Information Plan'. The capacity of the Commission to implement strategic information planning is seen as being influenced by three factors:

1 The organization's structure, equipment and systems
2 Its competencies and experience
3 Its culture.

(See Figure C2.2 on page 202)

Proposed methodology

The proposal recommended a combination of top-down (linking corporate strategy to essential information needs by critical success factors), bottom-up (mapping and analysing information resource entities by means of information auditing and structured interviews), and inside-out approaches (using focus groups to identify the opportunities afforded by IT, on similar lines to those for example described by Mumford, 1986), on the reasonable grounds that no single approach could cover all the essential aspects involved.

An eight-step process towards the development of a Strategic Information Plan was envisaged:

---

[2] The name given to unscrupulous companies which are set up for the purpose of accumulating assets on credit, then close down, and then open up as another company with the assets of the previous company.

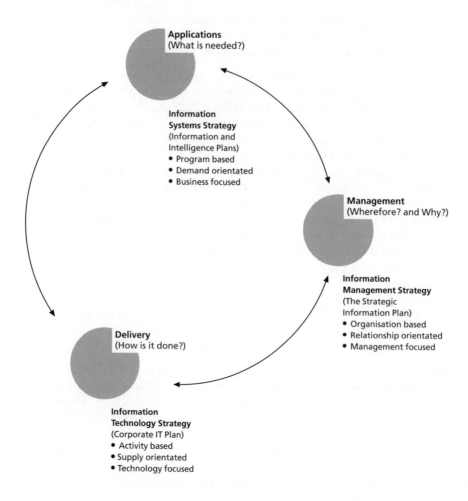

1 Appointment of an Information Manager[3], whose first task would be an 'internal literature review' to produce a first analysis of the ASC's information processes.
2 Setting up an Information and Intelligence evaluation group, whose membership would include librarians, intelligence staff and IT/IS staff, which would review information processes, flows, content and media within and between programmes.
3 Information audit of operational programmes (described in communications when the process actually started as 'Information Discovery' because this was seen as being 'a more friendly term than Audit' – a hint worth noting) in order to:
   • Make an inventory of information resources
   • Investigate costs associated with information processes
   • Gauge the importance of information to the ASC's programmes
   • Gauge whether ASC is a suitable case for information resource management.
4 Skills transfer – educating local information and intelligence staff in the principles of knowledge and information management.
5 Identifying, in conjunction with the information audit, the environmental information needs of ASC programmes, via focus groups, to discuss these questions:
   • What do I need to know? (information needed to achieve objectives, gaps in existing information, information needed for planning, external strategic information trends)
   • Where do I get the knowledge?
   • How will I make use of the knowledge now and in the future?
6 Preparation of a one- to three-year information management plan, identifying information needs and gaps, short- and long-term IT development needs, and information research directions
7 Implementation of knowledge management strategies within programmes
8 Re-evaluation of programmes' information needs (back to step 5).

Human resources implications

Besides the creation of the new Information Manager role, the proposal aimed to 'develop the historical role of libraries within a Government organisation', providing 'a charter for librarians to participate to a greater level in operational, management and research functions throughout the organisation'. (The

[3] Role:
• Coordinating the interests and activities of information users, processors and suppliers, and the means of managing information
• Ensuring that everyone receives and provides the information that best meets the needs of the ASC and that the way it is done matches the corporate culture
• Ensuring that information of all kinds flows within the ASC to all who need it in order to meet their work objectives
• Exploiting existing information stocks to the full, to meet the ASC's needs for decision making and problem solving
• Anticipating new information needs, and 'scanning the horizon' for new information in the internal or external environment which can offer new opportunities.

Commission has taken some useful steps in this direction recently, with the creation of Information Resource Centres in each state regional office and in the Office of the Chairman, the Internet Advisory Group, and the participation of librarians in the focus groups.) The proposal also envisages the development of the Regional Intelligence and Analysis Service towards undertaking, in collaboration with library staff, short-term research or analytical projects on information. The closer alignment of library and intelligence roles is seen as likely to create job enrichment. A new look at the divisions between information specialists as currently defined is contemplated; in the meantime, closer collaboration is envisaged.

Action on the proposal – first stages

The Operational Coordination Group agreed to the proposed process early in 1997 and work began on the stages set out above (see page 203). The results and observations on them are reported in the document which presented the Strategic Information Plan for approval at the end of that year (ASC, 1997b).

Information Manager

This appointment was made from inside; the person appointed was working on a special project developing performance management standards and was responsible for records management. He had previously worked for the New South Wales State Government as an IT manager, and had experience of private consultancy work as well.

Information and intelligence evaluation group

The group consisted of representatives of Information Specialist groups: Information Technology Services Branch; National Intelligence and Analytical Service; Information Resource Centre; and Information Management Centre. Meetings of the group were held at the end of each phase to review progress, disseminate non-strategic problems for solution, and review future plans.

Information audit

The audit process was entitled 'information discovery'. It aimed for an ambitious set of benefits, not all of which proved immediately achievable:
1 A credible estimate of information costs
2 A complete inventory of present information resources
3 Identification of where there is need or opportunity to improve information resources to help operational effectiveness
4 An on-line information resource directory
5 Measurement of the utility and value of information services within programmes
6 Measurement of the contribution of information services to attainment of organizational objectives.

A decision was taken at the start that the largest regional office (Sydney, New South Wales) would be the main project site, with sample testing of other regions. Structured interviews were held with a cross-section of 80 operational staff, 50 of them from the New South Wales regional office (the representation of various functions in the sample was proportional to the total percentages employed in them). Interviews were also held with National Directors, and a sample of the Regional executive, as well as with information experts from several external professional service organizations and government departments.

The interviewing was shared among a number of Information Specialists: the interviews were based on a methodology, and required direct input during the interview into a PC database. Training consisted of accompanying and observing an experienced interviewer. The interviews were designed to determine the types of information resources which people were using, the importance of those resources to the purposes for which they were used, and their effectiveness (in terms of completeness, accuracy, ease of use, timeliness, availability and accessibility – assessed on a five-point scale). Following Burk and Horton (1988), the interviewers invited respondents to rate the importance of the information resource entities they mentioned to the achievement of key business objectives, and to rate the resources under five categories relating to their effectiveness in achieving the business objectives, for example functionality and accuracy. They were also asked to mention additional, at present unmet, information needs.

A productive feature of this phase was the attempt to resolve problems with existing information resources as they were identified, rather than leaving them to accumulate for future attention. Concerns expressed during the interviews were progressively passed on to appropriate Information Specialists (in the National Intelligence and Analytical Service, IT and Services Branch, Informaation Resource Centre and Information Management Centre) for solutions. Of the many small problems raised, those with potential as short-term winners were personally followed up; others were referred to the internal service provider and the person who had raised them was informed that this had been done. The database being used made it possible to automate much of the communication.

Skills transfer

While there has not been a full skills transfer, there is certainly much better understanding and appreciation of the process, good collaboration, and involvement at specific points (for example business planning and actioning strategies – and participation in the review of the Strategic Information Plan in two years' time).

Environmental information needs

Half-day focus group sessions were held with several regional programme teams and two national programme teams (Managed and Personal Investment, and Small Business); here the aim was to extract and record tacit knowledge by leading the participants through an exercise aimed at gaining insight into the relationships between the environment in which the Commission operates and its business objectives. This, in turn, would lead to the identification of the types of information needed to support the strategic needs of the programmes concerned. These sessions involved conducting an environmental scan, building upon identified external trends most likely to impact the programmes within the next two to three years. Scenario-generation techniques were then used to build awareness of the potential threats to programme objectives and understand the types of information needed to support the strategic needs of the programmes concerned. The use of 'Influence Diagrams' provided a mechanism to capture the tacit knowledge and record the information needs.

Output from the information-gathering stages

The findings are in the form of two main analyses: a SWOT (Strengths, Weaknesses, Opportunities, Threats) analysis; and an analysis of influences and trends in the Commission's organizational and environmental context.

Strengths

Interviews revealed that the respondents rated the majority of the information resources available to them as being either an important or an essential support in achieving programme objectives, and that the major corporate systems which embody the information are heavily used. The systems were also found to be reliable and accessible. The other strength found was the effectiveness of the system that has been developed for reporting how efficient programmes are in achieving their target outcomes.

Weaknesses

The list here is a longer one; some of the key points are:
* A relatively low rating for the functionality of systems, in terms of difficulties in retrieval, and storage of relevant data in a number of different sources
* Lack of help in finding the right people to contact for help about information resources (over 350 'latent' requests of this kind were found)
* A low rating for data quality in the main corporate database systems
* A cultural issue of staff being 'too busy' to share information with their colleagues
* Most staff were very critical of how difficult it was to find files – although they did not accept personal responsibility for keeping record-tracking systems up to date. While they looked on records management as an administrative burden from a personal point of view, 94 per cent of them nevertheless regarded it as an important requirement
* There is no longer a formal national network to coordinate information-related projects – a consequence of the withdrawal of a senior executive position responsible for this form of coordination (the National Coordin-

ator for Information and Intelligence, who was responsible for the whole initiative)

- Most respondents wanted a more effective means of making integrated searches across a range of systems; while over 80 per cent rated the existing 'umbrella' system as very important, only just over 54 per cent found it very easy to use
- Although cost-effectiveness was a key proposed benefit of the information audit, it proved impossible to evaluate the cost-effectiveness of information resources, because of inadequate data on system use and costing, and lack of appropriate methods for establishing reliable costs and values
- Although there is an effective system for monitoring how the main internal processes of the Commission meet key performance standards, the same cannot be said of the means for monitoring the external environment for factors with an impact on programme direction
- Greater budgetary independence, outsourcing of IT support, the move to PCs and client server applications, and more IT knowledge within teams, all mean that the Commission has to find a balance between the need for centralized control against that for distributed information
- At the same time a more fluid organizational structure brings the danger of further fragmentation of the information management process, while increasing turnover of highly qualified technical staff will make it essential to 'capture and optimise knowledge resources'.

Opportunities

Potential for significant opportunities exists in:
- Using and managing the knowledge embodied in the Commission's staff to create new information and knowledge and capitalize on the results
- Integrated management of all information resources (including those contained in memoranda, e-mails, reports and correspondence) to allow finding everything relevant to a given issue regardless of format or location – a subject in which the Office of Government Information Technology is currently taking a keen interest
- Electronic management of the flow of information through business activity processes, using 'forms based workflow'
- Use of the Internet to promote both business transactions and informal interchanges with the regulatory organizations of other countries
- Collaboration in the development of information management with other Australian government agencies.

Threats

The greatest threat seen in the current situation is from the paralysing effect of perceived information overload; it needs to be countered by information management strategies which focus on:
- Better training for people in identifying the information essential to their own purposes

- Pre-analysis so that staff receive only the information which they need for effective work
- Rationalization and integration of available information resources and information content.

The environmental and internal contexts

The analysis suggests that the Commission has to respond to the implications of both domestic administrative changes, and world-wide changes in ideas. Closest at hand are the changes in its role during 1998 following the recommendations of the Financial Systems Inquiry (the Wallis Report). The Commission will now be responsible for the disclosure aspects of investments, licensing of financial intermediaries, and coordinating consumer protection in the financial sector.

It will also have to work towards fulfilling the 'whole-of-government access policy' contained in the Commonwealth Government Information Management Steering Committee's vision for government information:
- Using information fully as a national strategic asset for government, business and the community
- Managing information for better policy development and continuous improvement of services
- Sharing information easily across agency boundaries
- Improving information flows to promote collaboration across public service and with other levels of government
- Protecting personal privacy and public interest.

At the conceptual level, the Strategic Information Plan document fixes on the global trend to the idea of knowledge management. It gives a perceptive account which draws on the thinking of such authors as Nonaka and Takeuchi (1995), defining knowledge management as 'the discipline of systematically turning individual experiences relating to decision making and problem solving (tacit) and organisational recorded information (explicit) into improved productivity and decision making'. The report emphasizes the need to integrate the knowledge of individuals into 'corporate memory' so as to minimize the risk of knowledge loss as people move on, and points out the requirement for systems designed to support the process of conversion and access to corporate memory (see Figure C2.3 on page 209).

So far as the internal organizational context is concerned, the Commission's business planning, like that of many public organizations at the present time (see the British Library case study, page 213), is driven by four key factors:
1 Cost cutting, with emphasis on support and administrative overheads
2 Concentrating core activity on 'what makes the most difference'
3 Focusing support effort on what makes the core business most effective
4 Ensuring that the Commission retains its ability to respond to an uncertain environment while coping with these organizational changes.

Success depends strongly on maintaining organizational knowledge through well-managed information resources, in the context of a less hierarchical and more flexible organization.

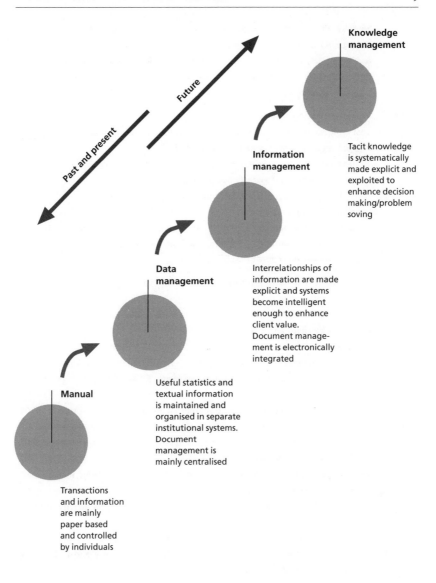

Fig C2.3   Information transition

A strategic information management plan

On the basis of the information-gathering and analytical work described above, a plan for strategic management of information was accepted for implementation at the end of 1997. Its objectives are to:

- Provide a framework to assist corporate management to monitor and make cost effective decisions on information resources
- Develop an effective linkage between information and business planning to assist programs to articulate and prioritise core business needs and be responsive to an uncertain environment

– Improve the quality of operational advice/decisions and overall productivity through better utilisation of knowledge and information resources
– Assess the impact of trends, both those within information management and those that affect the regulation of the financial services environment, on the provision of information resources.

The benefits are identified in these terms:

– Cost effective framework based on sound management practices
– Integration of all information based activities
– To have information to make its full contribution to ASC based on clear objectives and priorities and therefore be more effective
– Constant monitoring will assist rapid identification of environmental change enabling a flexible response
– Cooperation amongst those responsible for managing information within the ASC is promoted, limiting the 'information is power' principle
– Sound decisions on IT and other investment for information based activities.

A set of 'Information Management Principles' provides the policy framework for the strategy:

1 The provision of information resources must be linked to the annual business planning objectives and priorities.
2 Information is a corporate resource with no personal ownership.
3 Information management will comply with relevant legal requirements.
4 Information management does not discriminate between electronic or physical format.
5 We will support Commonwealth government information management principles and strategies, including the whole-of-government access policy.
6 We will apply the same management practices as we do to other strategic disciplines, e.g. human resources, finance, assets.
7 We must continually explore opportunities to leverage knowledge management and information management.
8 We are committed to nationally share, within the ASC, critical activity information.
9 We are committed to developing information management best practices.
10 We recognise information management as a key competency and will provide supportive tools and training.

Seven strategies

The Plan sets out seven strategies for implementation, and identifies the people with primary responsibilities for each, and the action they need to take in developing and implementing the strategies. A wide range of people from different functions is involved, and each strategy brings together Information Specialists, information systems/IT services staff, and stakeholders in the area concerned. The Information Manager is involved in all strategy development, and has the role of overseeing the process, in some cases directly, and in others in a monitoring capacity.

1 Build an effective national information management framework of policy, planning, standards, and collaboration.

2 Systematically identify and articulate core business information needs.

3 Improve business information processes and corporate data quality.

4 Develop an integrated information management structure for both electronic and physical documents and records.

5 Research and develop expertise to apply knowledge management tools and techniques.

6 Ensure that operational staff are able to make effective use of information resources.

7 Leverage use of the Internet.

Re-evaluation of programmes

Stage 8 of the process as originally proposed will mean revisiting national programmes during the business planning process each year (seen as 'an imperative') and then again in two years' time in connection with the new Strategic Information Plan.

Evaluation

The points to be made in this evaluation are all positive ones – with one exception, which had better be mentioned first: the withdrawal of a senior executive post with responsibility for coordinating intelligence and information throughout the organization (see the British Library case study, page 213, where a senior manager volunteered the suggestion that the Library probably needed such a post).

In other respects, this case study provides a very useful model, by virtue of a number of features:

- The orientation of the organization towards public service, with emphasis on accountability and open access to information for citizens
- The use of the Internet to provide public access to the company database
- The fact that a significant proportion of the Commission's running costs is spent on communication
- The organizational structure which has a grouping of information specialists that brings together Information Resource centres (including the library), Information Management Centres (including records management), IT and Services staff, and National Intelligence and Analytical Services.
- Initiatives for information strategy development were taken from a high level in the Commission's management
- The Information Manager reports to National Director level
- The 'quick wins' gained by picking up problems and dealing with them during the information audit, and letting people know about it
- Calling the audit 'information discovery' – which may well have helped to get away from the uncomfortable associations of being called to account before a hearing which has power to condemn
- The methodology adopted, which combined top-down, bottom-up and inside-out

- The use of a combination of personal interaction and appropriate technology in gathering information, which contributed towards economy of effort in analysing findings and preparing reports
- A sound analysis of the audit findings
- The interdisciplinary composition of the group undertaking development of the strategy
- A manageable set of information strategies
- Sensible timescales for carrying through the plan, and for implementing the information strategy
- The emphasis placed on monitoring and evaluation loops
- A sophisticated appreciation of what knowledge management means
- The adoption of the aim of building information management skills as part of jobs throughout the organization
- The emphasis placed on developing the role of libraries, with closer collaboration between staff in librarian and intelligence roles.

Since the completion of this case study, there have been further positive developments. National programmes are being established to develop information collection plans as part of normal business planning. In business planning reviews, Information Specialists will be called on to account for implementation of the Strategic Information Plan. The Information Manager is included as a key stakeholder on all information projects, a key stakeholder group of senior executives has been set up to take information planning forward, and the Deputy Chairman has taken on sponsorship. The level of interest in the Strategic Information Plan has been such that a page for information planning and management has been created on the Commission's intranet, and the Plan is being updated. And finally, there is a proposal for a 'Knowledge Management Collaborative Group' (representation including IT, Library, Intelligence, Records Management and Learning and Development) to explore trends and prepare recommendations.

References

AUSTRALIAN SECURITIES COMMISSION (1997a), *Annual Report 1996/97*, Sydney: ASC

AUSTRALIAN SECURITIES COMMISSION (1997b), *Strategic Information Plan*, Sydney: ASC

BURK, C. F., Jr and HORTON, F. W., Jr (1988), *Infomap: A complete guide to discovering corporate information resources*, Englewood Cliffs, NJ: Prentice Hall

MUMFORD, E. (1986), 'From bank teller to office worker: in pursuit of systems designed for people in practice and research', *International Journal of Information Management*, 6, 59–73

NONAKA, I. and TAKEUCHI, H. (1995), *The knowledge-creating Company; how Japanese companies create the dynamics of information*, New York: Oxford University Press

The British Library

Introduction

The whole business of the British Library can fairly be described as knowledge and information. As a national library, it exists to maintain and give access to a vast external store of human knowledge and ideas, embodied in print and to a growing extent in electronic form. That in turn requires it to manage information on a large scale: information about its activities and processes, its finances, its relations with users, its transactions with commercial partners and suppliers, its dealings with government over funding and policy; and about the economic, social and cultural environment in which it operates, nationally and internationally. So perhaps it is not overstating matters to suggest that its corporate strategy is in essence a knowledge and information strategy; and indeed senior managers of the Library interviewed in the course of this case study were prepared to entertain the suggestion.

That is one reason why a return to an institution which was the subject of a major case study in the first edition of this book is worthwhile. The others are that there have been major changes – some foreshadowed in that first study (carried out in 1989), and some unexpected – which exemplify the kind of events and pressures with which organizational information strategies have to deal, and that the British Library has dealt with them successfully, has overcome potential disasters from events outside its control (especially in matter of its new building at St Pancras), and has taken its own change initiatives.

This study concentrates on a number of concerns which are critical for the Library's information strategy:

1 Its relations with: sources of funding; users (on-site and remote); the research community in the library and information field; other institutions; customers and suppliers
2 Using and developing human resources to manage and create knowledge
3 Managing projects
4 Monitoring and evaluating its initiatives
5 Information technology and systems
6 Financial resources and management information
7 Looking ahead and thinking strategically about the future.

First, however, we need some context: the Library's historical background, major changes over the past decade, the mission and objectives which form the framework for strategy development and implementation, and the current organizational structure designed to help it achieve its objectives.

History

The history of the Library is outlined in Figure C3.1 (see page 215).

Major developments since 1990

When the original case study was in progress, the move to the new building at St Pancras was absorbing a great deal of planning, but it was still some distance away in time. Since then year by year it has moved inexorably closer to the centre of attention, until it became a magnet for resources and energies, to an extent that exceeded anticipation because of significant technical difficulties and slippage in the construction programme beyond the control of the Library. This culminated in the handover of the building for occupation more than six months later than the rescheduled programme promised, and a successful but exhausting and costly race against time to open the first reading room to schedule.

A decline in government Grant-in-Aid was causing anxiety in the Library at the time of the first case study, but it was small compared with the drastic cuts made since (see below, page 221), which have been compounded by the necessity of diverting money needed to maintain the Library's core operations to meet fully the costs associated with the move to St Pancras. At the same time, the government's pressure over the period on public bodies to help reduce public expenditure by seeking private finance has led the Library into the still fairly uncharted territory of Public Finance Initiatives (see below, page 222).

Not all changes and developments have been imposed from without; the Library has of its own decision moved away from an internally focused task orientation, and has turned outwards towards service to its users. It has also taken much further the attempts it was making in the late 1980s to move from the federal culture which was a legacy of its origins to a corporate culture. Since 1995, it has been bringing about a major change in organizational structure on functional lines, designed to help it to operate as a corporate entity. Initiatives in four key performance areas in 1994 (access, user satisfaction, collections development and collection management) formed the foundation for change in these directions.

The original case study reported on an automation strategy of 1988; that has formed the foundation for further developments, many foreshadowed, but some unforeseen – like the World Wide Web, and the Library's Portico site which offers, among other things, access to the catalogue through an OPAC. Today, while the emphasis is still on integrated access to records of the Library's total holdings, the Digital Library project is pointing ahead to access to the materials themselves (see page 225).

A final major change has been in the direction of a national information strategy – something hitherto conspicuous by its absence in the UK. In 1995 the Department of National Heritage established the Library and Information Commission, whose remit includes the development of a national strategy for information. The British Library has been closely involved in this process (see page 224).

Events

1753	The British Museum Act charged the British Museum to care for books, manuscripts and papers acquired by the State and to make them available for 'publick use to all Posterity'.
1828	The King's Library was built to house George III's personal collection, which he had given to the Museum.
1857	The great domed Reading Room opened.
1931	The National Central Library (formerly the Central Library for Students) was given a Royal Charter as the official clearing house for inter-library lending in the UK.
1932	The British Museum Newspaper Library was built at Colindale.
1949	The Council for the British National Bibliography Limited was set up as a non-profit consortium to provide bibliographic services to libraries.
1962	The National Lending Library for Science and Technology was set up at Boston Spa in Yorkshire, by the Department of Scientific and Industrial Research (transferred in1965 to the Department of Education and Science).
1965	The Office for Scientific and Technical Information was set up by the Department of Scientific and Industrial Research to sponsor and coordinate research in librarianship and information science.
1966	The Museum was entrusted with the National Reference Library of Science and Invention embodying the collections of the former Patent Office Library (re-named the Science Reference Library in 1973).
1972	The British Library Act brought together, under the British Library Board: • The library departments of the British Museum • The National Central Library* • The National Lending Library for Science and Technology* • The National Reference Library of Science and Invention • The Office for Scientific and Technical Information† • The Council for the British National Bibliography Limited
1976	A site at St Pancras was bought by the government for a new building for the British Library.
1980	The first stage of construction was approved by the government.
1983	The Library accepted responsibility for the India Office Library and Records, and the National Sound Archive (formerly the British Institute of Recorded Sound).
1984	Main building work began.
1988	The main shell of the Phase I building was completed.
1997 July	Building handed over.
1997 Nov 24	First reading room opened.

* Brought together under the Act to form the Library's Lending Division

† Not incorporated in the Act itself; incorporated in 1973 as the R&D Dept of the Library under the terms of a clause of the Act

Fig C3.1   **Major milestones in the history of the British Library**

Mission and objectives

The Library defines its mission in these terms (1998 mission statement):

> To foster the pursuit of knowledge by providing access to the Library's holdings and to information on the resources of other libraries for the benefit of scholarship, research and innovation.

Its strategic objectives for the period 1994–2000, are set out in its corporate plan (British Library 1997), in these terms:

> By the year 2000:
>
> – The British Library will operate as a single library from its two principal sites. Whether in the reading rooms or at remote locations, users will have the same access to the collection via automated catalogues.
> – It will be a major centre for the storage of, and access to, digital texts required for research.
> – It will achieve the funding necessary to allow it to restore budgets for its core programmes in acquisitions, preservation and research to levels appropriate to its standing as a national library.
> – It will maximise use of its reading rooms by providing ready access and prompt and convenient services. Readers in the reading rooms will be able to consult items in the collections, wherever they are housed.
> – It will significantly expand remote document supply both in the UK and overseas. It will seek to avoid the need for users to visit the reading rooms when their requirements can best be met by remote supply.
> – It will make remote document supply as fast and cheap as possible by exploiting digital storage and electronic transmission.

Organizational structure

The appointment of a new Chief Executive and the publication of new strategic objectives in 1993 marked a major shift towards the idea of a single collection, a single approach and a single form of access, together with a sense of the need to act more corporately. The first phase of a more functionally based structure was accomplished in 1995, to be completed with the full occupation of the St Pancras building. It represents the next phase of a move to a corporate Library structure which should promote a more homogeneous culture, and be user- and activity-oriented, appropriate to operations after the move, and flexible in response to future needs.

Developments which the structural change seeks to bring about include:

* Integrated presentation for users at St Pancras of reference, information and reading room services, and book delivery
* Integrating collection management activities
* Bringing research and innovation into the core of the Library's activities
* Strengthening corporate planning, and budgetary and performance monitoring
* Strengthening the structure in Finance and Personnel.

Financial constraints led to a decision to concentrate reductions on posts in middle and senior management grades in order to protect as much as possible

1994–1995

Income/expenditure (£'000)	
Income:	£
Grant-in-aid	83 324
Trading	25 317
Donations	2 640
Total Income	**116 605**
Expenditure:	
Staff costs	51 811
Other operating charges	45 761
Acquisitions	14 035
Total Expenditure	**116 258**

Service	No.
Reader visits	475 826
Items consulted in the reading rooms	5 401 705
Requests for information	666 107
Remote document supply (requests satisfied)	4 450 375
Research grants awarded	84

Holdings	No.
London reference material, includes:	
Monograph and serial volumes	12 169 000
Newspapers (volumes)	643 000
MSS (single & volumes)	293 000
Cartographic items	2 286 000
Music scores	1 429 000
Prints & drawings	22 000
Photographs	204 000
Patent specifications	40 585 000

Boston Spa document supply material, includes:	No.
Monographs	3 074 000
Serial titles	260 000
Reports in microform	4 100 000

Cataloguing	No.
Catalogue records created	843 942

Miles of shelving occupied		
London reference material	258	miles
Boston Spa document supply	95.2	miles

Fig C3.2   **Facts and figures: 1996–97 figures from Twenty-Fourth Annual Report**

staff levels in lower grades. The percentage of the total staff in the middle and senior bands will fall from 4.2 to 2.77 per cent by 1998/99, while allowing for investing senior staff time in new activities critical to the Library's future.

When the final phase of the new structure is accomplished, upon full occupation of St Pancras, the number of directorates will have been reduced from 14 to 9: Public Affairs; Planning and Resources; Collection Management; St Pancras Occupation and Estates; Information Systems; Research and Innovation Centre; Bibliographic Services and Document Supply; Reader Services (including the Science Reference and Information Service) and Collections Development; Special Collections (see the organization chart of Figure C3.3 on page 219).

Observations from people interviewed on the effect of the new structure suggest that it is succeeding in its aims. It is said that the distinction between Bibliographic Services and Document Supply is becoming less significant from the readers' point of view, and that the new structure supports reading room, outward-oriented and remote activities, and benefits marketing.

The collections: development and management

Both collection development and collection management were the subject of key initiatives, and each is represented by a directorate in the new structure.

Collection development

The remit of the collection development initiative was to:

- Examine the effects of existing acquisition and retention policies, and evaluate the extent of actual knowledge of the collection in relation to the information needed for effective co-operation on collection development.
- Consider the future characteristics of the Library's collections, by identifying trends in research, monitoring publishing trends, and assessing the impact of developments in technology.

The findings contributed to change in the management of collection development; it is now on a corporate basis with development policy, budget planning and monitoring spanning the whole of the collections rather than being carried out on individual collections. The view of those involved is that structural changes make the Library better able to take into account everything related to given issues – with opportunities to work across directorate boundaries as necessary, in particular between collection development and collection management. The forums provided for people to work across functional lines on an equal footing are said to be working well, as the Library becomes 'good at combining hierarchical and cross-hierarchical working'.

Processing

The collection management initiative (covering the range of processes from procurement and acquisition, through record creation and cataloguing, to preservation and retention) had as its aim to recommend corporate policies

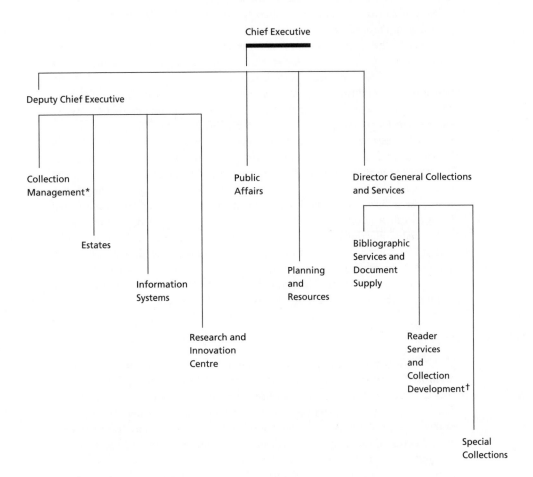

Chief Executive

Deputy Chief Executive

Collection
Management*

Estates

Information
Systems

Research and
Innovation
Centre

Public
Affairs

Planning
and
Resources

Director General Collections
and Services

Bibliographic
Services and
Document
Supply

Reader
Services
and
Collection
Development†

Special
Collections

* Combining in 1999/00 the current directorates
  of Acquisitions Processing and Cataloguing and
  Collections and Preservation.

† Incorporating in 1999/00 the current Science
  Reference and Information Service directorate
  (SRIS). Unil it moves to St Pancras, SRIS continues
  to operate separately.

Fig C3.3 **Organization chart**

and procedures for cost-effective management of the collection, and to develop performance measures which could be incorporated in the Library's planning and reporting.

Here too, the results led to moves towards integration; the first phase of the Library Processing Integration Programme has resulted in the transfer from London to Boston Spa of 23 posts involved with the acquisition, cataloguing and storage of mainstream material acquired by the Library. This programme can be viewed as an extension of the relocation programme carried out in the early 1990s when 250 posts were transferred northward. The purpose of the Library Processing Integration Programme, which is now embarking on phase 2, was to save on accommodation costs, to improve the speed with which items reach the shelf, and to achieve efficiencies. As a measure of this, 10 posts were deleted. Phase 2 of the Programme, which is under way, is looking at the scope for integration of the processing of more specialized material, where there is still a good deal of work carried out by service directorates such as Special Collections. There were also human resources and culture problems to be solved; holders of jobs were often unhappy with changes in job content, even when these involved getting rid of mundane tasks and offered in exchange the opportunity for exploiting the collections more fully, and of using their own knowledge more intensively and extensively.

Access

The terms of reference of the access initiative were to put forward a programme for improving access, with recommendations for options and resource requirements, and to identify management issues which might be acting as a barrier to progress. Their scope embraced further development of the concept of access to all collections regardless of location as if they were a single collection, catalogue provision, information services to users, ordering and delivery systems, collection policies, provision of surrogates, user demands, user registration, relations with other collections, and public access. While this has led to some advances, it is recognized that there is still a long way to go, as progress is constrained by severe limitations on the information systems budget. However, the principles are being applied in the areas where development is still pressing forward.

The access initiative was followed up by the Initiatives for Access programme, which grew out of and was linked with the four key initiatives, run by the Information Systems Directorate. The programme used digital techniques to create products in order to show and sell the idea of digital access. It comprised 15 projects, put forward by a group of directors, for example the electronic Beowulf project, an image-viewing system, on-desk staff Internet access, and the Library's Web site. The programme, which took about 10 per cent of the systems budget over a two-and-a-half-year period, generated great enthusiasm and proved very successful, both as a demonstration to the outside world and as a means of building confidence inside – and there were no expensive failures.

Another access project, OPAC 2000, for which funding is being sought, aims to make the reading room and Internet OPACs the same (at present they are quite different), to upgrade access and search capacities, and to bring in all the catalogues currently separate, such as those of the National Sound Archive and the manuscript collections.

While there is strong commitment to these activities and what they offer, anxieties were expressed about the potential dangers of relying on electronic access to the Library's own collections and to those of other institutions purely as a means of achieving economies. There were some suggestions in this connection that advisers to the government were overselling this aspect, and underestimating the practical problems and costs involved, both to users and to the Library.

We turn now to look at the Library's relations with the key players in its outside world: government and business partners, from whom it seeks sustenance to meet its objectives; the users it serves; the library and information research community; the institutions with whom it seeks to work; and its customers and suppliers.

Funding

When the first edition of this book was being written (see Orna, 1990, pages 139–141), the British Library had serious apprehensions about the government's approach to funding, which was not marked by any rash excess of generosity; this apprehension was compounded by the government decision to complete the building to meet the key requirements of the Library within a cash limit. The situation has changed a good deal since then, and not for the better; as more than one person remarked during the interviews for the present case study, today the late 1980s look something like a Golden Age. The same factors are at work, but in a much more intense form. As the Library's Corporate Plan for the years 1998/99 to 2000/01 puts it:

> It is paradoxical that as the British Library prepares to occupy its magnificent new St Pancras building, it simultaneously faces in 1998/99 the most serious funding crisis in its 25-year history.

The causes are not far to seek:
- The growth in the number of books and journals published, together with a trend in book and serial price inflation significantly higher than general indices (such as the Retail Price Index), increased use of the collection, heightened user expectations, and growing superannuation liabilities, means that each year the Library needs more funding just to stay in the same place in terms of service offered.
- The government grant in 1995 allocated over £9 million less in terms of the extra funds needed to meet the costs of occupying, operating from and running the new building than the £26.5 million which had been identified as the minimum by an independent assessment. The 1996 settlement reduced the Grant-in-Aid cash figure for the next four years by a further £5 million.

The upshot was that the Library had effectively to divert substantial sums from operational activities to ensure that the funding requirement of the St Pancras occupation was met. That meant reductions in spending on acquisition and conservation, and reduced and delayed investment in improvements to service, estates management, collection management and IT infrastructure.

In March 1997, in submitting a bid for additional funding to help rectify dangerous shortfalls in acquisitions and conservation expenditure, the Board of the Library pointed out that while so far it had felt able to live within the Government's planning figures, it now feared that if this bid were unsuccessful, and if the new PES (Public Expenditure Survey) settlement showed no increase above current indicative figures, it would have to re-evaluate its position on both services and the scope of collection.

In the event, the Library's Grant-in-Aid for 1998/99 was reduced by £2.25 million from the planning figure issued previously, and further cuts in acquisitions and conservation expenditure have been required. In the face of this, the Library is undertaking a strategic review and a zero-base budgeting exercise in order to re-focus its resources against key priorities.

The change of government in May 1997 introduced a further, and perhaps unexpected, complication: while its predecessor habitually gave planning figures for four years ahead, the new government was able only to give figures for one year, pending the outcome of a fundamental review of spending. Until the government finds itself able to move to longer-term planning, the Library will suffer from a lack of critical information, and be unable to plan adequately.

It will also carry for a long time the financial scars imposed by the circumstances of its move to the new building. When this case study was in progress, the Library was experiencing a period when the cuts in resources combined with the move to St Pancras were imposing the largest short-term burden; in 1997/98 and 1998/99 it had to pay both for St Pancras and for the other buildings it still occupied, carrying a double estate burden, though with some government help. While that situation will abate, long-term damage, which cannot be recouped, was inevitably inflicted.

Relations with private sources of finance

There has been a great change in the extent to which the Library seeks partnership with private sources of finance, and in the nature of the partnerships. Among key Corporate Plan targets for the period to 2000/01 is:

Exploit fully and effectively opportunities for achieving funding from other sources, including PFI (Private Finance Initiative), partnerships, sponsorship, and the Lottery.

The Library has embraced the PFI as a means of finding the investment for new developments that its Grant-in-Aid funding precludes. It has met with mixed success. No private sector partner could be found for its Financial Management Change Programme, and it had to abandon a PFI procurement for estates developments at Boston Spa and Colindale, for reasons that are set out below. However, the successful PFI procurement for the Corporate Bibliographic Programme has enabled the Library to replace some of its ageing IT systems, the investment for which would otherwise have put an insurmountable short-term strain on its finances. The Digital Library Programme will be a major PFI project, with a very large effect on document supply services, given the increasing demand for electronic versions. This involves intensive negotiations with publishers to gain their agreement on delivering material in electronic format. The PFI partnership may in fact extend beyond digital products, as the ultimate commercial partners may want to fold in traditional non-digital products and services to the partnership arrangements. At the time of the case study, three consortia were bidding; the project programme envisages that the contract will be awarded in November 1998.

The Library has encountered problems with PFI. Some arise from the newness of the concept. Others derive from the nature of the British Library's business: what it has to offer is not a product but a service, and there is not much in the way of opportunities for private sector partners to get innovative business opportunities out of the deal. The aim of building long-term partnerships, which is part of the ideology of PFI, also conflicts with the emphasis on short-term payback and acceptance of the cheapest tender implicit in the competitive tendering previously favoured by government. That apart, PFI constrains room for manoeuvre for a long period ahead and stage payment obligations bring penalties for non-fulfilment; in the case of the prospective estates developments, the PFI process started, but cuts in its overall budget meant that the Library could not afford the investment required to go through with the process.

The Library and its users

The way in which the Library regards its users has changed: it has 'recognized their importance whole heartedly', and now sees itself as a service organization in which the users are its partners with whom it interacts, and about whom it needs to know as much as possible. The fourth of its key initiatives was concerned with user satisfaction: it aimed to assess how well the Library was monitoring its performance and user satisfaction with it, and whether the services delivered to users were of the appropriate quality and effectively delivered.

Since then, it has established a special post for user feedback, covering all the reading rooms. The automated request system which interfaces with the OPAC will make it possible to collect information about use patterns; and more information is now available about readers themselves. It is clear that there are many different groups of readers whose interests have to be considered – at one extreme those who have at their disposal a full range of modern information technology, and can take advantage of remote electronic access to full text; at the other those who are likely always to remain dependent on printed tools for access and who lack the means and/or the wish to use technology intensively. One helpful result of the changes in organizational structure is that curators now work in the reading room, where their expertise can be directly available to readers. Another aspect of information directed to users is service standards; the Library took the previous government's Citizen's Charter initiative seriously, developed its own existing standards of service to make them more comprehensive, and published them.

Contribution to the research community

In the course of structural changes, the Library's Research and Development
Department became the Research and Innovation Centre. Traditionally it
had seen itself and been seen by the rest of the Library as something of a separate entity. It is now being drawn into the corporate mainstream, with a particular role in alerting the Library to trends in the area it monitors.

The Centre's mission statement now commits it to being more proactive
and focused in its programmes. New posts of Research Analysts have been introduced with the remit of analysing trends and context, building up knowledge, while administrative responsibilities are carried by a support unit. The
Centre's main role continues to be the disbursement of grants for research
and development in line with an overall mission of 'advancing the library and
information community'.

At the time of the original case study, in the absence of a national information policy, the British Library, as the national library, had to make the best
assumptions it could in that respect. In 1995, however, the Department of
National Heritage, with the help and advice of the Library, set up the Library
and Information Commission as a non-departmental public body, part of
whose remit was to develop national strategies for libraries and information services (the Commission is currently leasing premises from the British
Library, which has provided administrative support in the Commission's early
phase). One of its sub-committees has been responsible for developing a
national research strategy, in cooperation with the British Library (Library
and Information Commission, 1998). The strategy identifies a wide range of
'players' affected by research activity; sets out a thematic framework ('Con-
nectivity, Content and Competences', together with the value and impact and
the economics of library and information services); and proposes an action
plan for forward planning, funding, quality assurance, communicating, and
transferring research into practice and policy. Now that the strategy has been
published, the LIC, the British Library and the Department for Culture,
Media and Sport are considering the options for future management structures and fund-holding for library and information research; meantime, core
funding continues to be managed by the British Library, and collaboration on
research priorities continues between the LIC and the Research and Innovation Centre. A new British Library Research Plan (1998), developed by the
Library in cooperation with the Library and Information Commission and
covering the period 1998–2001, is based on the key themes of the LIC strategy.

The Research and Innovation Centre has a particular interest in the value
aspect and has called for proposals on the measurement of value and the impact of library and information services. Given the importance of evaluating
research, the Centre is developing an approach to tackling this aspect of its
programmes with the Tavistock Institute.

The innovation aspects of the Centre's work are reflected in the Digital
Library Programme – a PFI project aimed at establishing whether the Library's
digital services can be delivered in a partnership with the private sector. Other
innovation work includes promoting the need for legislation extending legal

deposit to non-print media and disseminating to British Library staff information on research outcomes elsewhere.

Relations with other institutions

The Library needs to manage information about its extensive network of relations with other institutions. A factor which makes for some difficulties in this respect is that in this country there is no single point of responsibility in government for funding both national libraries and major research libraries, in contrast to other countries where all of them are funded through the same government body.

The principal institutions of importance to the Library are:

- The universities: following a report from the Joint Funding Councils' Libraries Review Group (the Follett Report, 1993), discussions were held on collaboration in providing access to research collections; working parties were set up on the creation of a national bibliographic resource, a national approach to preservation and conservation, and a national approach to document supply and interlending
- Other national libraries: the Library cooperates with its counterparts in many other countries
- Other scholarly and research institutions.

The Library and its customers and suppliers

In one sense the users of the Library are its customers, and its relations with them are in many ways like commercial customer information and customer services. In addition, it has customers who purchase services and products from it and contribute to its revenues. They include the customers of specialist information services: SRIS the Business Information Service, Patents information, the Environmental Information Service, the Health Care Information Service, and Inside Information (a CD-ROM of periodical contents pages). There are also customers among a wider public: for its publications, its education service, and its 'Portico' World Wide Web site.

The Digital Library Programme offers opportunities to sell the Library to new audiences, with its potential for repackaging the rich content of the collection into products for diverse audiences. The Library is moving towards a market focus, following an approach already developed by the Document Supply Centre, which has designated territory managers and monitors sales segment by segment. Recognition of the importance of this approach, corporately and strategically, has implications for the kind of information about customers that the Library requires, and the ways in which it needs to use it.

The main suppliers with whom the Library deals are publishers. Although the expected switch to electronic publishing is taking place at a slower pace than originally anticipated, much effort has gone into changing the relationship with publishers, in order to be able to provide more services. The publishers themselves are wary about the financial implications, and are unwilling to relinquish the familiar transactions and known profits from printed products without appropriate guarantees. This had led to difficulty in gaining permission to use electronic versions of publications for tests and experiments. However, the Library now has a number of agreements on handling electronic publications.

Like customer information, information about suppliers is of growing importance for the Library. It now has a Contracts and Purchasing Unit which has become increasingly involved in procurements and contracts, with a resultant rise in professionalism. It is acknowledged that there is still a long way to go in building up and managing relevant information in this area, but progress should become possible when the new finance system is in operation. Information systems and IT procurement are seen as the most strategic domain of procurement, and here there is a stronger emphasis on building relations with suppliers and interchanging information with them.

The people who work for the Library – using knowledge

One of the noteworthy things about returning to the British Library nine years on is the number of people I found myself interviewing for the second time. It is characteristic of the Library that its staff at all levels tend to stay with it, and to be strongly committed to it. That does not, however, mean attachment to comfortable old ways and unwillingness to think differently, or that it cannot move quickly in emergencies (one of things commented on by senior managers was the way in which staff at all levels – with little time for training or familiarization – rose successfully to the move into the new building, despite a seven-month delay in the handover which left under five months for the move). The Library is very successful in retaining high-quality staff; it pays attention to development and to giving them responsibility for initiatives, and it does not expect them to jump to it and accept everything management tells them to do without question.

While the knowledge which people have about their work, and its value to the organizations that employ them, seems to be a wondrous new discovery for a lot of people in the business and IT world at present, it is an old and respected ally in the British Library. This means that the Library understands the value which staff set on their knowledge when it comes to changes in the way they apply it, and devotes time and effort to bringing about the necessary 'cultural' changes. It also underlies the management development programme at director level and the 'Change Group' that followed it (see page 230), and the emphasis on training and development at all levels.

Cross-departmental team building for specific purposes was mentioned in the first edition as a means of breaking down barriers; with the new corporate structure much more of this goes on now. But a 'matrix management' problem has to be solved. Restructuring means that people who formerly worked together in the same directorate are now in different directorates, and while the present job-holders keep the links going, as new staff come in, their primary allegiance is to line management, and there is a loss of the valuable lateral contact which the previous job-holders had.

Project management, benefit assessment and performance measures

The Library has a great deal of experience of managing large projects, and considers with good reason that it is getting better at it. It uses the Prince methodology, and today places much more emphasis than before on the 'back end' – the outcomes of projects and how far they conform to the expectations with which they started. It has devoted a great deal of effort to improving the way it manages and reviews projects to see if they are bringing the benefits proposed – something which is acknowledged to have been a weak point in the past. With current procurement, it seeks to build in a benefits management case from the start. A benefits management package has been built into the procurement process for the past two years, covering such performance criteria as costs versus budget and how the schedule has been kept to. Reviews of developmental changes, with the aim of looking at 'what should happen' against 'what did', and drawing the necessary lessons, have been commissioned from the Information Systems directorate, covering both major implementations of new systems, and run-of-the-mill developments such as the introduction of e-mail. To spread necessary knowledge, training programmes are run for middle managers on project management and team involvement.

Discussion of these issues elicited some interesting observations on the factors operating against taking a 'learning spiral' approach when tackling large-scale new projects. In a large organization there are pressures to carry such projects through in a single sweep with minimal pauses, and the motivation to this approach is intensified by public sector constraints such as procurement protocols, which demand a long time span and so introduce the risk of solutions that are outdated by the time they are implemented.

The reluctance of organizations to evaluate effectiveness of changes has often been remarked on. This discussion of the Library's attempts to do so produced a suggestion to account for it: rarely can we look at a single element of change against a static background; the conditions under which change takes place are themselves constantly changing; and change initiatives themselves change the environment in many complex ways. (The Middle Ages had a word for it – mutability.) This certainly makes evaluation a difficult task – though that is no excuse for not doing it.

Given the complexities, the Library tries not to become involved in too many major change projects at once, and this probably helps to account for its success in avoiding disastrous outcomes of projects.

IT and systems

The changes in the Library's approach to strategy and in its organizational structure have brought a new role for information technology and systems, in which they contribute as much to business development as to operations. The move brings them closer to corporate strategy, with more top management involvement in systems; their main contribution is now in the areas of the Library's 'key competencies' where return on investment is higher. Strategic management now occupies a high place in the job description of the Director of Information Systems: the emphasis is on creating systems through which the Library's strategic aims can be expressed and fulfilled, and on ensuring that relevant external developments in the technologies are available to the Library as a whole.

The Library's Information Systems Strategy (1995) has as its objectives to:

- Improve access to the collection by providing better information about it and better information services
- Build the collection of digital material
- Integrate the Library's services with the computer-based ways of working adopted by many of its users
- Establish a corporate records database describing the collection
- Set up digitization programmes to copy important material into digital form.

By the year 2000 the Library aims to become a major centre for storage and access to digital texts required for research, and to provide access to the world's catalogues, using digital network technology to supply documents to remote users. At the same time, it recognizes that the importance of existing materials and existing ways of using them will remain undiminished, and it seeks to enrich them by technological support. The strategy also aims to make acquisition, cataloguing, and finance and administration systems fully automated and more cost-effective.

Progress is being made towards achieving the objectives. Most of the catalogue can now be accessed via the Library's Portico World Wide Web site and the on-line OPAC is now being used 10 000 times a day. Within the Library there has been a major development in the use of networked information, bringing together financial, customer, management and planning information. An intranet for the directorates of Information Systems and Planning and Resources, with hyperlinks to relevant databases, has been developed.

The necessary systems investment is still a problem, however. Merely to achieve the priority programme in 1998/99 (for example a corporate bibliographic programme to replace legacy corporate bibliographic systems, some going back to the 1970s) will cost £14.5–£16.5 million, but the cuts in funding described earlier will require a reduction of £2–£4 million in this figure.

Management of financial resources

The Library has a good knowledge of the costs of what it does with information, has long experience of predicting how costs will change, and is making efforts to understand the interrelations between its activities and the effects of different options in allocating resources.

Financial Management Change project

This project introduced a different accounts structure, with activity-based costing from 1997/98. Financial management is said now to be better, with improved IT support. There are now budget coordinators in every directorate, who are responsible for much of the central information handling on corporate plans, budgets and staff numbers.

An economic model

At the same time as the initiatives in four key performance areas described earlier, an economic model was developed, with the aim of understanding 'how the Library's limited resources can best be invested to provide for an improved level of services to our users both in the short term and in the long term' in the four key performance areas. *ithink* software (combining systems diagrams and spreadsheets and used in business process reengineering, organizational development, etc.) was used to model operations, processes and activities, and to show interrelationships and dependencies between them, and the resources allocated. Performance indices were established for the four key performance areas. In the event, the model was not taken into further development. Its main value seems to have been in demonstrating at corporate level the implications of various scenarios for decisions and resource allocation, and in creating awareness among senior management of the relationships between different Library activities.

Risk management

The Library's 1997/98 Business Plan identified risk factors associated with the budget developed for that period. They included: no contingency provision for additional alterations or remedial work, for the effects of delays in occupation at St Pancras, for failure to achieve PFI solutions or for literature costs exceeding planning assumptions; dependence on projected growth in volumes and margins on remote document supply; and risks associated with earlier cost-cutting measures which were carried forward and increased.

Earned income

In the Business Plan for 1997/98 earned income is budgeted at 29.4 per cent of gross expenditure, compared with 28.8 per cent forecast for 1996/97. By 2000/01 total earned income is budgeted to rise to 35.3 per cent (£44.2 milion) of gross expenditure. The major part of revenue comes from core services.

In the late 1980s, the Library took the first steps towards rational criteria for charging for services and products, distinguishing three categories for pricing purposes:
1 Under full cost – 'national interest' services
2 Full cost recovery – most services
3 Full cost plus – selected services.

At that time the Library anticipated possible negative consequences, including:
• Complications in its cooperation with other libraries
• Problems of competition in the European single market from organizations in countries supplying comparable services with heavy government subsidy
• Users being unable to afford products that are essential for their needs

- Areas where charging even at rates below full cost recovery would still be above the going outside rates, or where charging could act as a deterrent rather than as a money maker
- Loss of long-term goodwill value of free services, which could affect potential collaborators or suppliers
- Failure to account for the cost of the development time required to establish cost recovery.

Since then it has developed clearer criteria for assigning services and products to the categories, but reconciling the principle of user pays with that of public good remains an unresolved problem; and it is said that the Library's Board will have to take a decision on whether it will be possible to sustain the 'merit good' argument. At present, management opinion is that while earned income has increased, the balance is still right, and that it is not detrimental to achieving the key objectives of the Library.

Thinking time

At the time when the interviews for this case study took place, a 'Change Group' of four senior managers had just started a two-month programme of work to which they were devoting 50 per cent of their time. The group followed from a nine-month senior management development programme in 1997, which in turn resulted from the need for team building following the restructuring of the previous year. The programme was devoted to learning about themselves: their behaviour, attitudes, personalities, and how others see them. The participants perceived that it was necessary to move on from what was described as excessive task orientation: 'We've done the short-term reacting to government; now we need space to think of longer-term strategy.'

The emphasis of the Change Group is on stopping to think, setting aside day-to-day management concerns for a time so as to consider:

- The role of the Library in the new political, economic, and technological situation
- Where, if the Library is to be subject to continuing attrition of Grant-in-Aid, to concentrate resources in order to take new initiatives, and where to release resources from what it is currently doing in order to undertake something new
- How to change the culture yet further, in particular to overcome the residual 'territoriality' which persists despite the reorganization, and to promote an information culture
- What further structural changes are needed in order to reduce the number of levels through which decision making has to travel up and down, and to take four senior managers out of line management so as to allow thinking.

Some interesting observations were made in the course of discussing this initiative. In connection with the earlier work on developing an economic model (see page 229), it was suggested that before the Library can do the things the model was intended to achieve, it needs, first, long-term strategic thinking, and then the systems to support it. For this, it is seen as critical that the senior management team can work effectively together and understand

one another's work at a deep level. A point was also made about potential con-
flict between thinking time and the demands of efficiency in the minds of new
staff of high quality who have recently come into the Library from a business
environment. They are described as dedicated, hard-working and able to
achieve great progress on tasks, but as finding it difficult to detach their minds
from the business in hand in order to think further ahead.

Integration

The Library is committed to integrating all aspects of its strategy, so that they
illuminate and support one another, and to creating systems which permit
integrated use of all its collections and all its information resources about itself
and its outside world. While it is now better able to look at everything related
to given issues, it readily admits that it still has further to go in this respect.
Comments to that effect were offered about financial management and
resource allocation, and about filing systems and records management. One
manager remarked, 'We probably need an information co-ordinator'; another,
agreeing with the proposition that corporate strategy and information are the
same thing in the Library's case, acknowledged that there was still more the
Library could do to synthesize and integrate its use of information; and a third
said that while the Library had progressed in its management information systems, it was not yet very good at distilling the meaning of the copious management information that emerged from them.

Evaluation

The British Library is living in difficult times; continuing cuts in its resources
limit its freedom of action, force hard choices, and expose it to high levels of
risk.

Fortunately, the Library is getting the best from the situation rather than
the worst; it is using the pressures as an occasion for learning about itself, and
for taking soundly based initiatives, rather than reacting in piecemeal panic.
While it acknowledges that it faces the threat that in future it may become
impossible to maintain the current scope and service levels of its activities in
support of its main purpose, it now has a strong framework for looking at the
issues on a corporate rather than a sectional basis, in relation to corporate priorities. It is moving towards an integrated strategy through its new corporate
structure though it acknowledges there is still further to go. Resource allocation is on the way to becoming more related to overall strategic needs, supported by long-term strategic thinking and the development of systems to
support it.

Information systems and IT fulfil a strategic role; their contribution is
increasingly focused on business development and concentrated on the
Library's 'core capabilities'. The Library takes justified pride in the high level
of success of its large projects, and is improving its capability for monitoring
and evaluating them.

It is able to capitalize on the traditional quality of its human resources: the
people who work for the Library at all levels have a strong commitment to the
institution, and draw on knowledge gained through years of experience. It is
good at retaining high-quality staff, who have scope for taking initiatives and
development opportunities. The Change Group is an example of its commitment to making time for thinking – it is interesting to note that this two-month
initiative is a follow-up to a long-term programme for cultural change for
senior managers; while bringing about cultural change needs a long time,
once mutual understanding among a group is established, productive thinking
can be achieved quite quickly. The Group has the potential to use knowledge
cooperatively to create new knowledge and take productive change initiatives.

References

British Library (1997), *Corporate Plan
1998/99–2000/01*

British Library (1995), *Information
Systems Strategy*

British Library (1998), *Research Plan
1998–2001*

FOLLETT, B. *Chairman* (1993), Joint
Funding Councils' Library Review Group:
A Report for the HEFC, SHEFC, HEFCW
and DENI, Bristol: Higher Education
Funding Council

LIBRARY AND INFORMATION
COMMISSION (1998), *Prospects: a strategy
for action. Library and information research,
development and innovation in the United
Kingdom,* London: LIC

ORNA, E. (1990), *Practical Information
Policies,* Aldershot: Gower

Credit Union Services Corporation (Australia)

The credit union movement

A credit union is defined as a group of people who join together to pool their savings and make loans to each other at reasonable rates of interest. Its business structure is that of a mutual, cooperative organization, based on the principles of one member one vote, which functions as an intermediary between savers and borrowers.

Credit unions came into being to provide low-cost loans for people who could not obtain credit without recourse to money lenders. They first appeared on the continent of Europe in the nineteenth century, in Germany, and later in Italy, France and Austria; the concept attracted little interest in the United Kingdom, where building societies, and later the Cooperative Bank, provided for British housing and consumer cooperative needs (Lewis, 1996). The movement spread to Canada and the United States at the beginning of the twentieth century. In the 1920s, the Credit Union National Extension Bureau was set up to promote credit unions throughout the USA and internationally; it merged in the 1930s with the Credit Union National Association (CUNA), and by the 1950s the CUNA World Extension Department was promoting credit unions in other parts of the world.

The members of the credit union own and control the organization and there are no external shareholders. By virtue of their organizational form, and perhaps thanks to their lack of size or expertise in this area, credit unions have been able to avoid the high-risk commercial lending that has brought many banks into difficulties in recent years. Each union is an autonomous legal entity, and they vary in asset size and membership base. In Australia some have over 100 000 members, while others number their members in hundreds; some are related to employee groups or professions, others have an industry, ethnic or parish basis.

Members' deposits are used to fund the loans to their fellow members, and the organization pays depositors interest for the use of their money. Borrowers' payments of interest on their loans form the credit unions' main source of income, and this is used to pay interest to savers, to meet operating expenses, and to provide reserves. Credit unions (CUs) may also fund additional financial services and education programmes. Any surplus can be returned to members in the form of benefits. CUs are becoming increasingly aware of the shortcomings and potential risk involved in relying on interest-only income and are starting to broaden their revenue streams; in Australia there is a very low margin on lending at present.

The basic philosophy of the credit unions is one of self-help and mutual aid among members. The international operating principles approved by the World Council of Credit Unions are based on: open and voluntary membership; democratic control; non-discrimination; service to members; equitable distribution of surpluses; financial stability; on-going education; cooperation with other cooperatives; and social responsibility.

Australia's credit unions

The first Australian credit unions began after World War II, developing in small geographic communities and church parishes. There was strong growth in the mid-1960s–1970s, and further rapid expansion in the 1980s. Today there are over 247 credit unions in the country (the number tends to change quite often, generally downward, mainly due to mergers and the like), with 3.5 million members; one in five Australian adults has a relationship with a credit union. Their asset base in 1996 was in excess of $A15.5 billion, and by December 1997 had increased to $A17.7 billion, and in terms of assets, credit unions come after the four major banks (National Australia Bank, Westpac, Commonwealth and ANZ) and the amalgamated St George–Advantage Bank. The gradual removal of statutory discrimination against credit unions over the past few years opens the way to their being able to provide deposit services to statutory authorities, businesses and community groups.

Australia's credit unions are supervised at the federal level by the Australian Financial Institutions Commission (AFIC). In addition, each state and territory has a State Supervisory Authority to register and directly supervise its credit unions and assist the AFIC. All states and territories also maintain their own contingency funds to provide deposit protection for credit union members in case of failure. Recently the Wallis Enquiry into Financial Institutions has made recommendations to government which, if passed, will enable CUs to operate under the same regulatory structure as other financial institutions.

CUs define their core values as: cooperation; moral integrity; trust; financial prudence; caring for members; and social responsibility. Their code of ethics enjoins them to:
- Encourage thrift among members and educate members and staff in financial awareness
- Cooperate with each other
- Act lawfully and within a spirit of justice and equity
- Avoid unfair discrimination
- Act efficiently and effectively, and strive for excellent quality of service
- Earn high levels of trust from members, other parts of the movement and from the wider community.

CUs recognize a number of stakeholder communities to which they owe ethical obligations:
- Credit unions to members
- Credit unions to credit unions
- Special service providers to credit unions
- Credit unions to special service providers
- The organization and its staff
- The general community
- Government and regulatory agencies

- Other suppliers
- The wider community.

A Credit Union Code of Practice, formalizing standards of disclosure and conduct and resolution of disputes, is monitored by the Reserve Bank of Australia and reviewed at regular intervals by a body authorized by the Commonwealth Government.

The Credit Union Services Corporation

The Credit Union Services Corporation is the major of two 'special service providers' to the credit unions. These institutions act, as wholesalers of products and services, like special credit unions whose members are individual credit unions; they provide facilities for investing funds, borrowing, and interfacing with other financial institutions.

Credit Union Services Corporation is an unlisted company, owned and funded by member credit unions (86 per cent of the credit unions in Australia). They hold shares in the Corporation (the number held is directly proportional to their asset size) and pay a membership subscription. The Corporation is managed by a Board of Directors, most of them elected by member credit unions; other directors are elected by the Board of Directors. A membership council facilitates links between affiliated credit unions and the Corporation. The Corporation's reason for being is to provide benefits of aggregation through economies of scale for the production and supply of products and services which CUs acting alone would not be able to provide to their members. The Corporation has therefore a responsibility to its owners to be profitable in its performance.

The Corporation's products and services

The main products and services offered by the Corporation include:
- Redicards for withdrawing money at credit unions or from autoteller machines, or for paying for purchases at retail point-of-sale machines
- Visa debit and credit cards
- Cheque accounts (the Corporation has an agency arrangement with one of the major banks to provide cheque books to CU members. At the moment government regulation means that CUs are not permitted to issue cheque books themselves, but the Wallis Enquiry report recommended that they should be allowed to do so, and the federal government is considering the relevant legislation)
- Superannuation trust
- Treasury services, managing $AI.7 billion credit union liquidity invested with the Corporation
- Provision of IT solutions (the Corporation's fully owned subsidiary, Credit Union Commercial IT, is one of the largest specialist financial software companies in Australia)
- Insurance for credit unions

- A national image advertising campaign, PR, publications and media liaison
- Dealing with legislative and regulatory issues on behalf of credit unions.

Goals, mission and vision

The Corporation's goals are:
- To deliver commercial services to credit unions at a profit
- To provide any commercial services at prices more competitive than any other long-term supplier
- To provide high-quality services that meet or exceed credit union expectations
- To assist credit unions in all ways possible to create the National Credit Union Network.[1]

It defines its mission as:

> To promote the principles of member-owned financial institutions, to make these institutions as accessible as possible to all people in Australia and to meet the financial needs of members with dignity, honesty and integrity.

and formulates its vision in these terms:

> Our vision is of a national coverage of financially strong credit unions, each with a leading position in its chosen market, supported by an efficient, competitive access network, the whole being marketed and sustained through a disciplined, democratic governance structure.

Organizational structure

In 1996 the Australian Financial Institutions Commission (AFIC) reviewed the corporate structure of the Corporation, as part of their ongoing role as regulator, with special attention to the relationship between the Corporation's primary business – defined as activities associated with the central banking function – and its secondary activities. The aim was to help the Corporation to develop a structure where the primary business was contained within the parent company and the secondary activities within a series of subsidiaries – following the Reserve Bank model of regulation of the banking industry, designed to protect depositors' funds from any claim in the event of failure of one of the subsidiaries. In pursuit of these aims the Corporation moved its funds management operation into a subsidiary – the Questor Financial Services Group, which handles personal investment services, and the stockbroking and funds administration business of the Corporation (this initial restructure was followed by similar movements of the insurance division and Credit Union Commercial IT into subsidiary operations). Questor also became the trustee for the Portfolio Service and for the Total Retirement Fund,

---

[1] Distinguishing features: differentiation through ethos and values; safety and security; national strategic marketing plan; accessibility; collective marketing of products; cost competitiveness; and cooperative unity.

and became a corporation regulated by the Australian Securities Commission – a move which put Questor on the same footing as the Corporation's competitors.

The Corporation is governed by its Board, to which the Chief Executive is responsible. At the next level are Group Corporate Services, Public Affairs and Governance, Movement Development and Business Services, Retail Banking, Credit Union Relationships, Subsidiary Operations and Third Party Relationships, Institutional Banking, and Group Information Services.

Areas of the Corporation with information-related responsibilities

A number of the divisions have important responsibilities for managing information. Public Affairs and Governance covers issues of management and political representation and is thus involved in presenting information to bodies and individuals which the Corporation needs to influence. Its Compliance Department is responsible for products and services to ensure awareness of compliance requirements, including a Compliance Note Service and Manual, with Internet access.

Relationship Management was introduced in mid-1997 as part of the restructuring of Credit Union Services Corporation, to address concerns raised by credit unions about the difficulty of getting direct contact, and to help the Corporation to become more customer-focused. The Credit Union Relationships Division brings together a group of Relationship Managers whose work is supported by a Communications, Data and Back-up Centre and the Research Department. As the primary point of contact between the credit unions and the Corporation, they are responsible for negotiating relationship plans with each credit union. Their role is defined as being 'To build and enhance the competitive position of member credit unions through an ethical and responsive partnership.' It is one which involves acquiring and managing key information about member CUs and their relationship with the Corporation, providing information to CUs, and information interactions with other parts of the Corporation on the basis of their specialist knowledge of member CUs. The Research Department's work is directed towards providing information to equip CUs and the Corporation to understand their market better, CUs to understand themselves better, and the Corporation to understand CUs better. It analyses data and information on aspects of the marketplace – the economy, the finance industry generally, the credit union movement, attitudes and financial behaviour of consumers, and socio-demographic trends. Databases and reports make the results available to the Corporation and the Unions (for details, see page 239). The Communications Department is responsible for helping the Corporation communicate with credit union boards, managements, suppliers, staff, the media etc, and for raising awareness of credit unions in the community. Its remit covers publications, education, media relations, promotions, etc. It carried out a communications audit during 1996/97, and went on to develop a strategy for communication using the Corporation's public Web site.

Group Information Services – headed by the Chief Information Officer – consists of four departments: Networks, Internal Systems, CU Technology

Services and On-line Service Delivery (Internet, intranet, etc), which provide the systems and IT infrastructure.

Corporate business strategy development

In 1996, the Corporation sponsored work on strategy in nine areas:

1 Business strategy – to develop understanding of major areas of retail banking activity
2 Marketing strategy – to make recommendations on an integrated national awareness programme
3 Technology strategy – work on a core banking-system technology strategy to support the needs of credit unions into the future, covering functionality, scalability, adaptability to new technologies, and suitability to credit unions of various sizes. This strategy embodies sets of 'Architecture Principles', including principles for information (see page 243) – which can be considered to form a nexus between the information technology strategy and the Information Management Policy which was proposed for approval in the summer of 1997 (see page 244)
4 Human resources strategy – the recommendations here include benchmarking human resources practices among credit unions
5 Cost reduction strategy – benchmarks have been established to identify areas where cost efficiencies can be gained and a process improvement programme designed to help CUs upgrade their business efficiency has been launched
6 Digital media strategy – electronic provision of products and services, together with reviewing opportunities to improve communication between credit unions
7 Capital formation strategy
8 Regulatory strategy – seeking a strong position for member-owned financial institutions in any new regulatory system (an inquiry into financial regulation in Australia is currently in progress)
9 Growth strategy – opportunities for establishing new credit unions and extending the services of existing ones to communities which have lost access to essential financial services.

These strategies have now been developed, and some, for example cost reduction, have been implemented.

Knowledge and information requirements, and how the Corporation meets them

The Corporation's mission and values imply a range of knowledge and information requirements. These are set out below, with an outline of the action it currently takes to acquire the information which it needs to feed its knowledge and keep it in good health. As will be seen, the Corporation invests a good deal of effort in acquiring essential information; the initiatives and the use of the results, however, are mostly within the various divisions involved, and there is very little coordination between divisions in this matter.

The Corporation's owners / customers, the credit unions, and other credit unions, in Australia and elsewhere

Information about the business of affiliated credit unions is available from two sources: the AFIC reports, which provide information about the health of the movement, market segments, etc; and the Annual Reports of credit unions which come to the Corporation in its capacity as a wholesale banker. As a recognized representative body on the international scene, in the World Council of Credit Unions, the Corporation has access to information about credit unions worldwide.

Developments in the economy, finance industry, consumers, socio-demographic trends

The remit of the Research Department covers collection of data on the economy, the finance industry, socio-demographic trends, etc; the material is converted into a range of information products, as described below. The department also maintains a central database of basic information on credit unions.

In 1995/96, comprehensive databases of economic and industry data, movement financial data and consumer research material were established. A database on movement marketing was set up from 1996, coming into operation by phases up to 1998. In the first phase analyses were made available to CUs at various rates, together with a core free service of basic market information related to each participating CU's catchment area. The second phase will bring in individual CUs' data; the third, benchmarks relating to cross-sell, retention, sales, product profiles, gaps/best practice; and the fourth, construction benchmarks against criteria selected by individual CUs.

A market research service is provided, with information about consumer behaviour and product usage. New consultancy services were initiated in 1997, offering syndicated market research, member survey design (questionnaires for CUs to explore their members' needs and attitudes); and a service to prepare research briefs for CUs who want to commission research. The Department also publishes research reports. Regular publications include:

- An annual overview (with quarterly updates) of the credit union operating environment – economy, finance industry trends, movement performance, political and regulatory issues, consumer perceptions and behaviour
- A quarterly statistical publication tracking the movement's performance across a range of growth indicators and key ratios
- State of the market – an annual report on market research findings, describing consumers' financial behaviour and attitudes towards various financial institutions.
- Consumer product needs – an annual report on market share by institution as well as consumers' key service expectations.

Legislation and regulatory requirements and bodies

Data on these topics are collected and managed on the initiative of the Public Affairs and Compliance division. This group is in the process of introducing a national electronic document management system, using Web technologies.

Relevant developments in information technology

Work here consists mainly of advances in technology centred on offering improved products or services to credit unions or their members. It includes focused activity relating to Internet banking, electronic commerce and new banking technology, such as non-branch banking, within the Retail Banking division – the Corporation's core business.

Customer response to products, services and communications

Information gathering may be reactive, in the form of sales figures and subscriptions; there is an annual customer satisfaction survey, which is generic in nature, and assessment is on a departmental basis. Additional responses are gathered during the annual district meetings and various credit union forums convened around Australia by the Corporation's business units and relationship managers. A customer listening programme is being developed which will be achieved in three phases to progressively encompass all externally focused business units. It has three levels of information gathering (basic: customer complaints; intermediate: follow-up of annual customer satisfaction survey; high: one-to-one interviews among credit unions which have a high impact on the business).

Staff – their skills, knowledge, training and education

While records about the training and ongoing education of employees are collected, until recently there has not been a competency system which would enable career or succession planning, identification of suitable internal applicants for vacancies or fast tracking of outstanding employees. A system is now being implemented by the human resources team.

The competition

Items such as the cost of transactions by the major banks and building societies are monitored by the Business Groups which offer products in the relevant markets, though the intelligence gathered is not coordinated throughout the organization.

Existing and potential markets

There is a keen focus on information about markets, especially during the annual planning process, when decisions are made on selling products and services outside the Corporation's traditional markets. The Research Department, as outlined above, is the main source.

Contacts

While information about contacts (particularly the individuals and institutions the Corporation needs to influence) is of great importance to the Corporation, and especially to such divisions as Public Affairs, which is responsible for lobbying federal and state governments, its acquisition and maintenance appears to be rather fragmented. The Research Department tries to ensure that its own contact information, which is meant to be the primary source, is maintained, and it has also set up an on-line system for collecting non-confidential information directly from credit union databases. Relationship Managers and most business units also collect and hold information on contacts.

Cost-effectiveness of its own activities

Costs are analysed on a quarterly basis. Business units are measured for efficiency and competitiveness where appropriate. The Corporation tracks the amount of resources dedicated to transforming raw materials to products and services and evaluates the effects in terms of customer profitability, by examining the fully loaded cost (direct cost of salaries + indirect costs + a proportion of corporate overheads + a proportion of costs allocated from internal services) of providing a service or creating a product, and comparing this to the revenue brought in by the product or service. These analyses are performed by a specialist in the area.

Results of monitoring and evaluation of its activities

The Board has established a framework for evaluation of its own performance and that of the Chief Executive and management of the Corporation. Every six months it conducts a survey of directors to assess progress with major functional responsibilities and performance of main areas of management. The results are input to the planning process.

For corporate performance issues, the customer satisfaction survey mentioned above is used to highlight areas where satisfaction is low, and the results of changes following such initiatives are monitored. Staff views on what is important in relation to what is being done well are collected through regular staff satisfaction surveys which are independently assessed. When the results are available, representatives from the senior management team meet staff to discuss areas of concern to staff, and explain new initiatives instituted in response to customer and staff feedback.

Information management

Not only does information need to be acquired; there are also things that need to be done to ensure that the right people get it and are able to transform it into knowledge.

Until 1997 there was no one functional area providing information management activities, and no allocation of responsibility for being aware of all the Corporation's information resources. Some management of information went on in various areas which are responsible for collecting, analysing and disseminating information, but it was described as tending to be 'generally rather disorganised', and not helped by the fact that until very recently 'the difference between IT and IM was not well comprehended'. In October 1997, however, the Corporation appointed a member of its staff with a background and qualifications in information management as an Information Management Consultant, with the remit of developing, implementing and maintaining an Information Management Strategy and providing advice in information management. The holder of the post reports to a matrix management structure involving the Head of the Corporation's Customer Focus Program and the Chief Information Officer

Intelligence gathering in relevant fields

Activities here are concentrated in Research, Retail Banking and Public Affairs, and to a certain extent in Communications. Until recently no formal scanning programmes have been in place, though some areas perform this function as part of their operations. Relationship managers are now involved in scanning activities which involve polling credit unions about specific business-unit-drive topics or queries.

Provision for storage, organization, access and dissemination in ways that meet work needs, via appropriate information systems and technology

There is some recent activity to support the new role of Relationship Managers (the call centre for data which is under development, and the support centre); a system to administer Quality documents; and the 'Quickdata' intranet. There is also a credit-union-only extranet, as well as the public Web site. Again, there is no enterprise-wide coordination or management of these resources or of their content, although developing strategies for the information content of the intranet and extranet are goals for the IM Consultant.

Identification of 'guardians' and 'stakeholders' of various information resources

Guardians are usually defined as the people entrusted by an organization with managing specific resources of information, and stakeholders as those who need the information in any given resource to support their knowledge and its application.

Until recently there were no attempts at identifying stakeholders, but work on this is now developing with an inventory of the Corporation's application systems, (information about the information systems) and the advent of the relationship management role. There is no formal record of who is responsible for the various information resources of the Corporation.

Identification of information interactions necessary for keeping knowledge up to date and applying it

This is what is usually called identification of 'information flows', and it covers the activities concerned with how information gets around within the Corporation, between it and its members and between it and its outside world. An example would be the way in which the Research Department collects information on activity indicators for the credit union movement and communicates it to the Communications Department, which then disseminates it to the outside world via press releases and other public relations activities.

As yet, nothing has been formally undertaken to find out 'who needs to tell whom about what'; although presumably this is well understood between the areas which participate in this process, it may become one of the issues for development of the information management strategy.

Monitoring information use

There is no provision as yet for monitoring information use and evaluating the results, but one of the critical success factors for the implementation of the information management policy is to set up measures which will assess information use and quality.

Assessing the cost and value of information and its use

No definitive answer has been found to the question of how the Corporation does this, but part of the inventory process mentioned above will be to assess the cost and value (after Burk and Horton, 1988) of the resources, and also the information value (based on Taylor, 1986) and the utility of the information (Orna, 1990).

Information strategy development

As mentioned earlier (page 238), the IT strategy embodies general principles for information, which form a link between information systems/IT strategy and information strategy. They can also be considered both as a top-level statement of some aspects of information policy (what is missing from them is the definition of what constitutes the 'right' information for meeting the aims of the Corporation).

'Information Principles'

The 'Information Principles' from the IT strategy are:
1 Information is a corporate resource, and as such must be accessible according to need (access to the right information, at the right time, by the right people, from the right location).
2 The master copy of data should be used to the broadest possible extent without re-copying or re-formatting.

3 Information supplied to credit unions and customers must be consistent, unambiguous, timely and accurate.

4 Data transfer between Credit Union Services and external parties will be electronic where feasible.

5 Data will be entered only once and as close as possible to the points of entry into the organization.

6 Valuable or confidential data must be protected against unauthorized access to them.

7 All sets of data will have a custodian (or owner).

8 Common definitions and standards for data shall exist organization-wide.

The Information Management Policy

A policy for information management was developed at Steering Committee level as the output from an Information Strategy Project in 1997. A series of briefing sessions with the Executive Management Group was held early in 1998 before formal presentation of the policy for approval.

Defining information management as a 'key organizational activity which exists to align information resources with corporate goals and objectives', the policy emphasizes the necessity for coordinating the information gathering and business intelligence creating process. Its objectives are to ensure that:

- The right information is acquired from the outside and generated from inside to achieve what the Corporation needs to do
- Information is exploited fully, to meet all current and future needs, and to help the Corporation adapt to changes in strategic direction or in the larger environment
- Information gets delivered in time and in the right format to the people who need to use it to support business operations or decision making
- Everybody who processes and uses information has the opportunity for learning the appropriate knowledge and skills for cooperating with one another in applying them to their work, and for developing new ways of using or processing information to help the Corporation achieve its objectives
- The technology in use is regularly reviewed to evaluate its appropriateness to the information objectives of the organization, and decisions on new technology are taken with regards to the Corporation's Information Policy and to the total socio-technical environment
- IM roles are recognized for managing and developing the information function and applying the information policy
- Relevant monitoring criteria are developed to evaluate implementation of the Information Policy, and feedback and redesign occur based on the effectiveness of the results
- There is close contact between policy makers and information specialists in identifying areas where information, which originates externally or is generated internally, is retained
- Systems are developed for disseminating the results of in-house research.

The policy identifies six critical success factors for the management of information:

1 Commitment to the principles of information management on the part of the CEO and senior management, demonstrated and supported by appropriate training and education for all staff
2 A framework of clearly defined information management policies and objectives, supported by standards and procedures, and understood within the organization
3 Accountability for carrying out the policies, clearly defined and accompanied by commensurate authority
4 Measurement of the organization's success in implementing information management practices, using appropriate measures, on a regular basis
5 Seamless integration of information management practices into normal business planning and operations of the organization
6 Culture: the creation of an environment which values information.

Basic principles for information management are set out as:
• Accountability for information of all kinds, including the obligation to collect and maintain only 'that information which is needed to fulfil the Corporation's responsibilities'
• Free information exchange between business units in order to meet corporate objectives
• Supply of consistent, unambiguous, timely and accurate information to credit unions and customers
• Accessibility of key information
• Compliance with legal and administrative requirements (including copyright and intellectual property)
• Preservation of information of enduring value
• Continuity of use of key information in all circumstances
• Privacy and confidentiality of personal information and of commercial-in-confidence information
• Leverage, by using information to increase cost-effectiveness, improve customer satisfaction, and to identify opportunities and threats in the internal and external environment
• A recognized custodian for every information resource.

The Corporation's approaches to information management are given an interesting presentation under the headings of Information Product, Information Leverage, and Information Business (see Table C4.1 on page 246).

The helpful principle of giving examples from the organization's own structure is followed in the definition of corporate information management functions. Each function (records management, collection management, data management, IS and IT management, value-added processing, environmental scanning, 'infopreneurial' activities, and support functions) is briefly described, and an example is given of areas in the Corporation which carry out the function. Environmental scanning, for instance, is defined as 'Activities which actively seek to obtain information about changes in the environment

Information Product

• Embed in products and services • Bundle and repackage • *Corporate Areas* – EPS, Chequing, Direct Entry	Existing processes generate or capture significant volumes of data as a by-product of transaction processing. Market for the by-product information is identified or created Product/service opportunities generated out of summarising or massaging transaction processing information by-products

Information Leverage

• Develop proprietary information for internal use • Increase performance at every level through information • Knowledge creation • *Corporate Areas* – SMP, On-Line Service Delivery, Financial planning systems	Fundamental strategy built on traditional basis (product differentiation, economies of scale) Information technology amplifies competitive dimensions of underlying base strategy. Information technology permits significant process innovation or redesign

Information Business

• Enhance the business around the organisation's information capacity • *Corporate Areas* – Communications, Public Affairs, Research, Institutional Banking	Excess capacity in internal information systems can be sold to other industry participants. Clear market demand exists for specific information product or services (e.g. abstracting services or information brokers).

Table C4.1   **Credit Union Services Corporation approaches to information management**

which may present opportunities or threats to the organization or may indicate opportunities for manipulation of the external environment to meet the aims of the organization ...', and the areas of the Corporation cited as examples are Public Affairs, Legal Counsel, and Retail Banking.

The policy also outlines the responsibilities, roles and required skills of information managers.

Implementation

The policy concludes with recommendations for its implementation:

- Link the information planning process to the annual strategic planning and goal setting process and activities.
- Perform in depth information audits throughout the organization to progressively establish corporate information needs and identify IM activities, functions and roles.

- Consolidate the information resources and requirements of the organization across divisions and departments.
- Highlight the roles and responsibilities of information managers within departments and divisions.
- Establish responsibility for adaptive behaviour mechanisms[2] within the Corporation and assign responsibility for these activities to appropriate areas.
- Create and maintain an information portfolio (meta-database – an information resource that contains details of all the organization's information resources) similar to the applications systems inventory.
- Identify the IM 'states' that exist within the Corporation and assist migration towards a federal model of IM (Davenport et al. 1992).
- Implement the Policy within two business units and then review and revise the implementation plan and the Policy itself.

The policy was accepted at Steering Committee level in mid-December 1997, and implementation is in progress in two areas: Commercial IT and the Customer Focus Project. The time scale envisaged is two years; it is intended to redeploy resources from within the Customer Focus Project and to identify people now performing information management activities within the business units. Presentation of the policy outwards into the organization will be:

1 Partly by evolution of an information culture
2 By business unit, where the approach will be 'What can we do to assist business units achieve their goals?'
3 By integrating the planning for information and the identification of information requirements into the strategic planning process; the Corporation's planning template has been amended to focus on information required to meet goals, and it will be used for the 1998–1999 planning cycle, commencing May 1998.

Figure C4.1 (see page 248), is an 'evolutionary diagram' which summarizes information management activities and projects over the period covered by this case study, including the planned action research project referred to below.

Evaluation

When I first began to learn about the Corporation, early in 1997, my judgement was that it was an information-dependent organization which was doing many of the right things with information, but which lacked a strategy for it, and did not have an overview of the role of information management to tie all the information-related activities together.

Since that time, much work has been done to bring that into being, and the process exemplifies many useful steps. Key ones among them include:

[2] How to identify areas of the organization which have a mandate for acting on information obtained from the environment to initiate projects (to produce new or improved products or services), or process improvement activities.

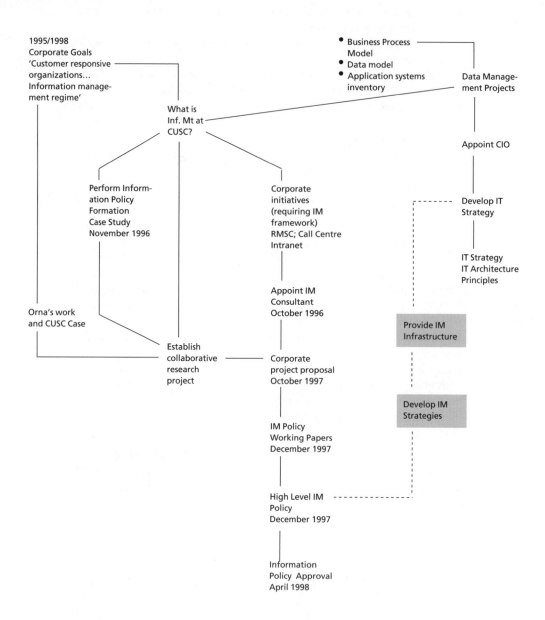

Fig C4.1   **Evolutionary diagram of information management activities and projects at Credit Union Services Corporation**

- The appointment of an Information Management Consultant from within the organization. The job description is an excellent one, and the job holder has experience of the Corporation, good standing within it, and appropriate authority confirmed by approval of the policy. She has also undertaken part-time postgraduate studies in information management, and is now planning further action research in the organization on the establishment of information management within the Corporation
- The fact that the IM Consultant had worked in the division concerned with information systems and IT is also helpful, because it makes for mutual understanding and facilitates incorporating the existing IT strategy into information policy
- The continuing role envisaged for the IM Consultant within the organization
- The policy itself is presented at the right level of principle, supported by examples of its application that should help people to relate it to their own work experience. It also gives a soundly based statement of 'what should be', and embodies critical success factors
- The orientation of the policy is towards people, as the transformers of information to knowledge, and knowledge to action
- The implementation proposals cover key issues
- A project approach is taken to implementation, with built-in monitoring as part of the projects.

The organization has started to move towards an information culture which, in the words of the Information Management Consultant, 'will be achieved when there is a common understanding of and corporate language for the management of information within Credit Union Services – in the same way that all employees understand the language of human resources management and the meaning underpinning the language'.

References

BURK, C. F., Jr and HORTON, F. W., Jr (1988), *Infomap: A complete guide to discovering corporate information resources,* Englewood Cliffs, NJ: Prentice Hall

LEWIS, G. (1996), *People Before Profit: the credit union movement in Australia,* Kent Town, South Australia: Wakefield Press

DAVENPORT, T. H., ECCLES, R. G., and PRUSAK, L. (1992) 'Information politics', *Sloan Management Review,* 34 (1) 53–65

TAYLOR, R. S. (1986), *Value Added Processes in Information Systems,* Norwood, NJ: Ablex Publishing Corporation

ORNA, E. (1990), *Practical Information Policies,* Aldershot: Gower

Health Canada Libraries: past, present and future[1]

Readers will find that this case study (one of two contributed by external authors) makes a helpful background to the British National Health Service case study (page 282). The initiatives described there drew on Canadian experience and in particular on the work of Professor Joanne Marshall, author of the present study.

Like that case, this one focuses on the contribution of libraries and librarians to the strategic use of information. It is important to be reminded of the continuing relevance of this irreplaceable element in an area as vital as the health of a nation.

This study is also exemplary from the point of view of management of the review process it describes, while the results reveal the value added by libraries and librarians in Health Canada in both financial (time-saving for users), and qualitative terms (support in decision making, suggesting new avenues, help in resolving problems).

The process also seems to have contributed to senior managers' understanding of information as a critical resource, and of the role of librarians in managing both traditional and electronic information, and as 'key people in developing information policy for the department'. EO

[1] Study contributed by Joanne G. Marshall, Faculty of Information Studies, University of Toronto.

ACKNOWLEDGEMENTS: This study was supported by Health Canada, and the contributions of Merle McConnell, Marty Lovelock, Greg Hunter, Weldon Newton and Carole Anne O'Brien are gratefully acknowledged.
Joanne G. Marshall

Introduction

In order to develop effective information policy in the organizational context, it is important to gather evidence from the past and to examine current outcomes. This report summarizes the history of the Health Canada Libraries and draws upon data gathered as part of the Health Canada Libraries Review to develop a best practices scenario for the future. The report was intended as a discussion document for consensus building about the future of the Health Canada Libraries. The report can also be seen as a basis for a more detailed model or policy plan that would put the vision into action.

Background

Health Canada is the federal ministry responsible for the Canada Health Act, which governs broad policies related to the provision of the national health care insurance programme. The ministry has shifted its responsibility in recent years from direct involvement in the provision of health care services through transfer payments to the provinces towards broader health care policy making and the development and maintenance of national standards. An exception to this trend is Health Canada's continuing responsibility for health care services to the First Nations peoples. The term First Nations is the preferred name used for Canada's indigenous populations.

In addition to its policy function, Health Canada is a scientific organization with responsibility for food and drug testing and disease surveillance. Health promotion and population health also continue to be important areas of activity within the ministry.

The Health Canada Libraries Review was initiated in response to a request from management in Corporate Services Branch (CSB) and the Health Protection Branch (HPB) to analyse the current state of libraries in the department and to position libraries in relation to the four critical areas of federal responsibility: health system renewal and support; services to First Nations; management of risks to health – products and disease control; and the population health strategy.

A Steering Committee was established to oversee the review process. The Committee consisted of the chief librarians for CSB and HPB and the managers to whom they report. For CSB this includes Marty Lovelock and Greg Hunter and, for HPB, Merle McConnell and Weldon Newton. The chief librarians are largely responsible for the planning and implementation of the review, while the Steering Committee provides overall direction and approval.

For technical advice and assistance on the review the Steering Committee selected Professor Joanne Marshall from the Faculty of Information Studies at the University of Toronto, who has extensive experience in library surveys and evaluation. The survey of the departmental staff, which forms part of the review, was carried out under Professor Marshall's direction by Carol Anne O'Brien.

Key informant interviews with senior department staff were conducted by Professor Marshall and the two chief librarians. A history of Health Canada Libraries was prepared by the chief librarians. Initial data entry and analysis was conducted at Carleton University and additional analysis took place at the University of Toronto. In August 1996, at the request of the Steering Committee, Professor Marshall agreed to enlarge her advisory role and to prepare this report. The report draws upon the past history and current performance of Health Canada Libraries as a basis for painting a broadly based, best practices scenario for the future. The report is intended as a discussion document that will aid consensus building around the future of Health Canada Libraries. It can also serve as the foundation for a more detailed model or business plan that will put the vision into action.

History and present organizational structure

A knowledge of the history and present organization of libraries in the department is essential to understanding the future vision described in this report. Until 1986, library services within Health Canada consisted of a Departmental Library and autonomous or semi-autonomous libraries in the Health Protection Branch and Health Services and Promotion Branch, as well as a resource centre in the Medical Services Branch. The original Departmental Library was dissolved in 1985 in favour of a branch library network consisting of four independent programme-responsive entities. Of these four, there are two remaining: the new Departmental Library and the Health Protection Branch Libraries.

The Departmental Library

The Departmental Library, as it presently exists, is the result of a merger of three former libraries. The Health Services and Promotion (HSP), and Medical Services Branch (MSB) Libraries were merged organizationally in 1987. In 1992, the Policy, Communications and Information (PC&I) Library, which had been created to serve four branches (Policy, Communications and Information; Social Services Programmes; Income Security Programmes; and Corporate Management Branch, as it was then called) merged with the HSP/ MSB Library to form the new Departmental Library.

Although brought together under one administration, the Departmental Library presently exists in three sites, a situation that is expected to continue until 1998. At that time, the three sites are scheduled to move to one location in the Jeanne Mance building with a satellite library in the Brooke Claxton building.

The Health Protection Branch Libraries

Health Protection Branch (HPB) Libraries have existed in one form or another since the 1940s. The development of a separate library organization within HPB is directly attributable to the sizeable information needs of a scientific organization. Prior to the formation of the HPB itself, the libraries in the Branch were part of particular directorates. In 1974, the Branch Management Committee agreed to transfer the Branch library resources to the former Departmental Library to enable it to administer library and information services on behalf of the Branch. When it became apparent that the Departmental Library was unable to meet HPB needs, an HPB library network was set up.

From 1974 to 1985, the HPB developed and operated a centrally administered network of libraries serving particular directorates while relying on the Departmental Library for centralized publication ordering, cataloguing and inter-library loan. For most of this period, the HSP libraries consisted of three libraries reporting to the Chief of the HPB Library Services Division: the Banting Library (serving the Food, Drugs and Former Field Operations Directorates); the LCDC Library; and the Environmental Health Library. The Chief of Library Services Division also had functional responsibility for HPB regional libraries in Montreal, Toronto and Vancouver. This meant that centralized services and collection support were provided to these libraries by the HPB Library Services Division in Ottawa.

When the original Departmental Library was closed in 1985/86, the Library Services Division in the HPB established its own centralized ordering, cataloguing and inter-library loan services for Ottawa and the regions. This arrangement with centralized services for a distributed network of HPB libraries has remained more or less constant to the present, with the addition of two libraries: the Drug Library in Holland Cross (formerly Place Vanier), funded by the Drugs Directorate, and the Radiation Protection Library on Brookfield Road, funded by the Environmental Health Directorate.

Current services and cooperative activities

Both the Departmental and HPB Libraries provide services to a wide range of Health Canada officials and employees in multi-disciplinary and professional fields in the National Capital Region (NCR) and in regional offices and locations across the country. These services include:

* Reference and referral
* On-line and CD-ROM database searching
* Current awareness alerting services (for example tables of contents, SDIs etc.)
* Circulation of library materials, inter-library loans and document delivery
* Journal routeing
* Acquisitions
* Library orientation and training

Selected services are also offered on a cooperative basis to external clients in other federal departments and agencies, as well as provincial, territorial and municipal governments, Members of Parliament, academic institutions, hospitals and community health centres, professional organizations and special interest groups, health-based industries and members of the general public with a specific interest in health-related issues.

The collections of the Health Canada Libraries reflect the evolving information needs of the department's programme areas. These areas rely heavily on their libraries, and programme staff, particularly in the HPB, want to be assured that the libraries will continue to provide the resources and services that their areas require. A cooperative acquisitions programme between the Departmental Library and the HPB Libraries optimizes the use of resources and minimizes duplication.

The Departmental Library focuses its acquisitions in the areas of health policy and reform, health insurance and finance, health promotion and preventive medicine, mental health, health of specific populations (Aboriginals, children, women and seniors), family violence, international comparative studies and documents (for example World Health Organization depository collection), general management and public administration, and statutory instruments and parliamentary papers.

The collections of the HPB Libraries include the following programme-related subjects: nutrition, pharmacology, toxicology, analytical chemistry and biochemistry, microbiology and immunology, epidemiology, communicable and chronic diseases, occupational health and safety, biotechnology and biostatistics, veterinary medicine, and environmental studies and pollution.

Collection resources in both libraries include not only traditional formats such as books and journals, but also electronic resources, such as CD-ROMs, on-line databases and Internet-based information. Services and collections are not static, but are continuously adapted to meet changing programme needs and shifts in policy initiatives within the department.

Results of the review

Three methods of data collection were used in the review: a survey of Health Canada staff; key informant interviews with managers and senior managers; and an examination of recent Health Canada policy documents and their relationship to library and information services. A summary of the results is presented below.

Survey of Health Canada staff

The first part of the survey of Health Canada staff was designed to determine the current importance of and satisfaction with existing library services and to gather ideas for new or changing service requirements from the client's perspective. A second part of the survey asked staff to answer a series of questions based on a specific use of the library. We were interested in the perceived value of the information, the amount of time saved (if any), and the equivalent dollar value and the relative importance of different information sources used in the particular situation, including the library. These measures are based on Professor Marshall's earlier research on the value and impact of specialized library services (Marshall, 1992, 1993).

The questionnaire was sent to a stratified random sample of 582 employees in the National Capital Region (NCR) and various regions across the country between October and December 1995. The overall response rate for the survey is 66 per cent ($n=382$). This response rate itself is a positive indication of the support for the libraries among Health Canada staff. In general, the results demonstrate the value and importance of libraries for Health Canada employees, reflecting the knowledge-intensive nature of the department's work. Almost three-quarters of the 382 participating employees say that the libraries are important to their job and only 9 per cent indicate that they do not need libraries to do their job. Over 80 per cent ($n=307$) of the employees were library users. Reported use was higher among HPB staff (90 per cent) compared to other branches (66 per cent).

Two thirds of the library users report that such use saves them time by relieving them of having to find some information themselves or helping them to find it more quickly. Reported time savings were translated into dollars by estimating the value of the respondent's time according to their classification and level using the 1995 salary tables. Based on an average of 30 reported uses of the HPB Libraries annually, and a conservative cost savings estimate of $100 per use, the extrapolated net savings to the department are over $1.6 million. A similar analysis of Departmental Library users, based on an average of 13 reported uses annually, shows savings of over $816 000. Actual savings are undoubtedly much higher, since 80 per cent of the total respondents reported that they were library users, but our conservative calculations are based only on a lower percentage of questionnaire respondents who provided an amount of time saved.

Cost savings were also reported in a 1993 study of special libraries in the United States. In organizations where a library was available, the annual cost per professional employee to acquire information was US$1700. When no library was available in the organization and information sources outside the organization had to be tapped, the annual cost rose to US$5010. The study also found that libraries in organizations increased productivity and enabled work to be performed faster, better and with higher quality (Griffiths and King, 1993).

Specific ways in which the information obtained from the libraries provides value for Health Canada staff are shown in Figures C5.1 and C5.2 (see page 256). Similar proportions from HPB and staff from other branches report that the information: refreshed their memory; made them more confident about making decisions; provided new information; verified previous knowledge; and made them think of a new dimension that they had not thought of before. In addition, the information contributed to better informed decision making and higher-quality reports. HPB staff were more likely to say that the information helped them resolve a problem. This result, and the slightly higher measures for HPB staff generally, may reflect the nature of scientific work and the importance of library and information services in these environments.

Health Canada staff use information from a variety of sources for decision making. When asked to rate the sources they had used in the particular decision-making situation, 283 respondents provided a rating for the libraries, 255 for their own materials, 233 for other employees, 212 for external contacts and 82 for the Internet. The library resources are rated as being of considerable or great importance by two thirds of the respondents, second only to the individual's own files and books. A comparison of HPB and respondents from other branches (see Figure C5.3 on page 258) shows that HPB staff rate the libraries considerably higher, while staff in other departments assign slightly greater importance to other employees and external contacts as information sources. The Internet is rated less highly as an information source. In addi-

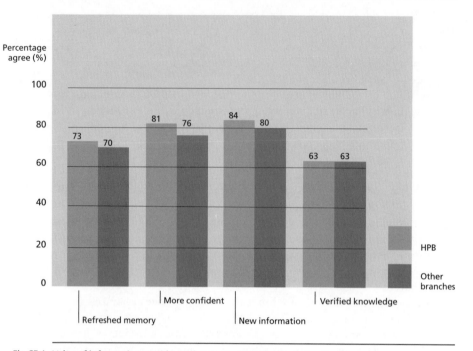

Fig C5.1   **Value of information.** HPB (n=208) compared to other branches (n=99)

Includes only those respondents who indicated that they had used the libray in the
past 12 months; total number of respondents varies by item

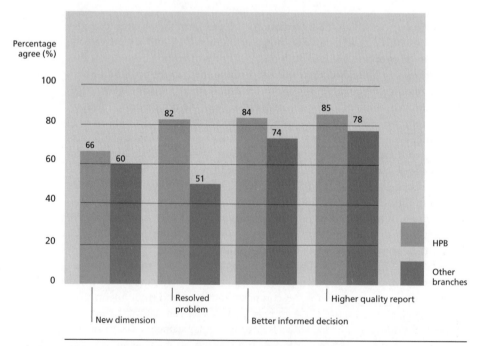

Fig C5.2   **Value of information.** HPB (n=208) compared to other branches (n=99)

	Importance rating*	Satisfaction rating**	Gap
Electronic access	89.6	67.6	22.0
Training on electronic sources	85.7	64.5	21.2
Ease of use	99.0	84.7	14.3
Convenient location	96.8	85.4	11.4
Journal collections	95.7	85.9	9.8
Speed of service	98.0	88.9	9.1
Library catalogue	93.3	85.6	7.7

*Rating based on the percentage of respondents who rated importance as high or medium.

**Rating based on the percentage of respondents who rated satisfaction as satisfied or very satisfied.

Table C5.1   **Importance/satisfaction gaps**

tion, the Internet was only used by 82 of the respondents, 58 of whom were at HPB and 24 in the other branches. These results suggest that, while the Internet is an important emerging information source, it is still problematic and not accessible to all.

When staff in the National Capital Region (NCR) are compared with the other regions (see Figure C5.4 on page 258), we note that libraries are rated slightly lower by staff in the regions, as are the individual's own files and books. Higher importance ratings for staff in the regions go to other employees and the Internet. Again the Internet results should be interpreted with caution, since only 11 Internet users were in the regions compared to 71 in the NCR. These results suggest that greater attention to regional library services is warranted.

An importance/satisfaction gap analysis of various aspects of library service provides some specific guidance for priority setting. As shown in Table C5.1, the greatest importance/satisfaction gaps are in electronic access, ease of use, training in electronic sources, and convenient location, followed by journal collections, speed of service and the library catalogue. A closer examination of the data shows an electronic access gap of 3.5 for HPB Libraries and 17.7 for the other libraries. This result is probably related to the restricted access to the Departmental Library catalogue in recent months and shows the importance of such services.

The former results are confirmed in the ratings given to potential new library services. Although all such services listed, including desktop electronic access, Internet training, electronic submission of document requests, electronic tables of contents, electronic environmental scanning and a database of Health Canada publications were all rated as highly desirable by the respondents, desktop electronic access was rated as the most important by 43 per cent of respondents.

Health Canada staff had an opportunity on the survey to write in one aspect of library services that they appreciated. Almost one third of the respondents noted the helpfulness of staff. When respondents were asked to list one way in

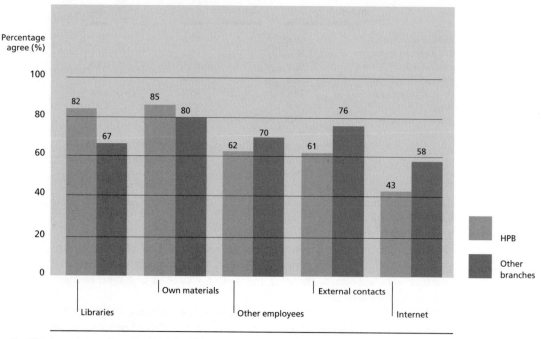

Fig C5.3 **Importance of sources.** * HPB (n=208) compared to other branches (n=99)

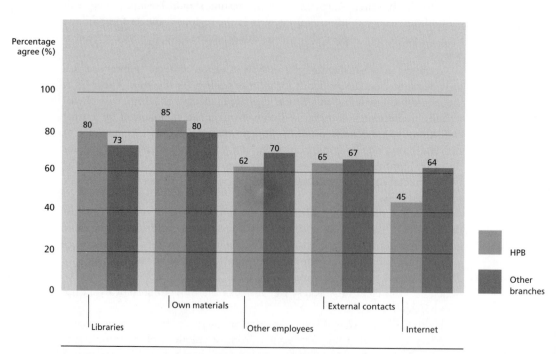

Fig C5.4 **Importance of sources.** * NCR (n=221) compared to other regions (n=86)

* Includes only those respondents who indicated that they had used the library in the past 12 months;
total number of respondents varies by item

which the libraries could improve services, the two most frequently mentioned items were improved electronic access and increased marketing of library services to promote awareness.

Key informant interviews

In addition to the survey results that gathered data on current experiences with library services, we were anxious to speak with senior managers representing various Branches and Directorates. We thought that these managers would be able to provide an aerial view of how and where the libraries could best position themselves to contribute to Health Canada's strategic directions in the future. Over 20 key informant interviews were conducted.

Our general finding was that organized and accessible information is seen as a critical resource for department work. As one senior manager in HPB said:

> We are basically a science-based organization ... we need scientific publications such as books and journals in print and electronic form. Libraries are critical because if we want to maintain our credibility as a science-based organization then we have to have the tools. We have to be assured that the science and technology information needs in our core businesses are addressed, i.e. the documentation required for people in the Branch to do their business has to be part of the overall core thrust.

Another manager commented on the need for library and information service by the Health Programmes and Services Branch:

> The Branch as a whole has an increasing interest in electronic dissemination of information with Internet being a likely vehicle. There are roles for the library in providing better and less expensive ways of obtaining information and providing improved access to international documents and developments, including having full documents in electronic form. The library should be the central access point for information of all types, including survey data.

A manager involved in population health noted that, even though the consequences of missing an article are not as serious as they are in other parts of the organization, the literature plays an important role for the directorate in identifying priorities and trends and identifying the need for change. Since topics of interest relate to health issues of the population, the need for information is very broad-ranging.

The new evidence-based approach to decision making in the department was seen as one that requires strong library and information services. There was also an indication that initiatives such as dealing with risks to the health of Canadians require a more interdisciplinary approach. As one manager put it, 'Risk assessment is scientific. Risk management is more policy oriented'.

Despite the perceived importance of information, many managers still report having difficulty obtaining and using the information that they and their staff need to work effectively. This includes both internal information in their own files and information from the libraries. The multiplicity of available information sources and the inadequacy of information technology to provide simple, convenient, and organized desktop access appear to be at the root of the problem. As a senior manager said:

> I consider information as an asset, but we have tons of data but no information
> ... we need better information from the provinces and from academia ... the real
> issue is information management.

There were strong indications in the interviews that the Health Canada
Libraries could play an important role in information management. Librarians have developed effective means of providing access to large, complex,
multiple-format collections of information and this expertise can be used to
assist the department in organizing its own internal information.

In the new world of electronic information, visionary managers saw the librarian as a facilitator or interface. As one manager said:

> I do not want my reviewers and researchers spending time tracking information
> down as opposed to analysing the information ... the more streamlined the inform-
> ation, the better ... this is professional librarianship. The sooner information is elec-
> tronic and coming to the user as opposed to the user going to it, the better. The
> more it is organized and rendered appropriate to the user, the better. The medium
> of libraries is changing, but not the whole. Libraries become the antennae to the
> organization, but with faster, broader electronic mechanisms. The role of the librar-
> ian as point person in knowledge identification and dissemination continues.

There was considerable discussion about the need for the concept of the
library to move away from a collection orientation towards a broader concept
of meeting information needs. There was strong support for a greater role for
librarians in developing an electronically accessible system of information
resources and provide training and support in the use of the system. There
was some scepticism about the Internet as a potential time-waster for Health
Canada staff and a role for the librarian was seen in identifying, selecting and
organizing access to appropriate Internet resources for department use.

There are many information-based initiatives ongoing in Health Canada,
such as the Public Health Information Network, Health Promotion On-line
and the LCDC Electronic Bulletin Boards; however, the interviews revealed
that direct links between these activities and the library have not always been
recognized or made. The libraries have the potential to provide consultation
and advice on the development of information products and services. Other
examples provided by senior managers where the libraries could play a role
include the development of an electronic environmental scanning service and
a database of Health Canada publications.

Another senior manager saw librarians as key people in developing information policy for the department and selecting the most appropriate electronic
products and services available externally. Such roles involve contract management and the ability to keep the overall information needs of the department in mind.

The most exciting idea to emerge from the key informant interviews was
that of Richard Van Loon, the Associate Deputy Minister, who identified an
important national leadership and policy role for Health Canada in the coordination of access to health library and information services. At the present
time, there are many health library resources located in universities, hospitals
and other public and private agencies in Canada, but there is no coordinated
national network for the development of health library and information
service policy and resource sharing. As a result, many practising health pro-

fessionals and others who need health information do not have access to
adequate and affordable library and information services.

In contrast, the US National Library of Medicine has developed such a network through its National Network of Libraries of Medicine (NN/LM) and
the National Health Service has appointed a Library Advisor to explore opportunities for cooperation and networking in the UK. During the course of
the libraries review, Professor Marshall prepared a brief concept paper for a
national health library network initiative and funding was approved to conduct a feasibility study. Health Canada has a great opportunity to provide the
national leadership required to meet this important need.

The lack of connection between library and information services and the
Health Canada business lines that was evident in the key informant interviews
prompted a further exploration of current initiatives and the possible linkages
with library and information services. The findings are discussed in the following section.

Health Canada business lines and library and information services

Two recent reports demonstrate the strong relationship between library and
information services and Canada's national health objectives: *Health Canada
Outlook 1996–97 to 1998–99* (April 1996) and *S&T at Work for the Health of
Canadians: The Science and Technology Action Plan of the Federal Health Portfolio* (1996).

Health Canada Outlook (1996, page 1) states that 'Leadership on health is
pivotal to all areas of the federal agenda.' The department is responsible for
ensuring that Canada has a strong health information and consultation network for anticipating, assessing and preventing emerging risks to the population through the public health intelligence network. This initiative and the
other three areas of federal responsibility – health system support and
renewal; services to First Nations; and the population health strategy – are all
knowledge-based, information-intensive activities that require strong health
library and information services.

As the report states, health issues will not stand still or decline due to fiscal
constraint. Rather, they are increasing in complexity and sometimes fre-
quency of occurrence due to Canada's shifting demographic structure and
the impacts of globalization and new technologies *(Health Canada Outlook
1996–97 to 1998–99*, page 5). As information becomes global and information
technology becomes available to provide access to information at an international level, it is important to reinvest in library and information services as a
mechanism for taking advantage of these opportunities.

The future role of Health Canada will be focused on policy, frameworks
and monitoring of results, all of which require strong library and information
support. Partnerships and complementarity of skills with provinces, territories
and stakeholders are emphasized (ibid, page 6). One of the key areas requiring
library and information support is Health Canada's goal of 'strengthening the
use of available research results and evidence in its own decisions and those of
its partners within the health system' (ibid, page 7). Health Canada Libraries
are the source for research results and evidence.

According to *Health Canada Outlook,* the department is 'strengthening the coverage, quality and dissemination of information derived from a broad range of internal and external sources' (ibid, page 9). A renewed focus on the science information base required for decisions across the health care system is evident through the implementation of the Health Services Research Fund (ibid, page 13). Information dissemination is also fundamental to the activities of the National Forum on Health which has established a dialogue with Canadians about the future of the health care system.

In the s&t document, the Minister again emphasizes that Canadians are looking to the federal government for leadership on health issues: 'With federal funding for health research less than a third of the Canadian total, and a tiny fraction of the worldwide investment, we need to make strategic investments in order to achieve the fullest and most effective use of available funds, ideas, facilities and highly qualified people in the future' *(S&T at Work,* 1996, Minister's message). Again, this statement points to the importance of research support through health library and information services as well as the role that libraries play in making the world's research available to Canadians.

In his message, the Minister states the importance of increasing the dissemination and use of health s&t information and addressing critical knowledge gaps. Excellent health library and information services are essential to the 'dynamic and internationally competitive health s&t capacity in the form of ideas, people and facilities' envisaged by the Minister.

A number of specialized programmes for disseminating health s&t information are highlighted in the report including HPB's Prevention of Adverse Drug Reactions, Food Safety and Heart Health (ibid, pages 29–30). In addition to these projects, Health Canada Libraries provide a wealth of knowledge as support for these programmes and others. The libraries themselves are a critical but, as our study suggests, less recognized element in Health Canada's s&t information dissemination strategy.

Health Canada's commitment to active use of the Internet through tools such as Health Promotion On-line and the LCDC Electronic Bulletin Board service is evident in the report (ibid, page 31). Health Canada Libraries have the potential to play essential roles in improving and maintaining the quality of these information resources by providing authoritative information and verifying the content of these electronic information products. Just as Health Canada Libraries have acted as depositories for collections of international print documents in the past, such as those from the World Health Organization, new opportunities exist for the libraries to develop linkages with the international electronic networks.

The promotion of a stronger science culture in Canada is among the new strategic directions of the health portfolio. Respect for the contribution of and reinvestment in health libraries and information services is a positive demonstration of such support that will benefit not only scientists and health care practitioners, but also the citizens of Canada.

The need for an information management strategy at Health Canada that takes a broad approach to internal and external sources of information, including libraries, was evident in our study results. The Treasury Board Document *Blueprint for Renewing Government Services Using Information Technology*

(1994), as well as the response to the document from the National Library of Canada (1994), contains the kind of broad-based thinking that will be required to address these issues. The report entitled *Gateway to a World of Information: Federal Government Libraries in the 1990s* provides additional detail about the changing role of libraries in the information age.

A best practices scenario for Health Canada Libraries

Health Canada Libraries will be a virtual network of library and information services providing one-stop electronic access to high-quality health information. The Health Canada librarians will be subject specialists who function as information resource system developers and managers, teachers and user support experts, and information consultants to Health Canada initiatives. Health Canada Libraries and library staff will be seen as integral to the business lines of the department because of their client-centred and evidence-based approach. The Health Canada Libraries will play a national leadership role in the networking and coordination of existing health library and information services in order to provide equitable access to health information for Canadians.

This scenario for the future of Health Canada Libraries emerges from the data collected in the review and our analysis of how the libraries could play a more fundamental role in assisting the Health portfolio to meet its objectives. Our vision of best practice builds on past success, but moves the libraries from a support to a leadership role within Health Canada, as well as nationally and internationally. To realize this scenario, the following are required:

- High-quality international data standards, such as MARC and Z39.50, must be adopted so that all Health Canada Libraries catalogues and electronic databases can function in a shared, seamless user interface.
- Health Canada librarians must become key players in the department's information management team so that library services can be integrated into other information-based applications for single-window access.
- A new, more integrated management model for Health Canada Libraries must be found that will cost-effectively combine key products, such as the catalogues, as well as other work processes and policies. Such a model must also ensure accountability and responsiveness to branch and directorate initiatives.
- The use of technological advances for the electronic delivery of information to the desktop in a uniform format must be maximized to the extent that existing resources allow.
- Library services must continue to be client-centred and based on information needs expressed by users. Librarians must adopt their own version of evidence-based practice in the efficient delivery of library and information services.
- Health Canada Libraries must continue to develop the highest-quality and most cost-effective collections, services and expertise that are oriented towards the business lines of the department.

- Health Canada initiatives, particularly those that are information-based, such as the Public Health Information Network and Health Promotion On-line, must be explored.
- Health Canada Libraries staff must be given the opportunity to develop the knowledge and skills required for the evolving roles that have been described in the report.
- Senior management and library staff must work together to ensure a broader and more collaborative vision of library and information services in the department.
- Library and information services must be marketed effectively so that Health Canada maximizes the return on its investment.
- New initiatives that will foster a broader vision of the library, such as the electronic environmental scanning service, database of Health Canada publications and full-text electronic documents, must be pursued.
- Strategic partnerships with other national and provincial libraries, including the National Library of Canada and the Canada Institute for Scientific and Technical Information, must continue to be explored.
- Health Canada's national leadership opportunity to facilitate the development of a National Network of Health Library and Information Services should be supported through an in-depth feasibility study.
- Health Canada Libraries must become the gateway to international health information for Canadians, as well as the gateway to Canadian health information for the rest of the world.

Conclusion

This report has drawn upon evidence gathered as part of the Health Canada Libraries Review to develop a broadly based best practices scenario for what the Health Canada Libraries could become. The basic requirements that need to be in place for the scenario to be realized are also enumerated. The report was intended as a discussion document for consensus building about the future of the Health Canada Libraries. The document is also an example of the type of initiative that librarians can take in order to position themselves in the organization and to work towards the development of library and information policies that will put their vision into action.

References

Gateway to a World of Information: Federal Government Libraries in the 1990s. Federal Libraries Study Final Report. *Liaison,* Special issue, January–February 1994

GRIFFITHS, JOSE-MARIE and KING, DONALD W. (1993) *Special Libraries: Increasing the Information Edge,* Washington, DC: Special Libraries Association

Health Canada Outlook 1996–97 to 1998–99, Ottawa: Government of Canada, April 1996

MARSHALL, JOANNE G. (1992), 'The impact of hospital libraries on clinical decision-making: the Rochester study', *Bulletin of the Medical Library Association,* 80 (2), 169–78

MARSHALL, JOANNE G. (1993), *The Impact of the Special Librarian on Corporate Decision-making,* Washington, DC: Special Libraries Association

National Library of Canada (1994), *A Response to the Treasury Board's Blueprint for Renewing Government Services Using Information Technology,* 29 May

S&T at Work for the Health of Canadians: The Science and Technology Action Plan of the Federal Health Portfolio, Ottawa: Minister of Supply and Services Canada, 1996.

Treasury Board of Canada Secretariat (1994), *Blueprint for Renewing Government Services Using Information Technology,* Ottawa

WALLINGFORD, KAREN T., RUFFIN, ANGELA B., GINTER, KAREN A., et al. (1996) 'Outreach activities of the National Library of Medicine: a five-year review', *Bulletin of the Medical Library Association,* 84 (2), Supplement, 1–60

Information Planning Board, Queensland Government

Introduction

Many governments have struggled without conspicuous success with national information policies, and some have attempted to ensure that at any rate their own departments have a policy for managing information and apply it (see page 16 for current UK developments). This case study looks at how the government of one of the Australian states is seeking, through an Information Planning Board, to get its departments and agencies (statutory bodies) to manage their information resources.

It is unlikely that information in any aspect, let alone the concept of managing it and making it accessible to the public, was a concern uppermost in the mind of the Queensland Government in power before 1989, which gained its reputation for quite other characteristics. In 1989, however, with a change of government, a review of the use of IT was set up. As with many such exercises, this one revealed that strategic planning for the use of information itself was in need of attention. The report from the review in 1990 stated that information was a government resource that must be managed. Two of the strategies proposed to this end were:

1 To develop procedures to define and review policies and guidelines for the management of information on a government-wide basis
2 To establish procedures to review how well they were being implemented.

An Information Policy Board (IPB) was set up on an interim basis in 1990 to coordinate IT and information management, and to spread good practice. Its formal establishment followed in 1992.[1]

In 1991 the interim body issued the first guidelines on information planning. These identified aims for the government's business strategy for the next five years, with indications of the information implications. The people concerned with producing the guidelines mostly came from an IT/systems background, and the guidelines had a strong focus on the systems side, with emphasis on the economic benefits of reducing the duplication of effort. The move towards information management came as the IPB started looking at how to make access to information easier both within government and for people outside.

---

[1] Following a further change of government in 1996, the name was changed to the Information Planning Board. The Board's members are the CEOs of central departments, together with representation from a line agency, and it is chaired by the Director-General of the Department of the Premier and Cabinet. It provides overall policy guidance and direction, while the Information Planning Branch (within the Department of the Premier and Cabinet) which reports to the Board, is responsible for implementing the information management agenda.

This approach was able to draw support from the 1992 report of the Public Sector Management Commission on *Managing Queensland's Public Sector,* which defined the objective of the Queensland Government as 'to advance the Queensland community economically, socially, educationally and culturally', as appropriate information and its management were clearly important for achieving the desired aim. As the IPB expressed it in its *Information Standard. Policies for the management of information within government* (Information Policy Board, 1994) outlined below:

> The Queensland Government collects information and also obtains information from other sources on behalf of the community, and is responsible to the public for the management of that information, in order to enhance Queensland's economic, social and cultural development, and to improve the quality of life of its people ... Information ... is needed at all levels of Government to assist in the achievement of business aims and objectives. ... [it] is essential for the provision of products and services to the public ...

Information serves as evidence of the way government operates and of the transactions it carries out. Failure to retain full records can result in enormous financial cost to government and/or severely disadvantage its citizens. And 'a significant percentage of each Agency's budget is spent on information handling activities'.

Policies for information management

The IPB's 1994 statement of policies for government agencies sets out their obligations in the matter in these terms:

> The Queensland Government is responsible to the community for effectively managing the information in its care. To facilitate this, all Agencies are required to develop, document, implement and review appropriate policies and practices for the management of information as a Government resource.

Eight principles are to be observed in information policies:
1 Accountability
2 Information exchange
3 Information accessibility
4 Compliance with legal and administrative requirements
5 Information preservation
6 Business continuity
7 Privacy and confidentiality
8 Copyright and other intellectual property.

The Board recognizes that implementation of information management policies within agencies will have significant resource implications and therefore recommends them to identify their priority areas for information and tackle them first.

The main part of the *Standard* consists of guidelines for managing information within government. Good-quality information is characterized as: accessible, accurate, auditable, complete, compliant, concise, consistent, current, effective, flexible/coordinated, precise, relevant, secure, and timely. The benefits from having and managing information to meet these standards are:

- More effective and efficient management of resources
- Improved decision making
- More responsiveness to external information requests
- An environment conducive to improved services, increased value
- Improved access, better opportunities for sharing information internally and externally
- Reduced costs from having complete, accurate and accessible information for legal proceedings
- Potential for increased value of information products and services, arising from combination of information from disparate sources
- Lower handling/storage costs
- Increased flexibility, faster response to change
- Improved consistency, reliability, and integration of information from various sources
- More stability – effectively structured data are more robust, requiring less maintenance
- Better response to situations requiring evidence of actions.

The critical success factors for an information policy that will give the benefits are:
- Commitment from CEOs and senior management
- A framework of clearly defined information management policies and objectives supported by standards and procedures, effectively communicated and understood by staff
- Accountability clearly defined and communicated throughout organization
- Measurement of successful implementation via regular auditing and review
- A culture in which information is valued.

Before setting out on the process of developing and implementing information policy and information management based on it, agencies need to have clearly defined business aims and objectives, roles and responsibilities, policies, standards, guidelines and procedures. They need to understand:
- How information supports the business – what its aims and objectives are, the information needed to support them, what is actually available and not available, how information can best be delivered to users, and the potential for further successful exploitation of specific information
- How effective it is in supporting the business
- The value/cost of supporting the business with enhanced access to information
- The potential value of information to public or individuals
- The potential of unfair gain by early or selective access to information.

And they need to know:
- What information the agency has
- What relevant information is collected, stored or used by other agencies, businesses or organizations
- Where it is stored and in what form
- Who manages and/or maintains it
- Who owns it

- Who has access to what information
- Who should have or should not have access
- How it can be accessed
- How and when information should be disclosed for equity between potential beneficiaries
- How comprehensive it is
- How accurate it is
- What it is worth.

In short, what the guidelines recommend is the kind of process described in Chapters 3–4 of determining what organizations need to do with information to achieve their objectives, matching it against the reality of what they are actually doing (for example by information auditing), and using that as a foundation for action, change initiatives, establishing costs and values, and monitoring progress.

The guidelines go on to give a framework of information management principles and strategies for agencies to adapt to their own needs.

1 *Accountability.* The Information Policy Board recommended that each department should set up an information steering committee with responsibility for coordinating the management and application of its information resource to support the corporate directions and business functions of government and the department. Departments should nominate custodians to assume responsibility and accountability to the information steering committee. Accountability also includes the obligation to document agency policies, and standards and procedures in respect of publications. Practices for such information management processes as compliance, review of economic value of the information portfolio, planning for future use of information resources, access rules, security, accuracy, etc. should be documented and communicated to all relevant staff. 'The "value" placed on information need not be economic but could be in terms of the impact on Agencies and stakeholders if information is lost, or in the context of "how easy is it to replace?"'

2 *Exchange.* Each agency is to develop, document and implement policies and practices for exchange or sharing of information across government, the private sector and the wider community, and to balance them as necessary with privacy considerations, which should be identified in policies and practices. Agencies should consider identifying information sets which may be of particular interest to the private sector, with a view to developing strategies for exploiting them in conjunction with information brokers or industry partners for mutual benefit, as a contribution to the state's economic growth.

3 *Accessibility.* Agencies should aim at continuous improvement through involvement of all staff with a common focus on quality outcomes. They should develop, document and implement appropriate standards to ensure the quality of the information resource; the standards should include those for data, technology and data exchange – for which a standards inventory should be maintained. They should assess the risk associated with incorrect key information: where it is high, stringent procedures should be applied

to ensure integrity. Quality assurance is needed for authoritative information; a single definitive source should be identified where appropriate, and information dissemination within agencies, especially in respect of publications, should be a central responsibility. Agencies should maintain an 'information portfolio' of their information holdings, linked to the relevant business or programme area, by documenting the functions which have an impact on information, as the basis for an 'enterprise information model'. The portfolio could be maintained by periodic information audits, a data dictionary, and guidance for comprehensive systems documentation.

4 *Compliance*. Agencies should ensure that legal deposit requirements are met; they should assign responsibility for monitoring new Acts for information management implications, and keep staff informed of those which could affect their area of responsibility.

5 *Preservation*. Agencies must provide for the preservation of information for administrative, evidential and historical purposes.

6 *Business continuity*. This principle covers physical security, disaster planning and recovery, archiving, retention and disposal.

7 *Privacy and confidentiality*. Agencies are to ensure that personal information, commercial-in-confidence information, and other sensitive information is not misused, in accordance with the Commonwealth Privacy Act, 1988.

8 *Copyright and other intellectual property*. Agencies must develop appropriate policies and practices to meet existing Information Standards on these issues.

Implementation

In the early period when the IPB was seeking to help agencies towards implementing the concepts and practices set out in the guidelines, two issues arose:
1 When information was known to exist, there could be reluctance to give other departments access unless they paid a commercial rate for it. This arose from a Treasury policy of encouraging departments and agencies to seek opportunities to gain financial benefit from giving access to their information. There has indeed been a constant tension within government between, on the one hand, making information more freely available for the greater economic and social good, and, on the other, the desire to obtain some return on the investment made in information.

The Information Standard of 1994 attempted to address the problem by identifying categories of users (for example, the general public, other Queensland government agencies) as a basis for charging policies. More recently, the Information Planning Branch developed a draft information access and pricing policy, which seeks to give freer access to government information. It states that certain classes of information (for example legislation) should be provided free of charge, while other government information (excepting information products) should be available at no more than the cost of provision. The Branch has been working with the Treasury and other departments to address some of the budgetary issues for departments. Subject to endorsement, the policy will be implemented stage by stage, with the support of the IPB and the Treasury for agencies which encounter any budgetary problems.

The Queensland Spatial Information Infrastructure Strategy (formerly Queensland Land Information Strategy, and led by the Department of Natural Resources) provided an early example of the recognition of the value of information and the need for effective information management practices. The participating departments took a cooperative approach to the development of policies and standards, including pricing arrangements; government departments are able to purchase information for non-commercial purposes at no more than the cost of provision.

2 Duplication across departments. A traditional IT approach was taken at first, via data models and data dictionaries, but it was found not to get very far, and the Board changed its approach to spreading good internal information management practice. It set up an inter-agency Information Management Network, to look at the management of information services; issues considered include privacy, archiving, charging, planning, for which working groups were set up. Regular briefing sessions were held for departments to pass on useful experience. With pressure on resources, the Network and working groups wound down.

The IPB also tried to collate departmental strategic information plans, in order to identify government-wide strategic trends and priorities; the attempt was, however, suspended following the restructuring of departments with the change of government in 1996.

The Information Policy Branch continues to promote awareness of the role and importance of information management in government to senior managers in collaboration with relevant agencies. There are problems of focus, and it is recognized that the training needs to be very concrete and related to their work.

While the Information Management Standard of 1994 has been generally accepted by agencies, the process of implementation is a lengthy one. Many people in government departments now understand the significance of information, but, as recognized by the IPB, they suffer resource problems. These problems have, among other things, prevented departments from following the recommendation in the standard that they should develop and maintain an 'information portfolio' or inventory of their information holdings and resources.

The Branch has made some attempts to broaden the focus of the IT industry to include information management. For a period in 1996/97 it worked with the Information Industries Board in an attempt to gain some common understanding among the stakeholders in the area of health information (for example government, clinicians, health industry software developers, etc).

Currently the Branch is working on an information management framework in conjunction with the Communication and Information Technology Branch of the Department of Public Works and Housing, who are developing the related IT framework. Both will support an on-line services strategy which is also to be developed. The key concept driving the strategy, which is also that of the information management framework, is the idea of 'seamless or transparent' access to government services, as a means of making citizens' transactions with government less burdensome and complicated. As the Branch points out, this can only succeed if it is based on a shared vision and approach across government, and on a common framework of policies and standards, supported by common technology platforms.

A relevant development in this connection is the shift that has taken place in the last few years in the larger departments, such as Education, Police, and Health to information management units consisting of IT, records, and libraries.

The Branch has also been working with the Commonwealth Government and other Australian states in looking at the issue of access to government information, and the possibility of a single entry point to Australian government information, which would allow searches on a given subject across all levels of government. So far the work has looked at such issues as navigation, searching and terminology, and at the cost justification for an initiative of this kind.

Evaluation

This case study records an encouraging initiative which has produced some sound foundations, in an area which has perplexed, if not defeated, many attempts at developing policies for managing information. Advantage was taken of one change of government which removed obstacles to such a policy, and while a recent further change has brought some problems, they have been met with perseverance – which is one of the main lessons to be learned. Teams which have a continuity of experience can draw a certain advantage from that, when the composition of the top level to which they are accountable changes. They can use their experience and knowledge to make strategic decisions on what has to be sacrificed at any rate for the present, what to seek to preserve at all costs, where to try to concentrate resources, and how to present the case to the 'new management'.

It is particularly to be hoped that pressure on resources will not stand in the way of action on such urgent requirements as a whole-of-government information architecture and a comprehensive picture of the data sets and major systems across government, which are essential if electronic service delivery is to mean something useful and helpful to all the parties concerned. There is a danger everywhere that governments – for lack of understanding of what information means, and failure to make modest investments in information strategy and information management – will waste large investments in information systems and technology to blunder their way into a version of electronic delivery which will mainly deliver a costly burden to the end users.

References

Information Policy Board (1994) *Information Standard Number 24. Policies for the management of information within government,* Brisbane: Queensland Government

Public Sector Management Commission (1992), *Managing Queensland's Public Sector*

Ministry of Agriculture, Fisheries and Food, Legal Department[1]

Case study

While a number of the case studies in this book include an account of information auditing as part of moves towards developing information policies and strategies, this is the only one which focuses in detail on the auditing process. For this reason, and because it is actually contributed by the person responsible for the audit described, it should have particular value for readers with a special interest in information auditing. EO

---

[1] Study contributed by Sue Westcott

The organization

The Ministry of Agriculture, Fisheries and Food (MAFF) has a wide-ranging remit. Its aims and objectives are:

1 To protect the public by:
- Promoting food safety
- Taking action against diseases with implications for human health
- Planning to safeguard essential supplies in an emergency
- Promoting action to alleviate flooding and coastal erosion.

2 To protect and enhance the rural and marine environment by:
- Protecting the rural economy, particularly in less favoured areas
- Encouraging action to reduce water and other pollution and safeguarding the aquatic environment, including its flora and fauna
- Improving the attractiveness and biodiversity of the rural environment.

3 To improve the economic performance of the agriculture, fishing and food industries by:
- Implementing MAFF's Common Agricultural Policy (CAP) obligations efficiently, and by seeking a more economically rational CAP while avoiding discrimination against UK businesses
- Creating the conditions in which efficient and sustainable agriculture, fishing and food industries can flourish
- Taking action against animal and plant diseases and pests.

4 To protect farm animals by:
- Encouraging high welfare standards.

5 To ensure the best use of internal resources in support of the Ministry's business by:
- Providing specialist support services
- Allocating resources where they are most needed
- Effective management and deployment of staff.

Among the specialist support services covered by the final aim is MAFF's Legal Department – the area where the information audit which forms the subject of this case study was carried out. Its objective is:

> To provide the Ministry and its agencies with legal and investigation services to a high professional standard, in a timely manner, and cost-effectively, so as to aid the attainment of their aims consistently with the requirements of the law and with principles of good administration.

In fulfilling this objective, the Department is required to have a thorough understanding of clients' businesses and their needs for legal and investigation services (clients in this context refers to Ministers and ministerial and agency staff); to keep under review the state of the law relevant to the clients' work and provide advance warning of any difficulties that may arise; and to ensure that there are adequate resources of people and finance for meeting clients' needs.

Background to the information audit

The audit carried out in MAFF Legal Department in 1995 was initiated by the librarian responsible for the Legal Library, initially as a result of the need to establish a way forward for the library in a rapidly changing environment. Various customer satisfaction surveys had been carried out, but nothing had ever looked at the way the customer base used (or wanted) information. The introduction of an office automation system was expected to produce business efficiencies but these had not been clearly identified. Customers were facing increasing pressure on their time just as information became more plentiful, easier to disseminate, and available in a variety of forms. The library also faced the problem of exploiting the new technology and maintaining existing paper collections within existing resources.

It was hoped that an audit would help establish the information needs of the business and give a clearer indication of the direction in which the library should target its resources. Senior management were happy to support the audit, and this led to full cooperation across the entire work group.

Office automation systems have been introduced into most UK government departments in the last five years. They consist of local and wide area networks, with e-mail and word-processing facilities, and they are now developing into the main work environment, in which information is easily created, copied, manipulated and disseminated. Shared work spaces allow work groups to develop information which is available to all from their desktop, and to develop databases which can improve management of information and projects. Communication is improved where people are geographically dispersed, and decision-making processes can be speeded up because many people can be consulted at once. The move towards packages such as Lotus Notes, which can automate workflow and encourage work groups to use shared work areas to create and discuss, and not just store, information will advance this process further.

Aims and objectives of the information audit

The purposes for which the audit was undertaken were:
* To look at the way information is managed. There was an increasing awareness that information is a resource, the same as staff, equipment, accommodation etc. It is estimated that government departments devote 50 per cent of their administrative budgets to handling information. Efficient management of this resource was therefore important.
* To identify information requirements. It is essential that the information requirements for any business are clarified. In Legal Department, it was vital to identify the link between information use and the achievement of business objectives. It was clear that opportunities existed, for example for using new technology to good effect (more opportunity to share information; time savings in consultation; information easier to update once, centrally; delivery of services such as CD-ROM products to people's desks). There was, however, no proof that any of this would be of benefit to the vast majority of the staff, who were somewhat suspicious of the technology. (In

the event, the audit provided useful information on the real potential benefits from IT, and where the difficulties still lay, which made it possible to
ensure that the opportunities identified were turned into real projects and
initiatives which met business needs. The findings from the audit also made
possible informed decisions on other aspects of information use, for example how to rearrange the library's collection to facilitate use.)
- To recommend specific actions to meet the information requirements.
- To look at practical ways to enhance local information management. This
  concerned not only the use of the facilities of the computer network, but
  also the way paper resources were managed, how the organization communicated, and ensuring that the principles of managing information were
  understood at a practical level
- To advise on the effective use of IT to facilitate this. The emphasis in MAFF
  was on delivering the equipment and ensuring that people could use the
  software to meet their own personal needs. Those in the Legal Department
  who were concerned with the provision of information services had increasingly realized that technology could do much more.

Methodology

First it was necessary to establish the business aims of the work group. In a
period when business plans and mission statements were commonplace, this
seemed superficially simple. However, it became clear that they were too general, and often represented an aspiration rather than a concrete set of proposals to work with. Key members of staff were approached, and a clearer picture
was gained of the direction Legal Department was taking and how they saw its
role within the Ministry. It was the detail which was helpful in this instance;
no mission statement would have given the detail I needed to target the services effectively. It was particularly gratifying to have such an open response,
and to observe the confidence of the senior staff with whom I spoke that the
audit would benefit the organization.

Second, existing resources needed to be identified. This involved not only
the library but also registered files, individual sets of documents, local databases, bulletin boards, etc.

The preliminary research gave a basic understanding of the needs of the
work group concerned, which could have been used to look for any obvious
discrepancies between what the information professional would expect to find
and what was found. This was difficult because the audit was a one-off and no
general picture would emerge. It was also important for me, as an insider carrying out the audit, to try to keep an open mind and not force the results into
an anticipated outcome. In retrospect, however, it would have helped to document the needs I expected to identify for later use as a point of comparison
with what was found.

Fifteen per cent of the work group was interviewed in interviews which
lasted between 45 minutes and one hour. These were carried out face to face
and followed a standard format. They covered these areas:
- How information was managed in the Legal Department
- Quality, currency and ease of use of information sources

- How information was processed
- How effectively it flowed
- Where and how it was stored
- What information sources were used.

The survey was followed up by a succinct report which was discussed with the Legal Adviser and others in the Department. The report included the quantitative data collected, and a summary of recommendations which covered the following areas:

- How information management could be improved across the work group
- What information was suitable for sharing
- What tools are suitable for disseminating shared information
- How storage and retrieval can be improved
- Information gaps.

Findings

The findings from the audit can be summarized as:

- *Identification of common requirements.* It was possible to isolate common information needs across the Department; these included contact and organizational information.
- *Clear specific benefits identifiable.* It was possible to suggest specific improvements in either processes or use of resources which would lead to better use of information. This was more often a case of exploiting the existing technology fully and appropriately than of the purchase of further systems or resources. It became possible, for instance, to make informed suggestions as to what sort of databases it might be helpful to develop in Microsoft Access – for example, we indexed the Reports of the Joint Committee on Statutory Instruments (the main body in the House of Commons which scrutinizes Statutory Instruments – SIs) and constructed the database in such a way that we could analyse the number of SIs which had been criticized which had come from MAFF, as well as identify specific SIs (there is no published index to them). We also used Access to produce a training database so that it was possible to keep track of which non-professional staff had attended which training courses – information we had to produce annually for the central training branch, a task which had hitherto always caused us problems.
- *Business objectives are hampered by poor information management.* Information on how specific legal questions had been dealt with was often hidden away in the files (or the head) of individual lawyers, and so often lost to the organization. As pressure increases on them to advise to very tight timescales, the lack of an adequate 'know-how' system was actually impeding their progress.
- *Users want help.* Many people felt overwhelmed by the new technology and the increasing tide of information. One of the group heads in Legal Department estimated that he received 50 messages a day through his e-mail, plus items by post, journal articles, etc. His support for the audit was based on the hope that it would give Legal Department a chance to see how it could

manage the information anarchy which our improved communication system had unleashed.

Benefits

The audit allowed me to break away from the traditional 'what do you think of the library services' survey, and to talk to users about their information needs and habits. This built up a more complete picture of information use in the department and the library's role in that. It was important to appreciate that the library's was a niche role, and to design and market the service accordingly. Realizing that you are competing for a very specific market is quite liberating, as it allows you to concentrate your resources where they are most needed, instead of feeling that you are not quite meeting anybody's needs.

The audit also identified 'new' users. These were the members of the investigations team, who are spread all over the country and often quite literally in the field. By giving me the opportunity for the first time of talking direct and building a working relationship with the individual inspectors in the investigations team, the audit revealed the full scope of their information needs. It had previously been concealed because of some misunderstanding of information-related job responsibilities on the part of a previous administrative staff member, through whom the inspectors' requests for information were channelled. The audit interviews made it clear that only very specific inquiries had been passed on to the library, and that the staff member who received the requests had used out-of-date sources to provide information on legislation rather than taking the inquiries to the library. Not surprisingly, the library had not known the true nature of the inspectors' information needs, and the inspectorate had been equally unaware of the full range of services the library provided, and, unimpressed by what they were receiving, were using other libraries and contacts. A clearer idea of the needs of this group meant that a strategy using the new technology could be drawn up to ensure that this part of the business was better served.

Opportunities to develop services were also identified. Previous customer service surveys had identified the journal circulation system as the least satisfactory service. Not enough copies of publications could be purchased, and these were often disposed of at the end of their lengthy circulation lists. Users, despite the pressure, resisted all attempts to reduce the number of journals they received or to move to an internal abstracting service. The Legal Department senior management team, however, clearly felt that the system and the staff were near breaking point, and the audit gave a firm basis to a move towards consideration of professional abstracting services, in electronic form, which could be networked to lawyers. A document supply service would supplement this. Funding would come from a reduction in the number of copies of publications purchased.

There was also an attempt to encourage use of a shared drive on the network to allow lawyers to comment on documents which were not necessarily drafted in their part of Legal Department – something which would go some way to alleviate the problems caused by those who draft failing to consult those who will later have to prosecute using MAFF legislation (MAFF is one of the few government departments which still carries out its own prosecutions). Although the potential benefits were quite clear and the technology easy to use, the opportunity was not taken up with any enthusiasm, probably because it was counter to a culture which did not formerly encourage drafting cooperatively. There is a valuable lesson here for all of us who seek to introduce change in the way in which people use information: changes which look logical and beneficial to the organization are not always immediately acceptable to those who would have to change the way they do things, and if such changes are to be achieved, time has to be given to negotiating and reaching understanding and agreement.

A clearer picture of the information flow became available to senior management. Information tended to flow down the management chain, and not to spread horizontally until group head level. Action is now being considered to coordinate information so that lawyers receive information across the Department as well as in the management chain.

Specific training needs were also identified, in terms of use of the technology and using the resources of the library. A programme addressing these needs was developed. The audit showed that users tended to react passively to the new technology but were not confident enough to begin to make it work for them – for example users would use databases which were provided over the network, but were reluctant to use File Manager to share information in their own work group or manage the information in their own work area. This too could be addressed through user training.

Finally, as Legal Department was about to embark on establishing a formal information technology strategy, the audit report supplied some of the information needed to establish information system requirements which met business needs.

Doing it yourself

There are undoubtedly advantages to carrying this work out across a department, as then the benefits of scale begin to emerge. The same programme can be used more than once, and cross-departmental benefits emerge. If this is not an option, and an audit might be appropriate, then the following things need to be borne in mind.

First the advantages: the internal auditor knows the business, knows the people involved and can build on the trust established with them. The auditor also has control over the process and the results.

The disadvantages are the time it takes (approximately two hours per interview, including writing up) whilst maintaining and developing a service; there is no benefit from being able to reuse the format (unless the audit is repeated regularly) and there is a definite risk of bias and emotional involvement. There is also the question of credibility if the auditor does not have sufficient status within the organization. The more the project is seen as an individual one, the harder implementation will be.

Support from the auditor's own management and senior management is key to the success of the report and the audit. The support and understanding of my own staff and others who have responsibility for information resources was also a major factor in the successful completion of the audit.

It is not possible to look at information needs in isolation from each other. The auditor needs to be aware that the findings may raise expectations to improve services over which the auditor has no control, and the results may well cause difficulties for others, for example system administrators and those who keep official records. The auditor also needs to respect the anonymity of those who impart confidences, even if these need to be presented as part of the findings – these can include poor communication and rivalry between work groups, both of which impinge on healthy information flow.

It is also important that the audit is seen as the start of a process and not the end. Auditors will need to follow up the recommendations of the report, and will need all their influencing skills to ensure that the recommendations become a reality.

In retrospect

Personally, I found that the audit process allowed me to see my own role from a different perspective and it gave me a chance to re-evaluate the library's position and aims. It also freed me from the need to provide traditional solutions to traditional (and seemingly intractable) problems.

Finally, it gave me, as a librarian, a chance to exercise my understanding of information management in a slightly different arena. It was also an opportunity to develop my own skills (project management, report writing, influencing skills, as well as research skills). It was above all a chance to use my expertise to consider and advise on one of Legal Department's most important assets.

The NHS – Information strategies to promote evidence-supported healthcare

Earnest lists appear of the changes that we are facing, and the skills and competencies that we must acquire if we expect to be employed in the future ... What I do believe is that people cope better with change if they are given practical help.
(Palmer, 1997)

A look back

In the first edition of this book, a case study (Orna, 1990, pages 241–263) looked at the steps the British National Health Service was taking in the late 1980s to develop a strategy for information, more broadly defined than the statistical data which had earlier been the focus of attention. At the time of writing, the White Paper *Working for Patients* had just been published, introducing the idea of a market in health care, with purchasers and providers, and foreshadowing self-governing hospital trusts, GP budget holders, and District Health Authorities placing contracts to buy services. It had been recognized that the new approach implied a high dependence on information for success, and the case study looked at how the implications were being explored at national level, and in a District Health Authority.

Things have moved on a good deal since then: the concept of the market is being re-examined; a new government has proposed reforms to the service (Department of Health, 1997a); studies of the effectiveness of health care on the basis of evidence have advanced rapidly; and attempts have begun to rectify the comparative neglect of the contribution of health service libraries and information services to the development of a health service information strategy (see Marriott, 1998).

The present case study looks at current initiatives to apply the concepts of evidence-based medicine in practice, and at the role of library and information services in developing strategies to support it. It focuses on two examples, one of which is well established and the other in the early stages: the Health Care Libraries Unit, funded jointly by the Anglia and Oxford NHS Region and the University of Oxford, and the West Midlands Evidence-supported Medicine Union.

Evidence-supported medicine

The ideas underlying evidence-supported medicine were first advanced by Archie Cochrane, a doctor who more than 30 years ago drew attention to the medical profession's ignorance about the effects of health care, and explained how evidence from randomized controlled trials (RCTs) could help towards the more rational use of resources. In his book (1972), he suggested that, because resources would always be limited, they should be used to provide equitably those forms of health care which had been shown in properly designed evaluations to be effective. He stressed the importance of RCTs because they were likely to provide much more reliable information than other sources of evidence.

Such evidence, however, is not easily accessible to those who have to make decisions about health care; though it exists in quantity, the original reports of the relevant research are dispersed and hard to locate. The traditional answer to this problem is the review of research, which seeks to act as the link between research findings and those who should be able to make use of them. Unfortunately, reviews of RCTs have in the past not been founded on respect for scientific principles, in particular the control of biases and random errors. The poor quality of most reviews has meant that advice on some highly effective forms of health care has been delayed for many years, and that other forms of care have continued to be recommended long after controlled research has shown them to be either ineffective or actually harmful. Initiatives to bring these ideas into effect started in the late 1970s in Oxford at the National Perinatal Epidemiology Unit. The opportunity to extend them into other fields came with developments in the NHS Research and Development Directorate, which gave initial support to a centre named after Cochrane in Oxford in 1992. This was one of three initiatives contributing to the Division's Research Information Systems Strategy; the others are the NHS Centre for Reviews and Dissemination at York University and a register of research projects.

Within a short time, an International Cochrane Collaboration developed world-wide, with centres in a number of countries. The work is carried out by collaborative review groups focusing on specific health topics. The Collaboration's overall mission is to help people make well-informed decisions about health care by preparing, maintaining and promoting the accessibility of systematic reviews of the effects of healthcare interventions (Cochrane Collaboration, 1996). One of the key principles in achieving the mission is promoting access by wide dissemination of outputs, taking advantage of strategic alliances, and promoting appropriate content and media to meet the needs of all kinds of users.

The work of the NHS Centre for Reviews and Dissemination at York University complements that of the Cochrane Collaboration; it commissions or carries out reviews on behalf of the NHS, focusing mainly on the effectiveness, cost-effectiveness, management and organization of health services, and disseminates the results in the NHS to enhance effective decision making. The Centre concentrates especially on the development of evidence-based clinical practice and service development.

'Turning evidence into everyday practice'

Improved access to research evidence on effectiveness from the developments described above has stimulated interest in evidence-based practice, with the aim of improving the quality of health care, reducing variations in delivery, getting better return on investment in research, and minimizing clinical risk. In 1993, as part of the NHS Executive's purchaser development scheme, Oxford Regional Health Authority was awarded a grant for a one-year project which came to be known as 'Getting Research into Practice and Purchasing' (GRiPP). The aim was to help clinicians and NHS purchasers to put health care programmes on a sounder research footing, and the project was carried out by teams in which local departments of public health played a leading role. The project raised awareness of the issues, and yielded many useful lessons on such matters as consulting and involving local professionals, reviewing evidence, developing evidence-based guidelines, and planning dissemination and evaluation strategy from the beginning.

The GRiPP project was followed by a two-year national programme designed to study how evidence-based practice can best be introduced. Promoting Action on Clinical Effectiveness (PACE) was launched in 1995, based at the King's Fund. As reported by Dunning et al. (1998) in 'Turning evidence into everyday practice', the programme covered 16 projects in various parts of the country, on a range of clinical conditions; the topics were:

- Hypertension
- Helicobacter pylori eradication (3 projects)
- Pressure sores
- Menorrhagia
- Continence (2 projects)
- Management of stroke patients
- Cardiac rehabilitation
- Congestive cardiac failure
- Post-operative pain control
- Leg ulcers
- Stable angina
- Low back pain
- Family support in schizophrenia.

The findings have shown that focusing on a clinical topic can encourage changes in clinical behaviour, and have indicated the necessary conditions to support such changes. They include cooperation among all the parties concerned to create organizations which 'support rather than stifle' delivery of evidence-based practice and which foster an 'inquisitive culture'. Essential elements in such organizations are information and library services, audit programmes to assess local practice and the need for change, education programmes to support clinicians who need to change, and information services to support the monitoring of practice and service delivery.

Support from library and information services

In all the changes of the last decade, including those in which the word 'information' figured prominently, libraries and information services in the NHS were largely overlooked in the service's managerial considerations, although, as the developments outlined above make clear, a research-based, information-seeking culture was gradually emerging.

Medical libraries and librarians have always taken a lead in innovation, and they have a long-standing tradition of networking and collaboration. This led in the early 1990s to work by a number of groups of health librarians on the problems precipitated by the recent NHS reforms. The results of their investigations made it clear that:

> Libraries were becoming increasingly marginalised, that librarians were facing competition from other information providers, that there were no recognisable national strategies, that there was massive duplication, fragmentation and information hoarding and worst of all that there was little research being done to investigate the contribution that libraries and information services might make to improving the quality of patient care. (J. Palmer, from an unpublished talk).

In response to this evidence, the British Library established a medical review panel, which sponsored a national seminar in 1992, followed by another the following year. The 'Cumberlege' seminars, as they came to be known (the Health Minister, Baroness Cumberlege, gave them active support), brought together health professionals from every sector to discuss information issues across disciplinary boundaries. The second seminar identified four objectives for a national health information strategy:

1 To improve the quality of the knowledge base and its coordination
2 To ensure that the knowledge base is disseminated widely using the technology that is becoming available
3 To identify, promote and disseminate good local practice
4 To improve the local organization and transmission of the knowledge base.

The case made by the seminars proved convincing; the NHS executive recognized the role of libraries in all these activities by establishing the post of NHS Library Adviser, whose role was to take forward the strategic objectives from the second Cumberlege seminar.

It is perhaps indicative of the years of neglect which preceded this step that the *Health Service Guidelines* published in 1997 by the Department of Health Library and Information Services (1997b) replaced a publication issued as long ago as 1970. As the executive summary puts it:

> Libraries are a key resource for clinical effectiveness, for research and for education and training, all of which are crucial to the delivery of high quality health care. The lack of recent national guidance on library and information services and the complex funding arrangements for library services has led to the fragmentation of information provision within the NHS and not all NHS staff have access to the health knowledge base. This Guideline sets out key principles and actions for improving access to information via the development of multi-professional library and information services.

While the concept of knowledge-based services has begun to result in increased demand for library and information services in the health service, the *Guidelines* suggest that effective development has been hampered by such factors as:

• Lack of a national policy for library and information services, or clear national links to R&D, education and training, or information management and technology strategies
• Complex funding from multiple sources
• Uncertainty about capital funding for development
• A legacy of libraries established to serve separate professional groups

- Uncertainty about whom libraries are funded to support, which can lead to inadequate services for nursing and other non-medical and community-based staff
- Transfer of nursing education into higher education and closure or absorption of College of Health libraries

Key principles are proposed to improve the situation:
- Access should be multi-disciplinary and meet the needs of all staff groups, including contractors, people undertaking career breaks, etc.
- Resources should include professional and clerical staff, stock, electronic information resources, computers, networks
- Funding needs to be better coordinated, and there should be clarity about the purposes and staff groups for which different funding streams are provided. Access should be free at the point of use
- There should be region-wide coordination of library services.

All NHS Trusts and Health Authorities are requested to draw up a library and information strategy covering all staff groups by autumn 1998. The strategy should demonstrate how they plan to achieve access to library and information services for all staff, by directly provided services, contracts or service-level agreements, and funding flows to support, and should include arrangements to monitor progress. Library and information services should be included in NHS Trust and Health Authority information management and technology strategies.

Anglia and Oxford Health Care Libraries Unit: Helping people to cope with change

The quotation at the start of this case study is from an article by the Director of the Health Care Libraries Unit in the University of Oxford. What follows here is an account of the practical help the Unit has given to health service librarians in the Anglia and Oxford Region of the National Health Service, to enable them to deal with one of the most significant of the many changes the NHS has introduced in recent years

The Region has a long-established Health Libraries and Information Network (HeLIN); founded in 1969, it includes 45 libraries in acute hospital trusts, psychiatric hospital trusts and health authorities. The Health Care Libraries Unit (HCLU) coordinates cooperative action in the network, and provides support, advice and training for its members; it is funded jointly by the NHS and the University of Oxford, and is also responsible for providing library and information services to the University's Faculty of Clinical Medicine for doctors in training. Its strategic aims are to:
- Ensure that health care professionals in the region have access to high-quality and up-to-date library and information services
- Ensure that library managers and staff are aware not only of current developments in their own profession but also of trends in clinical education and professional practice that may impinge upon library services

- Ensure that all customers obtain value for money by fostering cooperative and resource-sharing practices
- Promote innovative solutions through research and development.

The Unit's business plan identifies a number of important influencing factors in the environment which its strategy needs to take into account. First among them is 'the promotion of evidence-based health care and the role of research evidence to inform clinical practice and health care decisions'.

The 'Librarian of the 21st Century'

The core of evidence-based practice (Palmer, 1997) is a series of processes which all require core information skills:

1 Formulate a question
2 Search the literature
3 Critically appraise the results
4 Incorporate into practice
5 Evaluate the results.

When evidence-based medicine first became a prominent topic, however, it was difficult for librarians to realize that there was a role for their skills and knowledge in it, because it had originated in an academic environment in a non-traditional Canadian medical school at McMaster University. The McMaster philosophy was brought into the Oxford Region through a network of personal contacts which included the then Director of Public Health, and the originator of the Cochrane Collaboration, and the ideas became incorporated in the development of NHS strategy.

While the advancement of the idea benefited enormously from the fact that the NHS Research and Development Strategy underwrote evidence-based medicine and legitimized it in a way not achieved in other countries, librarians felt themselves on the fringes when NHS directives on the subject came out. This was the situation which the Director of the HCLU sought to address when she started her work there in 1993. It meant that she saw her first task as raising awareness among librarians, helping them to understand what happens in research, and to see a research role for themselves in relation to health information, and involving them in critical appraisal. (For an account of recent UK research projects on how information from NHS libraries might be used in clinical decision making, and by nursing professionals, see Urquhart, 1998.)

If libraries and librarians needed new attitudes, services and skills, then to make the changes acceptable, education and development were needed to enable people to 'feel comfortable with the new concepts and structure'. In 1994, with the support of the region's R&D Director, a programme of professional development for librarians – 'The Librarian of the 21st Century' – was developed. Its aim was:

> To ensure that all libraries and librarians in the Anglia and Oxford Region have the knowledge, skills and facilities to provide health care professionals with access to the knowledge base of health care, and thus to ensure that all decisions in health care are based upon the best available evidence.

Continuing Professional Development

Continuing Professional Development is a main focus of the programme, and is described (Palmer, 1997) as 'essentially a package for change management', taking account of both changes in the NHS and large-scale change in the library world. The skills and knowledge which health service librarians need for the twenty-first century are defined as:

* Organizational politics
* How to operate in a marketplace
* How to negotiate
* How to use and teach critical appraisal as a means to filter the literature
* Why research-based decision making is important in health care and in our own profession
* How to teach in all contexts – from individuals to large groups
* How to facilitate learning
* How to market, plan, evaluate
* How to locate and better search new information sources and products
* How to take quick advantage of new technologies
* How to exploit the resources of the Internet
* How to create personal storage and retrieval systems.

The programme was launched with a seminar led by Joanne Marshall (author of the Health Canada Libraries case study which appears in this book, see page 250) The first topic was critical appraisal, introduced via a workshop for librarians based on the workshops (originally developed as part of a collaboration between NHS Anglia and Oxford Region and the Department of Public Health, Hamilton, Ontario) for public health physicians, NHS purchasers etc. which are organized by members of the Critical Appraisal Skills Team.

Next came workshops to enhance the ability of participants to plan and provide effective teaching sessions with information users; these looked at effective adult learning and theories of learning, and provided micro-teaching practice.

Questionnaires to find out what participants themselves felt they needed led to further seminars on Internet searching and developments in on-line searching, and an overview of the work of the Cochrane Collaboration and of the Centre for Reviews and Dissemination (see page 283). A final workshop allowed participants to review the programme, decide what should become part of the regular repertoire of professional development in the region, identify new elements that should be added, and consider how to build on the knowledge and experience gained. Following the programme, the Regional Training Group (see below) assessed it and drew up a strategic plan for a programme of professional development to fill the gaps; this included workshops on facilitation skills, marketing and evaluating library services.

Benefits

The fact that the region has had a well established and active library and information network for many years allowed the benefits of the programme to be realized much more quickly. At the personal level, while some librarians have found difficulty in absorbing new concepts and different ways of working, all have gained confidence and report that their profile has been raised within their organization. They have come to recognize that they have unique skills which are of value within an evidence-based culture. For some, participation in the programme has opened doors; some have become involved in clinical effectiveness groups as equal partners; one is now a R&D coordinator for a group, and involved in cascading critical appraisal through county health authorities via critical appraisal groups.

Librarians in the region have now become partners in the teaching of critical appraisal skills (CAS), in connection with the workshops held in Oxford from 1992 onwards under the CAS Programme to introduce public health physicians and other health professionals to the techniques of critical appraisal. Participants in these workshops expressed an interest in learning how to find relevant information. As a result, HCLU and librarian members of the network worked with the CAS team to develop a pilot 'Finding the Evidence' workshop. Since 1995, over 25 of these workshops (each typically attended by about 30 people) have been held, for both multi-professional and single-professional groups, including nurses, doctors, physiotherapists, occupational therapists, psychiatrists and dentists. 'Training the trainer' workshops have also been started, to spread the ideas to other regions, and inquiries and applications to attend have come from other countries and continents. Librarians in the network have also been involved in running annual Search Clinics at the International Evidence-Based Medicine Workshops organized by the Centre for Evidence-Based Medicine in Oxford, and in the new Oxford University Masters Programme in Evidence-Based Health Care, one module of which is concerned with information skills.

The Training Group

The Training Group is one of a number of groups which fulfil part of the HCLU's role of supporting the Network and helping it to develop a strategic direction broader than that of individual organizations. It consists of representatives of the libraries in the Region and the Assistant Director of the HCLU. One of the longest-established groups, the Training Group has progressed from its initial role of planning meeting programmes to strategic thinking about training and development, and identification of emerging issues. The Librarian of the 21st Century programme has helped it to develop its role, especially in relation to teaching and learning, marketing and business planning. Its work is now described as helping people to enhance their skills by building on the skills of others. The experience and knowledge which Network members have gained as a result of its work is now feeding back into their local community.

'Retrospective strategic plans'

To the question of whether a strategy for information underlay the development activities described above, the answer was that the strategic planning was retrospective. At the start, the strategy was implicit, rather than explicitly formulated. Its aim was to equip librarians to take on a more active role in the changed situation of the NHS, to adopt a higher profile, and to 'learn the language' that would allow them to talk to people in other professions on equal terms (for reflections on the importance for information professionals of 'learning the language' of other disciplines in order to be taken seriously by them, see the case study of NatWest Markets, page 293, and Chapter 5, page 92). But it was only after the experience of the Librarian of the 21st Century programme that it was possible to give formal expression to the strategy.[1]

West Midlands Evidence-supported Medicine Union

By contrast with the initiatives described above, this is an organization which is in the early stages of seeking to bring about changes in practice to incorporate known evidence. It too is using libraries as one of the key agents in the process. The Union is funded by the Regional Levy Board, to develop ways of changing practice based on known evidence. There are three strands in this:

1 Education to change culture, bringing in external trainers and running workshops
2 Funding seed groups short-term
3 Picking up concepts – for example one expert is visiting all trusts in the area to check whether they have protocols for such schemes as treating schizophrenics at home by giving help with family therapy.

The role of the Regional Librarian is now recognized as being to enable cooperation across trusts, disciplines and sectoral boundaries, with the intention to increase the flexibility of resources (both staff and stock) and release opportunities for diversity of approach. This will be underpinned by using intranet/internet-based methods of resource management.

The Regional Library Unit has incorporated two trainer librarians, whose responsibility is to train librarians in the skills which will enable them to be key players in evidence-based practice. The training will involve, besides the relevant techniques, gaining understanding of the role of library staff in change management and development of the culture. Given the constraints imposed by short-term funding, the trainers will be expected to develop a complete self-learning package, which can be delivered as computer-based training with support from a mentor/coach, and which will include evaluation both of the process and the trainees. The total impact of the process will be evaluated in turn as part of the wider Evidence-supported Union activity.

[1] I suspect that the retrospective giving of shape to actions undertaken in the light of nature or tacit knowledge is quite common. The approach even has a name – constructionism; as Sless (1997) puts it, 'Theory from a constructionist view is simply the description given to what people do ... intertwined with practice, as a different aspect of the same thing ... an emergent property of practice. Theories are in part *post hoc* rationalizations – the plausible stories which we tell ourselves to account retrospectively for our actions.'

Evaluation

The work described in this case study arose from understanding that the knowledge and skills of librarians in the NHS are highly relevant to important new developments in health care, but that their relevance is mostly unrealized, by their possessors and by those who could benefit from them.

> '… if librarians are not to be increasingly marginalized, we must recognize that an investment in continuing professional development is one of the more important weapons we have if we wish to continue to be taken seriously by other professional groups, and by those who use our libraries' (Palmer, 1997).

A number of factors favoured the success of the Anglia and Oxford Region initiative. There was an existing strong network, with a culture of interaction and cooperation. The enterprise enjoyed the support of a management champion who understood the importance of libraries and information services. The HCLU director, who had recently come back into the NHS after a long period working elsewhere, was by virtue of that able to take a view of the whole picture; her own academic background also led her to appreciate that evidence-based medicine was a new and important concept. Another valuable contribution came from outside the United Kingdom; contacts with Canadian institutions (McMaster University with its unique approach to problem-based learning in medical studies, the Ontario Public Health Department, and the School of Information Studies at the University of Toronto) allowed the programme to draw on new approaches to the subject and to the learning process.

The outcome has been positive. It has shown librarians '*how* to enhance and improve their skills, not merely exhorted them to do so'. It has given a whole group of librarians in the region the same package of experience and training essential to support evidence-based patient care. This experience of shared learning is extremely important for a group which is in regular contact, because it helps to raise the quality of their contribution throughout the region. The content of the package, and the methods of delivery developed, is applicable in other regions of the NHS, and for areas other than health care.

The programme of professional development can properly be seen as promoting knowledge management, in that it has helped, and continues to help, the people concerned to value their own knowledge, to integrate new knowledge and skills with it, to apply it in new ways, to interact on an equal footing with those who use other kinds of knowledge, and to establish mutual professional respect in the process.

References

COCHRANE, A. (1972), *Effectiveness and efficiency: random reflections on health services,* London: Nuffield Provincial Hospitals Trust

COCHRANE COLLABORATION (1996), *Strategic Plan,* Oxford: UK Cochrane Collaboration

Department of Health (1997a), *The New NHS,* Cmnd 3807, London: HMSO

Department of Health (1997b), *Health Service Guidelines, HSG (97)47,* Library and Information Services

DUNNING, M. et al. (1998), *Turning Evidence into Everyday Practice,* London: King's Fund

MARRIOTT, R. (1998), 'The only way is up: an enhanced role for library and information service within the NHS beckons', *Library Review,* 47 (3), 166–170

ORNA, E. (1990), *Practical Information Policies,* Aldershot: Gower

PALMER, J. (1997), 'Skills for a virtual future', *Bibliotheca Medica Canadiana,* 19 (2), 62–65

SLESS, D. (1997), 'Theory for practice', *Communication News,* 10 (4), 1–5

URQUHART, C. (1998), 'Personal knowledge: a clinical perspective from the Value and EVINCE projects in health library and information services', *Journal of Documentation,* 54 (4), 420–442

NatWest Markets

Introduction

This case study is the story of an initiative which arose from the conjunction of an internal organizational impetus and ideas brought in from the outside environment. It tells of a strong and promising development that had to be halted for compelling reasons of major changes in the structure and the situation of the business. Though it did not bear the fruit its originators hoped for, this is not a story of failure; it is worth relating for the quality of the ideas underlying it, the original and imaginative approach taken, and the useful lessons to be learned from the outcome.

NatWest Markets

NatWest Markets is the corporate and investment banking division of the NatWest Group. At the time the knowledge management programme was initiated it had 7000 employees, working in 51 offices in 26 countries, and relationships with 3000 leading institutions. Its transactions amount to £60 billion through treasury, equities and capital markets businesses.

The knowledge management programme

In the autumn of 1996, the then Chief Executive of NatWest Markets was seeking a change of orientation for the business. The change was essentially a cultural one; the investment bank had been successfully created by an aggressive series of acquisitions which resulted in a range of very strong cultures rubbing up against each other – enterprises and teams which had, in the main, been successful because of very focused, even 'tribal', behaviour. While this culture had been appropriate for that purpose, now, in order to ensure that the investment paid off, it was necessary to break down the barriers between the 'feudal states' involved and develop cross-boundary approaches to products and clients; this was where significant future value could be reaped. At the same time, the broader organizational context – the NatWest Group to which NatWest Markets belongs – had identified knowledge as a cornerstone of desired cultural change throughout the group. The link between the two requirements was provided by a managing director in NatWest Markets, who had been the chief operating officer of NatWest Capital Markets and was about to assume a role in charge of account management for treasury and capital markets. She came across an article in the *Financial Times* about knowledge management, and realized that her whole career had been based on managing knowledge 'in the light of nature'. The effect of the article was 'like a light going on', which put her own knowledge and work practice – which were based on human resources development, and using information effectively – into a new context. She sent the article to the Chief Executive, and told him that this was the kind of job she would really wish to do should the opportunity arise in the company. The article arrived at the right moment. The managing director was invited to put forward a knowledge management programme to be carried through over a two-year period, with the aim of 'creating sustainable competitive advantage with our clients, based on continual creativity and innovation', and given the financial resources she requested and freedom to invest them.

Analysis and proposal

The process began as part of the follow-up work on global information flow done by an internal ten-member task force from a 'partnership forum' of some 50 of the younger managing directors. Its report (November 1996) identified the problems to be solved as:

1 Processes for capturing, structuring, filtering and distributing information
2 Generating value from and ownership of information processes
3 Cultivating ideas generation and innovation firm-wide.

The solution required actions from three sets of people – the 'building blocks':

* Insight – Capturing information
  The responsibility of 'Insight Teams', who would start by identifying what information exists, where it is, and who is responsible for it, and go on to capture useful information – internal and external, historic, current and future
* Navigation – Structuring, filtering, and distributing information
  To be undertaken by 'Navigation Teams', with a catalysis role of converting information to meet the needs of users. Their role would be central but not centralizing; and they would be business focused, because 'only business operators/practitioners really understand the validity of information'. This proved to be the key concept that led to the idea of knowledge coordinators and their role, which was one of the main strands of the programme which was developed.
* Plumbing – the enabling technology
  This requirement was defined as coordinated investment across the business in an infrastructure based on an intranet, the Internet, video-conferencing, voice-mail, and intelligent browsing software.

The effects of combining these activities were summarized in a 'KnowlEdge Formula©', which was intended to start fixing the main 'brand' ideas in people's minds:

$$[P + I] \times N = E$$
$$E \times O = R$$

Where P is Plumbing
I is Insight
N is Navigation
E is Edge (or KnowlEdge©)
O is Marketing/Business Opportunity
R is Revenue

Small-scale pilot experiments were proposed as a practical way of addressing the obstacles to effective information use which the task force had observed: the pressure of winning business taking precedence over information seeking outside individuals' own immediate network; fragmentation and duplation arising from decentralized investment in technology; product opportunities discovered by chance rather than by design; the skills and experience of the many recently recruited staff going unnoted and so not used to the full.

A retrospective analysis, from a presentation on the knowledge management programme made some months later, covers some of the same ground but adds some new factors about the cultural environment. It identified four groups of factors as governing the current environment in NatWest Markets:

1 Client, country and marketing knowledge
2 Product knowledge
3 Trading, risk, and reputation knowledge
4 Endemic social and cultural disorders.

The situation regarding the first three was characterized by missing opportunities or failing to exploit them fully, and finding things by hazard rather than by intention. The social and cultural disorders were summarized as:

* Fragmentation and duplication
* Fear of asking for help or giving it across boundaries
* 'Communities versus tribes. There are few meeting places to create cross-Firm communities with a common purpose'
* A poor record in project and change management
* Haphazard experimentation with new technologies, processes, and ways of team working
* Inability to acknowledge failure as an asset and to convert it to positive experience
* Lack of systematic briefing and debriefing on things that have been turned down
* No method for capturing and storing the experience gained by project teams for recycling
* Debate seen as a bad rather than a constructive way of finding new ideas.

There were, however, some excellent practices operating in areas of the firm which had either existed before (for example analytical processes in Credit, some of the technology projects, and team behaviours in such sections as Central Banks, Oil and Gas) or had been brought in with the new acquisitions (for example process mapping techniques in Greenwich Capital Markets), which could be replicated across the different business structures and infrastructure of the bank; and it was emphasized that they constituted a major opportunity.

The knowledge management team

With the proposals approved and resources given, the person designated as 'Chief Knowledge Officer' (CKO) appointed a management consultancy to audit the work on the project, compile a job description, propose performance targets and critical success factors, define human resources and support requirements, and suggest time allocation of team members to the key activities.

This step was taken to ensure an objective external view and to secure the benefit of outside experience in the field which the team was entering.

The Chief Knowledge Officer's[1] job was described as that of a catalyst for initiatives aimed at:

- Improving profitability through better use of information and more effective sharing of knowledge about clients, products, industries, and countries
- Strengthening NatWest Markets' competitive advantage by building a reputation for in-depth industry knowledge and creativity of deal ideas.

The job holder's key activities would be to:

- Support the launch of the knowledge management pilots, and provide resources and expertise for them
- Extract the lessons learned and use them for further initiatives
- Monitor projects against predefined performance targets, and report to the CEO and Chief Executives' Committee
- Oversee the development of tools to assist the effective use of knowledge
- Intervene to support initiatives when necessary
- Communicate progress, success, failures, and lessons to senior management and the broader organization
- Build enthusiasm about the practical business value to be gained from knowledge management
- Develop links with external groups
- Link with NatWest Group's knowledge management initiative.

The CKO would need to work with a small central team of three or four full-time members, and the team would require systems and IT support in the form of access to IT skills and close contact with the people responsible for monitoring and testing new applications.

Performance measures and critical success factors

Measures were defined for the short, medium, and longer term. At the end of one year there should be:

- A number of successful initiatives where the use of knowledge management had produced a positive, recognized impact on business performance
- A 'Knowledge Directory'
- A defined process for launching new knowledge management initiatives
- Operational IT-based tools for client contacts and product credentials, with a core of committed users
- Multiple examples of people fulfilling successful knowledge management roles, for example as experts on subjects or countries, or 'interest group co-ordinators'
- Widespread understanding of what knowledge management is
- A number of business areas eager to launch initiatives.

[1] The job title was one which the holder was reluctant to assume, as being too high-profile, and placing undue emphasis on the individual rather than the team. The reservations proved well founded.

A further year should see:
- Most practitioners in interest groups, active in sharing knowledge among the group
- A number of self-managed interest groups with only occasional input from the central knowledge management team
- Improvement in ratings for creative idea generation, with the majority of initiatives showing improvement against a baseline established at the start
- A programme aimed at creativity and idea generation, with rewards
- Knowledge management seen as a natural part of daily work
- Evaluation criteria which reflect the individual's contribution to NatWest Markets' knowledge and the knowledge management process
- Strong linkage between knowledge management and new strategic initiatives, in that the firm's existing knowledge is brought to bear on new growth opportunities, and the knowledge gained in new initiatives is shared with the rest of the firm.

Beyond the second year, the need for the CKO and central support team might well be reduced, though there would probably continue to be a need for a small group to support interest groups and initiatives that were meeting difficulties, to maintain and develop NatWest Markets' tools, and to ensure cross-fertilization between interest groups and the sharing of best practice.

Critical success factors were defined as:
- A high level of commitment by the CEO and the knowledge team
- Support from business heads to encourage initiative taking, accepting that some failures will be inevitable, allowing individuals to take some risks in the learning process
- Active support and encouragement from the CEO and the Chief Operating Officer to create an environment where people take the knowledge initiative seriously, to recognize and reward individuals who are early champions, and to give the programme time to prove its worth.

'Radical, distinctive and innovative'

The knowledge management team which was established undertook, in its own words, to (Ward and Alexander, 1997):
- Respond to and support the strategic goals of the firm
- Focus on people, viewing technology as an important enabler, rather than the object of the exercise
- Operate at the 'edge' of the company where innovation and learning happen
- Promote knowledge management values within the culture of the firm
- Be driven and shaped by the people who use it and their needs
- Be flexible to suit each user group's needs
- Be unbureaucratic and unhierarchical
- Be radical, distinctive and innovative in its presentation and channels of communication – never staid or ordinary
- Cut through organizational divisions, geographical boundaries, cultural differences and ingrained practices and attitudes'.

The team[2] took an 'information design' approach to communication, in that it looked to create information products, designed to match the users, the nature of the information content, and the ways in which people would want to use it. There was a strong emphasis on visualization in the whole development of the knowledge management programme; ideas would initially be expressed in graphic form, as diagrams showing concepts and their interrelation (see Figure C9.1 on page 299). A publisher of maps and charts provided training and education in the discipline of visual representation, and the team also used simple techniques to aid visualization, such as a printed-off whiteboard to run a daily log and to record and examine ideas.

Besides the visual approach, story-telling came to be seen as a vehicle for passing on useful knowledge, and conversation, rather than transmission or message sending and receiving, was taken as the model for interchange of knowledge. This metaphor came fairly late in the process, with the idea of the 'mapping and mining' and axes shown in Figure C9.2 on page 300. (See Nonaka and Takeuchi, 1995, for examples of how diagrams and stories help 'individuals internalize what they experience, thus enriching their tacit knowledge [and] facilitate the transfer of explicit knowledge to other people, thereby helping them experience the experiences of others'.)

The development of a metaphor was intentional; at the start there was something of a jumble of jargon from various fields, and it took the team some time to pick their way through the implications. They describe themselves as starting, mistakenly, by speaking in knowledge management and management consultancy jargon, which was very off-putting for the people they were addressing. Even the term 'piloting', chosen in preference to 'projects' (because projects fail, and the failure is seen as a bad thing, whereas pilots are experimental and allow for constructive failure), met with considerable suspicion. The next step was to translate the ideas into investment banking jargon, with the pilots described as assets and piloting as the creating of a portfolio of assets, so that the concepts could be readily understood and related to the appropriate business area.

The team encouraged potential participants to talk through pilots in their terms, describing, for instance, the sequence of events leading from an idea or opportunity through the creation of a deal team and the design of a product or execution of a transaction. It was then possible to probe with them what actions they could take at each significant point in the way of assembling, analysing or transmitting information, which would improve the effectiveness of their handling that stage, and to turn what was learned into a set of 'interventions' which they could undertake, with the team's support, to improve

[2] There was a clear conviction on the part of the CKO that the knowledge management team, products and services should be considered as a 'brand', because this was likely to encourage individuals to join, and would make products and projects easier to run and re-use. From the outset, there was also an intention that the team could become a 'semi-detached' business venture, an affinity business which would create third-party revenues, and to develop it as a 'practical roving think tank' which could look both at NatWest's own activities and at those of third parties. 'It was a critical founding premise that this should create a new revenue stream from a new venture which would have its own brand, but which would support and enhance the NatWest brand and reputation for being knowledgeable.'

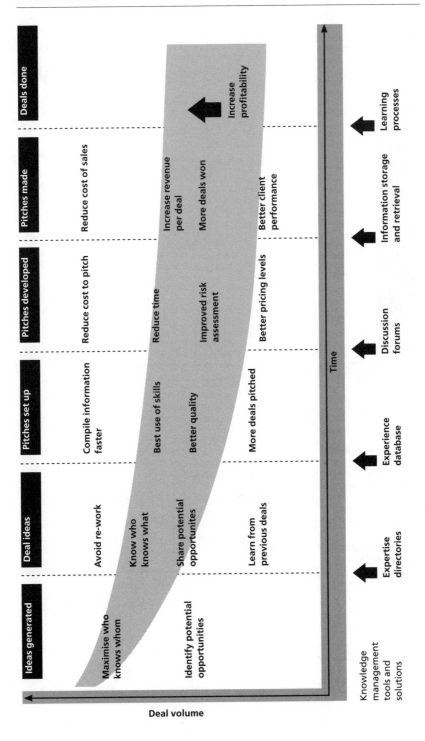

Fig C9.1   **Example of visualization. How knowledge management improves performance**

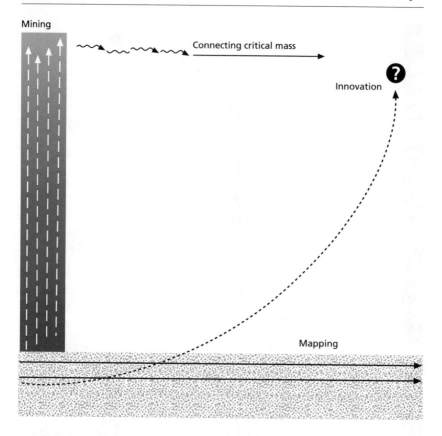

Mining

Connecting critical mass

Innovation ?

Mapping

Mining, depth of impact, experimentation

Series of experiments with high impact on relatively small, but cumulative number of people

Measured in value created/people involved

Connecting crtitical mass

Systematic and serendipitous creation of communities and communication with expected and unexpected results ... exchange of ideas and experience generates more innovation and productivity

Mapping, breadth, discovery

A small number of broadly based tools which achieve quick impact, and high visibility, and create maps from which to build navigation and chart a series of experiments and actions

Fig C9.2   **Knowledge management axes**

their hit rate – a process described as 'luring them' into talking the language of information and knowledge, having started the dialogue in their own language.

Over time, the team gained an understanding of the power of appropriate metaphor, which could be used on various levels, in creating a new 'space' for discussing issues and solutions. So the metaphor became part of the brand identity they were creating.

Use of resources

While the participants were enthusiastic, there was a lack of strong senior management backing. Nor did the prevailing circumstances allow for strong strategic alignment with human resources or IT, which might otherwise have been exploited, although both were informally very supportive. The situation was turned to advantage by using the 'venture capital' funding to market the ideas and bid for business, with the aim of reversing the position by the next stage so that units were competing to get in on the next pilots (this was actually achieved). The team's pitch to businesses was that they had funds available to invest in their projects if there were clear benefits for the team. The aim was to get the business to fund at least three-quarters of the effort; their return would be benefits from the pilots, while the payback for the knowledge management team would be further experience and new knowledge. The team developed a joint venture document for use with potential sponsors to help them understand the payoffs involved, the resources required, what interventions would be developed and what external expertise might be brought in. This was a very important step, because without it there was a tendency for some of the resourcing issues to 'fall down the gaps', particularly in clarifying who was responsible for detailed project management.

Pilots

The aim of the pilot projects was to 'stimulate ideas for better knowledge sharing from within the business units', to define a set of coordinating, 'editorial' and training roles, and to make advances without involving 'lots of administrators'. The team looked for projects which related to delivery to clients in some form, rather than to the internal workings of the business. The reasons were, first, that in an investment bank it was the revenue-generating potential of using knowledge that would capture attention, and second, that the team wanted to emphasize that this was an outward-looking initiative focused on the interface between the firm and the outside world, not an internally addressed productivity action.

One of the pilots chosen related to a product and one to a sector, since they represented contrasting issues. The first was a proposal from Global Structured Trade Finance, whose multi-skilled and multi-national staff (initially 75, then increased to 150), working in a number of countries world-wide, were concerned that some deals were being turned down or lost because of lack of information about the combined abilities of the group; the project also had a committed champion in the managing director, who was already looking at how to create an environment which would encourage knowledge sharing. The sector pilot was the Pharma Group, which brought together those interested in pharmaceuticals from a variety of aspects in different parts of the business. The aim of this pilot was to examine methods for stimulating innovation, and in particular to make more use of pure industry research and of client knowledge; it thus involved extracting tacit knowledge from individuals who were possibly unaware that what they knew was of value to others.

The two pilots were deliberately chosen to cut across one another. The first involved a specialized product area with a global team and a single head, which needed to exploit new ideas quickly in several countries because of the speed of replication in the market. Pharma, by contrast, was a community of interest of some people, under different heads across the firm, concerned with client rather than product issues, and focused on gaining access to tacit knowledge and putting it to work in improving the marketing interface and transaction winning with clients. Each could then provide a model for projects with other businesses; structured finance, for example, led on to securitization, derivatives and other product areas, while Pharma could be a model for bigger, more mainstream, sector groupings such as media and telecoms, and oil and gas. So the pilots allowed for developing different tools and skills, and provided a low-risk environment for testing models which could then be applied in more strategic areas of change, development and investment.

Criteria for choosing future pilots emerged from the experience of work on the first two.

- Committed, enthusiastic champions
- A clear local business purpose
- Interconnections to increase the ripple effect through other parts of the business
- A manageable scope, with flexibility and minimum bureaucracy, allowing the possibility of containing and learning from failures
- Benefits specified from the outset.

And piloting should be strategically planned, to allow systematic experimentation related to the organization's strategies, over a wide range.

One of the products of piloting was the metaphor/image of an analytical cube, whose three faces were:

1 Why are we doing this?
   - Revenue
   - Risk
   - Cost
2 Where are we doing it?
   - Client
   - Product
   - Geography
3 How are we doing it?
   - People
   - Process
   - Technology.

The intention here was to be able to build robust indicators and measures which would in time allow judgements about how given portfolios were performing, and what pilots would interact to provide the most valuable knowledge assets.

People and technology

The team responsible for the pilots consisted of seven people, described as a non-hierarchical community, at many different levels, and spread across the firm. The process of team building was a matter of seeking to use diverse experiences from within the firm; only one person was hired, and the CKO deliberately set out to complement the team's abilities with external skills to strengthen it. The external resources varied at different stages from 10–15 and the skills imparted included presenting stories in very simple and attractive terms, presentation of materials to potential pilot sponsors, mapping and chartting, and design and artwork; project management consultancy was brought in at one point when needed; and a very original independent designer worked with the team on planning their intranet. The total internal collaboration across the business, both on the pilots and on the *Green Book* (see page 304), comprised a community of 150–175 people (for example the knowledge and pilot coordinators, pilot sponsors, technical support).

As the work proceeded, a new role – that of knowledge coordinator – grew from the pilots. They were not envisaged at the start but proved to be a vital link in spreading the idea of knowledge management throughout the organization. Coordination was additional to their existing roles; they worked from within business groups rather than adding another administrative layer. They came from various jobs and levels; the key requirement was the ability to act as a 'navigator' through knowledge in the areas in which they themselves were concerned. The importance of their role is seen as underlining 'the fact that effective knowledge management is about people and changing their attitudes and working practices, not about introducing new technology'.

Establishing that this was in fact not a technology project was something that demanded a good deal of time, and was responsible for the pilots taking longer than expected. The role of technology was that of an enabler; unfortunately at the time of the pilots, the IT function was in the process of being decentralized, and so it was impossible to use it as an ally and a power-base to support the project. None the less, IT was essential for some of the products from the pilots; the technology used was at a quite modest level, based on Lotus Notes.

It should be emphasized that the team acknowledged the critical importance of technology, but that they wished first to make a statement about communities, and the roles of experts and expertise. They deliberately made the technology components of the project fairly basic and disposable, so that they could move fast without having to go through large upgrades in business areas before making anything happen. The technology used was 'more as a device to encourage collaboration and the development of the right roles, responsibilities and forums for meeting, finding solutions, establishing common ground between technology and the business, training, etc'. This also helped to sidestep the 'baggage' lying around in the form of technology projects which had been only partially successful. The longer-term aim, with new pilots, was to become increasingly inventive with technologies. Another useful initiative in the technology area was a 'knowledge tools audit' of technology projects in progress which appeared to have a connection with knowledge management; the findings made both a useful map for the team, and a defence against any attempt to get them to become foster-parents of ill-conceived technology projects which would become cuckoos in the nest.

Products

The Global Structured Trade Finance pilot led to three new prototype databases, which could act as models for replication in other areas: 'Experiences' (detailing skills and experiences of all the staff concerned); 'Product Innovations' (new products, deals and structures); and 'Opportunity' (an insider's guide to potential new deals). Similar work in the Pharma Group area led to a client contact planner, designed not just as a contact database, but also to allow people to put forward ideas and suggestions for forthcoming client meetings in which they were not directly involved.

The team found, however, that piloting would take a long time to yield good stories, so they needed something to offer more quickly; a hint of what that might be came from the frequent response that what was really needed was a 'new phone book'. While the team felt that a phone book was not the right answer, as a purely administrative product which did not significantly add value, they developed the idea of a product that could be used throughout NatWest Markets to give access to the whole range of expertise available – a particularly urgent need, created by the rapid growth of the business through acquisitions, which had brought in many new employees who could not know who to turn to for advice or information outside their immediate work environment. It would also fulfil the need for quick wins and could be used as a vehicle for ideas about knowledge management. It would also lead the team to local guides and knowledge coordinators, and help lay foundations for developing future projects and getting feedback.

The *Guide for exchange of experience* was designed to help individuals to exchange knowledge and experience. The people who agreed to feature in what became known simply as the *Green Book* were asked to state the terms under which they were prepared to share their knowledge of sectors, products or geographical areas, and to nominate a 'knowledge coordinator' for their area. The interviews with them were based on a structured guide, which sought among other things to learn from the people interviewed what kind of information was valued by the group to which they belonged, how they developed and shared it, and what information processes they would wish to improve. The questions would make a good basis for interviewing in the context of information auditing, too:

- What information do you currently value?
- How do you share information within the group?
- How do you share information with other areas of NWM?

- What information gathering, developing and sharing processes do you currently do well?
- What information gathering, developing and sharing processes could you improve?
- Is everyone in the group aware of the activities/expertise of other members?
- Is innovation important, and if so how well is this process effected in your business?
- How aware are you of the activities of other NWM product/sector areas?
- Do other areas of NWM have good understanding of your business?
- What information can the group provide?

The publication was compiled as quickly as possible, and designed to gain responses on how it should evolve. It was launched in July 1997 and contained references to 800 experts and 100 knowledge coordinators around the world. Originally it was intended as a first edition of 1000 copies, but as the deadline approached, some parts of the firm sought to block publication on the grounds that their areas were not well enough represented. At the same time, structural changes were taking place, and there was a real possibility that the publication might be stopped altogether. Its editor, however, took determined action, and gained agreement for production of a limited run as a working draft, with a reduced number of copies. The fact that the circulation was thus limited, mainly to the knowledge coordinators, turned what might have been disaster to good advantage, because it gave them status and created demand; people who wanted to use the guide had to go to them. At the same time, a mini-guide was produced which was widely distributed, and gave useful information about the programme and the knowledge coordinators.

It was a deliberate decision to make the product print-on-paper, because of the possibilities for more accessible learning for the people creating it: in management and marketing, keeping to schedule, and the basics of graphic and typographic design. They received appropriate training; and relevant external expertise was bought in, not only on the production side but also as part of an events programme for the knowledge coordinators, with a series of outside speakers visiting on a regular basis.

Outcomes

A presentation to the Chief Executive's Committee on the knowledge management programme (June 1997) summed up the development aimed at and undertaken, along both 'horizontal' and 'vertical' axes (see Figure C9.2 on page 300).

The horizontal axis

This involved mapping the firm – to create places of formal and informal information exchange, by means of:
- The *Green Book*
- The library – an 'unexpected development'. The experience of assembling the *Green Book* led to the team being given the task of reconfiguring the library. The aim here was to change it from a store of information to a

source of knowledge and innovation, a business intelligence service converting information to intelligence by means of expert filtering, editing, archiving and researching. The customers it would seek to serve were defined as 'client-facing people and product specialists' in search of information not held by interest groups or experts; knowledge managers from interest groups and business units, seeking help in information searches, guidance and coaching on how to gather information needed regularly, and advice on information sources; and knowledge managers receiving guidance, training and mentorship. The staffing, tasks and structure envisaged for it were those of a highly proactive modern library and information service (with the appealing addition of a café), operating in close proximity to an open learning centre.

- The intranet site
- Indexing, information design, storage, linking and retrieval of information
- 'Glass silos' – keeping knowledge/information resources intact, but allowing people to see what is in them; short cuts, feedback, debate, reporting of true stories
- Ordnance Survey Map: 'the conscious trapping of information for re-use' which gives greater flexibility in guiding, evolving, and dissolving temporary teams to deal with specific issues. Salient points were picked out and recorded by an intelligent cartographer. Figure C9.3 on page 308, shows the dimensions and the associated product series.

The vertical axis

Systematic small-scale experiments: 'Piloting can be seen as a kind of developing NWM clearing house for applied common sense and shared experience.' Its advantages are:
- A consistent framework to compare parallel developments and different perspectives on the same issues
- Real-life experience in a specific area, rather than assumptions, which can be used as the context for planning the future
- Failure converted to an asset; using the experience of doing things wrong to get it right next time
- An environment allowing conscious experiment, and then the use of successful experience quickly across different areas
- A framework of knowledge management around risk management to support knowledge-based risk decisions.

None of these things would of themselves create innovation, but they would provide foundations from which innovations could emerge and be effectively exploited as suggested in Figure C9.4 on page 309.

While the work of the knowledge team described above was going on, events in the business intervened to change the prospects for its future. About ten weeks into developing the programme, a major shift started to take place in the investment bank, which resulted, when six months' work had been done, in the resignation of its chief sponsor, the then chief executive. This was followed by a number of major structural changes, reorganizations, and cost-cutting initiatives, which both affected the short-term ability of the team to continue to develop along the original lines, and called into question the priority attached to the programme, given the other retrenchment that was going on. The knowledge management team understood as early as March, three months into the programme, that they were going to need a great deal of luck, as well as hard work and astute positioning, for the programme to last even beyond the summer, despite the indications of its potential for considerable success. The turbulence had a two-edged effect. On the one hand, waning political support for the programme was a serious obstacle, and the changes of management in technology and other key areas meant that the programme could not embed in a rational, logical way. On the other hand, senior managers were quite preoccupied, and this allowed the team to get on with it and secure ground for a period of time. The team also tried to interpret the changes and the direction in which they were taking the enterprise, and to move the priorities for pilots and products in the direction which would be most relevant to the future shape of activities. This meant a temporary move to considering productivity initiatives as a priority over client-facing ones, to support the short-term goals.

In the event, the planned programme in NatWest Markets could not be followed through, for valid reasons at group level. The knowledge management initiative closed down in October 1997, at a point when the prototype design for the electronic version of the main *Guide* was ready for testing with the knowledge coordinators, together with the design for the intranet site on which it would be available. The team put forward proposals for continuing with the original plans in other areas of the Group where less extreme change was in progress. In the end, however, the Group, while acknowledging the success of the work on knowledge management and appreciating that it had been enthusiastically received both within the firm and at presentations outside, decided that other priorities must take precedence. At this point the Chief Knowledge Officer moved out, to set up a virtual research-based business comprising a networked group of associates, which would undertake work of the kind initiated at NatWest Markets, and to sell it on.

Evaluation

Readers should find this valuable as an example of a process that primarily involves people, and negotiation among them about how they cooperate in using their knowledge to develop new knowledge, new products, and new uses. There are also lessons to be learned about combining firm guiding principles with a pragmatic approach. The whole process was one of knowledge exchange and interaction between people, development and self-discovery (exemplified in the CKO's discovery of knowledge and information management, and in the work of a team member who started as a secretary and went on to manage directory production). The outcome of the team-building strategy was a very satisfying one; by the end of their work, team members were starting to take ownership of their own parts of the programme, and coming to the CKO only for input on tactics and as a sounding board for their ideas,

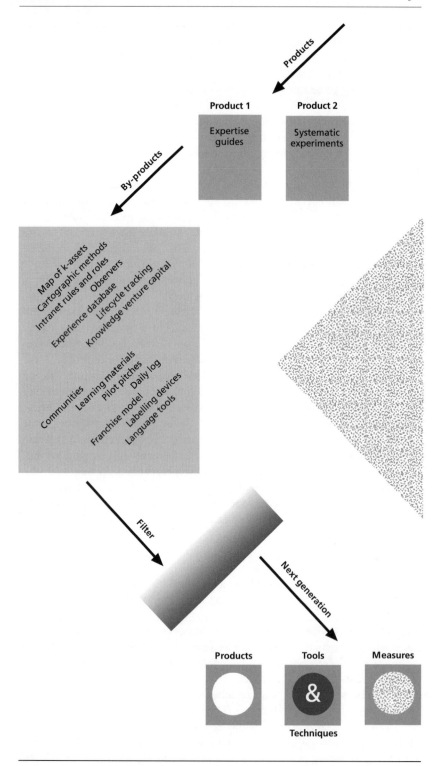

Fig C9.3   **Dimensions and associated product series**

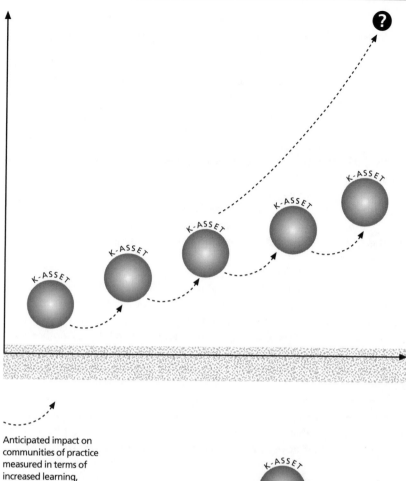

Anticipated impact on communities of practice measured in terms of increased learning, productivity, product delivery

Unplanned improvements from unforeseen events and by-products

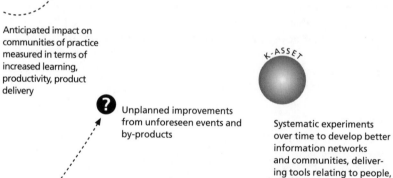

Systematic experiments over time to develop better information networks and communities, delivering tools relating to people, processes and technology and including continuous observation and feedback

Fig C9.4   **Business experiment**

rather than relying on her for decisions. That kind of experience is something that remains with people and enriches their work in the future.

Another aspect of the interactive conversational approach is the importance the team learned to attach to finding the right language for expressing their ideas in order to sell them. As suggested elsewhere in this book, if you want people to accept ideas which are familiar to you, but as yet alien to their own thoughts, you have to express them initially in language which is familiar to them. The combination of new ideas and strange language is death to success-ful selling, whereas familiar language can help people to start taking new ideas into their own knowledge structure, as happened during the pilots.

The use of pilot projects also provides an example of the 'learning spiral' approach recommended for the development of information strategy. It also gives rise to the idea (mentioned in the British Library case study as well) that when you have gained sufficient experience and knowledge through low-risk piloting, you can safely take a bounded risk on something larger and more way-out.

As the knowledge management team's own analysis makes clear, knowl-edge management at the time the initiative was undertaken could not be aligned to strategy in NatWest Markets; the organizational fabric was then too fragile and key issues too urgent for it to play a pivotal role, but it could pro-vide a base of experience for a more strategic approach in future. Another con-clusion was that creating and exploiting a 'coherent knowledge environment' required as an essential foundation a 'clearly mandated strategy across NWM for certain aspects of technology and information management'.

A final practical lesson is that one should be prepared to be ingenious and open-minded in making use of the things learned in initiatives that don't work out as planned, so that in the end they are not wasted. What can't be done in one organization or at one time can still find its use in other ways at other times. Experience teaches us that it is always worth looking for what we can usefully take from a situation that appears to have collapsed about our ears. That way, we live to fight and win another day.

References

NONAKA, I. and TAKEUCHI, H. (1995), *The Knowledge-creating Company: how Japanese companies create the dynamics of information,* New York: Oxford University Press, pp. 69–70

WARD, V. and ALEXANDER, J. (1997), 'Knowledge management: A case study', *Journal of Communication Management,* 2 (2), 167–171

Ogilvy & Mather

The company

The world-wide marketing communications company of Ogilvy & Mather was founded by David Ogilvy in 1948. Wholly owned by its financial parent, WPP Group plc, it is the sixth largest agency network in the world, with 312 offices in 89 countries and 10 000 staff working in more than 50 languages. Its clients include American Express, Ford, Hoover, IBM, Kodak, SmithKline Beecham, Samaritans, Unilever and the Worldwide Fund for Nature. It is structured around five geographical regions, supplemented by a world-wide client service organization which provides training, technology and staff to support the integration of resources for global and regional brands. Ogilvy & Mather was an early entrant into Europe, Latin America, Asia, Africa and Eastern Europe.

The company also operates in direct marketing, via OgilvyOne world-wide, a direct marketing company with 74 offices in 38 countries. This side of the business includes OgilvyOne dataservices – a consultancy network applying IT to marketing and sales which offers expertise in emerging communication technologies; international media planning and buying services; access to PR and sales promotion networks; and design and production services.

Vision and values

The Ogilvy & Mather vision is, appropriately, 'To be most valued by those who most value brands'. Under the heading of values, the company describes itself as:
- Working for brands, in brand teams representing its own skills and those of its clients
- Encouraging 'individuals, entrepreneurs, inventive mavericks'
- Valuing 'candor, curiosity, originality, intellectual rigor, perseverance, brains – and civility'
- Preferring 'the discipline of knowledge to the anarchy of ignorance' (and expressing the preference by pursuing 'knowledge the way a pig pursues truffles')
- Prizing both analytical and creative skills: 'Without the first, you can't know where to go; without the second, you won't be able to get there.'
- Respecting the intelligence of its audiences
- Expecting its clients to hold it accountable for its stewardship of their brands, and its success to be judged by making their brands more valuable to both users and owners.

Information strategy development

The company's approach to information in the late 1980s was a fairly common one in advertising agencies, and so was its fate: a conventional library serving the information requirements of account executives, the creative department and senior managers, which fell a victim to recession. A similar story could be told of other agencies – nothing is ever static in organizations, and no one can afford to rest on the laurels of a currently successful strategy, and some are still struggling with the consequences. Ogilvy & Mather's experience of doing without managed information resources (which included trying to cope with two on-line services without an intermediary), however, showed that something was needed to replace what had been dispensed with, though of a different kind. An information manager with experience in the advertising world was appointed with the remit of developing a new strategy for the London business. The fact that there had been a clean break with traditional library services, and the experience since then of doing everything on an *ad hoc* basis, combined to overcome what could be described as a 'cultural resistance to new methods of accessing information'. The resistance to the traditional version is hardly surprising given the organizational values with their emphasis on individualism and personal pursuit of knowledge.

Sensibly, the information manager took these characteristics as the starting point for developing a strategy. In the process of sorting out some pressing problems with the on-line services and arranging for access to new databases, it was borne in upon her that the whole process of briefing an intermediary in the constantly changing context of advertising led to a static rather than a dynamic account of requirements, and reduced the possibility of interaction between users and the information found for them. This discovery informed consultations with managers, planners, creative staff, and media executives, at various levels up to that of directors on the board, about their current sources of information, how they used it, and the way of receiving it that would best fit in with their way of working. The discussions also laid the foundation for keeping up to date with developments in the business through continuing informal interaction and integration with various groups.

The findings from the consultation process, as presented to the Board, were:

- Fragmented use of information
- Time pressures
- Lack of awareness of available information
- Information overload
- Financial disincentives (the requirement to provide a job number each time a request was made meant that users felt penalized for seeking information)
- Current awareness is a key weakness.

The information strategy which is under development is founded on the idea that knowledge and information cannot be delegated, but should be part of the job responsibility of each individual. As sources of information multiply, people must take responsibility for being knowledgeable and identifying what information they need to feed their knowledge. (As readers of the case studies will observe, this idea is also an essential strand in the information strategies of other very different organizations; see, for example the studies of the University of North London, page 349, and Thomas Miller, & Co. Ltd, page 343.)

The basic aims of the information strategy are that individuals should have more personal control over the information they require to use in their work, and that information provision should match the time constraints under which they work. Information is needed in this business not just to answer questions relevant to immediate tasks in hand, but also to provide insights into clients' businesses which have the potential to lead to productive ideas. Quality and applicability are of the greatest importance; sheer quantity is a negative feature.

What was presented to the Board in 1997 was at the level of principles, described as 'somewhere between a policy and a strategy':

Strategic principles
– Information on demand
  Just in time v just in case
– End user access
  Better awareness
  Personal control
  Integrated business tool

The recommendations for the lines an information strategy should follow were:

– Give individuals more control over information resources through direct access
– Maximise current awareness applications of information
– Raise awareness of what information is available
– Maximise use of corporate information assets
– Create a more sympathetic financing arrangement by establishing a basic level of information which could be freely accessed (ie Reuters/Mintel/Internet) with only more specialized sources attracting specific charges.

The approach appealed to management as appropriate for the nature of the business, and likely to be cost-effective, and the strategy was accepted.

If the aims of the strategy are to be achieved, information finding and managing skills will no longer be limited to a small professional group; instead, they will have to become part of the 'tools of the mind' at the disposal of all knowledge workers in the business. This also means using the technology intelligently, so that getting and handling information becomes like any other part of the business process, and can be approached in the same way as any other application.

Implementing the strategy

Given the wide range of clients, the constantly changing subjects on which the agency works for them, and the lack of predictability in the business, bought-in on-line services directly accessible by the end users were the chosen immediate means of putting the strategy into operation. The first choice was Reuters Business Briefing, and within four months 200 staff were on-line to it. The next step will be a move to Reuters Advertising and Media Briefing, a more tailored version of the basic product; the objective is for this on-line service to meet about 80 per cent of the agency's needs. While access to such services takes care of information from the outside world, there is an as yet unfulfilled need to get at internally generated information. Planned developments to this end include integrating internally generated information with external information via an intranet.

Reporting and feedback on implementation of the strategy and its results are informal, and at the initiative of the Information Manager. Apart from the figures available from the system on how much it is used, monitoring of user response is also informal; as with most such services, there are a number of users who find it indispensable, and at the other extreme others who never use it. Unfortunately, major technical problems arose when there was a change in the environment in which it was implemented (a move from Windows 3.1 to Windows 95); interaction between the internal system and the technology of the product caused serious difficulties. The resultant disruption to the service has inevitably had a negative impact on users' perceptions of the product's performance and the benefits of direct access.

Evaluation

Despite technical difficulties like the one just described (which are a salutory reminder that nothing can be taken for granted, even with well-established applications and widely used environments), there are strong positive features in this case study. The strategy is based on individual responsibility, with professional information management support. The choice of information source is related to the nature of the business and its information needs, and the methods adopted in working towards an information strategy match the agency's organizational culture.

There are also issues still to be tackled in order to ensure the success and durability of the information strategy:

- Essential education and training without which the staff cannot use the information provided successfully, and the strategy cannot work
- Provision for repeated access to what has been found once, so that full value can be gained from it. It is hoped that the intranet, when introduced, will help to meet this need
- Integration of internal information with that originating externally (another point where the intranet should help)
- Relating the information strategy to the overall business strategy
- Developing means of assessing added value from this approach to information use.

Singapore Productivity and Standards Board

The origins of Singapore's vigorous national information policy ... can be traced back to the Economic Committee's desire in the mid-1980s to restructure the economy so that more value was added by each worker. Information is seen as a resource that will not only improve the productivity of industry and commerce, but that will also permit the evolution of new industries. The information services sector is increasingly seen as one of those new industries. (Moore, 1997)

The institution which forms the subject of this study is an example of the distinctive approach to combining national and organizational information policies which characterizes the East Asian region. As described by Moore in the article quoted above, this approach rests on the idea that the key to sustainable economic development lies in the partnership between the state and the private sector; the state should plan and largely finance the infrastructure, and support the development of the private sector. The attitude to competition is different from that of Western economies; it is seen as 'a powerful force but one that needs to be managed' (Moore, page 143) by a variety of supporting actions on the part of the state to give companies 'time and space to grow before they can compete effectively' (ibid., page 142). A further difference lies in the way in which people are seen in relation to the 'information society'. While in the West they are primarily regarded as recipients and consumers, who will be sold the new products of information technology, in such countries as Japan, Singapore and Korea people are recognized as having an active rather than a passive role. Singapore is singled out as having 'created further and higher education institutions that are equipping people with high-level skills' and promoting 'a culture that encourages constant retraining and re-education' (ibid., page 146).

This approach is exemplified in initiatives taken under the Library 2000 report produced by a committee appointed by the Minister for Information and the Arts 1992. Its terms of reference were to produce a master plan for library services, determine how IT could be fully exploited for this and to report on the library manpower and skills required.

The committee's report, accepted by the government in 1994, recommended as main strategic thrusts: an adaptive public library system, a network of borderless libraries, a national collection strategy, a quality service based on market orientation, symbiotic linkages with business and the community, and global knowledge arbitrage (that is, capitalizing on Singapore's business experience of many cultures to act as mediator between expanding and developed economies).

The report pointed out that investment so far had been mainly in the hard infrastructure. In the next phase of development, local enterprises needed to 'grow and regionalize and co-evolve with other multinational companies ... What is further needed is more investment in the soft infrastructure to help businesses and individuals to increase their competitiveness through knowledge and information ... More should be done to invest in our people ... it is resourcefulness, not resources, which will increasingly determine winners from losers.'

One of the outcomes was Tiara (Timely Information for All, Relevant and Affordable), a digital library cluster (DLC), proposed by the Library 2000 report. In 1995, the National Computer Board (NCB) formed DLC to review how information could be brought to the masses rather than just to the research community. The aim is to bring information to the people through a network of borderless libraries and information providers. Led jointly by the National Library Board and the NCB, Tiara's key champions and partners include the Productivity and Standards Board. Tiara projects include a library services network, an information services network, development of local and regional databases and content hosting (encouraging information providers to set up information hubs in Singapore). Access will be via the Internet from home, schools, libraries and community centres.

Tiara will be supported by Singapore 1, part of the country's IT2000 master plan for a broad-band information infrastructure, for delivering IT applications and services to all sectors of society. Singapore 1 is a step on the way – a national high-capacity network platform to deliver multimedia services to workplace, home and school. It has two levels: an infrastructure of networks and switches, and applications and multimedia services. The infrastructure will consist of a core broad-band network connecting several LANs (Local Area Networks), which will be built, owned and operated by an industry consortium. Applications will be developed in the areas of government, home, education and business. A pilot network will be running by 1998; initially government will be the 'anchor tenant', making its services electronically available to the public; over the years to 2004 the private sector will gradually take over.

Background to the establishment of the Board

The Singapore Productivity and Standards Board (PSB) came into existence in 1996 as a new statutory board under the Ministry of Trade and Industry (MTI), following the recommendations of a Task Force on Institutional Reform for Productivity and Quality and Improvements. The purpose of this multi-agency task force, formed in 1995, was to propose the appropriate institutional reform to take Singapore's productivity growth to a new height, so as to enhance Singapore's economic capability and competitiveness. Its recommendation for the formation of PSB underlined the need for a holistic approach to total factor productivity (TFP) improvement in order to achieve maximum synergy.

PSB integrates the functions previously undertaken by two institutions: the National Productivity Board (NPB) and the Singapore Institute of Standards and Industrial Research (SISIR). With the formation of PSB, the 'soft' aspects of productivity represented by NPB's activities in training, consultancy and promotion were integrated with the 'hard' aspects represented by SISIR's work in technology, quality, standards and industrial research. PSB also took over from the Economic Development Board (EDB) the responsibility of developing small and medium-sized enterprises (SMEs).

The mission of PSB is 'to raise productivity so as to enhance Singapore's competitiveness and economic growth for a better quality of life for our people'. It has adopted six key thrusts to achieve this mission:

- Manpower development
- Technology application
- Standards and quality development
- Industry development
- Productivity promotion
- Incentives management.

Structure

PSB is governed by an 18-member Board of Directors, comprising representatives from employer groups, the National Trades Union Congress (NTUC), the government, and professional and academic bodies. Its current chairman is the Minister without Portfolio and Secretary-General of the NTUC.

It has three main groups:
- Resources and Corporate Development
- Industry and Manpower
- Standards and Technology.

A restructuring in 1997, following a business process reengineering (BPR) exercise, brought together the main information functions within the Planning and Information Division, which forms part of the Resources and Corporate Development Group. On the basis of a recommendation from the BPR exercise, a centralized unit was established to plan the Board's information infrastructure. This Information Management Unit (IMU) is headed by the Chief Information Officer (CIO) who is also the Divisional Director of Planning and Information. The restructuring also brought the Information Systems Department (previously called the Computer Services Department) into the Planning and Information Division, with the aim of providing close and strong support for information management initiatives. Also part of the Division is the Information Resource Centre, which provides information services to industry.

Towards a systematic approach to information management

The recent restructuring of the Planning and Information Division has brought into focus the important role of information management. This role entails not only the management of vast amounts of information to meet the needs of PSB staff, but also the provision of relevant information to the workforce and industry – the target groups of the PSB's programmes. Hence there is a strong orientation to the outside world, through the provision of technical and business information, skills and training, and industry assistance – all focused on how PSB's clients need to use information.

More important, grouping all the information-related functions within the Planning and Information Division underlines the point that information initiatives must be strongly aligned to the strategic plans of the organization. Without that orientation, information initiatives could focus on the wrong areas, while the strategic plans would not have the benefit of strong support from information initiatives. The appointment of the Divisional Director of Planning and Information as the CIO was thus an important step in crystallizing the bond between information management and strategic planning in the Board.

When the IMU was set up, it scoured the literature and studied the practices of organizations that had a reputation for good information management policies. It could not, however, find a suitable comprehensive model for PSB. It then put up a policy paper outlining the proposed scope of information management in PSB, which synthesized the useful points from the literature and the practice of other organizations, and introduced a number of its own ideas.

The paper quoted interesting statistics in support of the case for managing information. In a Reuters (1997) survey of six countries in both East and West, 80 per cent of Singapore executives reported themselves as suffering stress from information overload, among other factors – the highest percentage in the survey. However, Singapore had a low percentage of firms offering training to their staff in managing information – 42 per cent as against an average of 58 per cent.

The IMU emphasized at the start of its policy paper that, while 'the scope of information management is in many organizations largely confined to database development and management', this alone is not enough to 'transform information into knowledge', and that information technology is most effectively used when it is aligned with the organization's strategic plan. The CIO's job is thus defined in broad terms (broader than the general usage of the term in the United States, where it tends to be strongly IT-oriented) as being to:

1 Organize and manage the information planning process
2 Develop an information architecture that integrates information systems in the organization and supports its strategic business plan
3 Develop information systems that support the organization's strategic and operational objectives
4 Formulate policies and guidelines pertaining to information management
5 Oversee investments in IT infrastructure and competencies
6 Identify opportunities to improve the relevance and adequacy of the information activities undertaken.

With the CEO's endorsement of the paper, information management has become a core part of the work of PSB and is expected to play a key role in helping the Board to achieve its vision.

PSB's information architecture, and the scope of information management

The framework for developing PSB's information plan (see Figure C11.1 on page 320), starts from its mission, thrusts and goals, and progresses through an analysis of the information requirements for meeting them to the development of an information architecture. This in turn (as shown in Figure C11.2 on page 321) forms the basis for formulating the strategic information plan, which defines and prioritizes the various information systems projects.

The framework for the information architecture has a three-tier structure, and a range of information flows and interactions, internal and with the external environment. Transaction processing systems (which are not necessarily all IT-based) cover such things as call and contact management systems and the corporate MIS. The central Enterprise Decision Support System, of which a 'knowledge-based system' is an important element, is intended to pool information from all areas of the Board so that it can be used for decision making, problem solving and answering queries. At the top level, the Executive Information System is designed to 'filter and organise information into categories and reports' that senior management use to make effective decisions. The knowledge-based system has the central role of linking the three tiers of information, drawing on the Transaction Processing Systems and providing the key information for the Executive Information System. It will hold and make accessible internally generated and externally originated information, to both the Board's staff and its customers in industry.

The work of the IMU covers five broad areas:

1 Information planning, which includes establishing the strategic direction for Board-wide information management
2 Information architecture development
3 Managing the Knowledge-based System
4 Formulating information management policies and guidelines
5 Reviewing the strategy for information management and the information architecture to ensure they are fully responsive to changing business requirements.

The IMU works in collaboration with all departments and centres in the Board which are responsible for managing information resources of various kinds, in particular the Information Systems Department, the Information Resource Centre, Internal Audit Department, Planning and Research Department, and Corporate Communications Department (see below for more detail about the role of the first two). It aims to bring the major stakeholder user departments into 'full partnership in managing the information resources'.

The PSB intranet is an example of the close cooperation and collaboration among the various departments in PSB required to make information management an organization-wide function. It is seen to benefit both PSB staff and the organization in two ways:

1 It serves as a knowledge base that makes possible information pull rather than push.
2 It builds teamwork across the Board as it connects all staff to information as well as to each other.

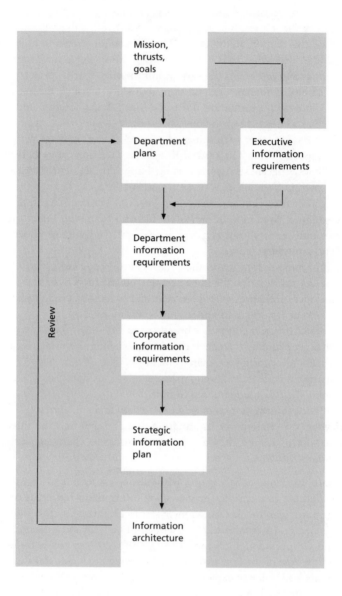

Fig C11.1   **Information planning framework**

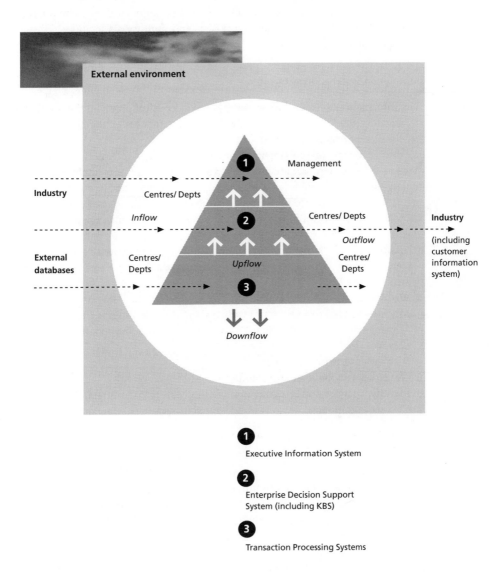

Fig C11.2   **PSB information architecture**

The PSB intranet will be developed in stages. The first phase, already implemented, focuses on important corporate information, including PSB's standard operating procedures, statistics, calendar of PSB events, library resources, publications and other operational information. The later phases will allow for staff interaction and transactions. Future facilities and services to be offered on the PSB intranet include bulletin boards and multimedia facilities, as well as electronic commerce.

Information Systems Department

The Information Systems Department (ISD) is a critical player in the information management initiative in PSB. While the IMU focuses on the management of business information content and flow, the ISD plays a leading role in meeting the IT needs of the organization. It manages IT technical operations, systems development, and technology evaluation and transfer, including technology deployment, network and systems management and integration testing. It is also responsible for developing the competencies of IT professionals. Its roles and responsibilities in respect of information management in the Board are of:

1 Identify and implement information systems to support management decision-making activities, as well as to enhance the internal operational efficiency of the Board
2 Work with end-users to achieve their goals through the innovative use of IT
3 Manage the effective use of IT resources and provide support to end users
4 Manage and enhance the Board's computer network and its office automation systems
5 Manage enterprise databases
6 Set IT security policies and standards
7 Identify, transfer and integrate new technologies into the IT framework
8 Oversee and manage vendors and external providers of IT services.

Information Resource Centre

The provision of information to industry and to the Board's own staff is mainly the responsibility of the Information Resource Centre (IRC). It plays a key role in the Singapore Business Library Network, which services the information needs of the business community. It drives the User Needs and Interests Group (UNIG) for Business, set up under the National Computer Board's Digital Library Initiative.

The IRC's vision is to be the one-stop information resource centre for productivity improvement in Singapore. To realize its vision, it has adopted a three-fold strategy:

1 Provide industry with access to information on productivity
2 Process and package information on productivity, using appropriate tools and technologies
3 Establish and maintain linkages and networking with information providers on a national, regional and international level.

The IRC is unique in offering access to the largest and most comprehensive range of materials on productivity, patents and standards in Singapore. Its services include general reference, information retrieval, current awareness, patent information, standards information and intelligence.

Another unique feature is its publication of a wide range of productivity-related information in print and electronic form. Its information products range from periodicals to thematic publications, guidebooks, casebooks, directories and comics. Examples of its publications are the *Productivity Digest,* the *Guidebook Series* with titles such as *Benchmarking* and *Business Excellence,* and the *Primer* series, with such titles as *Total Factor Productivity.*

The Centre recognizes that creating business networks and contacts is vital to an organization's long-term effectiveness and competitiveness. It therefore actively engages in networking, becoming more multi-disciplinary and multi-faceted, and building partnerships with specialist agencies and institutions. Its alerting and intelligence services, for example, now go beyond conventional current awareness to the development of information packages on emerging issues. One such example is its *Insights* series in the area of the environment; another is the booklet *BizInfo: Your Guide to Business Information in Singapore,* a joint publication of the PSB, the National Library Board, the Singapore Trade Development Board and the National Computer Board.

Evaluation

This case study is a good practical example of the characteristically Singaporean approach as set out in the introduction, in particular of the kind of initiative recommended in the Library 2000 report for 'more investment in the soft infrastructure to help businesses and individuals to increase their competitiveness through knowledge and information'. The merging of two institutions has been constructively used, without wasting any time but with a good investment in thinking, as an opportunity to work towards strategic use of knowledge and information.

The structural change which brought together a range of activities concerned with information – strategic information management, systems and IT, and information services – within a Division primarily concerned with planning the Board's strategies, created a sound basis for a new unit responsible for the strategic management of information. (See also the case studies on Amnesty International, Surrey Police, and the Australian Securities and Investment Commission, where similar structural changes have been made.)

It is encouraging to see that the unit began its work from first principles, by defining what PSB needs to know and the information it requires to support its knowledge, and that, while it studied the literature and the practice of other organizations, it has had the courage of its own convictions. The 'information architecture' which it has developed is more fundamental and more concerned with information content and its transformation to knowledge than the usual run of information architectures. The knowledge base is seen as its core, and it recognizes the range of information resources on which PSB needs to draw and the necessity of their integrated management. The role of IT and information systems is clearly defined, and the emphasis on helping people to use information technology innovatively in their work is welcome as an indication of concentration on areas where investment in IT and systems can bring the highest return. The outward orientation of the PSB is supported by the initiating actions of the Information Resource Centre, which go well beyond the traditional library role.

Not all the case study institutions described in this book have the fortune to work in a national context so favourable to the development of information strategies, but the supportive environment of the PSB does not detract from its rapid progress. When I visited the Board in August 1996, it had only recently been set up; in little over a year it has done a great deal of intensive thinking and has moved to the point where it can describe itself, with justice, as being 'poised to take on future challenges and opportunities, brought about by its recognition of the strategic importance of information; and ... to serve its stakeholders, both external and internal, more efficiently and effectively.'

References

MOORE, N. (1997), 'The information policy agenda in East Asia', *Journal of Information Science*, 23 (2), 139–147

Surrey Police

Introduction

The interest of this case study lies in three facts which are unusual taken singly and unique in combination. The organization concerned is a police force – representative of a public institution whose approach to information has tended to the traditional and bureaucratic; its senior managers have deliberately spent a long time thinking about the meaning of knowledge and information in the context of their work; and it is making a serious attempt at information auditing.

Surrey Police

Three parties are concerned with policing in Britain: the Home Secretary, the police authorities which are responsible for individual police forces, and the Chief Constables of police forces. Surrey Police consists of around 1700 police officers, 850 civilian personnel and 260 special and parish constables. The Force's headquarters, in the county town of Guildford, provides direction to the Force from the senior management team and support to divisions. Its departments are responsible for Administration of Justice; Complaints and Discipline; Finance and Administration; Human Resources; Information Technology; Mobile Support; Performance Management; the Safer Surrey Partnership; and Territorial Support.

The Force's geographical area covers approximately three-quarters of the administrative county, and it serves 774 000 of its 1 000 000 residents. Surrey is a mixed rural and urban area and, as a commuter region for London, it has double the shire counties' average traffic volume and *pro rata* the longest motorway network in the country. Although this makes it extremely vulnerable to travelling criminals, particularly from the London area, Surrey has one of the lowest recorded crime rates in the country.

Surrey Police adopts a geographical policing style, based on local teams of officers responsible for meeting the policing needs of their local communities, which it pioneered in 1989. The geographic areas are the building blocks of policing in Surrey. Each of the six divisions into which Surrey Police is divided is led by a divisional commander. Within the divisions are the areas, each with its own dedicated team of police officers, special constables, traffic wardens and civilian support staff. Policing of each area is the responsibility of an inspector. The role of these officers is vital to the geographic system; each has responsibility for the area 24 hours a day, 365 days a year. The approach which they take to their work is defined as a problem-solving one. To understand what needs to be done and to build productive partnerships with individuals and organizations, the area inspectors have to know their ground.

They and their teams build up a continuously changing profile of the area, containing information on people, places and events, which enables them to anticipate problems and tailor policing activities to local needs. The inspectors are well known to the community leaders and in contact with influential local groups, providing information and advice to support partnership working (see below). The area teams' good local knowledge allows them to maintain a 'menu' of policing tasks; some items stay on it permanently, others come and go as situations dictate.

In Surrey, policing activities fall into one of three categories:

1 Reacting to events as they occur and returning the situation to a 'state of stability' (the normal situation of those affected)
2 Planning for events by responding to information about criminal or disruptive activities, leading to enforcement intervention
3 Developing preventative and partnership policing. The partners include the community, business, voluntary groups and statutory services.

The policing plan is monitored by means of a Management Information System introduced in 1996, with the aim of allowing managers to 'monitor performance; set targets; identify strengths and weaknesses; identify areas of enquiry through exceptions and trends; support and develop strategic and tactical plans; plan resources; prioritization and deployment to match demand; identify accountability and value for money' (Surrey Police Authority Policing Plan 1997/98, page 26).

First steps towards a policy for information

The origins of the senior management interest in information go back to a project about rationalizing retention schedules for archiving documents early in 1993. The officer who carried out the project came to be more and more aware that the decision on whether to dispose of material or archive it was but the final stage in a much longer process, covering acquisition, storage methods, retrieval and use. And that in turn led to reflecting that not only does information go through a 'life cycle' of processes, it also contributes to other processes.

These considerations found expression in the diagram which is reproduced as Figure C12.1 on page 327.

With the encouragement of a senior manager who sponsored this work, he extended his reading into the fields of information management, systems strategy and policy, using definitions from HM Treasury, CCTA, and various books (including the first edition of this one). The outcome was an informal paper on 'Information strategy', which argued that information is a resource for the police service, standing alongside the traditional ones of personnel and finance. If effectively managed, it contributes to improving the quality of policy making, enables effective operation and higher service quality, produces more accurate and cost-effective management information, saves costs on unnecessary information, and gives a better focus to systems investment. These considerations were very relevant to areas of work which were coming to the fore at the time, including the development of ideas about what 'Level 3 policing' required.

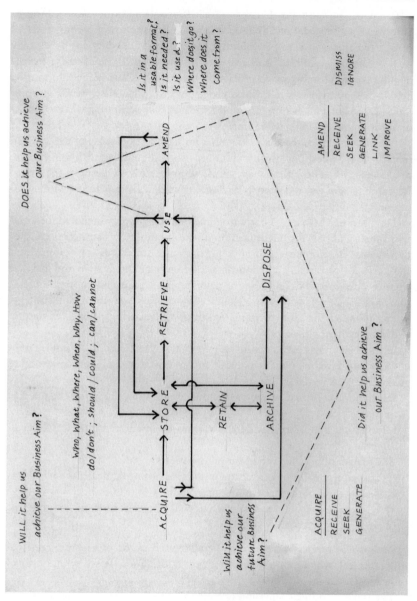

Fig C12.1   **Information life cycle and its contribution to other processess**

The paper pointed out that many police forces had undertaken a form of 'information audit' and had as a result instituted changes at great expense and considered themselves to be 'information efficient' – a belief not necessarily well founded. 'Regrettably this may not be the case. Although these Forces may be handling information efficiently they rarely know if the information held is the best available to achieve Force objectives.' In other words, it is not much use making an information audit without first examining what the organization should be doing with information.

The conclusion of the paper was that an information strategy was needed to address the questions of what the Force should be doing with information to achieve its business aims – apparently a pioneering suggestion; the Police Research Group was reported as having no examples of any forces with an information strategy.

The proposed scope of a corporate information strategy included information values and policies; identification of the organization's strategic information needs; development priorities for systems; structures, procedures and standards for controlling and coordinating to reduce duplication and increase sharing of information; and training priorities for creating an information culture. The Force was said to be well placed to develop an information strategy, in that it already had a clear statement of objectives and priorities, structure, and management philosophy.

In the following year, a 'position paper' was put forward on information strategy and management. It pointed to the waste in managing information created by such situations as:

* Information captured in one part of the organization not being exploited to the full
* Information that is used widely having to be re-entered into a number of different systems
* The danger of missing important information
* Information vital for one department that may be squandered as a worthless by-product by another
* The introduction of new systems for collecting information without first finding out what already existed.[1]

The paper proposed questions to be addressed by an information management project which should try to align information flows with business processes:

* The Force's strategic aims and objectives
* The information needed to support them
* The information available (audit)
* Differences between needs and provision
* What to do to match needs with provision
* How best to deliver information to users.

---

[1] Actual examples include:
* An activity analysis exercise which gathered information which was already available
* People responsible for a number of systems requiring vehicle descriptions were unaware that information in a format that exactly met their needs was available on site in a program used by the Force Garage, which provides industry-standard details of all models.

A major consequence was the creation of a high-level Information Management Steering Group, through the continuing support of the sponsoring senior manager, who set going a process of introducing members of the group to information strategy concepts. Thereafter there was what looked like a protracted pause with a good deal of talk but no discernible action – the group was reported as 'discussing principles at length but not initiating any projects'. (In retrospect, however, this is now seen by those concerned as a critical stage when time was well spent in allowing senior managers to take ownership of the relevant ideas and to feel at home with them.) In the meantime, it was agreed that the officer who had introduced the subject into the Force should become its professionally qualified specialist in information management, and he did a part-time MSc in information science.

One formal report was accepted; this set out proposals on a range of information issues: the role of library services, including computer-based cataloguing; the role of the registry; the need for an archive, and for Internet and intranet facilities – all brought together within the remit of an expanded Information Services Department. All the recommendations were accepted and they formed the basis of the current Information Services Department structure. Further progress had to wait on an appointment to the new post of Director of Information Services.

In mid-1995, the Chief Constable's policy conference had before it an agenda item on Information Management, in the form of a proposal that 'Surrey Police recognize that information is a key resource and its acquisition, storage, availability, use, maintenance and dissemination should be subject to the management disciplines which apply to any valuable asset'. This was accepted. The essence of the concept was embodied in a simple diagram, as shown in Figure C12.2 on page 330.

The final product of the Information Management Steering Group before it disbanded, on the appointment of the Director of Information Services, was a statement of information policy. The key points were:

- Information is a corporate resource to be made available to all who require it in order to perform their duties. All members of staff have a responsibility to seek out and use information pertinent to their daily tasks. Information should be withheld only to safeguard security, privacy, legal requirements, private opinion, confidentiality, privileged etc. information, and operational activity.
- Information resource requirements and value are best informed by users of the information. So stakeholders must be involved in information resource development; user requirements should be reflected in information systems and information technology, for which there should also be strategies.
- Information should be made readily available to complement decision making, and it should be timely and accurate.
- The costs of acquiring and maintaining information resources must be justifiable. So costs should be quantified, justified and subject to normal planning and budgetary controls, and owners of information resources should provide for their maintenance.
- Information must be acquired, processed and managed in a planned integrated and economic way. It should be possible to combine information from

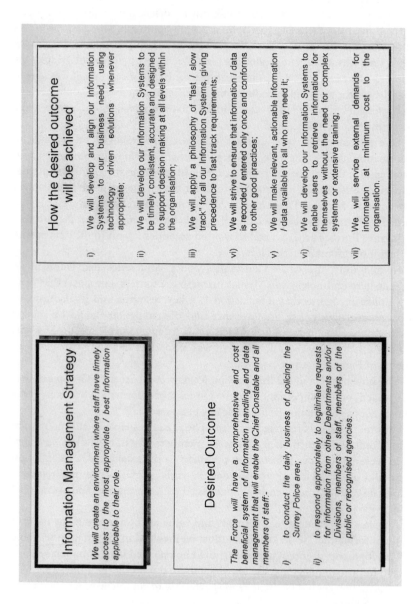

Information Management Strategy

We will create an environment where staff have timely access to the most appropriate / best information applicable to their role.

Desired Outcome

The Force will have a comprehensive and cost beneficial system of information handling and data management that will enable the Chief Constable and all members of staff:-

i) to conduct the daily business of policing the Surrey Police area;

ii) to respond appropriately to legitimate requests for information from other Departments and/or Divisions, members of staff, members of the public or recognised agencies.

How the desired outcome will be achieved

i)   We will develop and align our Information Systems to our business need, using technology driven solutions whenever appropriate;

ii) We will develop our Information Systems to be timely, consistent, accurate and designed to support decision making at all levels within the organisation;

iii) We will apply a philosophy of "fast / slow track" for all our Information Systems, giving precedence to fast track requirements;

vi) We will strive to ensure that information / data is recorded / entered only once and conforms to other good practices;

v)   We will make relevant, actionable information / data available to all who may need it;

vi) We will develop our Information Systems to enable users to retrieve information for themselves without the need for complex systems or extensive training;

vii) We will service external demands for information at minimum cost to the organisation.

Fig C12.2   **Based on IM strategy in one sentence + Desired outcome, and How it will be achieved; and Open Information Strategy, Desired Outcome, How it will be achieved?**

different sources; there should be common processes, techniques, structures, retention periods; where possible information should be acquired once and stored in one place; the nature and whereabouts of information should be publicized and appropriate access provided.

- Information is a valuable resource for all staff and its importance to the Force should be recognized through appropriate resource allocation and skills development. So information owners must recognize the need to maintain and develop their information resources; and users must be fully trained to meet the demands of their own role.

Action

The next step was the appointment of a Director of Information Services – and here problems arose over the wording of the advertisement, which had to make clear that someone with an understanding of information as well as of IT was required. Once this difficulty had been overcome, and an appropriate appointment had been made, the former standstill was transformed into pressure from management to implement everything at once.

The Director of Information Services, who joined Surrey Police in 1996, has a background which complements that of the Information Manager, who is a long-standing member of the Force. He is a systems specialist, whose experience in developing the predecessors of intranets led to an interest in the information management aspects of unstructured information, and awareness of issues of ownership, control, and guardianship of information.

Infrastructure and organizational structure

Two critical enabling aspects needed tackling: the infrastructure of systems and technology, and an appropriate organizational structure. The strategy aims to deliver a basic utility to everyone, with access to internal and external information sources in a consistent way that facilitates their inputs and takes account of people's work needs. A new network based on Windows has been introduced which offers consistent access. The front-end screen for all systems is designed as a Web browser screen which allows access to corporate databases. This is an outcome of what is described as a 'common vision among systems people' which now prevails.

The Information Services Department that was set up in 1996 covers systems, technology, and related services, library, records and registry. (For a similar structure, see the Amnesty International case study.) The underlying perception is that all the people involved need one another's expertise. It was justly observed that the functions now brought together were previously 'organizational nomads' who did not fit a bureaucratic structure; the managers responsible for them did not understand their role, and a low level of practice prevailed.

A high-level Information Steering Group was set up to oversee all pilot projects undertaken by the Department. The most significant project concerned information auditing.

Information auditing

From the outset the team responsible for developing and implementing information strategy were certain that an information audit was the necessary basis for their work; having analysed 'what should be' at a level of principles, it was now time to investigate the actuality.

The immediate impetus came from a report from Her Majesty's Inspector of Constabulary in November 1996. It dealt with an inspection on form processing in another police force, which led to large financial savings, and suggested that all forces should make a similar review. As this was analogous with the retention scheduling question which had led to the original initiatives on information management (see page 326), the Information Manager was asked to look at the matter. His recommendation was that form processing was not the fundamental problem, and that it would be more useful to do an information audit to get a real picture of how information was being used. This was something that could be done regularly, and by virtue of that was more likely to contribute to a long-term improvement.

The Director of Information Services had a particular interest in auditing in relation to the concept of information as an asset. He saw it as a mix of flow/process and physical stocktake concepts and wanted especially to use it to learn about owners and users of information.

The account of the information audit which follows is a first-hand one; it is contributed by Graham Robertson, the external consultant who worked with Surrey Police on the information audit.

▼

In introducing information auditing, two principles were followed. The first was that leadership and implementation should come from within the organization, using traditional managers, who do not have an information background but do understand the organizational context, to lead selected auditing pilot projects. The other was that external experience and advice should be drawn on to start the process, to promote understanding of the basic information concepts, and to give support in the very early stages of implementation. Consultants with a particular interest in and experience of information auditing provided this external support.

Planning

With the assistance of the consultants, a brief scope document was drawn up to set the scene for internal discussion and to secure the necessary senior executive project commitment and resources. The scope document:
* Summarized how the organization had arrived at this point, and defined the information audit as part of a developing information strategy, set within a recently established information policy
* Set out a specific information auditing approach
* Considered immediate and potential benefits
* Highlighted possible concerns and issues.

It also suggested a broad project timetable of three years, to start once the scope document had been discussed and approved, and recommended that an Information Steering Group (ISG), including individual managers from operational and administrative sections, should manage and coordinate the whole process. This pre-project 'planning' stage actually took just under six months.

The scope document proposed these stages for the programme:

1 Executive awareness (three months)

2 Pilot programme set up (three months)

3 Pilot programme activity (six months)

4 Prospective full programme roll-out (two years).

It did not attempt to define the resources required, other than to state that they would be addressed within each stage, for the next stage, as the project progressed and specific needs arose. The first stage would simply require executive time, which might be considered, in budgeting terms, as an experiential learning process, and therefore could even draw on training budgets if need be.

The scope document was agreed, and accepted by the Director of Information Services, in January 1997, and was then submitted to an internal project control group, which approved and authorised it.

Stage 1: Executive awareness

The development project was launched in April 1997. The executive awareness programme was based initially on eight seminar/workshop sessions for members of the ISG, and included an internal communications exercise. The workshop sessions were incorporated into regular ISG meetings, and began with some of the theory of managing information as an organizational resource, in line with such other accepted resources as people and finance.

Three audit concepts were introduced: audit techniques, domains of activity, and whether it was possible to use or adapt a standard audit programme model, which had been developed by the external consultants, to suit the requirements of this particular organization.

The audit techniques discussed, drawn in part from financial auditing, were: observation; inspection and verification; interview and inquiry; quantification and benchmarking; any other special methodologies that the organization might already be using were also allowed for. These techniques provide a mixture of assessment, checking and evaluation skills, which then act as a basis on which the audit team can 'form an opinion'.

The domains of activity are: physical stocktakes; information mapping; information needs analysis; workflow and process charting; and overall monitoring, compliance and control processes.

The standard information audit programme model presented contained seven items, each covering a general category of issues which could require attention in any area of an organization which is to be the subject of information auditing (see Robertson, 1997). They are listed here in no particular order of priority:

• Information processing

• Information control and security

• Information cost, price and value

• Information presentation, use and dissemination

- Information storage, maintenance and destruction
- Information ownership, responsibility and accountability
- Other general operating issues.

One session of the workshop programme included a demonstration of information needs analysis within a workgroup; this led on to consideration and determination of suitable candidates for the pilot projects. It was agreed that suitable candidates for pilot projects should have target objectives which were achievable over a three- to four-month period, without adding too much additional workload to the existing and continuing staff responsibilities of the audit team. The pilots should tackle a variety of subjects to test the relevance of this information audit approach and the variety of audit techniques mentioned above. They should address issues that needed resolution within the Force at that time, and they should, wherever possible, cover operational as well as administrative information activities. Another important selection criterion was that the project should, if possible, bring some immediate benefit (or quick win) for the organization.

Some ISG members found these early sessions straightforward and were evidently keen to get on with the fieldwork. Others found the theory difficult to accept, even though they accepted that policing was very much an 'information business'. It was helpful that most members had some prior knowledge of experiential learning.

The existing and changing responsibility of some members presented obstacles to be overcome in managing the early ISG meetings, particularly as one objective of the first stage was to bring everyone together in their understanding of the concepts of managing information as a resource and information auditing. Regular and consistent attendance at ISG meeetings certainly became an issue in the first two months, and as a result the number of workshop sessions was reduced, and the internal communications programme was deferred.

Stage 2: Pilot programme set up

Initially, two pilot projects were proposed. They dealt with, respectively, a simple operational process and a generic organizational information resource/repository, both of which were in common use throughout the Force. Subsequently, two additional candidates emerged. One dealt with issues where information flowed between two different areas of functional responsibility in an administrative area, and the other was concerned with issues where information was received from external authorities and required systematic operational analysis.

A member of the ISG (usually, the proposer) was designated as the pilot manager or coordinator for each pilot. The external consultants, who had attended the ISG meetings whenever the information auditing project was on the agenda, then withdrew from this management role and concentrated on helping with the launch of the pilot projects.

Induction training for the pilot managers

Each pilot manager/coordinator was given the opportunity of some support from the external consultants. All four managers/coordinators elected to participate in a brief two-hour introductory and individual session led by one of the consultants, where the process or the resource that was to be the subject of the pilot was discussed, and basic audit techniques were illustrated once again. Specific project definitions, timetable matters and the issues of managing the actual audit teams were also explored. Pilot managers were asked, wherever possible, to see that their teams recorded tasks, comments, reactions, and opinions as appropriate and logged all the time spent. They were also asked to keep the ISG informed of their activity as necessary. It was emphasized that any audit activity at this level should be seen as a continuous learning process for everyone involved.

It became evident from this stage that police officers were intuitively familiar with audit techniques, once they saw the similarity with their own investigative skills. Some civilian staff, however, were more concerned about 'learning how to audit', and expected a more detailed methodology to be set down. While the brief summary of audit techniques and domains of activity proved useful, audit programme elements proved harder to introduce and were abandoned for the third and fourth pilots. Where they were mentioned, these programme elements proved useful only as a guide, until the audit teams had begun to tackle their subject areas, when they provided a reminder of the issues and concerns that they should be addressing during their fieldwork.

Pilot manager/coordinators felt reassured to have an external consultant present at the early meetings with the 'audit team'. As their confidence grew, the need for external support diminished.

The Department of Information Services asked each pilot manager to submit a project definition form, setting out the issue addressed, objectives to be achieved, and reporting timetables. This procedure was an established process within the organization and it both gave purpose to initial induction meetings and provided clarity and discipline as the pilots proceeded (see the University of North London case study, pages 357 to 359, which also used a project definition document).

Induction training for the audit teams

Each audit team undertook a series of induction meetings, at the beginning of their projects. For three of the four pilots, an external consultant attended by invitation. Support for the fourth pilot was provided in a different way, as the audit team members were confident that they could deal with the task without external assistance. (It is perhaps significant that, in this case, members of the audit team were nominally senior to the pilot manager.) In the event, it became clear that this degree of independence was not constructive, although it proved useful to gain experience from it.

In all the other pilots, the meetings covered such matters as the context of the overall programme, key ideas in information resources management, understanding an information audit approach, determining the actual pilot programme objectives, workload recognition and diary management. In all cases, there were 'brainstorming' exercises, focusing particularly on where information came from, what was done to it, and where it might be used. In some cases, the audit teams had to be pulled back from classic process improvement and development to the more basic audit approaches of discovery and identification, which in time might well act as a precursor to future process improvement. In some cases, attention was paid to the development of suitable collection mechanisms (usually based on MS Excel spreadsheets). Teams were encouraged to keep an open mind about how they might present their conclusions until they approached the end of their projects. They were also reminded that a good/satisfactory audit report might simply say that 'everything was working perfectly'. Other critical elements included how to determine boundaries to the audit process, manage expectations, and be aware of such political issues as the ownership of information and the power associated with that ownership. Audit teams were made aware that some information audit programmes were unfortunately associated with 'downsizing' exercises and that if they encountered concerns on that aspect they must tread cautiously. Their purpose was simply to gather information and assess the position rather than challenge existing organizational resources, and if they wished to 'discover' what they needed to know, they would need to win cooperation and collaboration, rather than create resistance and fear. At all times, audit teams were encouraged to look out for 'quick wins' which would ensure benefit to the organization and assure credibility of the audit process. Two pilots actually secured such benefits.

The pilot projects were initially designed to run over a three- to four-month period, with some time remaining for analysis, comparison and conclusion, but some pilots took more time to launch than others because of existing work pressures and diary coordination. As a result the pilot programme actually took nearer to nine months to complete. At the time of writing, three out of the four pilots have reported conclusions or outcomes.

Stage 3: the pilot projects

Partly by design, and partly by good fortune, the four pilot projects offered an excellent variety of issues to test the different audit techniques and approaches, and provided useful experience at many different levels. Each pilot offered a different mix of management issues and audit challenges.

Pilot 1: A routine information processing task

The subject of this pilot was originally defined as a simple routine information processing task, with great potential for rationalization and improved integration with other information resources through further automation. There were operational and administrative implications to some of the internal and external information resources to which it contributed.

The 'simple process' actually turned out to be more complex, with considerable interdependencies, and required an analysis of an extremely labour-intensive, paper-based information flow, that currently involved multiple re-keying of data. There were inconsistencies in content and style, and local value was being added on an occasional basis at different stages. Although this project was proposed by the Information Manager, the pilot was actually coordinated by a member of the civilian staff who was involved in quality assurance matters. The two members of his 'audit team' were or had been senior police officers. While both 'auditors' had good operational experience and evidently held suitable management responsibilities in the 'Administration of Justice department', they were both nominally 'senior' to the pilot coordinator. This meant that in practice the audit approach was clearly determined by individual members of the audit team.

Apart from a limited introductory session with the pilot manager, there was no further request for support, and the audit team immediately started to chart the information flow and illustrate inter-dependencies as they arose. It rapidly became evident from the resulting flowcharts that the subject area was far from 'simple' and some work was devoted to analysing and elaborating these interdependencies from the coordinator's quality assurance experience. A data collection form was also developed, which expanded from some twenty data items to nearly fifty items as discovery continued.

The project then ran into difficulties, as its coordinator was assigned additional duties and was unable to give further time. A statement summarizing the findings to date lists ten major findings and suggests areas of further study. Examples of the major findings were: 'the whole information flow is large and complex, using many forms, some logging progress, some multi-sectioned for different uses, and a vast amount of internal post and paper trails'; '… large sections which are duplicated … And some information that is redundant or just not worth collecting'; 'there are … data protection issues'; '[data] input requires a lot of detailed input and time, demands precision, does not always get it'.

Suggested areas for further study included: improvement of forms and use of information gathered; streamlining the paper trail; consideration of various performance parameters; identification of critical areas where small improvements would have a large effect; whether simple technology, in conjunction with the recent intranet services, could improve or replace some parts of the process; and the (real) costs and benefits associated with automating complex systems.

The interim conclusions are interesting: The process that was the subject of the audit, was considered to be important to everyday policing and demanded proper prior evaluation of changes with the involvement of practitioners at each stage of the process, if costly mistakes were to be avoided. The team took a pragmatic approach to information auditing by devising a methodology based on standard formats, linked to the audit theories that were provided. The training that had occurred was considered to be more thought-provoking than oriented towards a practical application.

Pilot 2: A physical stocktake of a major operational information resource

This pilot project emerged early in the selection stage, and was proposed (and subsequently managed) by one of seven Divisional Development Inspectors (DDIs) in the Force (who was also a member of the ISG). DDIs have a specific and important role of providing development support throughout the organization and acting as a communication channel linking strategic developments (with which they are familiar) with practical issues in the 'front line'.

Standing Orders require that the information repositories covered by the audit should be maintained at different levels throughout the fourteen operational 'Areas' of the Force. The audit team was made up of one other DDI and two other police officers. Although they were initially concerned about needing to 'learn auditing techniques', it became clear that since their normal duties make police officers naturally inquiring and intuitively investigative, no actual time needed to be devoted to this aspect.

An external consultant was invited to join three of the initial meetings of the group. Considerable time was spent in working over and agreeing the project aims and objectives, and clarifying the subject area and any potential interrelationships with other projects or initiatives. Some time was then also spent in developing a MS Excel spreadsheet application to act as a collection and analysis mechanism.

Initially, it was suggested that only a sample of the known repositories should be tested during this pilot, but this approach was altered to become a full audit (physical stocktake). As a result, 65 repositories were reviewed and tested. To enable field researchers to obtain as many answers as possible in one inspection visit to each location, the audit team developed a basic audit checklist, selecting relevant items such as information dissemination, presentation and use. Working from this checklist made field research easier to complete, and ensured, as far as possible, a standardized approach to data collection.

A variety of information attributes were tested, including information content, information currency, information ownership and contribution to organizational objectives. Both qualitative and quantitative results were obtained on each repository; all the results were noted and compared within the spreadsheet format of the MS Excel application.

The audit team had hoped to try all the audit techniques mentioned earlier (see page 333), but in view of their decision to carry out a full physical stocktake on the subject area, it proved impractical within the given time-frame. None the less, the team's report shows that they were able to draw clear and useful conclusions. For instance, one weakness, identified from the 'currency' test, was that few information entities within the subject area included dates of origin. Age, relevance and accuracy were therefore more difficult to judge. Another conclusion from this pilot was that 'in general, the use of information auditing techniques [lent] a discipline and a clarity to the task'. However the process of information auditing carried implications of resource time, and if benefits were to outweigh costs, smaller test samples should be addressed on future occasions.

Shortly after the audit fieldwork had been completed, and basic results summarized, the team held a 'Design workshop', inviting representatives of various ranks and roles from across the Force, in order 'to obtain the views of users' as to what these information repositories should usefully contain. The output from this workshop provides a rich supplement to the more traditional 'project report' subsequently presented to the ISG. This workshop also usefully demonstrated a further audit technique of reviewing specific information needs of the organization within a particular area, by actively involving the actual users of such information. For instance two workgroups set out to explore independently what the repositories should be, and came up with virtually identical conclusions. As a result, delegates to the workshop were able to 'sign up' to an agreed definition that these information repositories, rather than being simply paper based, should become: 'a dynamic system which identifies ... [operational information] ... which is likely to create a policing demand'. Outputs from the design workshop were also made available to the ISG as appendices to the closing audit report.

Towards the end of its activity, and on the basis of its audit findings and results, the subject area of this pilot was redirected towards a wider operational programme within the Force, and was incorporated in it. Further development work on these information repositories could therefore be pursued within the short, medium and long terms. The ISG considered this to represent an extremely satisfactory 'quick win' for the information audit process.

Pilot 3: Identifying and resolving conflicts in information processes between two administrative departments

At face value, the subject area of this pilot project seemed a surprising choice. Management of staff accommodation did not seem to be a natural place to test information auditing techniques. In the event, however, it proved to be a valuable choice. The pilot manager, in this case a civilian member of staff, was responsible for managing Property Services and Capital, and was a member of the ISG. He was familiar with audit processes within a financial arena, and suggested tackling the information issues around maintaining and managing the occupancy of staff accommodation. One of the principal issues here was that several different organizational functions were involved, including operational managers, the personnel department and financial staff. One objective was to identify information ownership and policy issues across the various departmental functions and thereby assess existing procedures and existing responsibilities in information terms.

The audit team comprised three line managers (civilian staff) and a representative (also civilian staff) from the finance area. An external consultant attended the first two induction meetings in full, and then joined a subsequent meeting for its conclusions. Two points became clear on this pilot. Firstly, there were immediate initial differences about information objectives and needs which had to be resolved between managers of some of the functions involved. Secondly, there was a definite desire to 'carry out a development project' to resolve the problem, rather than concentrate on basic audit processes. This second point required some careful external guidance to ensure that attention was focused initially on an audit approach (in this case information gathering and collation exercises) before going on to define how a proper and more effective system could be established and developed. Some time was spent in clarifying the aims and objectives of this pilot with the team, before defining particular areas of audit activity for each member. These areas of activity included a general search for relevant staff policies or procedures, in whatever form they might take, in each of the functional areas; gathering information on the actual *status quo* of staff accommodation from existing records, to test completeness and accuracy of existing information, and visiting external organizations with similar responsibilities to compare processes.

Once again, an MS Excel spreadsheet was developed and used as a simple collection mechanism. By the end of the pilot, the team was able to comment on existing policies, determine and prove the actual status of staff accommodation and occupancy states, and compare existing in-house procedures with those of comparable external organizations. The team then moved into development project mode and made firm proposals as to further work which should be undertaken both at an administrative and at a technical level. A further outcome of this pilot was that the pilot manager was able to reassure senior managers that apparent issues surrounding room availability did not exist in this area and that certain operational problems that were arising could be resolved immediately, with only a small amount of additional redecoration expenditure. This outcome was also considered to represent a 'quick win' by the ISG.

Pilot 4: Evaluating the benefit of processing specific operational information

Once again, the suggestion for this pilot came from a member of the ISG, because it represented serious issues relating to the allocation of time and manpower resources in connection with the processing and dissemination of externally sourced operational information. Here, the audit team comprised two members of the pilot manager's own staff, responsible for acquiring, organizing and analysing operational information, which was delivered by an external authority, and two members who were potential users of such information at the operational level. All members of this team were police officers.

An external consultant was invited to join in the induction process and attended three meetings. Considerable time was spent at these meetings in defining the overall information flow process and illustrating different sources and audiences. Another issue which required careful discussion was the fact that the process involved the use of externally sourced information, and confidentiality issues needed to be respected. The audit team was concerned that any results of such an 'audit process' might be misused if they were not presented in a proper manner and within the right context. This type of work did not lend itself to statistical analysis of 'successes' versus 'failures'. As a result, it was suggested that the team follow through particular cases, drawing conclusions on the quality of the process, rather than 'the value' of any outcome, and then, in a separate exercise, quantify the effort that had to be applied, highlighting achievements whenever they occurred. The method of reporting could be left until the end, and it was emphasized that 'audit reports' did not need to be detailed, but could simply illustrate an opinion of accuracy and relevance. At the time of writing, this pilot project is yet to be completed.

Time and costs to date

It is unusual and welcome to have information about the amount of time and costs involved in such an information audit project as this. The organization is happy to report the following:

Stage 1 required 30 days of internal staff time with 12 days of external consultancy support. Internal staff time for activities in stages 2 and 3 (which, in practice, merged into one stage), probably required at least 100 days (although it is difficult to be precise about this figure), with nine days of external consultancy support.

A (very approximate) guide to internal staff cost could be set at £200/day for police officers and £120/day for civilian staff, which gives, broadly speaking, an overall internal staff cost of around £18 000.

External consultancy costs over the first year amounted to £10 500, with travelling expenses not exceeding 10 per cent of this amount. At a day rate of £500/day, stage 1 therefore cost £6000, and stages 2/3 £4500.

For comparison, it is worth noting that the organization's IT budget (1977/ 98) is of the order of £3.6 million/year, and this includes the Information Management (IM) function at £0.5 million. A substantial part of both these figures is represented by staff costs. Within the IM budget, the sum set aside for development work and special projects is still only some 10 per cent (that is, approximately £50 000) of overall budget.

However in this context it must also be emphasized that these information audit pilot projects have only addressed a very small part of the whole organization as yet, and that there is still considerable work to be done if information auditing is to be rolled out across the whole organization, with corresponding impacts on staff costs, and hence possibly the IM budget. None the less, the cost comparison between the organization's IT budget and those incurred in respect of the information audit project prompts this observation from one of the external consultants associated with the project.

> **IT projects require specification, cost benefit analysis and justification; initial high capital input (risk/trust); commitment and effort ... and long term patience before any predicted return on investment is secured ... if indeed it ever is. Thinking through how information is and should be used and managed in any organization is relatively cheap... and yet can yield enormous benefits over reasonable time frames.**

The next steps

As the organization completes its pilot project programme and reviews the various conclusions from all the pilots, it is evident that there is now considerably more expertise within the ISG on information resources management (IRM) and information auditing (IA) than in the rest of the organization. Work has begun on developing an information management policy to support the information policy that is already in place, and attention is being paid in it to establishing some reliable means of measuring benefit.

Proposals are also now in hand to develop better understanding in IRM and information auditing and expand awareness, through organizing induction workshops in specifically different directions:

- Incorporation into the system development philosophy: IT applications teams should be introduced to IRM and IA so that these concepts are borne in mind during system development (particularly concentrating on information needs analysis)
- Communicating through to the users/front-line officers: IRM and IA should be introduced to all Divisional Development Inspectors (DDIs), so that these ideas and concepts can be cascaded throughout existing channels of communication. (This effectively reintroduces the communication strategy which was deferred in stage 1)
- Performance measurement: those already responsible for performance measurement should also become aware of the principles of IRM, so that appropriate metrics and other measuring mechanisms may be developed, wherever possible in line with other existing processes in the Force
- Existing and new projects, designed to 'reduce bureaucracy': information-auditing, and in particular information-needs-analysis, techniques can provide a helpful framework for these projects.

It may well be that further pilot projects will develop out of these initiatives as the organization continues to learn about how it uses information and what its actual information needs are. The first stages of the information audit development programme have provided a useful working experience of a generic set of skills, which can now be used in a variety of different ways, to support the continuing improvement of the management of information.

Evaluation

The 'Open Information Strategy' described in this case study contains both information systems and information strategy. It seeks to move the organization towards better use of its existing policies by supporting its staff in their work in the field with necessary information and enabling them, through the technology, to feed in their own information to the organization. It won ready acceptance by senior managers because, through long-term exposure to basic ideas about information management, they had come to absorb and own them. The background of preliminary work, supported by a management champion, meant that there were 'no axes to grind, no historical positions to defend, once we were over the IT barrier'. It also made it possible to change the organizational structure so that information content, information systems and information technology were managed within the same framework, with a management team who thoroughly understand the relationship between information management and information systems management.

Many of the ideas which became important for the organization's thinking were brought in from the outside world through reading, conversation and encounters with such bodies as the Aslib Information Resources Management Network. They were 'acclimatized' by being presented in a way that matched a well-understood organizational context and culture. One of the encouraging lessons from the story told in this case study is the discovery that in information auditing it worked to give responsibility to managers without an information background; their own professional knowledge and habits of inquiry meant that they did not have difficulty with building the concepts involved into their existing knowledge.

Serious first-hand accounts of information auditing in action are rare, and readers planning to make an audit should find many useful lessons and ideas in the one that forms part of this case study.

For the future, the development and implementation of the information strategy should lead to more freedom of action for the staff of Surrey Police, and it is foreseen that this is where a cultural challenge will be encountered. The meeting between the traditional self-image of police services – tough, active, practical people out in the street, solving problems in the front line – and the concept of an information-based knowledge-using organization will be an interesting one. The challenge will be met, and the two cultures linked, by continuing to capitalize on the tacit knowledge of the Force, and by emphasis on gaining reputation through informing the public and interchanging information with them.

Reference

ROBERTSON, G. (1997), 'Information auditing: the information professional as information accountant', *Managing Information*, 4 (4), 31–35

SURREY POLICE AUTHORITY (1997), *Policing Plan 1997/98,* Guildford: Surrey Police Authority

Thomas Miller & Co. Ltd

The company

The origins of the independent professional firm which forms the subject of this case study go back to 1884. The company and its subsidiaries manage a number of non-profit-making insurance companies based in London – most of them dating back to the nineteenth century; they also act as London agents for the managers of similar overseas insurers, and provide consultancy services or contact offices for them. The insurance companies concerned are all mutuals; known as 'clubs' and operating mainly in the area of liability insurance, they are solely for the benefit of policy holders. Their members decide overall policy via a board of elected directors, and delegate the day-to-day running of clubs to the professional managers.[1]

The clubs include the UK P&I Club, the largest insurer of third-party liabilities for ocean-going ships; the UK Defence Club which provides cover for costs and expenses incurred by shipowners and charterers in connection with uninsured disputes; war risks clubs for Greek- and British-owned ships; the TT club, providing liability and equipment insurance for the multi-modal transport industry – containers, terminals, depots, freight forwarders etc.; and ITIC, a provider of professional indemnity and public liability insurance for ship agents, brokers and managers. The professional clubs include those for barristers, solicitors, patent and trade mark agents, surveyors and housing associations.

The company describes itself, with justice, as a 'knowledge business', whose main asset is the specialized and varied knowledge of its 550 staff world-wide; while it is an insurance but not a legal business, it acts more as a specialized consultancy for client organizations. It identifies the value of its services as related to the insights deriving from 'vision, tolerance at the edges, and acceptance of failure' – a combination of organizational culture and supporting technology.

Information and knowledge needs

A range of high-level professional skills is required of staff, who carry large responsibilities for negotiating, often under time pressure. They need, besides professional qualifications, a good knowledge of insurance, law and the relevant business sectors, and knowledge of specific geographical areas. They also have to be (as an information product about the company addressed to

[1] There are interesting parallels and comparisons to be made with another of the case studies in this book – that of the Credit Union Services Corporation of Australia, see page 233.

graduates puts it) 'numerate, resourceful, a proficient communicator and negotiator with commercial acumen'. As described below, the company makes a large investment in in-house and other training, with particular emphasis on skills for accessing and using appropriate information to the best possible advantage.

Information support

The responsibility for providing information services to the company's staff rests with its Business Intelligence Centre (BIC), which was set up in 1993, when the Chairman decided it was an essential support for remaining competitive (previously there had been no information service). The Centre is headed by the Group Director of Information, one of two directors reporting to the Chairman; the post is funded by the businesses, which means that the holder has to prove to them the value of the information provided. Currently the BIC registers 2500 'sales' a year. The Director of the information team has several years' experience in one of the company's businesses, and key contacts in all; the rest of the team are information specialists without a background in business, so at present the BIC relies on her knowledge in making judgements.

The BIC has a range of information roles. Its own brochure defines them under the headings of managing (filtering information, centralized negotiation of information contracts, and managing Lotus Notes databases); providing information (inquiry answering, current awareness products); research (assisting with Going for Growth ideas, for example background research for launching new businesses), library services (organization of Miller libraries world-wide, book and periodical orders/subscriptions); 'electronic tools of the trade' (for example Reuters Insurance Briefing, FT Profile, and Lloyd's Shipping Index); and Lotus Notes databases. The databases include:

- Miller TeamWork – all documents etc. about the internal activities of any Miller team (with its own good practice guide)
- Miller Directory – of all employees, departments, etc.
- Catalogue of all books, files, periodicals, speeches, presentations held world-wide
- Internet sourcebook – a directory of useful sites on the World Wide Web
- Miller Encyclopaedia – a database of knowledge and information about P&I, TT, Defence, War Risks and ITIC subjects
- MRC Status reports – transport company reports.

The BIC maintains and manages information in Lotus Notes databases; contributors are responsible for accuracy and detail of content, with help available from BIC.

A learning centre is associated with the BIC – it offers internal and external courses on such subjects as computer training, legal maritime training, as well as master classes and videos by partners.

Towards an information strategy

As in a number of organizations, the realization that an information strategy was needed came in Thomas Miller & Co. Ltd from the experience of developing an IT strategy. In 1990, the underwriting director of the company, a lawyer who had worked there since 1978, was asked by the Chairman to join the information technology partners in devising an IT strategy to help overcome such major problems as the large paper files about individual claims coming in from all over the world and requiring long-term storage. Given nine months to look around, they found a fairly typical problem: there was no very clear business strategy, and so they had to make assumptions about it.

IT strategy

On the basis of the assumptions, they produced an IT vision for the 1990s. The strategy developed from that led to the establishment of an IT infrastructure. The main features are document storage and shared creation of documents, with full-text search capacities; some expert systems of high quality; a very advanced image and workflow system is also under development, driven by the need to give users access to available relevant knowledge. Communications are seen as a critical area, demanding the highest level of IT skill. The company has had a local area network for about 15 years, and a wide area network for ten years; e-mail and Lotus Notes are used for communication and group working; today the basic principle is that everyone working for Thomas Miller, wherever they are in the world, should have the same desktop. A five-layer Internet site is under development; the levels are:

1 Public information
2 Registration process
3 Access gained by registration to useful material on transport (for example a collection of useful shipping sites on the Web)
4 General client information, available to all clients, but to no one else, offering the 'Miller Encyclopaedia' (see below), and other reference material, full-text-searchable.
5 Material private to individual clients, on their own claims information, which is of high value to them, given that the policies concerned are very complex, and claim payments can take a long time.

To support bridging between the www site and internal material, a move has been made to Domino (a Notes facility for putting material on to the Internet).

As described in a case study in a DTI publication (DTI, 1996), the lessons of the process of developing an IT strategy were:

* Identify and concentrate on people desperate for a business solution
* Start by making available existing information and knowledge, not by creating new information
* Set up an information department as a business unit with specific metrics
* Continuous collaboration to help all users master the system and use it effectively
* Help people to understand new priorities and acquire new skills for career development in a changed business and professional environment
* Turning any form of expertise that used to be done by hand, paper or brain into a system will take longer than expected 'because the process forces you to re-think how you work.'

- You have to use the new system immediately and regularly once trained, otherwise training is wasted
- Make the electronic system the only place for key information; abandon paper.

As will be seen, many of the lessons pointed in the direction of information strategy. To quote the person responsible, 'we decided that success depended on expertise in information sharing and learning'. In 1993–94 a new chairman asked him to focus on information, and he became Group Director of Information, and a new appointment of Director of Learning was made. The role of Group Director of Information has remained much the same now that a colleague has taken it over. The original holder of the post is now involved in exploring new opportunities, for new business development, but retains a strong interest in information aspects, and in the development of knowledge management (see below).

Information strategy development

Development of the information strategy is the responsibility of the Group Director of Information, who heads the company's Business Intelligence Centre. A strategy accepted by the Board in 1997 covers internal and externally generated information. Its purpose is described as:
- To prevent information overload caused by rapidly developing technology
- To maximize the use of information held in the firm
- To increase the accessibility and reduce the cost of information
- To help the clubs improve their service to members
- To ensure that those not located in London are kept informed
- To provide research capabilities.

So far as internally generated information is concerned, the strategy states that is essential for people in the organization to be able to get at whatever information they need and to be able to interchange it. The strategy also covers the obligations of all staff to be aware of requirements on compliance and copyright issues, and to exercise responsibility in their work for the proper use of information, and the quality of information.

The strategy sees it as essential to balance the information service offered, as between gaining new business and keeping existing clients happy. Service to clients includes 'information for profit' for example by offering members of two of the clubs access to the 'Environmental Encyclopaedia' (material on international and local legislation and environmental and safety issues), and to the 'Miller Encyclopaedia' – a database of information about subjects of significance to the clubs to which the company provides services; the electronic equivalent of general filing systems, it covers such topics as conventions, trading conditions, legal, port, loss prevention, travel, stowage, etc. After a period of piloting, access to the 'Miller Encyclopaedia' is now provided on-line to all clients. A balance is also sought in determining the cost-effectiveness of information – as between measuring for financial value (which could take too much time) and logging the trail of inquiries; the measure of success is the straightforward one of whether users return for more.

The strategy requires significant changes in behaviour within the organization; the BIC is working with the Personnel Department on employment contracts, with the aim of having information obligations – covering information interchange as well as confidentiality – written into the contracts given to staff. At the same time, 'guardians' and 'stakeholders' have been identified: each area of the business and each team in each business has a leader whose obligation is to ensure communication and interchange of information, and to act as a catalyst for renewing information. So, for example, each section of the Encyclopaedia has a named author who is responsible for keeping it up to date.

When the Board accepted the strategy, the BIC team started brainstorming, looking at their own training in knowledge of the business. At the same time they began a process of making sure that everyone was aware of what they could and should have; visits were made to identify key contacts world-wide.

The future

Information management in implementation of information strategy to date has been a matter of gathering information, managing frameworks, identifying gaps, changing the culture, adding value in meeting inquiries, and giving new ways of access to old types of information. The company now sees itself as moving towards knowledge management; which it views as being similar to the management of information, but more oriented to humans, the knowledge they possess and act upon, and their obligations to self and others. A step in this direction is the revision of the existing internal directory to give access to what staff are expert in (a revival in electronic form of the 'index of expertise' of the 1960s). Longer term, it envisages the possibility of becoming a knowledge broker, with 'more brain power than financial capital', bringing thinking to bear on capital, including bringing it in from outside.

Evaluation

This case study of a business whose staff need large knowledge resources to operate effectively has some useful lessons. The initiatives which led towards the current development of information strategy came from the top of the company and support has continued from that level, which has given stability and continuity to the process. Some of the people who have taken responsibility for information strategy are from the core businesses, with long experience and high standing, reflected in the level of the posts they hold.

This is one of a number of examples of successful organic development from IT strategy towards information strategy. The fact that the originator of the IT strategy was also the initiator of the moves to information strategy has made for continuity, and the IT strategy itself was soundly based on the understanding that its success depended on expertise in information interactions and in learning. This is followed through both in the close association between the Business Intelligence Centre and the Learning Centre, and in the emphasis which the information strategy places on the responsibility of staff for making proper use of information in their work and maintaining the quality of information. It is good to see these responsibilities expressed by the incorporation of information obligations in contracts, and by the identification of guardians and stakeholders of information resources.

The company is thus well placed for the next stage of moving towards the management of knowledge, though there is a realistic recognition that it will take time for full understanding of information obligations and the action implicit in them to permeate and become embodied in everyday practice.

Reference

DEPARTMENT OF TRADE AND INDUSTRY
(1996), *Profit from improving your message
flows*, London: IT Skills Forum

University of North London

'The University is a Paradise, Rivers of Knowledge are there, Arts and Sciences flow from thence. Counsell Tables are hortes conclusi *(as it is said in the Canticles) Gardens that are walled in, and they are* fontes signati *Wells that are sealed up; bottomless depths of unsearchable Counsels there.'* John Donne

One measure of how much things have changed in the time since the first edition of this book is the raised awareness of information in institutions of higher education. In 1992, in a talk at a conference rather ominously entitled 'Campus information: the electronic answer?', I took this quotation from John Donne as my text, and suggested that, whatever may have been the case in the seventeenth century, in the late twentieth century the paradise wasn't doing any too well in the matter of 'campus information':

> **Rivers of knowledge leak away into the sand; Arts and Sciences do not always flow to all the places they might nourish. The deliberations of the Counsell Tables are sometimes walled in and sealed up – though more often they flood forth as a tide of too many words on too many pieces of paper. The depths of Counsels are all too often literally unsearchable, inaccessible and irretrievable. (Orna, 1992)**

And as to the 'electronic answer', the technology was not THE answer; it was an essential part of an answer, but success would depend on 'human thought, human understanding of complex organizations, human cooperation, and human decisions' about how to use it.

An initiative from the Funding Councils for Higher Education

Writing six years on from that time, it is possible to feel somewhat encouraged. It is now an obligation for institutions of higher education to have an information strategy as part of the strategic plans which the Higher Education Funding Council requires from them each year. The *Guidelines* (1995) from the Joint Information Systems Committee of the Funding Councils for Higher Education, in the very first sentence, say this is about 'the ways in which a higher education institution makes major decisions about the future of its teaching and research. *It is not just about computing or libraries*'.

The last point is emphasized by an analysis of the weakness of information systems and IT strategies (technology-driven; focused on management-related information to the exclusion of information for teaching and research; concerned with improving current ways of doing things rather than seeking new ones), and of the risks inherent in relying solely on them (fragmentation within the academic community; inappropriate investments, unaccompanied by changes in working practices, and not adequately evaluated).

The *Guidelines* suggest that the best way to think of an information strategy is 'as a set of attitudes rather than as a report', and as a process rather than as a product. The attitudes are those which would lead to:

* Most information being available for sharing, and accessible
* Quality of information matching the purposes of its users
* All staff knowing and exercising their responsibilities towards information
* Priorities being clearly identified and acted on.

The information with which the strategy is concerned is defined as: 'teaching and learning materials (in all media), research information and data and the management information needed to plan and monitor the delivery of teaching, learning and research' – wherever it exists, not solely on computers or in libraries. Given the importance of the matter with which information strategy deals, 'its creation and maintenance justifies the close attention and support of the Vice-Chancellor/Principal'.

The process suggested for developing an information strategy consists of six elements:

1 Set-up – defining the scope, terms of reference, people involved
2 Context – understanding of the overall direction of the institution and the environment in which it works, and of the opportunities presented by emerging information technologies
3 Information needs – what information resources the strategy covers, the standards they should meet, the infrastructure required to support them; and mismatches between what the institution needs and what it actually has and does
4 Roles and responsibilities – identifying the people concerned, and ensuring that they understand and accept their roles and responsibilities in relation to information
5 Implementation – priority list of projects, project management plans, change management programmes
6 Monitoring and review – of the strategy and the contexts in which it needs to operate.

Figure C14.1 on page 351 shows the information strategy framework proposed in the *Guidelines*.

Pilot sites in six institutions which reflect the diversity of higher education and represent the four funding councils in the UK, were selected and started work on developing information strategies in 1996. This case study is an account of how one of them has set about its work. (For an interesting account of how some other institutions approached the process, see Allen, 1998.)

The University of North London

The origins of the University of North London (UNL) go back to 1896. A leading polytechnic in the public sector of higher education from the 1960s, it became a university in 1992. Today it has 16 000 home and overseas students. The institution's history and the character of its student body influence its mission statement, which emphasizes:

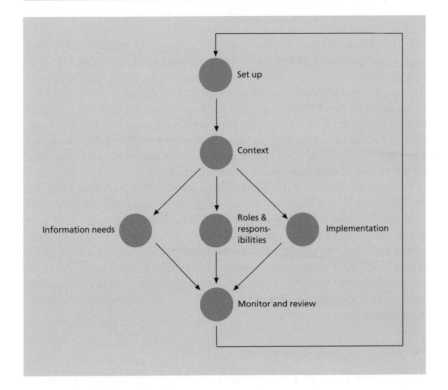

Fig C14.1   **An information strategy framework**

- Access to opportunity (life-long learning; supporting the development of self-reliant and capable graduates)
- Quality (education which adds value to the capabilities, skills and qualifications of students)
- Regional development (partnerships which support the social cultural and economic development of the region where the university is located)
- Internationalism (delivering a curriculum and learning experience which reflect and promote its international and European context).

Its faculties also reflect its established specialisms: the Business School; Environmental and Social Studies; Humanities and Teacher Education; Science, Computing and Engineering.

The management of the university is led by its Vice-Chancellor/Chief Executive, supported by a senior management team consisting of the Directors of Academic Affairs, Corporate Services, Human Resources and Research, the Secretary and Clerk to the Board, and the Deans of faculties. Its academic governance is the responsibility of the Board of Governors to which the Vice-Chancellor, Chair of the Academic Board, reports; the Academic Board in turn has a sub-structure of faculty boards, committees, working groups and sub-committees.

The information strategy pilot project

The JISC *Guidelines* were published in 1995; pilot sites were selected early in 1996 and started work on their information strategies in June of that year. The different pilot institutions took their own approach, mainly determined by their culture and structure, though there are similar themes in the work of different sites. Distinctive features of the UNL pilot, according to the staff running it, are the information management 'toolkit' for managers which is being developed (see page 359) and the use of a strategy framework document (see page 353) as a starting point; other pilot sites are said to have implemented projects first and then developed frameworks from them.

The UNL pilot began with setting up a structural framework to manage the project, consisting of an Information Strategy Steering Group (ISSG) and an Information Strategy Task Group (ISTG). The Steering Group's role is to oversee and coordinate the work, and report on it to the Vice-Chancellor; to ensure resources; to agree priorities for implementation; and to ensure monitoring. The Task Group is responsible for doing the job, reporting to the ISSG, recommending on monitoring methods, and highlighting external, internal or technological changes which might require review of the elements of the information strategy.

Definition and purpose of the strategy

The broad definition of information strategy adopted by the ISTG was based on that in the first edition of this book: 'the detailed expression of information policy in terms of objectives, targets and action to achieve them for a defined period ahead. Information strategy provides the framework for the management of information.'

The focus of the UNL's information strategy is set out in the *Information Strategy Framework Document* produced by the ISTG (UNL, 1997) as

> the way in which information, in whatever format, is received, used, managed and disseminated. It will cover the core areas of the University's work: teaching, learning and research. It will cover course materials in a variety of media and the management information needed to plan for and monitor the delivery of the core activities ... [it] will also include policies on information, and individual and organizational responsibilities for information and information systems.

The overall purpose (as stated in the university's Strategic Plan) is defined as to:
* Support the delivery of strategic aims
* Support operational, functional and management processes – through effective use of information, promoting sharing to avoid duplication of effort, and improving management of information as an asset
* Facilitate involvement and participation of members of the university – communication between staff and between staff and students; development of responsible attitudes towards information; training and development in information management
* Support interaction between staff and students – with timely and consistent information and information systems that 'enhance the student experience'

- Deliver external requirements and support accountability – with emphasis on the quality of information going out of the university as well as on internal information flows
- Support external relationships and partnerships – through 'effective communication with key players outside the university'
- Promote external awareness of the university – by management of its 'external image'.

In approaching their task, the Steering Group and the ISTG aim to develop good information management practice. In line with the aim of making information management part of the job of all members of the university, they seek to create a set of 'tools' which managers and others can use with confidence to carry out information management projects in their own areas.

Scope of the strategy

The key areas for which the strategy is being initially planned relate to those parts of the university's Strategic Plan which deal with 'Academic Identity and Academic Profile':
- Learning and teaching – all parts of the university use, process and generate information as an integral part of their work. 'The transformation of information into knowledge is at the heart of the University's academic work.'
- Research – sound information management is at the core of the research function
- International activities – the information strategy will support delivering a curriculum reflecting and promoting the international and European context of the university
- Information systems and IT strategies – in line with the priorities of the Strategic Plan
- Management and decision making – to reduce duplication, support good practice, increase accountability for information, and achieve benefits and cost savings
- Academic and administration systems – these systems too are largely information-based.

The wide scope of the strategy implies that it will have to provide for integrated management of information as part of processes that involve contributions from different functions. There is said to be as yet no institutional way of looking at information as a resource distributed across the whole university, and so some of the implementation projects involve interaction between different functional areas.

Information strategy and information systems/IT

The *Information Strategy Framework* describes the role of the information strategy *vis-à-vis* information systems and IT as providing an 'overarching framework for supporting and informing the development of information systems'.

As such, it is envisaged as embracing 'information management and information technology systems and their interrelationships'. In this respect, it will:

- Start from specific information needs, clarify existing and potential mechanisms for meeting them, and chart current information flows
- Support ways in which information requirements are handled – help managers and staff in taking a 'self-critical approach' to current practice, and give opportunities and means to improve work practices by developing good information management practice
- Define information systems required to underpin the management of information and define the IT to deliver it – this approach will help to guide investment decisions.

A university IT strategy already exists; but once it was developed its impact was limited. It is described as having some useful features, but lacking an agreed programme for implementation and clear criteria for monitoring. One of the implementation projects will therefore be an audit of IT strategy, in relation to its relevance to the institution today, and to the information strategy and the information systems strategy. An IT strategy manager is now a member of the Task Group. The Management Information Systems Group (MISG) has the specific task of looking at information systems in relation to their appropriateness and ability to deliver. A systems strategy will come from its work.

The place of human resources

The Information Strategy will identify and define clear roles, responsibilities and structures related to information and information management. In this area an information management approach is seen as having a contribution to make to the university's regular process reviews, in relation to functional analysis, roles and responsibilities and competence-based job descriptions. As part of the university's staff development programme, information strategy workshops have been run and more are planned.

How the work has developed

A progress report from the Task Group after its first nine months of work outlined its major activities to date, and its plans for the next period.

Information policy

An information policy, highlighting good practice, was defined at an early stage to gain acceptance and support for practically oriented proposals for good information management practice. The elements of the policy were:

1 *Assessing and measuring good practice.* The aim of this part of the policy is to ensure that those accountable for achieving the university's strategic goals adopt principles of good information management – to be measured against such criteria as:

- Acquisition and full exploitation of appropriate information to meet current needs and to cope with change
- Delivery of appropriate information to users at the right time and in the right format
- Understanding between the people who process information and those who use it
- Opportunities for them to gain appropriate knowledge and skills – including information sharing
- Constant review of technology to evaluate how appropriate it is in relation to the university's information objectives
- Appropriate organizational structures and human resources both for managing and developing the information strategy and for implementing the information policy.

Performance measures are being identified for assessing the positive impact of good information management practice. The measures are similar to those suggested in the first edition of this book, and the approach is comparable to that of the Investors in People programme. For each measure, criteria statements with a five-point scale are being developed.

2 *Objectives for good practice.* These cover:
- Management of information assets (based on the Hawley Committee's work, 1995 on information as an asset)
- Information quality (in relation to what people need to know to do their job; access policies; reliability; integrated use of information; consistency; and costs of dissemination)
- The proper use of information (legal, regulatory, operational, and ethical standards; responsibility for information belonging to other organizations and individuals).

Work is in progress to enumerate the obligations that must be met, and to ensure and monitor compliance; the terms 'owner', 'custodian', and 'user' will be defined in respect of information.
- Risks and protection (mechanisms to assess the type and level of risk associated with key information assets, and to protect them)
- IS and IT strategy (regular monitoring as part of, or alongside, the information strategy).

The performance of information systems is being monitored to identify opportunities for using information systems and IT to support delivery of the information strategy. The strategy will also inform the work of the Management Information Systems Group; key staff involved with information strategy belong both to the ISTG and the MISG.

3 *Monitoring and review* (constant review and updating of the information strategy in the light of changing strategic aims and priorities).

The interesting concept of information budgets is also being developed; the aim is:

> for managers and staff to regard information management as an integral part of their work and as an accepted part of the University's management cycle. Just as there is a financial budget round and an annual calendar for academic quality, so a cycle for monitoring local information budgets will be established.

The project approach

In line with the JISC ideas about information strategy as a process rather than a product, the university's pilot is advancing by a series of projects in areas identified by the Steering Group and the Senior Management Team. During the 1997/98 implementation phase a series of projects is being managed by Steering Group members in cooperation with relevant functional areas of the university.

1 *Promoting technology innovation in teaching and learning.* This project is intended to highlight key information issues in transforming delivery of course units. It will entail the development of technology-based teaching on a course unit. An information audit will be done of an agreed subject, and priority areas for development will be determined on the basis of the audit findings

2 *The student information life cycle.* The aim is to develop an institution-wide map of student information flows, from application through to after the completion of their studies.

3 *Strategic management information: a 'road map'.* A statement of the university's needs for strategic information will be produced, as the basis for evaluating existing systems and specifying appropriate new management information systems.

4 *Knowledge management.* Knowledge – defined as deriving from 'the human interface with information' is recognized as 'one of the most valuable and least managed assets in the University'. This project will focus primarily on the knowledge of teaching staff; it will audit existing practice and consider how to facilitate the sharing of knowledge and experience.

5 *Information strategy and process reviews.* A project which will use the methodology developed by the Task Group for analysing information flows, roles and responsibilities (see page 359 for a description of the pilot audit) to supplement the existing programme of departmental process reviews carried out by Human Resources. The project should test the usefulness of information strategy in supporting and facilitating organizational change.

6 *Auditing the university's IT strategy.* Audit and evaluation will be made of the current IT strategy in terms of its potential and actual contribution to the Information Strategy. The objective will be to highlight issues that should be addressed as part of an agreed review of IT strategy.

Each plan has a brief protocol, which sets out a summary of the subject area, the people responsible, goals, objectives, scope, organization, risks and actions, control systems, and activities and the resources of time and money required for them. Figure C14.2 on pages 357 and 358, shows an example.

UNIVERSITY OF NORTH LONDON
Information Strategy Task Group

IMPLEMENTATION PROJECT PLANS 1997/98

TITLE   Promoting technology innovation in teaching and learning

SUMMARY
The Information Strategy and the toolkit developed to implement it will be
used to promote and facilitate the development of technology-based
teaching in a subject area (provisionally in the HP&CS area of Humanities).
An information audit will be carried out in the agreed subject. Priority areas
for development and input will be determined. Internal and external
materials will be gathered and integrated into course delivery in line with
the information needs outlined in the audit. Revised information flows will be
mapped. The project will highlight the key information issues to be addressed
in transforming the delivery of course units. These will be encompassed in
guidelines and indicators which should be applicable elsewhere within
the University.

Lead ISTG members	Grainne Conole; Peter Holmes
ISSG Consultants	Greg Condry
UNL Constituencies involved	Deans, Teaching staff, ISS staff

GOALS

1   To support the delivery of those aspects of the Strategic Plan which
relate specifically to the integration of technology in the learning and
teaching domain by using the Information Strategy and the
accompanying 'toolkit'.

2   To show the relevance of the Information Strategy in helping to
transform content delivery across a subject area.

OBJECTIVES

1   To identify an appropriate subject area in discussions with the Deans
and teaching staff.

2   To carry out an information audit of the agreed subject area.

3   To identify develop and apply appropriate innovations for application
within the subject modules.

4   To identify current cross-subject information flows and indicate potential
improvements.

5   To cascade project outcomes across the university.

6   To demonstrate, through the project, the benefits of the Information
Strategy toolkit to teaching staff, Deans and other academic managers.

SCOPE
The project will be undertaken within a defined subject area. Similar projects
in other subject areas can only be carried out if appropriate resources are made
available. The project will run from September 1997 to June 1998.

C:\WORK~WPDOCS\ISIMPALL.WPD December 8 1997

Fig C14.2   **Example of an implementation project plan.** *Continued on next page*

STRUCTURE

The project leaders will work closely with staff in the selected subject area and report regularly to the ISTG and the ISSG.

ORGANISATION

The project will be jointly managed by the two ISTG members. The work will be carried out by the project working group, in consultation with the appropriate Dean.

RISKS AND ACTIONS

The close involvement and enthusiasm of the Dean, teaching staff and ISS are seen as critical to the success of the project. Wider dissemination and implementation will require the support of both ISTG and ISSG members for full effectiveness.

CONTROL SYSTEMS

The project will be steered by ISTG and monitored throughout by the two ISTG members who will be managing the project. Feedback and evaluation will be obtained by relevant interviews and questionnaires as appropriate throughout the project.

RESOURCES

Establish a working task group consisting of the relevant faculty staff, two ISTG members and appropriate members of ISS. Arrange meetings/ presentations to update the project team on the Information Strategy and the aims and development of the project. 3 days.

Conduct an information audit for the agreed subject area, involving teaching, staff. students, ISS and administrative staff as appropriate. 15 days.

Analyse essential information from the audit to help establish priority areas for development. 5 days.

Gather external and internal relevant materials, courseware and IT solutions for application to the issues raised by the project. Demonstrate and make recommendations. 5 days

Integrate and embed the innovations in compliance with the information needs outlined from the audit. Apply, evaluate and iteratively improve within the subject modules. 20 days

Identify good practice for information flow within the subject area and monitor performance using the toolkit. 5 days

Disseminate project findings through ISSG and ISTG, via the web, staff development sessions and externally through conference presentations. 5 days.

Totals

58 Project Officer days @ £84 per day = £4,872.

(Some expenditure on materials, licences etc may be required for this project.)

C:\WORK~WPDOCS\ISIMPALL.WPD December 8 1997

Fig C14.2   *End*

In all the projects, the Task Group seeks to develop a collaborative relationship with the managers responsible for the project area, in which its members act as consultants and facilitators of change rather than taking direct responsibility for it. On 'political' grounds it was felt necessary to establish an arms-length role, and not to be seen as coming in to impose solutions. In reality, the Task Group members all have other jobs which take their full attention, and it is therefore important to spread responsibility for applying the strategy among those who manage the areas for which it has been developed.

The project outcomes will be used to assess the effectiveness of the outline information policy and good practice recommendations described above, and a revised statement will be delivered, taking into account changing strategic aims and priorities.

Monthly project reports are presented; the specified outcomes will be monitored, and the Information Strategy Task Group and the Information Strategy Steering Group will take an overview of the project results in order to inform revision and development of information strategy.

Developments in information auditing

As the outline of the implementation projects makes clear, nearly all of them involve finding out what is actually happening with information in the project area, and matching it against a picture of what should be happening, as the basis for proposing an appropriate strategy for using information. This is the essence of information auditing (see Chapter 4, page 68), and one of the most interesting aspects of this case study is how the Task Group has extended information auditing into new fields and has started to develop new methods.

As part of the preparation for the projects, a detailed audit case study was made of assessment in the university, with the participation of academic and administrative staff and students. A questionnaire was used to find out how the process was carried out and how it was perceived by different parties to it, in different areas. Flow diagrams were created (using data flow analysis software) and were discussed with the people engaged in assessment. Figure C14.3 on page 360 shows an example.

The questionnaire asked respondents who was responsible for ensuring they got the information they needed, what quality controls were used, and details of everything that happened in the assessment process. They were also asked what information they needed to do their job, and how that related to departmental strategy. The information sought was in fact more detailed than immediately required.

Key issues emerging from the audit were:
- The roles and responsibilities of academic and administrative staff
- Waste and duplication of effort
- Differences in practice in different parts of the university.

This work has led to a contribution to the suite of tools which is being developed to help managers and others to carry out information management projects in their own areas. It has yielded an information audit questionnaire, a methodology for translating the responses into a functional analysis of individuals' 'tasks', and the use of a software package for mapping the information

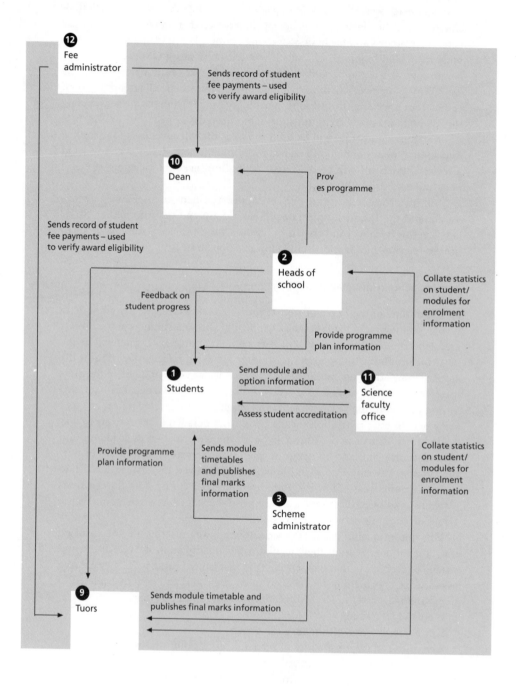

Fee administrator ⑫

Sends record of student fee payments – used to verify award eligibility

Dean ⑩

Prov
es programme

Sends record of student fee payments – used to verify award eligibility

Heads of school ②

Collate statistics on student/ modules for enrolment information

Feedback on student progress

Provide programme plan information

Students ①

Send module and option information

Assess student accreditation

Science faculty office ⑪

Provide programme plan information

Sends module timetables and publishes final marks information

Scheme administrator ③

Collate statistics on student/ modules for enrolment information

Tuors ⑨

Sends module timetable and publishes final marks information

Fig C14.3   Part of a flow diagram from the audit study of assessment

flows involved. It has also helped the group to learn about getting the right level and range of questions. Their general judgement is that they have what 'looks like the bones of a useful methodology'.

Learning from the pilot

The process of producing an information strategy is seen as important and valuable in itself, and the Task Group describes itself as having developed into a 'creative, cross-university team'. One discovery from experience was that it was necessary to go beyond what the JISC *Guidelines* proposed as a methodology. They were found to be too narrow by themselves and other sources were used to supplement them, including Burk and Horton (1988) on Infomapping, material from the KPMG IMPACT initiative and the Hawley Committee, and the first edition of this book. In practice, the *Guidelines* are said not to have proved workable as a methodology for the actual business of developing an information strategy. Other sites are said to have had a similar experience, and a revised edition is in preparation by JISC.

While outside consultancy was available through JISC, the Group felt that more access to 'knowledge of issues in the field' would have been helpful. Sometimes it was difficult to know whether they were progressing the project at the right level. And the work was 'more onerous and time consuming than predicted' (an observation that could be made for just about any project of this kind). Changes in working practice became necessary when the university was unable to allocate staff resources for support at a time when it was urgently needed. The position was retrieved with some JISC funding, and having learned from experience, the Group made a more ambitious request for resources (which was successful) to the university for the next year. Resources for that period were £10 000 from JISC granted against deliverables, and the £15 000 asked for from the university.

Monitoring

Once developed and implemented, the strategy will be monitored and maintained to ensure that it becomes 'embedded in the workings of the University and aligned to changing institutional needs and priorities'. The elements of the process will be monitoring of implementation projects and development of performance indicators against benchmarks, which will be incorporated in the university's quality systems. Figure C14.4 on page 362 shows an example of the indicators which have been developed.

Evaluation

This case study is in a notoriously difficult area for information strategy development, where there is little past experience to draw on in attempting to consider information in an integrated way across the whole of very diverse institutions. It shows many positive and encouraging features, as well as useful

100 per cent	75 per cent	50 per cent	25 per cent	0 per cent
A list has been drawn up and agreed of the University's information needs and the potential benefits from its information sources. Appropriate action has been agreed to ensure meeting these needs and full exploitation of these resources. A timetable for review has been agrred and implemented.	A list has been drawn up and agreed of the University's information needs and the potential benefits from its information sources however no action has been taken as a result of it. No review has taken place.	A list has been drawn up but not yet agreed and no action has therefore been taken.	A list has not been agreed but ad hoc actions have been taken to exploit information resources and meet the University's needs.	No list has been drawn up and there is no evidence to suggest any ad hoc actions being taken to meet this indicator.

2.3 The drawing up and regular review of a clear and detailed list of the University's information needs and the benefits which are potentially attainable from the information available to it.

3   Information gets to the people who need to use it at the right time and in the right format.

3.1 Clear understanding of who the customers are for information.

3.2 Clear understanding of customers' needs, including deadlines.

3.3 Good communication/liason/conultation between supplier and customers.

3.4 Re-working, re-formatting and checking minimised through information sharing.

3.5 Duplication of effort and waste eliminated.

Fig C14.4   **Performance indicators for good information management practice**

lessons which have been learned by the people responsible for a pioneering effort.

Perhaps the most distinctive feature is the Task Group's insistence on thinking through 'what should be' and then systematically finding out 'what is' – an approach which has incidentally extended the concept and methods of information auditing in useful ways. Equally important is the commitment to a project approach, which constitutes a learning spiral and appears to be having the desired effect of gaining commitment from Steering Group members who manage projects. The use of a partnership-type approach to project areas and their staff shows sensitivity, which seems to be bearing fruit. The indications are that people in the university are absorbing new ideas and beginning to understand what information is about. Among encouraging signs is the fact that responsibility for information is appearing in job descriptions in some parts of the university, and the recognition of the precedence of information over IT in various important areas such as MIS development. However, it is acknowledged that there is still a long way to go and some of the feedback on the *Information Strategy Framework Document* indicates that 'we need to continue our efforts to explain and involve'.

Lessons have also been learned about the resources of time and support for staff needed. While the process has been supported by a strong management and reporting structure, which is taken seriously by top management and by the Steering Group, the Task Group realizes that more progress could have been made had more energetic support from the top been possible; this, however, was prevented by other demands on the time and energies of people concerned. So, while the Task Group has been given scope and encouragement, it has not been possible for much of the project to be actually driven by the Senior Management Team.

To quote one of the key people concerned, 'We have learned the hard way in many respects. The time and effort to achieve even the fairly modest progress we have made has been far more than we (or the JISC *Guidelines*) envisaged.' It is now perceived that one or more secondments at the outset would probably have ensured smoother progress and greater permeation of the information strategy. But realistically it was 'only ever going to be done in the way we have done it, given institutional resource issues and other priorities. This hasn't prevented it feeling at times like rolling a large stone up a hill – which is of course very therapeutic ...'.

There is another valuable lesson in these quotes, which can be commended to anyone embarking on a similar process: perseverance, awareness of what is possible, a degree of detachment, and a sense of humour are all useful assets.

References

ALLEN, D. (1998), 'Information, technology and transformational change in the HE sector', *Library and Information Research News*, 22 (7), 40–51

BURK, C. F., (Jr) and HORTON, F. W., (Jr) (1988), *Infomap: A complete guide to discovering corporate information resources*, Englewood Cliffs, NJ: Prentice Hall

HAWLEY COMMITTEE (1995), *Information as an Asset: the Board Agenda*, London: KPMG IMPACT Programme

JOINT INFORMATION SYSTEMS COMMITTEE (1995), *Guidelines for Developing an Information Strategy*, Bristol: JISC (Higher Education Funding Council for England, Scottish Higher Education Funding Council, Higher Education Funding Council for Wales, Department of Education Northern Ireland)

ORNA, E. (1992), 'Information policies and information management', in *Campus information: the electronic answer?*, papers presented at the Second IUCC/SCONUL Conference, Bournemouth

UNIVERSITY OF NORTH LONDON (1995), *Strategic Plan*, London: UNL

UNIVERSITY OF NORTH LONDON (1997), *Information Strategy Framework Document*, London: UNL

Index